TEAM

THE 17 INDISPUTABLE
LAWS OF TEAMWORK

WINNING WITH PEOPLE

JOHN C.
MAXWELL

THOMAS NELSON
Since 1798

NASHVILLE DALLAS MEXICO CITY RIO DE JANEIRO BEIJING

Published in Nashville, Tennessee, by Thomas Nelson. Thomas Nelson is a registered trademark of Thomas Nelson, Inc.

Published in association with Yates & Yates, www.yates2.com

Thomas Nelson, Inc., titles may be purchased in bulk for educational, business, fund-raising, or sales promotional use. For information, please e-mail SpecialMarkets@ThomasNelson.com.

Unless otherwise noted, Scripture quotations are from THE NEW KING JAMES VERSION. © 1982 by Thomas Nelson, Inc. Used by permission. All rights reserved.

Scripture quotations noted *The Message* by Eugene H. Peterson. © 1993, 1994, 1995, 1996, 2000. Used by permission of NavPress Publishing Group. All rights reserved.

Scripture quotations noted KJV are from the KING JAMES VERSION.

ISBN 978-1-4002-8042-1

Printed in the United States of America
08 09 10 11 QW 5 4 3 2 1

Contents

The 17 Indisputable Laws of Leadership

1. THE LAW OF SIGNIFICANCE   5

One Is Too Small a Number to Achieve Greatness

What's your dream? Lilly Tartikoff's is to cure cancer. She's not a scientist—nor does she need to be. All she needs to know is the Law of Significance.

2. THE LAW OF THE BIG PICTURE   19

The Goal Is More Important Than the Role

What would prompt a former U.S. president to go cross-country by bus, sleep in a basement, and do manual labor for a week? The answer can be found in the Law of the Big Picture.

3. THE LAW OF THE NICHE   32

All Players Have a Place Where They Add the Most Value

If you were the leader of the free world, how would you decide what job to give the person who's capable of doing *any* job—including yours? If you wanted everyone to win, you'd use the Law of the Niche.

4. THE LAW OF MOUNT EVEREST

As the Challenge Escalates, the Need for Teamwork Elevates

Tenzing Norgay and Maurice Wilson were experienced climbers with the right equipment. So why did one man die on the mountain while the other conquered it? Only one knew the Law of Mount Everest.

5. THE LAW OF THE CHAIN

The Strength of the Team Is Impacted by Its Weakest Link

Does it matter if thousands of your employees are doing a great job and only one person makes a wrong turn? Just ask the company that paid more than $3 billion in damages and was bound by the Law of the Chain.

6. THE LAW OF THE CATALYST

Winning Teams Have Players Who Make Things Happen

What do you do if December 31 is rapidly approaching and your salespeople are hopelessly behind on their goal for the year? Dave Sutherland can tell you. His team made its goal because he's always lived by the Law of the Catalyst.

7. THE LAW OF THE COMPASS

Vision Gives Team Members Direction and Confidence

When Abby Kohnstamm began working for IBM, she found that the company that had set the pace for innovation in American business for much of the twentieth century was adrift and losing billions of dollars a year. Why? The answer can be found in the Law of the Compass.

They were expected to crush the competition. They had the talent and the ambition to win. But instead of dominating, they self-destructed. If only they'd known about the Law of the Bad Apple.

Maybe people don't die in your organization when somebody drops the ball. But it can happen to people in this family business. That's why the Law of Countability is so important to them.

The company could have been the world's largest retailer. Instead it was forced to close its doors after 128 years of business. Why? The leaders were paying for ignoring the Law of the Price Tag.

Thousands of Web-based companies have failed. Many "successful" ones are still waiting to make a profit. Yet this company keeps winning and growing and making money! Why? Because it has always played by the Law of the Scoreboard.

12. THE LAW OF THE BENCH 165

Great Teams Have Great Depth

Who is usually an organization's MVP? The CEO? The chairman? The top salesperson? Would you believe it might be someone from HR? You would if you knew the Law of the Bench.

13. THE LAW OF IDENTITY 182

Shared Values Define the Team

How do you get thousands of people excited about working in warehouses, wearing bright orange, and catering to the customer's every need? Bernie Marcus and Arthur Blank did it by building their company's foundation on the Law of Identity.

14. THE LAW OF COMMUNICATION 197

Interaction Fuels Action

The team had ten leaders in ten years. Employees were burned out and bitter, and the company was bleeding cash. So how was Gordon Bethune going to save this last-place airline from crashing? He started by using the Law of Communication.

15. THE LAW OF THE EDGE 214

The Difference Between Two Equally Talented
Teams Is Leadership

The team had major problems. The participants had everything they needed to go the distance—talent, support, resources—everything but the most important thing. Their only hope for turning things around was someone who fulfilled the Law of the Edge.

What would prompt a fifty-year-old man who couldn't even swim to endure the pain of training for the toughest triathlon in the world? No, it wasn't a midlife crisis. It was the Law of High Morale.

Have you ever been tricked into taking a job? Morgan Wootten was, and as a result, he has changed the lives of thousands of kids. His life of giving will teach you everything you need to know about the Law of Dividends.

CONTENTS

Winning with People

THE 17 INDISPUTABLE
LAWS OF TEAMWORK

Embrace Them and Empower Your Team

ACKNOWLEDGMENTS

Every book I write is an act of teamwork. And this one is no exception. I'd like to thank the people who helped me to create *The 17 Indisputable Laws of Teamwork:*

The INJOY Team, who helped me to think through and refine the laws.

Margaret Maxwell, my wife, best friend, and number one teammate, who gives good advice.

Linda Eggers, who always takes care of all the details of my life.

Kathie Wheat, who did such wonderful research for the book.

Stephanie Wetzel, who sharpened the manuscript by proofreading and editing every word.

Charlie Wetzel, whose writing extends my influence around the world.

INTRODUCTION

Every day, in some way, you are a part of a team. The question is not, *Will you participate in something that involves others?* The question is, *Will your involvement with others be successful?* You can find the answer to that question in this book.

Everyone knows that teamwork is a good thing; in fact, it's essential! But how does it really work? What makes a winning team? Why do some teams go straight to the top, seeing their vision become reality, while others seem to go nowhere?

These questions don't have simple answers. If they did, sports would have more back-to-back world champions, and the list of Fortune 500 companies would never change year after year.

One of the challenges of learning about teamwork is that even people who've taken a team to the highest level in their field sometimes have a hard time identifying what separates a great team from a collection of individuals who can't seem to get it together. Some will say the key to winning is a strong work ethic. But haven't you known plenty of hardworking individuals who never worked together to reach their potential? Others believe that great teams are the result of chemistry. But they often say, "I can't explain how you create it, but I definitely know it when I see it." How can you get your hands around that and learn from it to build *your* team?

As a communicator who spends countless hours speaking to live audiences every year, I am always looking for straightforward ways to teach people complex truths. That's what a communicator does—he takes something complicated and makes it simple. In 1998, I wrote *The 21 Irrefutable Laws of Leadership.* My desire was to share what I had learned from three decades of leading people. The response was overwhelming. The book landed on bestseller lists of the *New York Times* Business Books, the *Wall Street Journal, Business Week,* and the Christian Booksellers Association (CBA) marketplace. For that I am truly grateful. But more important, during the last several years as I have taught the laws throughout the United States and on five continents, I have had the delight of seeing people connect with the laws, apply them to their lives, and improve their leadership. Learning the laws changed people's lives, and I knew that I had found an effective handle for helping people learn leadership.

My desire is to make team building as simple to grasp, retain, and put into practice as leadership. I want to take the mystery out of it. That's why I've worked hard to identify the Laws of Teamwork. The wonderful thing about a law is that you can depend on it. No matter who you are, what your background is, or what circumstances you face; you can take a law to the bank.

As I teach you the laws, you will find that I often approach the subject of teamwork from a leader's point of view—that makes sense since leaders are the ones who bring teams together and lead them to victory. But you don't have to be a leader to benefit from this book. Just about everything you do depends on teamwork. It doesn't matter whether you are a leader or follower, coach or player, teacher or student, parent or child, CEO or nonprofit volunteer worker. No matter who you are, if you learn and apply the laws, your teamwork capacity will increase. The greater the number of laws that you and your teammates learn, the more likely you are to be transformed from a group of individuals into a winning team.

Teams come in all shapes and sizes. If you're married, you and your spouse are a team. If you are employed by an organization, you and your colleagues are a team. If you volunteer your time, you and your fellow workers are a team. As Dan Devine joked, "A team is a team is a team. Shakespeare said that many times." Although the gifted playwright might not have said exactly that, the concept is nonetheless true. That's why teamwork is so important.

At a recent conference where I was teaching, a young leader who was just getting started in his career came up to me and asked, "John, what's the one thing I need to know about teamwork?"

"One thing?" I replied. "That's not an easy answer to come up with."

He persisted: "But just get me started. I want only the thing that's most important."

"All right, if you insist," I said. "The one thing you need to know about teamwork is that there is more than one thing you need to know about teamwork."

At first he looked at me questioningly. Then he became a bit irritated. But then I could see a sudden understanding in his eyes.

"Oh, I get it," he said. "It's a process. Okay, okay. I'm ready to dive in. I'm willing to take the time to learn."

I want to encourage you to do the same, to devote yourself to the process of learning to be a great team member and team builder. As you read about the Laws of Teamwork and begin to apply them, I think you will find that they have a positive impact on every aspect of your life. As you proceed, also remember this: None of the laws stand alone, but they all stand together really well. The greater number of laws you learn, the better you will become.

Enjoy the process, give it your best, and never forget that no matter what you want to do in life, it takes teamwork to make the dream work.

THE LAW OF SIGNIFICANCE

One Is Too Small a Number to Achieve Greatness

Who are your personal heroes? Okay, maybe you don't have heroes exactly. Then let me ask you this: Which people do you admire most? Who do you wish you were more like? Which people fire you up and get your juices flowing? Do you admire . . .

- Business innovators, such as Jeff Bezos, Fred Smith, or Bill Gates?

- Great athletes, such as Michael Jordan, Marion Jones, or Mark McGwire?

- Creative geniuses, such as Pablo Picasso, Buckminster Fuller, or Wolfgang Amadeus Mozart?

- Pop culture icons, such as Madonna, Andy Warhol, or Elvis Presley?

- Spiritual leaders, such as John Wesley, Billy Graham, or Mother Teresa?

- Political leaders, such as Alexander the Great, Charlemagne, or Winston Churchill?

- Film industry giants, such as D. W. Griffith, Charlie Chaplin, or Steven Spielberg?

- Architects and engineers, such as Frank Lloyd Wright, the Starrett brothers, or Joseph Strauss?

- Revolutionary thinkers, such as Marie Curie, Thomas Edison, or Albert Einstein?

Or maybe your list includes people in a field I didn't mention.

It's safe to say that we all admire achievers. And we Americans especially love pioneers and bold individualists, people who fight alone, despite the odds or opposition: the settler who carves a place for himself in the wilds of the frontier, the Old West sheriff who resolutely faces an enemy in a gunfight, the pilot who bravely flies solo across the Atlantic Ocean, and the scientist who changes the world through the power of his mind.

THE MYTH OF THE LONE RANGER

As much as we admire solo achievement, the truth is that no lone individual has done anything of value. The belief that one person can do something great is a myth. There are no real Rambos who can take on a hostile army by themselves. Even the Lone Ranger wasn't really a loner. Everywhere he went he rode with Tonto!

Nothing of significance was ever achieved by an individual acting alone. Look below the surface and you will find that all seemingly solo acts are really team efforts. Frontiersman Daniel Boone had companions from the Transylvania Company as he blazed the Wilderness Road. Sheriff Wyatt Earp had his two brothers and Doc Holliday looking out for him. Aviator Charles Lindbergh had the backing of nine businessmen from St. Louis and the services of the Ryan Aeronautical Company, which built his plane. Even Albert Einstein, the scientist who revolutionized the world with his theory of relativity, didn't work in a vacuum. Of the debt he owed to others for his work, Einstein once remarked, "Many times a day I realize how much my own outer and inner life is built upon the labors of my fellow men, both living and dead, and how earnestly I must exert myself in order to give in return as much as I have received." It's true that the history of our country is marked by the accomplishments of many strong leaders and innovative individuals who took considerable risks. But those people always were part of teams.

> *The belief that one person can do something great is a myth.*

Economist Lester C. Thurow commented on the subject:

> There is nothing antithetical in American history, culture, or traditions to teamwork. Teams were important in America's history— wagon trains conquered the West, men working together on the assembly line in American industry conquered the world, a successful national strategy and a lot of teamwork put an American on the moon first (and thus far, last). But American mythology extols only the individual . . . In America, halls of fame exist for almost every conceivable activity, but nowhere do Americans raise monuments in praise of teamwork.

I must say that I don't agree with all of Thurow's conclusions. After all, I've seen the U.S. Marine Corps war memorial in Washington, D.C., commemorating the raising of the flag on Iwo Jima. But he is right about something. Teamwork is and always has been essential to building this country. And that statement can be made about every country around the world.

THE VALUE OF TEAMWORK

A Chinese proverb states, "Behind an able man there are always other able men." The truth is that teamwork is at the heart of great achievement. The question isn't whether teams have value. The question is whether we acknowledge that fact and become better team players. That's why I assert that *one is too small a number to achieve greatness.* You cannot do anything of *real* value alone. That is the Law of Significance.

> *"There are no problems we cannot solve together, and very few that we can solve by ourselves."*
>
> —LYNDON JOHNSON

I challenge you to think of *one* act of genuine significance in the history of humankind that was performed by a lone human being. No matter what you name, you will find that a team of people was involved. That is why President Lyndon Johnson said, "There are no problems we cannot solve together, and very few that we can solve by ourselves."

C. Gene Wilkes, in his book *Jesus on Leadership,* observed that the power of teams not only is evident in today's modern business world, but it also has a deep history that is evident even in biblical times. Wilkes asserts,

- Teams involve more people, thus affording more resources, ideas, and energy than would an individual.

- Teams maximize a leader's potential and minimize her weaknesses. Strengths and weaknesses are more exposed in individuals.

- Teams provide multiple perspectives on how to meet a need or reach a goal, thus devising several alternatives for each situation. Individual insight is seldom as broad and deep as a group's when it takes on a problem.

- Teams share the credit for victories and the blame for losses. This fosters genuine humility and authentic community. Individuals take credit and blame alone. This fosters pride and sometimes a sense of failure.

- Teams keep leaders accountable for the goal. Individuals connected to no one can change the goal without accountability.

- Teams can simply do more than an individual.

If you want to reach your potential or strive for the seemingly impossible—such as communicating your message two thousand years after you are gone—you need to become a team player. It may be a cliché, but it is nonetheless true: Individuals play the game, but teams win championships.

WHY DO WE STAND ALONE?

Knowing all that we do about the potential of teams, why do some people still want to do things by themselves? I believe there are a number of reasons.

1. *Ego*

Few people are fond of admitting that they can't do everything, yet that is a reality of life. There are no supermen or superwomen. As Kerry Walls, one of the people on my INJOY Group team, says, "Spinning more plates doesn't increase your talent—it increases your likelihood of dropping a plate." So the question is not whether you can do everything by yourself; it's how soon you're going to realize that you can't.

> *Teamwork is birthed when you concentrate on "we" instead of "me."*

Philanthropist Andrew Carnegie declared, "It marks a big step in your development when you come to realize that other people can help you do a better job than you could do alone." To do something really big, let go of your ego, and get ready to be part of a team.

2. *Insecurity*

In my work with leaders, I've found that some individuals fail to promote teamwork because they feel threatened by other people. Sixteenth-century Florentine statesman Niccolo Machiavelli probably made similar observations, prompting him to write, "The first method for estimating the intelligence of a ruler is to look at the men he has around him."

I believe that insecurity, rather than poor judgment or lack of intelligence, most often causes leaders to surround themselves with weak people. As I stated in *The 21 Irrefutable Laws of Leadership*, only secure leaders give power to others. That is the Law of Empowerment. On the other hand, insecure leaders usually fail to build teams because of one of two reasons: Either they want to maintain control over everything for which they are responsible, or they fear being replaced by someone more capable. In either case, leaders who fail to promote teamwork undermine their own potential and erode the best efforts of the people with whom they work. They would benefit from the advice of President Woodrow Wilson: "We should not only use all the brains we have, but all that we can borrow."

> *"We should not only use all the brains we have, but all that we can borrow."*
>
> —WOODROW WILSON

3. Naïveté

Consultant John Ghegan keeps a sign on his desk that says, "If I had it to do all over again, I'd get help." That remark accurately represents the feelings of the third type of people who fail to become team builders. They naively underestimate the difficulty of achieving big things. As a result, they try to go it alone.

Some people who start out in this group turn out okay in the end. They discover that their dreams are bigger than their capabilities, they realize they won't accomplish their goals solo, and they adjust. They make team building their approach to achievement. But some others learn the truth too late, and as a result, they never accomplish their goals. And that's a shame.

4. Temperament

Some people aren't very outgoing and simply don't think in terms of team building and team participation. As they face challenges, it never occurs to them to enlist others to achieve something.

As a people person, I find that hard to relate to. Whenever I face any kind of challenge, the very first thing I do is to think about the people I want on the team to help with it. I've been that way since I was a kid. I've

> *"People have been known to achieve more as a result of working with others than against them."*
>
> —DR. ALLAN FROMME

always thought, *Why take the journey alone when you can invite others along with you?*

I understand that not everyone operates that way. But whether or not you are naturally inclined to be part of a team is really irrelevant. If you do everything alone and never partner with other people, you create huge barriers to your own potential. Dr. Allan Fromme quipped, "People have been known to achieve more as a result of working with others than against them." What an understatement! It takes a team to do anything of lasting value. Besides, even the most introverted person in the world can learn to enjoy the benefits of being on a team. (That's true even if someone isn't trying to accomplish something great.)

A few years ago my friend Chuck Swindoll wrote a piece in *The Finishing Touch* that sums up the importance of teamwork. He said,

> Nobody is a whole team . . . We need each other. You need someone and someone needs you. Isolated islands we're not. To make this thing called life work, we gotta lean and support. And relate and respond. And give and take. And confess and forgive. And reach out and embrace and rely . . . Since none of us is a whole, independent, self-sufficient, super-capable, all-powerful hotshot, let's quit acting like we are. Life's lonely enough without our playing that silly role. The game is over. Let's link up.

For the person trying to do everything alone, the game really is over. If you want to do something big, you must link up with others. *One is too small a number to achieve greatness.* That's the Law of Significance.

You Can See the Difference

When you look at the way people conduct their lives, you can tell fairly quickly who recognizes and embraces the truth of the Law of Significance. That is certainly true of Lilly Tartikoff. I don't know whether Lilly always knew the value of teamwork, but I suspect she learned it early since she was once a professional ballet dancer. If dancers don't work together, then their performances never reach the caliber of Lilly's. Beginning at age seven, she spent ten hours a day, six days a week, practicing or performing ballet. As a result she became a member of the New York City Ballet Company and performed with them from 1971 to 1980.

At a tennis party in Los Angeles in 1980, Lilly met Brandon Tartikoff, the newly named president of entertainment for NBC. At that time he was the youngest network president in history at age thirty. They soon became friends. Then they began to see each other romantically. In 1982, they were married. And that started a whole new life for Lilly. She went from a nontelevision watcher to the spouse of a network executive immersed in the L.A. culture of the entertainment industry. But that adjustment was nothing compared to the other challenge she faced that year. For the second time in his life, Brandon was diagnosed with Hodgkin's disease.

Amazing Science

On the advice of a physician friend, Brandon went to see a young oncological researcher at UCLA named Denny Slamon. In August 1982, Dr. Slamon started Brandon on two kinds of treatment, one of which was experimental. Brandon would usually be treated on a

Friday, and afterward Lilly would drive him home and take care of him while he suffered from horrible side effects all weekend. They followed that pattern for a year, and all the while Brandon continued in his role of network president. It was a difficult time for them, but they chose to face the cancer as a team, and in time Brandon recovered.

Out of that ordeal came many things. For one, Brandon's network, NBC, went from worst to first in the ratings. In his autobiography he wrote, "Cancer helps you see things more clearly. The disease, I've found, can actually *help* you do your job, and there's a very simple reason why: There's nothing like cancer to keep you focused on what's important."[1] That focus enabled him to air some of the most popular and groundbreaking shows in television's history: *The Cosby Show, Cheers, Hill Street Blues, Miami Vice, The Golden Girls, The A-Team, St. Elsewhere,* and others.

For Lilly, though, there was a different outcome. Once Hodgkin's disease had been driven from her husband's body, she didn't simply move on.

"Brandon was at the receiving end of some pretty amazing science," she observed. The medical research that had extended Brandon's life intrigued her. So when she had an opportunity to help others benefit from that same science, she couldn't say no. That occurred in 1989 when Dr. Dennis Slamon, the UCLA scientist who had treated Brandon seven years before, asked Lilly for her help.

Nobody Can Do It Alone

For years Dr. Slamon had been studying breast cancer. He believed he was on the verge of developing a radical new treatment that would not only be more effective in treating the disease than anything previously developed, but he could do it without all the usual side effects of chemotherapy. He had the expertise and skill necessary to do the work, but he couldn't do it alone. He needed someone to help with funding. He thought of Lilly. She was only too happy to agree to assist him.

The plan she developed showed keen insight into teamwork and strategic partnerships. Lilly had once worked as a beauty adviser for Max Factor, formerly connected to Revlon. She sought to get Ronald Perelman, the CEO of Revlon, together with Dr. Slamon. At first that wasn't easy, but once Perelman realized the potential of Slamon's research, he pledged $2.4 million to the scientist's work with no restrictions. It was a partnership unlike anything that had been done before. What resulted was the creation of the Revlon/UCLA Women's Cancer Research Program—and a successful new treatment for cancer was soon saving women's lives.

A TASTE OF TEAMWORK

For Lilly, cofounding the research program was just a beginning. She had gotten a taste of what teamwork could do, and she was hungry to do much more. She quickly realized that she could enlist others to her cause. She would build a larger team, and she would use her show business connections to do it. That same year she established an annual Fire and Ice Ball in Hollywood to raise money. A few years later, she enlarged her circle and partnered with the Entertainment Industry Foundation (EIF) and created the Revlon Run/Walk, first in Los Angeles, and then in New York. So far, those events have raised more than $18 million for cancer research. And in 1996, she helped create the National Women's Cancer Research Alliance.

In 1997, her husband Brandon's cancer recurred a third time, and it took his life. He was only forty-eight years old. Despite the personal setback, Lilly continues to build teams to fight cancer. When she met Katie Couric, who had lost her husband to colon cancer, Lilly was again inspired to action. With the help of Couric and the EIF, she formed the National Colorectal Cancer Research Alliance in 2000.

"When I sat down with Katie," said Lilly, "to hear that, with an early diagnosis, you could turn the cancer around, and literally, it's 90 percent curable and preventable. Well, this was like putting a steak in front of a hungry dog . . . I thought, we've got to do this. So I brought in all my partners: the Entertainment Industry Foundation and Dr. Slamon . . . and Dr. Slamon brought together an agenda and a mission . . . So we created the NCCRA [National Colorectal Cancer Research Alliance]. You have no idea how exciting and gratifying it is."[2]

An individual cannot do the incredible, significant task that Lilly Tartikoff and her partners are trying to accomplish. No single person can take on cancer. But that's true of anything worth doing. If it's significant, it takes a team. That's something Lilly realized, put into practice, and now lives by every day. *One is too small a number to achieve greatness.* That is the Law of Significance.

Teamwork Thought

You may be good—but you're not *that* good!

BECOMING A BETTER TEAM MEMBER

What major goals are you working toward achieving right now? Write some of them here:

1. _____

2. _____

3. _____

Now, reflect on how you are working toward these goals. What approach have you been taking to achieve them? Are you going it alone? Or are you building a team to accomplish them?

If you're not trying to be part of a team, figure out why. Is it a matter of ego? Are you insecure? Have you misjudged the size of the challenges? Or does your temperament incline you to work alone? If you answer yes to one of these questions, work to overcome the difficulty immediately. The sooner you become a team player, the sooner you will be able to achieve your dreams.

BECOMING A BETTER TEAM LEADER

Think about the greatest dream you have for your life. Now ask yourself,

- "Is it bigger than I am?"

- "Does it benefit others as well as myself?"

- "Is it worth dedicating part of my life to?"

If you answer yes to all of these questions, then think about what kinds of people should join you to achieve that dream. Make a list of the like-minded people you know who might want to join you in the process. Then invite them to take the journey with you. And be on the lookout for others who would benefit from being part of the team.

THE LAW OF THE BIG PICTURE

The Goal Is More Important Than the Role

Years ago, I was invited to participate in an important conference that was being planned by a highly respected national organization. I was one of about a dozen speakers who had been selected to speak to an audience of more than sixty thousand people drawn from all parts of the country. It was for a worthy cause that I valued, and I considered the invitation to be an honor.

Several weeks before the conference was to occur, all the speakers were scheduled to meet together along with the founder of the organization to talk strategy, discuss the topics about which we would speak, and give one another support and suggestions. I was really excited about it because the group included some extraordinary leaders. It promised to be an electric time, but the reality of the meeting turned out to be different from what I expected.

When we all got into a room together, it didn't feel like a strategy-and-support session. As we discussed the upcoming day, a few of the speakers seemed to be jockeying for position. Because they were good communicators, they understood that the speaking order, the time of day, and the amount of time allotted would make a big difference in how their messages would be received. The role each speaker was to play seemed to be of more interest than the goal of the conference.

But I also noticed something else. When one speaker briefly informed us about his topic, I sensed immediately that his speech would be the real hinge pin of the whole conference. All of the other messages would be subordinate to it. Yet the man was not fighting for the best place. He wasn't jockeying. He didn't seem to want any part of that kind of maneuvering.

In that moment when everyone was focusing on himself, I realized that we had lost sight of the big picture of why we were there. So I said to the group about this speaker, "I believe his message will be the difference maker in the lives of the people attending this conference. And I think the audience will receive it better if it's delivered when I am slated to speak. Please," I said to the person who wasn't trying to promote himself, "take my spot."

It was almost as if somebody had struck each person in the room. Suddenly everybody regained perspective. After that, instead of looking out for themselves and protecting turf, all of the speakers were willing to give everything for the common good. We all remembered that the goal was more important than our individual roles. That is the essence of the Law of the Big Picture.

WHAT'S IN IT FOR ME?

In a culture that sings the praises of individual gold medals and where a person fights for rights instead of focusing on taking responsibility, people tend to lose sight of the big picture. In fact, some people seem to believe that they *are* the entire picture: Everything revolves around their needs, their goals, and their desires. I saw a message on a T-shirt that expresses the attitude well: "My idea of a team is a whole lot of people doing what I tell them to do."

A team isn't supposed to be a bunch of people being used as a tool by one individual for selfish gain. Members of a team must have mutually beneficial shared goals. They must be motivated to work together, not manipulated by someone for individual glory. Anyone who is accustomed to pulling together people and using them to benefit only himself isn't a team builder; he's a dictator.

> *If you think you are the entire picture, you will never see the big picture.*

If you want to observe team dynamics in action, look at the world of sports where you can easily see whether people are working together. The outcome of a game is immediate and measurable. For that reason it's easy to see when an individual is thinking only of himself and not the shared goals and values of the team.

To win in sports, members of the team must always keep the big picture in front of them. They must remember that the goal is more important than their role—or any individual glory they may desire. NBA superstar David Robinson remarked, "I think any player will tell you that individual accomplishments help your ego, but if you don't win, it makes for a very, very long season. It counts more that the team has played well."

IT'S ALL ABOUT THE TEAM

The acclaimed football coach of Oklahoma during the 1950s, Bud Wilkinson, put it this way in *The Book of Football Wisdom:* "If a team is to reach its potential, each player must be willing to subordinate his personal goals to the good of the team."

> *"If a team is to reach its potential, each player must be willing to subordinate his personal goals to the good of the team."*
>
> —BUD WILKINSON

Some sports teams seem to embrace an "everyone-for-himself" mind-set. Others weave the attitude of subordination and teamwork into the fabric of everything they do. For example, football teams such as Notre Dame and Penn State don't put the names of the players on their jerseys. Lou Holtz, former coach of the Fighting Irish, once explained why. He said, "At Notre Dame, we believed the interlocking ND was all the identification you needed. Whenever anyone complained, I told them they were lucky we allowed numbers on the uniforms. Given my druthers, I would have nothing more than initials indicating what position the wearer played. If your priority is the team rather than yourself, what else do you need?"

Winning teams have players who put the good of the team ahead of themselves. They want to play in their area of strength, but they're willing to do what it takes to take care of the team. They are willing to sacrifice their role for the greater goal. That's the Law of the Big Picture.

SEEING THE BIG PICTURE

People who build successful teams never forget that every person on a team has a role to play, and every role plays its part in contributing to the bigger picture. Without that perspective the team cannot accomplish its goal, whether the team's "game" is sports, business, family, ministry, or government.

Leaders at the highest level understand the Law of the Big Picture. They continually keep the vision of the big picture before themselves and their people. An outstanding example involves Winston Churchill. It's said that during World War II when Britain was experiencing its darkest days, the country had a difficult time keeping men working in the coal mines. Many wanted to give up their dirty, thankless jobs in the dangerous mines to join military service, which garnered much public praise and support. Yet their work in the mines was critical to the success of the war. Without coal the military and the people at home would be in trouble.

So the prime minister faced thousands of coal miners one day and told them of their importance to the war effort, how their role could make or break the goal of maintaining England's freedom.

Churchill painted a picture of what it would be like when the war ended, of the grand parade that would honor the people who fought the war. First would come the sailors of the navy, he said, the people who continued the tradition of Trafalgar and the defeat of the Spanish Armada. Next would come the best and brightest of Britain, the pilots of the Royal Air Force who fended off the German Luftwaffe. Following them would be the soldiers who had fought at Dunkirk.

Then last of all would come the coal-dust-covered men in miners' caps. And Churchill indicated that someone from the crowd might say, "And where were you during the critical days of the struggle?"

And the voices of ten thousand men would respond, "We were deep in the earth with our faces to the coal."

It's said that tears appeared in the eyes of those hardened men. And they returned to their inglorious work with steely resolve, having been reminded of the role they were playing in their country's noble goal of preserving freedom for the Western world.

> *"Everybody on a championship team doesn't get publicity, but everyone can say he's a champion."*
>
> —EARVIN "MAGIC" JOHNSON

That's the kind of mind-set it takes to build a team. It takes the courage and the resolve to recognize that *the goal is more important than the role*. It's no small thing for people to do what's best for the team. Often it means sacrificing professional satisfaction, individual statistics, or personal glory. But as NBA star-turned-successful-businessman Earvin "Magic" Johnson says, "Everybody on a championship team doesn't get publicity, but everyone can say he's a champion."

WHAT'S UP WITH BIG PICTURE TEAMS?

So how do people start to become a more unified team? How do individuals make the shift from independent people to team players who exemplify the Law of the Big Picture? It's not something that happens overnight. It takes time. Here is my best take on how to get the process started.

1. Look Up *at the Big Picture*

Everything starts with vision. You need to have a goal. Without one you cannot have a real team. Hall of Fame catcher Yogi Berra joked, "If you don't know where you're going, you'll end up somewhere else." An individual without a goal may end up anywhere. A group of individuals without a goal can go nowhere. On the other hand, if everyone in a group embraces the vision for achieving the big picture, then the people have the potential to become an effective team.

Leaders usually have the role of capturing and communicating vision. They must see it first and then help everyone else to see it. That was what Winston Churchill did when he spoke to the coal miners during the war. That was what Dr. Martin Luther King Jr. did as he spoke to people about his dream from the steps of the Lincoln Monument in Washington, D.C. That was what GE CEO Jack Welch did when he let his people know that a division of GE that couldn't be first or second in its market wouldn't be a part of GE. The people on a team will sacrifice and work together *only* if they can see what they're working toward.

If you are the leader of your team, your role is to do what only you can do: Paint the big picture for your people. Without the vision they will not find the desire to achieve the goal.

2. Size Up *the Situation*

One value of seeing the big picture is that it helps you recognize how far you really are from achieving it. For someone determined to do everything alone, seeing the gulf between what is and what could be is often intimidating. But for people who live to build teams, seeing the size of the task ahead doesn't worry them. They don't shrink from the challenge—they savor the opportunity. They can't wait to put together a team and a plan to accomplish that vision.

At a meeting of all three divisions of The INJOY Group, CEO Dave Sutherland stood before our people and outlined a few of our goals for the coming year. (Some of those goals were huge.) During that process, Dave said, "Some people see the size of the goal, and they get scared. That doesn't bother me a bit. We've already got a great team. To make it to the next level, we just need a few more people like the ones we already have." That's the mind-set of a team builder!

3. Line Up *Needed Resources*

Hawley R. Everhart believes, "It's all right to aim high if you have plenty of ammunition." That's what resources are: ammunition to help you reach a goal. It doesn't matter what kind of team you're on. You cannot make progress without the support of the appropriate equipment, facilities, funds, and so forth—whether your goal is climbing a mountain, capturing a market, or creating a ministry. The better resourced the team is, the fewer distractions the players will have as they try to achieve their goal.

4. Call Up *the Right Players*

When it comes to building a successful team, the players are everything. You can have a distinct vision, a precise plan, plenty of resources, and incredible leadership, but if you don't have the right people, you're not going to get anywhere. (I'll talk more about this in several of the other laws.) You can lose with good players, but you cannot win with bad ones.

5. Give Up *Personal Agendas*

Teams that win have players who continually ask themselves, "What's best for the rest?" They continually set aside their personal agendas for the good of the team. Their motto can be expressed by the words of Ray Kroc, founder of McDonald's, who said, "No one of us is more important than the rest of us."

A remarkable sports story from several years ago was the success of the U.S. Women's Soccer Team. They won the Olympic gold medal and the World Cup in a few brief years. A key player on that team was Mia Hamm. In her book *Go for the Goal*, she gives her perspective on her sport and the attitude a player must bring into the game to achieve the goal of becoming a champion:

> *"No one of us is more important than the rest of us."*
>
> —RAY KROC

Soccer is not an individual sport. I don't score all the goals, and the ones I do score are usually the product of a team effort. I don't keep the ball out of the back of the net on the other end of the field. I don't plan our game tactics. I don't wash our training gear (okay, sometimes I do), and I don't make our airline reservations. I am a member of a team, and I rely on the team. I defer to it and sacrifice for it, because the team, not the individual, is the ultimate champion.

Mia Hamm understands the Law of the Big Picture. And by doing whatever it took to help her team—including washing the gear—she demonstrated that the goal was more important than the role.

6. Step Up *to a Higher Level*

Only when players come together and give up their own agendas can a team move up to a higher level. That's the kind of sacrifice required for teamwork. Unfortunately some people prefer to cling to agendas and pursue the paths of their own inflated egos instead of letting go of them to achieve something greater than themselves.

It's just as philosopher Friedrich Nietzsche said: "Many are stubborn in pursuit of the path they have chosen, few in pursuit of the goal." And that's a shame because people who think only of themselves are missing the big picture. As a result their potential goes untapped, and the people who are depending on them are bound to be let down.

SUBORDINATE ROLE FOR THE TEAM'S SUCCESS

President Abraham Lincoln once remarked, "Nearly all men can stand adversity, but if you want to test a man's character, give him power." Few people have more power than an American president. Being the so-called leader of the free world can certainly go to a person's head. But not to Jimmy Carter's. If you review his career—from the time he was a school board official to his term in the White House and beyond—you can see that he was willing to take on nearly any role to achieve a goal he believed in. He has always embraced the importance of the big picture.

There is possibly no more vivid example of the Law of the Big Picture in Carter's life than his work with Habitat for Humanity. Habitat was officially founded by Millard and Linda Fuller in 1976, though the two had been exploring the idea for many years before that, first in the U.S. and then overseas. The goal of the organization is a huge one—to eliminate poverty-level housing and homelessness from the world.

In the late seventies and early eighties, they began their bold venture. After six years they had built houses internationally in Mexico, Zaire, and Guatemala. And in the U.S., they had affiliates building houses in San Antonio, Texas; Americus, Georgia; Johns Island, South Carolina; and other locations in Florida and Appalachia. Groundwork was being laid for them to build in many other cities, but the process was a struggle. They had found a successful formula for their goal: Offer home ownership to the neediest people able to make a house payment, build low-cost housing using volunteer labor, involve the future home owner in the building process, and create no-interest loans to finance the houses. It was an inspired idea, and it was catching on. To reach the world as they desired, however, the Fullers knew they would have to take Habitat to a whole new level.

From their headquarters in the town of Americus in southern Georgia, the Fullers saw a possibility. Ten miles away in the tiny town of Plains was a man who might be able to help them: Jimmy Carter. The former U.S. president had spoken at a couple of Habitat functions. Following Carter's speaking in 1983, Millard Fuller got the idea to approach Carter about helping the project along. And in early 1984 they made contact. When Carter said he was very interested in Habitat for Humanity, Fuller decided to boldly propose a list of fifteen possible roles the former president could take, hoping he would agree to one or two. His list included serving on Habitat's board, making media contacts, helping to raise money, doing a thirty-minute video, and working on a building crew for a day.

To Fuller's surprise, Carter did not agree to do one or two items on the list. He agreed to do *everything* on it. Ironically the task that captured the attention of the public most was Carter's willingness to serve on a building crew and swing a hammer to help construct a house. At first people thought Carter would just stop by for brief publicity photos. But the former president put together a work crew, traveled with them via Trailways bus to the Brooklyn, New York, building site, worked tenaciously every day for a week, and slept in a church basement along with everyone else. That first time was in 1984. Carter has raised a team and served in similar fashion every year since then. And his dedicated service has attracted people from every walk of life to serve in similar roles.[1]

A SHARED GOAL

Habitat for Humanity is the brainchild of the Fullers, and its success is the result of the efforts of hundreds of thousands of people from around the globe. But Jimmy Carter is the one who put it on the map. His selfless service inspired people rich and poor, famous and obscure, powerful and not so powerful to see the huge goal of helping people at the lowest level of society by providing them with a decent place to live. And he inspired them to get involved.

So far Habitat and its volunteers have built more than 100,000 houses sheltering more than a half million people all over the world.[2] Why? Because they, like Carter, wanted to be part of something bigger than themselves. They understood that the goal was more important than the role. They embraced the truth of the Law of the Big Picture.

TEAMWORK THOUGHT

When you see the big picture correctly,
you serve the team more quickly.

BECOMING A BETTER TEAM MEMBER

What goal in your life is bigger than you are? Are you currently participating in something greater than yourself? If not, set aside some time to spend alone reflecting on your goals and priorities. If you are trying to accomplish something big, then ask yourself what you are willing to do to accomplish it. Are you willing to take a subordinate role if necessary for the good of the team, as President Carter did? If not, you may become a hindrance to the success of the team.

BECOMING A BETTER TEAM LEADER

Think about a team you are currently part of (preferably one with a big goal). What kind of attitude do team members have when it comes to the big picture? Are they team players who desire to do whatever it takes for the team to succeed? Or do they desire to benefit only themselves?

Begin to foster a team mind-set in others by modeling a willingness to serve the big picture rather than yourself. Then think about ways you can help your teammates to embrace the Law of the Big Picture. Motivate people by painting the big picture. Publicly honor team play. And give rewards to people who sacrifice for the good of the team.

3

THE LAW OF THE NICHE

All Players Have a Place Where They Add the Most Value

On January 26, 2001, the United States experienced a historic first: An African-American assumed the post of secretary of state, the highest cabinet post in the United States government. The man who took that position was Colin Powell. Columnist Carl Rowan remarked of the appointment, "To understand the significance of Powell's elevation to this extremely difficult and demanding post, you must realize that only a generation ago it was an unwritten rule that in the foreign affairs field, blacks could serve only as ambassador to Liberia and minister to the Canary Islands."

Powell's appointment was remarkable, but not just because it was groundbreaking. It was significant because, to put it simply, Colin Powell was the best individual in all of the United States to take on the role of secretary of state. George W. Bush, the president who appointed him, stated, "In this cause, I know of no better person to be the face and voice of American diplomacy than Colin Powell," citing his "directness of speech, his towering integrity, his deep respect for our democracy, and his soldier's sense of duty."[1] Bush recognizes that *all players have a place where they add the most value.* Powell's is running the State Department. That's the Law of the Niche.

A Place for Him

A soldier's sense of duty has been a vital part of the character of Colin Powell since he was in his early twenties. Something of a late bloomer, Powell entered college uncertain of what he wanted to do with his life. But it didn't take him long to find his identity: in an ROTC unit called the Pershing Rifles at the City College of New York. It was there that he discovered real teamwork for the first time in his life. In *My American Journey*, Powell wrote:

> My experience in high school, on basketball and track teams, and briefly in Boy Scouting had never produced a sense of belonging or many permanent friendships. The Pershing Rifles did. For the first time in my life I was a member of a brotherhood . . . The discipline, the structure, the camaraderie, the sense of belonging were what I craved. I became a leader almost immediately. I found a selflessness among the ranks that reminded me of the caring atmosphere within my family. Race, color, background, income meant nothing. The PRs [Pershing Rifles] would go the limit for each other and for the group. If this was what soldiering was all about, then maybe I wanted to be a soldier.[2]

As he got closer to graduation from college, there was no doubt in his mind. He gladly chose military life.

NO ORDINARY JOURNEY

In the army Powell seemed to achieve success everywhere he went and quickly rose in rank. His love was commanding troops, and when he received those assignments, he did well. Yet he was constantly tapped for special jobs and responsibilities. When that happened again and again, keeping him from leading soldiers in the field, he became frustrated. But a mentor, General John Wickham, wisely told him, "You're not going to have a conventional army career. Some officers are just not destined for it."

Wickham was right. Powell's career did turn out to be unusual. And it ultimately prepared him for a cabinet post, sharpening his gifts and giving him broad experience. As an infantry officer who did tours around the globe (including two in Vietnam), Powell learned command and leadership. His work with soldiers also taught him to communicate and connect with people. As a White House Fellow, he got his first exposure to American politics and world governments. Besides his interaction with high-level U.S. officials, he met with leaders of Japan, the Soviet Union, China, Poland, Bulgaria, and West Germany.

Powell moved to a whole new level in his post at the Pentagon during the Carter and Reagan administrations. It was there that he learned how to work with civil servants and he expanded his understanding of government and military politics. As the senior military assistant to Secretary of Defense Caspar Weinberger, Powell traveled the world and attained in-depth comprehension of the complex relationships between the United States and foreign powers.

But in the office of the national security adviser, Powell stepped into the big leagues. As the deputy assistant to the president for national security affairs, he gained valuable experience in foreign policy. In fact, he was so adept that when his boss, Frank Carlucci, was asked to be secretary of defense, Powell stepped into Carlucci's former position as national security adviser. There he not only advised President Reagan, but Powell worked side by side with Secretary of State George Shultz as the statesman negotiated nuclear missile treaties with the USSR, organized summits between heads of state, and worked with Soviet President Mikhail Gorbachev to end the cold war.

COMMAND PERFORMANCE

How does someone like Colin Powell top off a successful term as the nation's first African-American national security adviser? By achieving the military's highest rank of four stars, and then by becoming the youngest chairman of the Joint Chiefs of Staff in the history of the nation. (He was also that position's first African-American and first ROTC graduate.) And once again, Powell shone in his position. Les Aspin, former secretary of defense, commented about Powell following a meeting in the Clinton White House, "It was so clear to all of us that he could do any job in the room, up to and including president."[3]

When President-elect Bush approached him about becoming a cabinet member, there was only one logical place for him to serve, the place where he would add the most. At a town hall meeting on January 25, 2001, Powell remarked,

---

I didn't know I would be coming back into government when I left the Army seven years ago and went into private life . . . But when Governor Bush asked me to consider it, I was ready for it. I was anxious to see if I could serve again. I think I have something to contribute still. And when he specifically said, I would like you to go to the State Department, it was almost as if I had been preparing for this in one way or another for many, many years. My work in the Pentagon, my work as a Deputy National Security Adviser, National Security Adviser, Chairman of the Joint Chiefs of Staff, and seven years in private life watching the world change, suggested to me this is something I should do.[4]

President Bush, his cabinet, and everyone in the country have a lot to gain from Powell. Not only is he the best person for the job, but he has given the newly elected president and his team greater credibility with a constituency inclined not to trust them. Powell's appointment is tangible proof of Bush's claim to inclusiveness. But that's the power of the Law of the Niche. When the right team member is in the right place, everyone benefits.

Good things happen to a team when a player takes the place where he adds the most value. Great things happen when all the players on the team take the role that maximizes their strengths—their talent, skill, and experience. That's the power of the Law of the Niche.

WHEN PEOPLE ARE IN THE WRONG PLACE

Just about everyone has experienced being on some kind of team where people had to take on roles that didn't suit them: an accountant forced to work with people all day, a basketball forward forced to play center, a guitarist filling in on keyboard, a teacher stuck doing paperwork, a spouse who hates the kitchen taking on the role of cook.

What happens to a team when one or more of its members constantly play out of position? First, morale erodes because the team isn't playing up to its capability. Then people become resentful. The people working in an area of weakness resent that their best is untapped. And other people on the team who know that they could better fill a mismatched position on the team resent that their skills are being overlooked. Before long, people become unwilling to work as a team. Then everyone's confidence begins to erode. And the situation just keeps getting worse. The team stops progressing, and the competition takes advantage of the team's obvious weaknesses. As a result the team never realizes its potential. When people aren't where they do things well, things don't turn out well. That's the Law of the Niche.

Having the right people in the right places is essential to team building. A team's dynamic changes according to the placement of people:

The Wrong Person in the Wrong Place	=	Regression
The Wrong Person in the Right Place	=	Frustration
The Right Person in the Wrong Place	=	Confusion
The Right Person in the Right Place	=	Progression
The Right People in the Right Places	=	Multiplication

It doesn't matter what kind of team you're dealing with, the principles are the same. David Ogilvy was right when he said, "A well-run restaurant is like a winning baseball team. It makes the most of every crew member's talent and takes advantage of every split-second opportunity to speed up service."

I was reminded of the Law of the Niche by something I did a few years ago. I had been asked to write a chapter for a book called *Destiny and Deliverance,* which was tied to the DreamWorks movie *The Prince of Egypt.* It was a wonderful, delightful experience. During the writing process, I was invited to go to California and view parts of the movie while it was still in production. That made me want to do something I had never done before: attend a movie premiere in Hollywood.

My publisher managed to get me a pair of tickets for the premiere, and when the time arrived, my wife, Margaret, and I flew out to the movie capital. Movie stars and moviemakers, along with many other people in the industry, attended the high-energy event. Margaret and I enjoyed the movie—and the whole experience—immensely. In short, we had a blast.

Now, anybody who's gone to a movie, show, or sporting event with me knows my pattern. As soon as I am pretty certain about the outcome of a ball game, I hit the exit to beat the crowds. When the Broadway audience is giving the ovation, I'm gone. And the second the credits begin to roll in a movie, I'm out of my seat. As *The Prince of Egypt* came to a close, I started to get up, but not a person in the theater moved. And then something really surprising happened. As the credits rolled, people began to applaud the lesser-known individuals whose names appeared on the screen: the costume designer, the gaffer, the key grip, the assistant director. It was a moment I'll never forget—and a distinct reminder of the Law of the Niche: *All players have a place where they add the most value.* When each person does the job that's best for him, everybody wins.

PUT PEOPLE IN THEIR PLACE

NFL champion coach Vince Lombardi observed, "The achievements of an organization are the results of the combined effort of each individual." That is true, but creating a winning team doesn't come just from having the right individuals. You may have a group of talented individuals, but if each person is not doing what adds the most value to the team, you won't achieve your potential as a team. That's the art of leading a team. You've got to put people in their places—and I mean that in the most positive way!

To be able to put people in the places that utilize their talents and maximize the team's potential, you need three things:

You Must Know the Team

You cannot build a winning team or organization if you don't know its vision, purpose, culture, or history. If you don't know where the team is trying to go—and why it's trying to get there—you cannot take the team to the height of its potential. You've got to start where the team actually is; only then can you take it somewhere.

You Must Know the Situation

Even though the vision or purpose of an organization may be fairly constant, its situation changes constantly. Good team builders know where the team is and what the situation requires. For example, when a team is young and just getting started, the greatest priority is often to gather good people. But as a team matures and the level of talent increases, fine-tuning becomes more important. At that time a leader must spend more time matching the person to the position.

You Must Know the Player

It sounds obvious, but you must know the person you are trying to position in the right niche. I mention it because leaders tend to want to make everyone else conform to their image, to approach their work using the same skills and problem-solving methods. But team building is not working on an assembly line.

As you work to build a team, evaluate each person's experience, skills, temperament, attitude, passion, people skills, discipline, emotional strength, and potential. Only then will you be ready to help a team member find his proper place.

START BY FINDING THE RIGHT PLACE FOR YOU

Right now you may not be in a position to place others on your team. In fact, you may be thinking, *How do I find my niche?* If that's the case, then follow these guidelines:

- *Be secure.* My friend Wayne Schmidt says, "No amount of personal competency compensates for personal insecurity." If you allow your insecurities to get the better of you, you'll be inflexible and reluctant to change. And to grow, you must be willing to change.

- *Get to know yourself.* You won't be able to find your niche if you don't know your strengths and weaknesses. Spend time reflecting on and exploring your gifts. Ask others to give you feedback. Do what it takes to remove personal blind spots.

- *Trust your leader.* A good leader will help you start moving in the right direction. If you don't trust your leader, look to another mentor for help. Or get on another team.

- *See the big picture.* Your place on the team makes sense only in the context of the big picture. If your only motivation for finding your niche is personal gain, your poor motives may prevent you from discovering what you desire.

- *Rely on your experience.* When it comes down to it, the only way to know that you've discovered your niche is to try what seems right and learn from your failures and successes. When you discover what you were made for, your heart sings. It says, *There's no place like this place anywhere near this place, so this must be the place!*

> *When you discover your place, you will say, "There's no place like this place anywhere near this place, so this must be the place!"*

A PLACE FOR EVERYONE AND EVERYONE IN HIS PLACE

One organization that strives to match its people to the right places is the U.S. military. That is particularly true now that it employs an all-volunteer force. If each function in a military command doesn't work at top efficiency (and interact well with all the other parts), then terrible—and sometimes deadly—breakdowns occur.

Nobody is more keenly aware of that than a combat pilot. Take, for example, Charlie Plumb, who retired as a captain of the U.S. Navy. A graduate of Annapolis, he served in Vietnam in the mid-1960s, flying seventy-five missions from the aircraft carrier USS *Kitty Hawk.*

An aircraft carrier is a place where you can readily observe how all the pieces of the military puzzle come together to support each other. A carrier is often described as being like a floating city with its crew of 5,500 people, a population greater than that of some towns in which its crew members grew up. It must be self-sustaining, and each of its seventeen departments must function as a team accomplishing its mission.

Every pilot knows of the team effort required to put a jet in the air. It takes hundreds of people utilizing dozens of technical specialties to launch, monitor, support, land, and maintain an aircraft. Even more people are involved if that plane is armed for combat. Charlie Plumb undoubtedly recognized that many people worked tirelessly to keep him flying. But despite the efforts of the best-trained air support group in the world, Plumb found himself in a North Vietnamese prison as a POW after his F-4 Phantom jet was shot down on May 19, 1967, during his seventy-fifth mission.

Plumb was held prisoner for nearly six grueling years, part of the time in the infamous Hanoi Hilton. During those years, he and his fellow prisoners were humiliated, starved, tortured, and forced to live in squalid conditions. Yet he didn't let the experience break him. He now says, "Our unity through our faith in God and in our love for country were the great strength which kept us going through some very difficult times."

TURNING POINT

Plumb was released from his imprisonment on February 18, 1973, and continued his career in the navy. But an incident years after his return to the United States marked his life as surely as his imprisonment. One day he and his wife, Cathy, were eating in a restaurant when a man came to the table and said, "You're Plumb. You flew jet fighters in Vietnam."

"That's right," answered Plumb. "I did."

"It was fighter squadron 114 on the *Kitty Hawk.* You were shot down. You parachuted into enemy hands," the man continued. "You spent six years as a prisoner of war."

The former pilot was taken aback. He looked at the man, trying to identify him, but couldn't. "How in the world did you know that?" Plumb finally asked.

"I packed your parachute."

Plumb was staggered. All he could do was struggle to his feet and shake the man's hand. "I must tell you," Plumb finally said, "I've said a lot of prayers of thanks for your nimble fingers, but I didn't realize I'd have the opportunity of saying thanks in person."[5]

What if the navy had put the wrong person in the position of parachute rigger, the anonymous and the rarely thanked job that man performed during the Vietnam War? Charlie Plumb wouldn't have known about it until it was too late. And we wouldn't even know where the breakdown had occurred because Plumb wouldn't have lived to tell the tale.

Today, Charlie Plumb is a motivational speaker to Fortune 500 companies, government agencies, and other organizations. He often tells the story of the man who packed his parachute, and he uses it to deliver a message on teamwork. He says, "In a world where downsizing forces us to do more with less, we must empower the team. 'Packing others' parachutes' can mean the difference in survival. Yours and your team's!"[6]

That's just another way of communicating the Law of the Niche. Are you packing parachutes for your teammates? Or are you functioning at less than 100 percent? *All players have a place where they add the most value.* I want to encourage you to make sure you've found yours.

TEAMWORK THOUGHT

You are most valuable where you add the most value.

BECOMING A BETTER TEAM MEMBER

Have you found your niche? As you fulfill your responsibilities, do you find yourself thinking something like, *There's no place like this place anywhere near this place, so this must be the place*? If so, then stay the course and keep growing and learning in your area of expertise. If not, you need to get on track.

If you know what your niche is but aren't working in it, start planning a transition. It could be as simple as a change in duties or as complex as a change of career. No matter whether it will require six weeks or six years, you need a transition plan and a timetable for completing it. Once you're certain of your course, have the courage to take the first step.

If you have no idea what you should be doing, you need to do some research. Talk to your spouse and close friends about your strengths and weaknesses. Ask for your leader's assessment. Take personality or temperament tests. Look for recurring themes in your life. Try to articulate your life purpose. Do whatever it takes to find clues concerning where you should be. Then try new things related to your discoveries. The only way to find your niche is to gain experience.

BECOMING A BETTER TEAM LEADER

A sign of a great team leader is the proper placement of people. Use the guidelines in the chapter—know your team, the situation, and the players—to begin improving your placement process. And remember this: To help people reach their potential and maximize their effectiveness, stretch them out of their comfort zones, but never out of their gift zones. Moving people outside their gifts leads to frustration, but motivating people out of their comfort zones leads to fulfillment.

> *A sign of a great team leader is the proper placement of people.*

THE LAW OF MOUNT EVEREST

As the Challenge Escalates, the Need for Teamwork Elevates

In 1935, twenty-one-year-old Tenzing Norgay made his first trip to Mount Everest. He worked as a porter for a British team of mountaineers. A Sherpa born in the high altitudes of Nepal, Tenzing had been drawn to the mountain from the time that Westerners began visiting the area with the idea of climbing to the mountain's peak. The first group had come in 1920. Fifteen years later, climbers were still trying to figure out how to conquer the mountain.

The farthest this expedition would go was up to the North Col, which was at an altitude of 22,000 feet. (A col is a flat area along a mountain's ridge between peaks.) And it was just below that col that the climbing party made a gruesome discovery. They came across a wind-shredded tent. And in that tent was a skeleton with a little frozen skin stretched over the bones. It was sitting in an odd position, with one boot off and the laces of the other boot between its bony fingers.

HARSHEST PLACE ON THE PLANET

Mountain climbing is not for the faint of heart because the world's highest peaks are some of the most inhospitable places on earth. Of course, that hasn't stopped people from attempting to conquer mountains. In 1786, the first climbers made it to the summit of Europe's highest mountain, Mont Blanc in France. That was quite a feat. But there's a big difference between climbing the highest of the Alps at 15,771 feet and climbing Everest, the world's highest peak at 29,035 feet, especially in the days before high-tech equipment. Everest is remote, the altitude incapacitates all but the hardiest and most experienced climbers, and the weather is ruthlessly unforgiving. Experts believe that the bodies of 120 failed climbers remain on the mountain today.[1]

The body Tenzing and the others found in 1935 was that of Maurice Wilson, an Englishman who had sneaked into Tibet and tried to climb the mountain secretly, without the permission of the Tibetan government. Because he was trying to make the ascent quietly, he had hired only three porters to climb the mountain with him. As they approached the North Col, those men had refused to go any farther with him. Wilson decided to try to make the climb on his own. That decision killed him.

MEASURE THE COST

Only someone who has climbed a formidable mountain knows what it takes to make it to the top. For thirty-two years, between 1920 and 1952, seven major expeditions tried—and failed—to make it to the top of Everest. Tenzing Norgay was on six of those expeditions, as well as many other high climbs to other mountains. His fellow climbers joked that he had a third lung because of his ability to climb tirelessly while carrying heavy loads. He became respected, and he learned a lot. The greatest lesson was that no one should underestimate the difficulty of the climb. He had seen people do it at the ultimate cost to themselves.

On one climb, for example, when conditions became difficult, Tenzing and the other Sherpas put on their crampons (spikes that attach to climbing boots). But George Frey, an experienced mountaineer, decided not to wear his because he thought he didn't need them. He slipped and fell one thousand feet to his death below. Tenzing regretted the man's death, but his view was realistic. He wrote of careless climbers, "Like so many men before them—they had held a great mountain too lightly, and they had paid the price."[2]

NOT A CASUAL STROLL

In 1953, Tenzing embarked on his seventh expedition to Everest with a British group led by Colonel John Hunt. By then, he was respected not only as a porter who could carry heavy loads at high altitudes, but also as a mountaineer and full-fledged expedition member, an honor unusual at that time for a Sherpa. The year before he had climbed to a height of 28,250 feet with a Swiss team. Up to then, that was the closest any human being had come to the top of the mountain.

Tenzing was also engaged to be the British group's sirdar for the trip, the Sherpa leader who would hire, organize, and lead the porters for the journey. That was no small task. To hope to get just two people from base camp up to the summit, the team brought ten high-altitude climbers, including a New Zealander named Edmund Hillary. Altogether, the men would require two and a half *tons* of equipment and food. Those supplies couldn't be trucked or air-lifted to the base of the mountain. They had to be delivered to Kathmandu and *carried* on the backs of men and women 180 miles up and down Himalayan ridges and over rivers crossed by narrow rope-and-plank bridges to the base camp. Tenzing would have to hire between two and three hundred people just to get the supplies in the vicinity of the mountain.

Supplies needed by the party above the base camp would have to be carried up the mountain by another forty porters, each a Sherpa with extensive mountain experience. The best third of that team would continue working higher up the mountain, carrying up the 750 pounds of necessary equipment in 30-pound loads. Only Tenzing and three other porters would have the strength and skill to go to the high camps near the summit.

IT TAKES A TEAM

For each level that the climbers reached, a higher degree of team-work was required. One set of men would exhaust themselves just to get equipment up the mountain for the next group. Two-man teams would work their way up the mountain, finding a path, cutting steps, securing ropes. And then they would be finished, having spent themselves to make the next leg of the climb possible for another team. Of the teamwork involved, Tenzing remarked,

> You do not climb a mountain like Everest by trying to race ahead
> on your own, or by competing with your comrades. You do it slowly

and carefully, by unselfish teamwork. Certainly I wanted to reach the top myself; it was the thing I had dreamed of all my life. But if the lot fell to someone else I would take it like a man, and not a cry-baby. For that is the mountain way.[3]

The team of climbers, using the "mountain way," ultimately made it possible for two pairs to make an attempt at reaching the summit. The first consisted of Tom Bourdillon and Charles Evans. When they tried and failed, the other team got its chance. That team consisted of Tenzing and Edmund Hillary. Tenzing wrote of the first team:

> They were worn-out, sick with exhaustion, and, of course, terribly disappointed that they had not reached the summit themselves. But still . . . they did everything they could to advise and help us. And I thought, Yes, that is how it is on a mountain. That is how a mountain makes men great. For where would Hillary and I have been without the others? Without the climbers who had made the route and the Sherpas who had carried the loads? Without Bourdillon and Evans, Hunt and Da Namgyal, who had cleared the way ahead? Without Lowe and Gregory, Ang Hyima, Ang Tempra, and Penba, who were there only to help us? It was only because of the work and sacrifice of all of them that we were now to have our chance at the top.[4]

They made the most of their chance. On May 29, 1953, Tenzing Norgay and Edmund Hillary accomplished what no other human being ever had: They stood on the summit of Mount Everest, the world's highest peak!

Could Tenzing and Hillary have made it alone? The answer is

no. Could they have made it without a great team? Again, the answer is no. Why? Because *as the challenge escalates, the need for teamwork elevates.* That's the Law of Mount Everest.

WHAT IS YOUR EVEREST?

You may not be a mountain climber, and you may not have any desire to reach the summit of Everest. But I bet you have a dream. I say that with confidence because deep down everybody has one—even the people who haven't figured out what theirs is yet. If you have a dream, you need a team to accomplish it.

How do you approach the task of putting together a team to accomplish your dream? I think the best way to start is to ask yourself three questions:

1. "What Is My Dream?"

It all starts with this question because your answer reveals *what could be.* Robert Greenleaf remarked, "Nothing much happens without a dream. For something really great to happen, it takes a really great dream."

What lies in your heart? What do you see as a possibility for your life? What would you like to accomplish during your time on this earth? Only a dream will tell you such things. As Harlem Renaissance poet Langston Hughes wrote:

> Hold fast to dreams for if dreams die,
> Life is a broken-winged bird that cannot fly.
> Hold fast to dreams for when dreams go,
> Life is a barren field frozen with snow.

If you want to do something great, you must have a dream. But a dream is not enough. You can fulfill a dream only if you are part of a team.

2. "Who Is on My Team?"

This second question tells you *what is.* It measures your current situation. Your potential is only as good as your current team. That's why you must examine who is joining you on your journey. A mountain climber like Maurice Wilson, who had only three halfhearted companions, was never able to accomplish his dream of climbing the mountain. However, someone like Tenzing Norgay, who always climbed Everest with the best mountaineers in the world, was able to make it to the top. A great dream with a bad team is nothing more than a nightmare.

3. "What Should My Dream Team Look Like?"

The truth is that your team must be the size of your dream. If it's not, then you won't achieve it. You simply cannot achieve an ultimate number ten dream with a number four team. It just doesn't happen. If you want to climb Mount Everest, you need a Mount Everest–sized team. There's no other way to do it. It's better to have a great team with a weak dream than a great dream with a weak team.

> *Your team must be the size of your dream.*

FOCUS ON THE TEAM, NOT THE DREAM

One mistake I've seen people repeatedly make is that they focus too much attention on their dream and too little on their team. But the truth is that if you build the right team, the dream will almost take care of itself.

Every dream brings challenges of its own. The kind of challenge determines the kind of team you need to build. Consider a few examples:

> *Many people focus too much attention on their dream and too little on their team.*

Type of Challenge	Type of Team Required
New Challenge	Creative Team
Controversial Challenge	United Team
Changing Challenge	Fast and Flexible Team
Unpleasant Challenge	Motivated Team
Diversified Challenge	Complementary Team
Long-term Challenge	Determined Team
Everest-sized Challenge	Experienced Team

If you want to achieve your dream—I mean really do it, not just imagine what it would be like—then grow your team. But as you do so, make sure your motives are right. Some people gather a team just to benefit themselves. Others do it because they enjoy the team experience and want to create a sense of community. Still others do it because they want to build an organization. The funny thing about these reasons is that if you're motivated by *all* of them, then your desire to build a team probably comes from wanting to add value to everyone on the team. But if your desire to build the team comes as the result of only one of these reasons, you probably need to examine your motives.

How to Grow a Team

When the team you have doesn't match up to the team of your dreams, then you have only two choices: Give up your dream, or grow up your team. Here is my recommendation concerning how to do the latter.

> *When the team you have doesn't match up to the team of your dreams, then you have only two choices: Give up your dream, or grow up your team.*

1. Develop Team Members

The first step to take with a team that's not realizing its potential is to help individual team members to grow. If you're leading the team, then one of your most important responsibilities is to see the potential that people don't see in themselves and draw it out. When you accomplish this, you're doing your job as a leader.

Think about the people on your team, and determine what they need based on the following categories:

- Enthusiastic beginner—needs direction

- Disillusioned learner—needs coaching

- Cautious completer—needs support

- Self-reliant achiever—needs responsibility

Always give the people who are already on your team a chance to grow and bloom. That's what early British explorer Eric Shipton did with a young, inexperienced kid named Tenzing in 1935, and his country was rewarded eighteen years later with a successful climb of the world's highest peak.

2. Add Key Team Members

Even if you give every person on your team a chance to learn and grow, and all of them make the most of the opportunities, you may find that you still lack the talent needed to accomplish your dream. That's when it's time to recruit that talent. Sometimes all the team needs is one key person with talent in an area to make the difference between success and failure. (I'll talk more about this in the Law of the Bench.)

3. Change the Leadership

Various team challenges require different kinds of leadership. If a team has the right talent but still isn't growing, sometimes the best thing you can do is to ask someone from the team who has previously been a follower to step into a leadership role. That transition may occur only for a short season, or it may be more permanent.

> *The challenge of the moment often determines the leader for that challenge.*

The challenge of the moment often determines the leader for that challenge. Why? Because every person on the team has strengths and weaknesses that come into play. That was the case for the Everest team as they faced every stage of the journey. Colonel Hunt chose the climbers and led the expedition, casting vision, modeling unselfish service, and making critical decisions about who would take which part. Tenzing chose the porters, leading, organizing, and motivating them to build the camps at each stage of the mountain. And the climbing teams took turns leading, cutting the trail up the mountain so that Hillary and Tenzing could make the final climb to the summit. When a particular challenge emerged, so did a leader to meet it. And everyone worked together, doing his part.

If your team is facing a big challenge, and it doesn't seem to be making any progress "up the mountain," then it might be time to change leaders. There may be someone on the team more capable for leading during this season. (Learn more by reading the myths of the head table and the round table in the Law of the Edge.)

4. Remove Ineffective Members

Sometimes a team member can turn a winning team into a losing one, either through lack of skill or a poor attitude. In those cases you must put the team first and make changes for the greater good.

Tenzing faced that situation during the Everest expedition of 1953. During early days of travel, there were continual flare-ups between the porters and the British team of climbers, and as sirdar, Tenzing was constantly stuck in the middle trying to work things out. After repeatedly negotiating the peace between the two parties, Tenzing discovered that the source of the problem was two Sherpas who were stirring up dissension. He promptly fired them and sent them home. Peace was quickly restored. If your team keeps breaking down or falling short, you may need to make changes in your team.

Growing a team is demanding and time-consuming. But if you want to achieve your dream, you have no other choice. The greater the dream, the greater the team. *As the challenge escalates, the need for teamwork elevates.* That is the Law of Mount Everest.

NOT EVERY CHALLENGE IS A DREAM

The challenges that our teams face are not always ones we select. Sometimes they are thrust upon us, and we have no choice but to do the best we can with the team we have, or give up and suffer the consequences. That was certainly the case for the crew and support team for Apollo 13.

If you saw the movie *Apollo 13* starring Tom Hanks (or remember some of the coverage on television during the actual flight as I do), then you know the basic story. On April 13, 1970, at 10:07 P.M. EST, an oxygen tank in the service module of the *Odyssey* spacecraft exploded, causing the ship to lose its oxygen supply and all normal power. In addition, the ship's main engine was rendered nonfunctional. Since the ship was 200,000 miles away from earth and on a course that would put it into a permanent orbit around the moon, it was a potentially disastrous—and possibly fatal—challenge.

The astronauts in the *Odyssey*, James Lovell, John Swigart Jr., and Fred Haise, would not be able to make it back to earth on their own. Their survival depended on teamwork at a level that the space program had never experienced—and it was used to having people work together like a well-oiled machine.

TEAMWORK AT A NEW LEVEL

The flight control team on the ground immediately instructed the command crew to shut down the ailing command capsule and move into the lunar module (LM) *Aquarius* for their safety. That put the crew out of harm's way for the moment. But they still faced two major challenges:

1. Getting the command module, *Odyssey*, and the lunar module, *Aquarius*, on the quickest course home.

2. Conserving the "consumables" that kept the astronauts alive: power, oxygen, and water.

Accomplishing both would severely test everyone's abilities and know-how.

During a typical Apollo mission, Houston's mission control employed four teams of controllers, each designated by a color: white, black, gold, and maroon. Each team had technicians responsible for various specific areas required to keep the ship on course. The usual procedure was for each team to take a six-hour shift under the guidance of one of three flight directors. But with the lives of three astronauts on the line, every member of every team jumped in to help. And one team was pulled from the usual rotation by Gene Kranz, the lead flight director, and dubbed the Tiger Team. Those fifteen men worked as a crisis management team.

As Kranz gathered them together, he told them,

> For the rest of the mission, I'm pulling you men off console. The people out in that room [the other teams] will be running the flight from moment to moment, but it's the people in this room who will be coming up with the protocols they're going to be executing . . . For the next few days we're going to be coming up with techniques and maneuvers we've never tried before. I want to make sure we know what we're doing.[5]

In addition, NASA promptly sent word out to contractor representatives, such as the people at Grumman Aerospace, who had built the lunar module. (And when word got out that there was trouble with Apollo 13, virtually *everyone* in the organization showed up at the facility in the middle of the night to pitch in.) They also pulled in every top specialist and experienced astronaut they had, quickly building a coast-to-coast network of simulators, computers, and experts. NASA records state:

Astronauts Alan Shepard and Ed Mitchell operated one of the LM simulators at the Manned Spacecraft Center in Houston, and Gene Cernan and David Scott worked in the other. At Cape Kennedy, Astronaut Dick Gordon simulated emergency procedures in a third LM. One team of simulator specialists worked around the clock without a break. No procedure, no maneuver instruction, no checklist was relayed to the crew that hadn't been thoroughly proved out.[6]

AS EASY AS ONE, TWO, THREE

The team's first task was to figure out how to get the lunar module, which had been designed to support two men for 49.5 hours, to sustain three men for 84 hours. They did that by determining how to get the ship to run using the bare minimum number of systems, which would use less than one-fourth of its normal power.

Next, they had to get the spacecraft on a course that would return it to earth. That was no simple task since they would have to use the lunar module's tiny engine, and the guidance systems were off-line. But between the efforts of the crew, the expertise of the lunar module's manufacturer, and the calculations of Tiger Team, they were able to do it. And they also boosted the craft's speed to shorten the flight time. That would preserve precious water and energy.

The third major challenge the team faced was making the air that the crew was breathing safe. Oxygen was not a problem because the small lunar module was well supplied. But carbon dioxide was building up to dangerous levels because the small craft intended to land on the moon had not been designed to remove so much of it.

The crew on the ground worked out a clever way to adapt the lithium hydroxide filters from the command module so that they would work with the lunar module's noncompatible system.

Each time NASA's massive team faced an obstacle that threatened to leave the crew stranded in space, their pooled ingenuity, inherent tenacity, and incredible cooperation enabled them to overcome it. As a result, on April 17, 1970, the crew of the *Odyssey* made it safely home. NASA likes to call the mission a "successful failure." I call it a lesson in the Law of Mount Everest. *As the challenge escalates, the need for teamwork elevates.*

Putting men on the moon is an incredible challenge. But getting them home when things go wrong 200,000 miles away from earth is an even greater one. Fortunately for those men, the dream team was already in place when they got in trouble. And that is one of the lessons of Apollo 13. The time to build your team is not in the midst of a life-or-death challenge, but long before one can happen. If you haven't already, start building today so that when a formidable challenge occurs, you and your team will be ready.

Teamwork Thought

The size of your dream should determine the size of your team.

Becoming a Better Team Member

What is your natural first reaction when a challenge becomes more difficult? Do you go off alone to think? Do you try to solve the problem alone? Do you stay away from other people to avoid the pressure? Or do you lean on your teammates and let them lean on you?

If you don't already do it, teach yourself to rally with your teammates. You cannot win a great challenge alone. As Tenzing asserted, "On a great mountain, you do not leave your companions and go to the top alone."[7]

BECOMING A BETTER TEAM LEADER

What kinds of adjustments do you need to make to create your dream team, one that can meet the challenges ahead? Do you need to spend more time developing your people? Do you need to add key team members? Or should you make changes to the leadership? And don't forget that you, too, need to keep growing. What's true for a teammate is also true for the leader: If you don't grow, you gotta go.

THE LAW OF THE CHAIN

The Strength of the Team Is Impacted by Its Weakest Link

O n March 24, 1989, the news broke that an environmental disaster had occurred in Alaska's Prince William Sound. The oil tanker *Exxon Valdez* had run aground on the Bligh Reef, damaging the hull of the ship and rupturing eight of the vessel's eleven cargo tanks. As a result, 10.8 million of the ship's approximately 53 million gallons of oil poured out of the ship and into the sea.

The negative impact on the area was immense. Fishing and tourism came to a halt, harming the local economy. The environment suffered. Experts estimate wildlife losses at 250,000 seabirds, 2,800 sea otters, 300 harbor seals, 250 bald eagles, 22 killer whales, and billions of eggs for food-fish species such as salmon and herring. Though it wasn't the largest oil spill on record, experts consider it to be the worst spill in history in terms of the damage done to the environment.[1]

Of course, Exxon, the company that owns the ship, also paid a price. The company's representatives estimate that the incident cost Exxon $3.5 *billion:*

- $2.2 billion in cleanup costs

- $300 million in claims paid

- $1 billion in state and federal settlements[2]

But that's not all. In addition to what Exxon has already paid, the company stands to lose an additional $5 billion in punitive damages, a judgment it is still attempting to reverse through the appellate process more than a decade after the incident. What was the cause of such an expensive and far-reaching accident? The answer can be found in the Law of the Chain.

THE BROKEN CHAIN

When the *Exxon Valdez* cast off from the Alyeska Pipeline Terminal on the evening of March 23, the voyage began routinely. An expert ship's pilot guided the vessel through the Valdez Narrows and then returned control of the ship to its captain, Joe Hazelwood. The captain ordered that the ship be put on a particular course, turned control over to Third Mate Gregory Cousins, and left the bridge. Thirty-five minutes later, the *Exxon Valdez* was stranded on a reef and leaking tons of oil into the sea.

Investigation following the accident painted an ugly picture: neglect of safety standards, indifference to company policy, and unwise decision making. The ship's captain had been drinking in the hours before he took command of the ship. One officer, rather than the required two, remained in the wheelhouse as the tanker navigated the Valdez Narrows and again after the pilot left the ship. (And that officer, Cousins, had been so overworked that fatigue is thought to have contributed to the navigation error that followed.) Nor was a lookout always present on the bridge while the vessel was under way.

There were also discrepancies between what Captain Hazelwood told the Vessel Traffic Center he was doing and the orders he actually gave on the ship. At 11:30 P.M., the captain radioed that he would take a course of 200 degrees and reduce speed to wind his way through the icebergs that sometimes float in the shipping lanes. Yet the engine logs showed that the ship's speed kept increasing. Nine minutes after that, the captain ordered that the ship take a course of 180 degrees and be put on autopilot, but he never informed the traffic center of the change. Then at 11:53, he left the bridge.

At four minutes after midnight, the ship was on the reef. For almost two hours, first Cousins and then Hazelwood tried to get the ship free, all the while leaking oil into the sea. In the first three hours, it's estimated that 5.8 million gallons poured from the distressed tanker. By then, the damage was done, and the weak link had caused the "chain" to break. Alaska's coastline was a mess, Hazelwood's career as a ship's captain was over, and Exxon was stuck with a public relations nightmare—and massive financial obligations.

As much as any team likes to measure itself by its best people, the truth is that *the strength of the team is impacted by its weakest link.* No matter how much people try to rationalize it, compensate for it, or hide it, a weak link will eventually come to light. That's the Law of the Chain.

YOUR TEAM IS NOT FOR EVERYONE

One of the mistakes I often made early in my career as a team leader was that I thought everyone who was on my team should remain on the team. That was true for several reasons. First, I naturally see the best in people. When I look at individuals with potential, I see all that they can become—even if they don't see it. And I try to encourage and equip them to become better. Second, I truly like people. I figure the more who take the trip, the bigger the party. Third, because I have vision and believe my goals are worthwhile and beneficial, I sometimes naively assume that everyone will want to go along with me.

But just because I wanted to take everyone with me didn't mean that it would always work out that way. My first memorable experience with this occurred in 1980 when I was offered an executive position at Wesleyan World Headquarters in Marion, Indiana. When I accepted the position, I invited my assistant to come with me to be a part of the new team I was building. So she and her husband considered my offer and went to Marion to look around. I'll never forget when they came back. As I excitedly talked about the coming challenges and how we could begin to tackle them, I began to realize from the expressions on their faces that something was wrong. And that's when they told me. They weren't going.

That statement took me completely by surprise. In fact, I was sure that they were making a mistake and told them so, doing my best to convince them to change their minds. But my wife, Margaret, gave me some very good advice. She said, "John, your problem is that you want to take everybody with you. But not everyone is going to go on the journey. Let it go." It was a hard lesson for me to learn—and sometimes it still is.

From that experience and others I've had since then, I've discovered that when it comes to teamwork . . .

1. Not Everyone Will Take the Journey

Some people don't want to go. My assistant and her husband wanted to stay in Lancaster, Ohio, where they had built relationships for many years. For other people the issue is their attitude. They don't want to change, grow, or conquer new territory. They hold fast to the status quo. All you can do with people in this group is kindly thank them for their past contributions and move on.

2. Not Everyone Should Take the Journey

Other people shouldn't join a team because it's a matter of their agenda. They have other plans, and where you're going isn't the right place for them. The best thing you can do for people in this category is wish them well, and as far as you are able, help them on their way so that they achieve success in their venture.

3. Not Everyone Can Take the Journey

For the third group of people, the issue is ability. They may not be capable of keeping pace with their teammates or helping the group get where it wants to go. How do you recognize people who fall into this category? They're not very hard to identify.

- They can't keep pace with other team members.
- They don't grow in their area of responsibility.
- They don't see the big picture.
- They won't work on personal weaknesses.
- They won't work with the rest of the team.
- They can't fulfill expectations for their area.

If you have people who display one or more of those characteristics, then you need to acknowledge that they are weak links.

That's not to say that they are necessarily bad people. In fact, some teams exist to serve weak links or help them become stronger. It depends on the team's goals. For example, when I was a senior pastor, we reached out to people in the community with food and assistance. We helped people with addictions, divorce recovery, and many other difficulties. Our goal was to serve them. It's good and appropriate to help people who find themselves in those circumstances. But putting them on the team while they are still broken and weak doesn't help them, and it hurts the team—even to the extent of making the team incapable of accomplishing its goal of service.

What can you do with people on your team who are weak links? You really have only two choices: You need to train them or trade them. Of course, your first priority should always be to try to train people who are having a hard time keeping up. Help can come in many forms: giving people books to read, sending them to conferences, presenting them with new challenges, pairing them with mentors. I believe that people often rise to your level of expectations. Give them hope and training, and they usually improve.

But what should you do if a team member continually fails to meet expectations, even after receiving training, encouragement, and opportunities to grow? My father used to have a saying: "Water seeks its own level." Somebody who is a weak link on your team might be capable of becoming a star on another team. You need to give that person an opportunity to find his level somewhere else.

THE IMPACT OF A WEAK LINK

If you are a team leader, you cannot avoid dealing with weak links. Team members who don't carry their own weight slow down the team, and they have a negative effect on your leadership. Several things may happen when a weak link remains on the team:

1. The Stronger Members Identify the Weak One

A weak link cannot hide (except in a group of weak people). If you have strong people on your team, they always know who isn't performing up to the level of everyone else.

2. The Stronger Members Have to Help the Weak One

If your people must work together as a team to do their work, then they have only two choices when it comes to a weak teammate. They can ignore the person and allow the team to suffer, or they can help him and make the team more successful. If they are team players, they will help.

3. The Stronger Members Come to Resent the Weak One

Whether strong team members help or not, the result will always be the same: resentment. No one likes to lose or fall behind consistently because of the same person.

4. The Stronger Members Become Less Effective

Carrying someone else's load in addition to your own compromises your performance. Do that for a long time, and the whole team suffers.

5. The Stronger Members Question the Leader's Ability

Anytime the leader allows a weak link to remain a part of the team, the team members forced to compensate for the weak person begin to doubt the leader's courage and discernment. You lose the respect of the best when you don't deal properly with the worst.

Many team members may be able to avoid the hard decision of dealing with subpar members, but leaders can't. In fact, one of the differences between leaders and followers is action. Followers often know what to do, but they are unwilling or unable to follow through. But know this: If

> *You lose the respect of the best when you don't deal properly with the worst.*

other people on the team make decisions for you because you are unwilling or unable to make them, then your leadership is being compromised, and you're not serving the team well.

STRENGTHENING THE CHAIN

Weak team members always take more of the team's time than strong ones. One reason is that the more competent people have to give their time to compensate for those who don't carry their share of the load. The greater the difference in competence between the more accomplished performers and the less accomplished ones, the greater the detriment to the team. For example, if you rate people on a scale from 1 to 10 (with 10 being the best), a 5 among 10s really hurts the team where an 8 among 10s often does not.

Let me show you how this works. When you first put together a group of people, their talents come together in a way that is analogous to addition. So visually a 5 among 10s looks like this:

$$10 + 10 + 10 + 10 + 5 = 45$$

The difference between this team and great ones with five 10s is like the difference between 50 and 45. That's a difference of 10 percent. But once a team comes together and starts to develop chemistry, synergy, and momentum, it's analogous to multiplication. That's when a weak link really starts to hurt the team. It's the difference between this:

$$10 \times 10 \times 10 \times 10 \times 10 = 100,000$$

and this:

$$10 \times 10 \times 10 \times 10 \times 5 = 50,000$$

That's a difference of 50 percent! The power and momentum of the team may be able to compensate for a weak link for a while, but not forever. A weak link eventually robs the team of momentum—and potential.

Ironically, weak links are less aware than stronger members of their weaknesses and shortcomings. They also spend more time guarding their turf, saving their positions, and holding on to what they have. And know this: When it comes to interaction between people, the weaker person usually controls the relationship. For example, someone with a good self-image is more flexible than a person with a poor self-image. An individual with a clear vision acts more readily than someone without one. A person with superb ability and high energy accomplishes more and works longer than an individual with lesser gifts. If the two people journey together, the stronger member must constantly work with and wait on the weaker one. That controls what happens on the journey.

If your team has a weak link who can't or won't rise to the level of the team—and you've done everything you can to help the person improve—then you've got to take action. When you do, heed the advice of authors Danny Cox and John Hoover. If you need to remove somebody from the team, be discreet, be clear, be honest, and be brief. Then once the person is gone, be open about it with the rest of the team while maintaining respect for the person you let go.[3] And if you start to have second thoughts before or afterward, remember this: As long as a weak link is part of the team, everyone else on the team will suffer.

No Weak Links!

Nobody particularly wants to have a weak link on a team, someone who causes the team to fail at its objectives. Yet we've all had to work with weaker team members. And sometimes good experiences have come out of it. There is rich personal reward to be reaped by helping a teammate go from being a weak link to a solid team member—and sometimes even to becoming a star player. But for good or bad, dealing with subpar performers is an inevitable part of being on any team, right? There's no such thing as a team that has no weak links, is there?

As I already mentioned, the goal of the team often determines how well it can work with a weak link. Sometimes the stakes for a team are so high that its members cannot afford to have a weak link. And that is the case for the U.S. Navy SEALs. The jobs they do are so demanding that a weak person on the team will get everyone on the team killed.

In recent years the SEALs have generated a lot of popular interest. They've been the subject of numerous novels and movies. They've captured people's imaginations because they are considered the best of the best. As one former SEAL remarked, "No group of men is closer to perfection in their chosen field."

The SEALs were first commissioned by President John F. Kennedy in 1962. They evolved from the underwater demolition teams who were developed during World War II to clear the amphibious landing areas of obstacles in such locations as Omaha and Utah Beaches in Normandy and later on the islands of the Pacific. Like all the special operations forces in the various branches of the U.S. military, they are experts in weapons, hand-to-hand combat, and demolition, and they have trained to parachute from airplanes. But their expertise is in operations based on and in water. That's the origin of their name: SEALs indicates that they are capable of operating in the SEa, from the Air, and on LAND.

FORGING THE CHAIN

The key to the success of the SEALs is their training—the real emphasis of which is not learning about weapons or gaining technical skills; it's about strengthening people and developing teamwork. Weapons change, and so do methods of conducting operations, but the intense mental and physical training has remained much the same for all the years that the SEALs have been in existence. Peter J. Schoomaker, commander in chief of U.S. Special Operations Command, says, "Everything but our core values are on the table; we have to be ready to change anything but those values to get the job done. The core value for a SEAL Team is the people."[4]

Having the right people on the team starts with the selection process. Only a certain kind of person will even apply to go through SEAL training. And of those who apply, only one in ten is accepted. (The navy recommends that candidates be running at least thirty miles a week and swimming long distances *before* they apply.) Those who do make it into the program then undergo twenty-six weeks of intense physical, psychological, and mental stress. The physical and emotional rigors of that training make marine boot camp look like a picnic. John Roat, who went through the training, was one of the first members of the newly formed SEAL teams in 1962. He said that more than 1,300 men tested to get into the training, but the program accepted only 134. The bar for physical training was so high that people began dropping out the first day. And he saw that as a good thing. He explained:

> There were still some 130 guys when the instructors broke us up into ten-man boat crews and gave us our boats . . . The men of each crew carried their boat on their heads, and until a crew got its ducks in a row, everyone in it suffered. There was no chance of a boat crew's learning how to work as a team until it got rid of the men who didn't belong in training. Until they were gone, they were just an added harassment factor. Sounds cold, but that's life.[5]

For the first five weeks, the training is torturous and the physical demands incredible. Then comes Hell Week, five days of constant physical and mental challenges where the trainees are kept awake and training for all but four or five hours during the entire week. It's the trial that eliminates remaining weak links and at the same time forges the class into a real team. Roat described the impact of that part of the training:

> Each training class still learns the same things during Hell Week: You can go farther than you ever thought possible, but you can't do it alone, and everyone left standing belongs there. Hell Week has changed less than any part of training, for one simple reason: The instructors cannot find a better way. You can't pick the ones who can

hack it by their looks. No written test will find out if a man is a Team player. If it was possible to get good operators by letting some shrink interview trainees and say yea or nay, the navy would love it. The big problem is, the psychologists can't predict who will survive five-plus days of no sleep, with constant harassment, and impossible physical demands with an easy way out. That's still the test.[6]

SEAL training is so intense that there have been classes from which *no one* completed the training. In the end, 49 of the 134 people who started training with Roat graduated. The hearts of those who made it through the stress and pain can be represented by the words of one of Roat's classmates: "I couldn't quit; I would have let my classmates down. I just couldn't do it."

Many people consider the Navy SEALs to be the elite among the already elite company of special operations forces in the U.S. military. Their interaction is the definition of teamwork, and they depend upon each other at a level that most people cannot understand and will never experience. Their survival depends on it. And for that reason, they cannot afford to have any weak links.

Although you may never have to face the pressures that SEALs do, you can be sure of this: *The strength of the team is impacted by its weakest link.* No matter what kind of team you're on, that's always true. That's the Law of the Chain.

TEAMWORK THOUGHT

The team cannot continually cover up its weakness.

BECOMING A BETTER TEAM MEMBER

Most people's natural inclination is to judge themselves according to their best qualities while they measure others by their worst. As a result, they point to areas where their teammates need to grow. But the truth is that every person is responsible for his own growth first.

Take a hard look at yourself. Using the criteria from the chapter, examine yourself to see where you may be hindering the team. Mark the box under the word *Self* for any issue that applies to you. And if you have real courage, ask your spouse or a close friend to evaluate you by marking the boxes listed under the word *Friend*.

Evaluated by		Possible Issues
Self	*Friend*	
❑	❑	*Have trouble keeping pace with other team members.*
❑	❑	*Am not growing in my area of responsibility.*
❑	❑	*Have a hard time seeing the big picture.*
❑	❑	*Have difficulty seeing my personal weakness.*
❑	❑	*Have a tough time working with the rest of the team.*
❑	❑	*Consistently fail to fulfill expectations in area of responsibility.*

If you (or the other person who evaluated you) checked more than one box, you need to put yourself on a growth plan so that you don't hinder your team. Talk to your team leader or a trusted mentor about ways you can grow in any weak area.

BECOMING A BETTER TEAM LEADER

If you're a team leader, you cannot ignore the issues created by a weak link. For the various kinds of teams, different solutions are appropriate. If the team is a family, then you don't simply "trade" weak people. You lovingly nurture them and try to help them grow, but you also try to minimize the damage they can cause to other family members. If the team is a business, then you have responsibilities to the owner or stockholders. If you've offered training without success, then a "trade" might be in order. If the team is a ministry and training has made no impact, then it might be appropriate to ask the weak people to sit on the sidelines for a while. Or they might need some time away from the team to work on emotional or spiritual issues.

No matter what kind of situation you face, remember that your responsibilities to people come in the following order: to the organization, to the team, and then to the individual. Your own interests—and comfort—come last.

THE LAW OF THE CATALYST

Winning Teams Have Players Who Make Things Happen

Most teams don't naturally get better on their own. Left alone, they don't grow, improve, and reach championship caliber. Instead, they tend to wind down. The road to the next level is always uphill, and if a team isn't intentionally fighting to move up, then it inevitably slides down. The team loses focus, gets out of rhythm, decreases in energy, breaks down in unity, and loses

> *Catalysts are get-it-done-and-then-some people.*

momentum. At some point, it also loses key players. And it's only a matter of time before it plateaus and ultimately declines into mediocrity. That's why a team that reaches its potential always possesses a catalyst.

THE DEFINITION OF A CATALYST

Catalysts are what I call get-it-done-and-then-some people. The most outstanding one I've ever had the privilege of seeing in action is Michael Jordan. In the opinion of many people (including me), he is the greatest basketball player ever to play the game, not only because of his talent, athleticism, and understanding of the game, but also because of his ability as a catalyst. His résumé as an amateur, and as a professional with the Chicago Bulls attests to that ability:

- Won NCAA Division I Championship (1982)

- Named the *Sporting News* College Player of the Year twice (1983, 1984)

- Received the Naismith and Wooden Awards (1984)

- Won 2 Olympic gold medals (1984, 1992)

- Won 6 NBA world championships (1991, 1992, 1993, 1996, 1997, 1998)

- Selected NBA Rookie of the Year (1985)

- Selected to the NBA All-Rookie Team (1985)

- Selected for All-NBA First Team a record 10 times (1987, 1988, 1989, 1990, 1991, 1992, 1993, 1996, 1997, 1998)

- Holds the NBA record for highest career scoring average (31.5 points per game)

- Holds the NBA record for most seasons leading the league in scoring (10)

- Holds the NBA record for most seasons leading the league in field goals made (10) and attempted (10)

- Ranks 3rd in NBA history in points (29,277), 3rd in steals (2,306), and 4th in field goals made (10,962)

- Voted NBA Defensive Player of the Year (1985; after being criticized that he was "only" an offensive player)

- Selected to the All-NBA Defensive First Team 8 times (1988, 1989, 1990, 1991, 1993, 1997, 1998)

- Named NBA MVP 5 times (1988, 1991, 1992, 1996, 1998)

- Named NBA Finals MVP 6 times (1991, 1992, 1993, 1996, 1997, 1998)

- Named 1 of the 50 greatest players in NBA history

Statistics make a strong statement about Jordan, but they really don't tell the whole story. For that, you had to see him in action. When the Bulls needed to get the team out of a slump, the ball went to Jordan. When a player needed to take the last shot to win the game, the ball went to Jordan. Even if the team needed to get things going in practice, the ball went to Jordan. No matter what the situation was on the court, Jordan was capable of putting the team in the position to win the game. That's always the case for championship teams. *Winning teams have players who make things happen.* That's the Law of the Catalyst.

STILL MAKING THINGS HAPPEN

As you know, Michael Jordan has retired from basketball as a player. But he is still in the game. In early 2000, Jordan became part owner and president of basketball operations of the Washington Wizards. Only a week after becoming part of the organization, Jordan put on a number 23 Wizards jersey and joined the team for a practice.

Wizards forward Tracy Murray, who guarded Jordan during some drills, remarked afterward, "He's definitely moving the same way . . . dunking the ball, shooting a jump shot, fade away. Still got the same game, hasn't gone anywhere."

Nobody expected his talent to be diminished, especially not just two years after his retirement. But his ability as a catalyst hadn't diminished either. Murray continued, "And as soon as he sets foot in that gym, he starts talking trash, so of course the intensity is going to pick up."

Every catalyst brings intensity to the table. One commentator remarked of Jordan's visit to the court, "By being himself, he turned a Wizards practice into something it hasn't been in a while—energetic and fun."

"Which is what we should expect every day," was Jordan's reaction. "Actually, I told them they shouldn't have to wait for me to come out to show the energy that they had today. I just tried to keep them focused, challenge them, say whatever I have to say. If they can play hard against me, they can play hard against anybody. It was fun."[1]

That's the way it always is for a catalyst. Having fun. He loves stirring up the team, making things happen, doing whatever it takes to push the team to the next level. When a catalyst does that consistently, the team becomes expectant, confident, elevated, and ultimately amazed. That's the Law of the Catalyst. *Winning teams have players who make things happen!*

THREE KINDS OF PLAYERS

When crunch time comes, a catalyst becomes critical, whether it's the salesperson who hits the impossible goal, the ballplayer who makes the big play, or the parent who gets a child to believe in himself at a critical moment in life. A team can't reach big goals or even break new ground if it doesn't have a catalyst.

My experience with teams has taught me that what is true for sports is also the case for business, ministry, and family relationships. When the clock is running down and the game is on the line, there are really only three kinds of people on a team:

1. People Who Don't Want the Ball

Some people don't have the ability to come through for the team in high-pressure situations, and they know it. As a result, they don't want the responsibility of carrying the team to victory. And it shouldn't be given to them. They should be allowed to play in their areas of strength.

2. People Who Want the Ball But Shouldn't

A second group contains people who can't carry the team to victory. The problem is that *they don't know* that they can't. Often the cause is that these players' egos are greater than their talent. These people can be dangerous to a team.

3. People Who Want the Ball and Should

The final group, which is by far the smallest, consists of people who want to be "go to" players at crunch time and who can actually deliver. They are able to push, pull, or carry the team to new levels when the going gets tough. They are the catalysts.

Every team needs catalysts if it wants to have any hope of winning consistently. Without them, even a team with loads of talent cannot go to the highest level. I saw an illustration of this in the late 1990s and again in 2000 with the Atlanta Braves. They had the best starting pitchers in baseball. They had strong hitters, Gold Glove fielders, and talent in the bull pen. They possessed team members who had been league MVP or rookie of the year. But they lacked the catalytic players they needed to become World Series champions.

CHARACTERISTICS OF A CATALYST

It's easy to point out a team's catalyst after he has made an impact on the group and spurred the members on to victory, especially in the world of sports. You can point to particular moments when the person went to a whole new level and took the team there at the same time. But how do you recognize a catalyst *before* the fact? How do you look for catalytic people for your current team?

No matter what kind of "game" you're playing or what kind of team you're on, you can be sure that catalysts have certain characteristics that make them different from their teammates. I've observed that these nine are often present in the catalysts with whom I've interacted. They are . . .

1. Intuitive

Catalysts sense things that others don't sense. They may recognize a weakness in an opponent. They may be able to make an intuitive leap that turns a disadvantage into an advantage. They are able to use whatever it is they sense to help the team succeed.

For different kinds of teams, the way the intuition plays out changes. That makes sense because the goal of the team determines what the team values. Another reason is that people are most intuitive in their areas of natural strength. So for a small business, the catalyst may be an entrepreneur who can smell an opportunity when no one else is aware of it. For a ministry or other nonprofit organization, the catalyst may be a person who intuitively recognizes leadership and can recruit talented volunteers. For a football team, it may be a quarterback who senses that a defense isn't adjusting well and calls the play that wins the game. In each case the situation is different, but the result is the same: A catalyst senses an opportunity, and as a result, the team benefits.

2. Communicative

Catalysts say things that other team members don't say in order to get the team moving. Sometimes they do it to share with their teammates what they have sensed intuitively so that they will be better prepared to meet the challenge. Other times their purpose is to inspire or incite other team members. And they usually know the difference between when a teammate needs a boost—and when he needs a boot.

Anytime you see a team of people suddenly turn around or crank their play up to another level, you'll see someone on the team talking, directing, inspiring others. You'll see it, too, with strong political leaders. People such as Churchill, Roosevelt, and Kennedy changed the world with their words. They were catalysts, and catalysts communicate.

3. Passionate

Catalysts feel things that others don't feel. They are passionate about what they do, and they want to share that love with their teammates. Sometimes the passion explodes as a controlled fury to achieve goals in their area of passion. Other times it manifests itself as a contagious enthusiasm. But however it comes out, it can inspire a team to success.

Legendary baseball player Pete Rose of the Cincinnati Reds has experienced his share of problems, but he was certainly one of the great catalysts of his sport in the twentieth century. He was once asked which goes first on a baseball player: his eyes, his legs, or his arm. Rose's response was telling. He said, "None of these things. It's when his enthusiasm goes that he's through as a player." And he's also through as a catalyst.

4. Talented

Catalysts are capable of doing what others cannot do because their talent is as strong as their passion. People rarely become catalysts outside an area of expertise and gifting. That's the case for two main reasons. First, talent knows what it takes to win. You can't take the team to the next level when you haven't mastered the skills it takes to succeed on a personal level. It just doesn't happen.

The second reason people must have talent in an area where they desire to be a catalyst is that part of being a catalyst is influencing other team members. You can't do that if you have no credibility with them because of your own poor performance. Part of being a catalyst is sharing your gift with others to make them better. You can't give what you don't have.

5. Creative

Another quality commonly found in catalysts is creativity. Catalysts think things that others do not think. While most team members may do things by rote (or by rut), catalysts think differently from their teammates. They are constantly looking for fresh, innovative ways to do things.

Business and sports team consultant Carl Mays asserts that "creativity involves taking what you have, where you are, and getting the most out of it." Sometimes what they come up with can change the tempo of a game. Other times their ability to rewrite the rules changes the whole way the game is actually played.

6. Initiating

I enjoy creative people, and I've worked with many through the years. In fact, I consider myself to be creative, especially in the areas of writing and teaching. But my experience with creative people has taught me something about them: While all creative people have more than enough ideas, not all of them are good at implementing those creative thoughts.

Catalysts don't have this problem. They do things that others cannot do. Not only are they creative in their thinking, but they are disciplined in their actions. They delight in making things happen. That initiative can take almost any form: a baseball manager arguing with an umpire to stir up his players, a parent changing jobs or moving the family to help a struggling child, or a business owner putting up financial incentives for employees to break through barriers. So they initiate. And as a result they move the team as they move themselves.

7. Responsible

Catalysts carry things that others do not carry. My friend Truett Cathy, the founder of Chick-Fil-A, has a saying: "If it's to be, it's up to me." That could very well be the motto for all catalysts.

Not long ago a commercial appeared on television that showed a pair of consultants giving a company's CEO advice on how he could take his business to the next level. They explained how the company's computer system should be overhauled, how the distribution system could be improved, and how marketing channels could be changed to make the company much more effective and profitable.

The CEO listened carefully to everything they had to say, and finally he smiled and said, "I like it. Okay, do it."

The consultants looked confused for a moment, and one of them stammered, "We don't actually *do* what we recommend."

Catalysts are not consultants. They don't recommend a course of action. They take responsibility for making it happen.

8. Generous

Catalysts give things that others don't give. A true mark of people's taking responsibility is their willingness to give of themselves to carry something through. Catalysts display that quality. They are prepared to use their resources to better the team, whether that means giving time, spending money, or sacrificing personal gain.

> *Catalysts are not consultants. They don't recommend a course of action. They take responsibility for making it happen.*

A vivid example of someone giving of himself for the team can be found in the life of New York businessman Eugene Lang. On June 25, 1981, Lang stood before sixty-one graduating sixth graders in P.S. 121, the East Harlem elementary school from which he had graduated decades before. He knew that statistically, 75 percent of the children would probably drop out of school during the next six years and would never graduate from high school. And he wanted to try to do something to change that.

He began by encouraging them to work hard, telling them that if they did, success would follow. But then on the spur of the moment, Lang moved from consultant to catalyst. He promised those kids that if they would stick with it and graduate from high school, he would provide each of them with scholarship money for college. That promise was the start of what became the "I Have a Dream" program.

Four years later, all 61 students were still in school. Six years later, 90 percent of the 54 kids who remained in touch with Lang graduated from high school, and two-thirds of them went on to college. Today, I Have a Dream sponsors 160 projects in 57 cities, and it touches the lives of 10,000 kids—all because Lang decided to become a catalyst.[2]

9. Influential

Catalysts are able to lead teammates in a way that others cannot. Team members will follow a catalyst when they won't respond to anyone else. In the case of a highly talented team member who is not especially gifted in leadership, he may be an effective catalyst in an area of expertise. But people with natural leadership ability will have influence far beyond their own team.

Michael Jordan, once again, is a wonderful example. Obviously he had influence with his teammates in Chicago. But his influence stretched far beyond the Bulls. I got a taste of that firsthand at the NBA 2001 All-Star Game. I had the pleasure of speaking at the chapel for players and officials before the game, and later I got to spend time with the referees who had been picked to officiate. During my talks with them, I asked what player they respected the most in terms of his honesty. Their answer was Michael Jordan.

One ref then recounted that in a close game, Danny Ainge, whose team was playing against the Bulls, made a shot near the three-point line. The officials had given Ainge only two points for the basket since they were not sure whether he was outside the three-point line. During the timeout immediately after the shot, one of the refs asked Jordan whether his opponent's score had been a valid three-point shot. Jordan indicated that it was. They gave Ainge the three points. Jordan's integrity—and influence—caused them to reverse their call.

When you see many of those nine qualities in someone on your team, then take heart. When crunch time comes, he is likely to step up to a whole new level of performance and attempt to take the team there too.

My Own Go-to Guy

At my company, The INJOY Group, a number of team members are catalysts within the organization. But none are stronger than Dave Sutherland, the CEO.

Dave came on board in 1994 as the president of ISS, the division of The INJOY Group that helps churches with fund-raising through capital campaigns. Just prior to his coming on board, I had given serious thought to shutting down that arm of the organization. ISS wasn't supporting itself financially, it was draining time and re-sources from other more productive areas of the company, and it wasn't having the positive influence I had hoped for. But I believed that Dave Sutherland's leadership could make a difference. And soon after I hired him, I began seeing progress at ISS.

The second year that Dave was with me, the company had some pretty aggressive goals. That year the company's goal had been to partner with eighty churches, more than twice as many as it had the previous year. And each partnership could come only after a personal presentation to a church's board and their acceptance of our offer to help.

One day during the first week of December, I stopped by Dave's office and spoke to his wife, Roxine, who works with Dave as his assistant. I hadn't seen Dave in a while, and I asked where he was.

"He's on the road making a presentation," she said.

I thought that was a little odd because the company had several key people whose job it was to make the presentations to churches.

"On the road? When will he be back?" I asked.

"Well, let's see," said Roxine, "when he left the Monday after Thanksgiving, we still needed twenty-four more churches to reach our goal. Dave said he won't be home until we reach it."

And reach it he did. Dave was on the road until December 19. But that was no great surprise. My writer, Charlie Wetzel, told me that in a sales and marketing career that spans three decades, Dave has *never* missed a goal. Not once.

His tenacity and ability serve Dave well. But they also serve the team well. By reaching that goal, Dave made every person on the team a winner that year. And everyone in the company used the momentum he created to take ISS to a whole new level. A year later, ISS became the second largest company of its type in the world. And by the end of the year 2000, it had helped more than one thousand churches across America raise more than $1 billion.

When you have a Michael Jordan or a Eugene Lang or a Dave Sutherland, your team always has a chance to win. They are get-it-done-and-then-some people. Why is that important? Because *winning teams have players who make things happen*. Without them, a team will never reach its potential. That is the truth of the Law of the Catalyst.

TEAMWORK THOUGHT

Games are won by get-it-done-and-then-some people.

BECOMING A BETTER TEAM MEMBER

How are you when it comes to crunch time on your team? Do you want the ball, or would you rather it was in someone else's hands? If there are more talented and effective catalysts on your team, then you should not want to be the go-to player in a pinch. In those cases, the best thing you can do is get an "assist" by helping to put those people into position to benefit the team. But if you avoid the spotlight because you are afraid or because you haven't worked as hard as you should to improve yourself, then you need to change your mind-set.

Start to put yourself on the road to improvement by doing the following things:

1. *Find a mentor.* Players become catalysts only with the help of people better than themselves. Find someone who makes things happen to help you along the way.

2. *Begin a growth plan.* Put yourself on a program that will help you develop your skills and talents. You cannot take the team to a higher level if you haven't gotten there.

3. *Get out of your comfort zone.* You won't know what you're capable of until you try to go beyond what you've done before.

If you follow these three guidelines, you still may not become a catalyst, but you will at least become the best you can be—and that's all that anyone can ask of you.

BECOMING A BETTER TEAM LEADER

If you lead a team, you need catalysts to push the team to its potential. Use the list of qualities in the chapter to begin identifying and enlisting people who can get it done and then some. If you see that potential in some of your current teammates, encourage them to take initiative and become positive influencers on the team. If the people on the team can't or won't step up to that level of play, then start recruiting people from outside the team. No team can go to the highest level without a catalyst. *Winning teams have players who make things happen.*

THE LAW OF THE COMPASS

Vision Gives Team Members Direction and Confidence

F or nearly a hundred years, IBM has been a rock of American business standing firm in a stream of competition. Even during the Great Depression of the 1930s, while thousands of companies were disappearing, IBM kept growing. The source of its strength was business and technological innovation.

INTRODUCING TECHNOLOGY

For a half century, IBM continually broke ground in the area of computers, beginning in the 1940s with its Mark I. In the 1950s and 1960s, the firm introduced innovation after innovation. By 1971, IBM was receiving $8 billion in annual revenues and employed 270,000 people. When people thought of blue-chip companies, IBM is likely the first one they pictured.

But for all its history of advances, by the late 1980s and early 1990s, the company was struggling. For a decade IBM had been slow to react to technological changes. As a result, by 1991, it suffered $8 billion in *losses* every year. And even though IBM fought to regain ground technologically, consumers' favorable perceptions of the company were at an all-time low. Where IBM had once been seen as dominant, people looked upon it as hopelessly behind the times—a slow-moving dinosaur among new companies that moved like cheetahs. If something didn't change, IBM was going to be in big trouble.

Then in 1993, IBM got a new CEO, Lou Gerstner. He quickly began recruiting key members for his team, IBM's executive committee. Perhaps the most important addition was Abby Kohnstamm, whom he invited to be IBM's senior vice president of marketing.

INTRODUCING . . . A COMPASS

Kohnstamm was eager to get started. She believed the company's products were strong enough, but its marketing was weak. When she arrived at IBM, what she found was much worse than she had expected. Not only was IBM failing to reach customers effectively; when it came to the marketing department, employees weren't even sure who did what or why. For example, when Kohnstamm asked how many employees were in the marketing area, she couldn't get the same answer from any two employees. Greg Farrell of *USA Today* described the situation: "The company was a fragmented, decentralized organization with more than a dozen quasi-autonomous businesses, and 70 ad agency partners worldwide."[1]

Kohnstamm immediately dismissed all those agencies and hired one to replace it: Ogilvy & Mather Worldwide. Her desire was to give the entire IBM team a single unifying theme for the hardware, software, and services they had to offer. Before long, she had found it. The company adopted the concept of e-business. Kohnstamm asserts, "E-business is the single focal point for the company, and is the single largest marketing effort ever undertaken by IBM."[2]

The vision seems to be working. Steve Gardner, an ad agency owner who once promoted Compaq, says, "The most stunning thing about e-business was that it transformed IBM from perceived laggard to leader in the Internet space without any real change in its lines of products or services. That's an astonishing achievement."[3]

Where once IBM was struggling, it now has renewed direction and confidence. Bill Etherington, senior vice president and group executive over sales and distribution, notes that the marketing focus has had an incredibly positive effect on IBM's employees. And he should know. He's been with IBM for thirty-seven years. He says, "We all had enthusiasm for this wonderful campaign. It had an edge to it and portrayed the company in a much more modern light."[4] Maureen McGuire, vice president of marketing communications, agrees: "The campaign has galvanized employees. We're trying to get all those people to sing the same song, read from the same book." For a company that hadn't sung for a long time, that's a momentous achievement. And it just goes to show you, *vision gives team members direction and confidence.* That's the power of the Law of the Compass.

DON'T GET LOST

Have you ever been part of a team that didn't seem to make any progress? Maybe the group had plenty of talent, resources, and opportunities, and team members got along, but the group just never *went* anywhere! If you have, there's a strong possibility that the situation was caused by lack of vision.

Great vision precedes great achievement. Every team needs a compelling vision to give it direction. A team without vision is, at worst, purposeless. At best, it is subject to the personal (and some-times selfish) agendas of its various teammates. As the agendas work against each other, the team's energy and drive drain away. On the other hand, a team that embraces a vision becomes focused, energized, and confident. It knows where it's headed and why it's going there.

> *Great vision precedes great achievement.*

Field Marshal Bernard Montgomery, a leader of troops during World War II who was called a "soldier's general," wrote that "every single soldier must know, before he goes into battle, how the little battle he is to fight fits into the larger picture, and how the success of his fighting will influence the battle as a whole." People on the team need to know why they're fighting. Otherwise, the team gets into trouble.

THE LEADER'S RESPONSIBILITY

Field Marshal Montgomery was adept at connecting with the sol-diers on his team and casting vision for their battles. That ability brought him and them success. He understood that leaders must be vision casters. Author Ezra Earl Jones points out,

> Leaders do not have to be the greatest visionaries themselves. The
> vision may come from anyone. The leaders do have to state the

vision, however. Leaders also have to keep the vision before the people and remind them of the progress that is being made to achieve the vision. Otherwise, the people might assume that they are failing and give up.

If you lead your team, then you are responsible for identifying a worthy and compelling vision and articulating it to your team members. However, even if you are not the leader, identifying a compelling vision is still important. If you don't know the team's vision, you can't perform with confidence. You can't be sure you and your teammates are going in the right direction. You can't even be sure that the team you're on is the right one for you if you haven't examined the vision in light of your strengths, convictions, and purpose. For everyone on the team, the vision needs to be compelling.

CHECK YOUR COMPASS!

How do you measure a vision? How do you know whether it is worthy and compelling? You check your compass. Every team needs one. In fact, every team needs several. A team should examine the following six "compasses" before embarking on any journey.

A team's vision must be aligned with:

1. A Moral Compass (Look Above)

Millionaire philanthropist Andrew Carnegie exclaimed, "A great business is seldom if ever built up, except on lines of strictest integrity." That holds true for any endeavor. There's only one true north. If your compass is pointing in any other direction, your team is headed the wrong way.

A moral compass brings integrity to the vision. It helps all the people on the team to check their motives and make sure that they are laboring for the right reasons. It also brings credibility to the leaders who cast the vision—but only if they model the values that the team is expected to embrace. When they do, they bring fuel to the vision, which keeps it going.

2. An Intuitive Compass (Look Within)

Where integrity brings fuel to the vision, passion brings fire. And the true fire of passion and conviction comes only from within.

In *The Leadership Challenge,* James Kouzes and Barry Posner explain that "visions spring forth from our intuition. If necessity is the mother of invention, intuition is the mother of vision. Experience feeds our intuition and enhances our insight." A vision must resonate deep within the leader of the team. Then it must resonate within the team members, who will be asked to work hard to bring it to fruition. But that's the value of intuitive passion. It brings the kind of heat that fires up the committed—and fries the uncommitted.

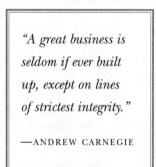

"A great business is seldom if ever built up, except on lines of strictest integrity."

—ANDREW CARNEGIE

3. A Historical Compass (Look Behind)

There's an old saying that I learned when I lived in rural Indiana: "Don't remove the fence before you know why it's there." You never know: There might be a bull on the other side! A compelling vision should build on the past, not diminish it. It should make positive use of anything contributed by previous teams in the organization.

Anytime you cast vision, you must create a connection between the past, the present, and the future. You must bring them together. People won't reach for the future until they have touched the past. When you include the history of the team, the people who have

> *People won't reach for the future until they have touched the past.*

been in the organization a long time sense that they are valued (even if they are no longer the stars). At the same time, the newer people receive a sense of security, knowing that the current vision builds on the past and leads to the future.

What is the best way to do that? You tell stories. Principles may fade in people's minds, but stories stick. They bring relationships to the vision. Tell stories from the past that give a sense of history. Tell stories about the exciting things that are happening now among team members. And tell the story of what it will be like the day that the team fulfills the vision. Stories are like thumbtacks that help to keep a vision in front of people.

4. A Directional Compass (Look Ahead)

Poet Henry David Thoreau wrote, "If one advances confidently in the direction of his dreams, and endeavors to live the life which he has imagined, he will meet with a success unexpected in common hours." As I already mentioned, vision provides direction for the team. Part of that direction comes from a sense of purpose. Another comes from having goals, which bring targets to the vision.

A goal motivates the team. NFL referee Jim Tunney commented on this when he said, "Why do we call it a goal line? Because eleven people on the offensive team huddle for a single purpose—to move the ball across it. Everyone has a specific task to do—the quarterback, the wide receiver, each lineman, every player knows exactly what his assignment is. Even the defensive team has its goals too—to prevent the offensive team from achieving its goal."

5. A Strategic Compass (Look Around)

A goal won't do the team much good without steps to accomplish it. Vision without strategy is little more than a daydream. As Vince Abner remarked, "Vision isn't enough—it must be combined with venture. It is not enough to stare up the steps; we must step up the stairs."

The value of a strategy is that it brings process to the vision. It identifies resources and mobilizes the members of the team. People need more than information and inspiration. They need instruction in what to do to make the vision become reality and a way to get there. A strategy provides that.

6. A Visionary Compass (Look Beyond)

The vision of the team must look beyond current circumstances and any obvious shortcomings of current teammates to see the potential of the team. A truly great vision speaks to what team members can become if they truly live out their values and work according to their highest standards.

If you are your team's leader, getting people to reach their potential means challenging them. As you know, it's one thing to have team members show up. It's another to get them to grow up. One of the things about having a far-reaching vision is that it brings "stretch" to the team.

Without a challenge many people tend to fall or fade away. Charles Noble observed, "You must have a long-range

> *"You must have a long-range vision to keep you from being frustrated by short-range failures."*
>
> —CHARLES NOBLE

vision to keep you from being frustrated by short-range failures." That's true. Vision helps people with motivation. That can be especially important for highly talented people. They sometimes fight lack of desire. That's why a consummate artist like Michelangelo prayed, "Lord, grant that I may always desire more than I can accomplish." A visionary compass answers that prayer.

Someone said that only people who can see the invisible can do the impossible. That shows the value of vision. But it also indicates that vision can be an elusive quality. If you can confidently measure the vision of your team according to these six "compasses," and you find them all aligned in the right direction, then your team has a reasonably good chance at success. And make no mistake. Not only can a team fail to thrive without vision—it cannot even survive without it. The words of King Solomon of ancient Israel, reputed to be the wisest man who ever lived, are true: "Where there is no vision, the people perish."[5] *Vision gives team members direction and confidence,* two things they cannot do without. That is the critical nature of the Law of the Compass.

COFFEE MAGIC

Some people capture a vision, as Abby Kohnstamm did at IBM, and they use it to focus their teams. Others are captured *by* a vision, and the power of it changes the courses of their lives.

That was certainly the case for Howard Schultz, the man who bought Starbucks Coffee Company in 1987.

Schultz was no stranger to Starbucks. In 1982, just six years out of Northern Michigan University, he had walked away from a great job as vice president in charge of U.S. operations at Hammarplast, a Swedish company that specializes in housewares, to join Starbucks. He had discovered the Seattle coffee retailer when he saw that their four stores sold more of Hammarplast's drip coffeemakers than Macy's in New York.

Schultz remembers the vision he had for Starbucks the day after his first visit to the company:

> It was like a shining jewel . . . There was something magic about it, a passion and authenticity I had never experienced in business. Maybe, just maybe, I could be part of that magic. Maybe I could help it grow. How would it feel to build a business? . . . How would it feel to own equity, not just collect a paycheck? What could I bring to Starbucks that could make it even better than it was?[6]

Schultz was captivated by a vision to expand Starbucks beyond Seattle, perhaps even across the entire country. When he began working for Starbucks as their director of retail operations and marketing, he started helping them to expand. But after Schultz had been with Starbucks for about a year, his vision for the coffee business itself also began to expand.

MAKE MINE A GRANDE!

After a visit to Italy, Schultz saw the huge potential of putting a coffee bar with espresso drinks in each Starbucks location. He believed that move held the greatest promise for the company, but he couldn't convince the owners to buy in to his vision. Since its inception in 1971, Starbucks had been a retailer of fresh whole coffee beans, not a seller of coffee by the cup.

Despite his love for Starbucks, Schultz left after three years to start his own company, which he made into a success. But two years later, when the owners of Starbucks let him know they wanted to sell the company, Schultz jumped at the chance. In 1987 the two companies merged and became the Starbucks Corporation.

Two factors drove Howard Schultz as he began the work of expanding Starbucks. The first was his love of coffee. The second was his desire to create a workplace that valued people and treated them with respect and dignity. That mattered to him greatly after a childhood of seeing his father struggle to support his family. Schultz says,

> I have a lot of respect for my dad. He never finished high school, but he was an honest man who worked hard. He sometimes had to take two or three jobs just to put food on the table. He cared a lot about his three kids, and played ball with us on weekends . . . But he was a beaten man. In a series of blue-collar jobs—truck driver, factory worker, cab driver—he never made as much as $20,000 a year, never could afford to own his own home. I spent my childhood in the Projects, federally subsidized housing in Canarsie, Brooklyn, [New York] . . . He had tried to fit into a system, but the system had crushed him.[7]

When it came to the coffee part of his vision, Schultz didn't worry about Starbucks. However, the working environment was another matter. In the two years he had been away from the company, the employees at Starbucks had become demoralized. Schultz says, "People were cynical and wary, beaten down and unappreciated. They felt abandoned by previous management and anxious about me. The fabric of trust and common vision that Starbucks had when I first joined had frayed badly."[8]

Recasting the Vision

Schultz began to address the issues immediately—starting with this statement to employees:

> Five years ago, I changed my life for this company. I did it because I recognized in it your passion. All my life I have wanted to be part of a company and a group of people who share a common vision. I saw that here in you, and I admire it.
>
> I'm here today because I love this company. I love what it represents . . . I know you're scared. I know you're concerned. Some of you may even be angry. But if you would just meet me halfway, I promise you I will not let you down. I promise you I will not leave anyone behind.[9]

Schultz had cast the vision. And in the coming months, he proved that he still valued great coffee. But he also went further. He began doing things that showed he valued the team. He called the people working for Starbucks "partners," and he backed it up with how he ran the company. He created a health plan that covered everyone, including part-timers. He clarified the company's mission and put into place a system in which hourly employees could hold management accountable to them. He even offered stock options to everyone, right down to the hourly employee who worked twenty hours a week making cappuccinos.

Schultz was trying to create the kind of company that people wanted to work for, the kind of place where someone like his father could have worked with dignity and respect. And he did it while making the company highly profitable. Starbucks is now a publicly traded company worth over $6 billion.[10] It serves more than 20 million people each week in more than 5,000 stores around the globe with plans to keep growing.[11] And it ranks high on the Forbes list of the best companies to work for.

Schultz sums up his role at Starbucks this way:

> I started off as a dreamer . . . Then I moved to entrepreneur . . . Then I had to become a manager, as the company grew larger and I needed to delegate more and more decisions. Today, my role is to be Starbucks' leader, its visionary, cheerleader, and keeper of the flame. [12]

Today Starbucks' customers, partners, and stockholders can clearly see the company's direction and have confidence in it. That's what vision does for a team. That's the power of the Law of the Compass.

❧

TEAMWORK THOUGHT

When you see it, you can seize it.

BECOMING A BETTER TEAM MEMBER

What is the vision for your team? You'd be surprised how many individuals are part of a group that works together but isn't clear about why. For example, that was the case when I became the leader of Skyline Church in the San Diego area. The church's board was comprised of twelve people. When I asked each member to articulate the church's vision the first time we met, I got eight different answers. A team can't move forward in confidence if it has no compass!

As a member of your team, you need a clear understanding of its vision. If the team doesn't have one, then help it to develop one. If the team has already found its compass and course, then you need to examine yourself in light of it to make sure there is a good match. If there isn't, you and your teammates are going to be frustrated. And everyone will probably be best served by a change.

BECOMING A BETTER TEAM LEADER

If you are the leader of your team, then you carry the responsibility for communicating the team's vision and keeping it before the people continually. That's not necessarily easy. Jack Welch, CEO of General Electric, observed, "Without question, communicating the vision, and the atmosphere around the vision, has been, and is continuing to be, by far, the toughest job we face."

I have found that people need to be shown the team's compass clearly, creatively, and continually. Whenever I endeavor to cast vision with the members of my team, I use the following checklist. I try to make sure that every vision message possesses . . .

❑ *Clarity:* brings understanding to the vision (answers what the people must know and what I want them to do)

❑ *Connectedness:* brings the past, present, and future together

❑ *Purpose:* brings direction to the vision

❑ *Goals:* bring targets to the vision

❏ *Honesty:* brings integrity to the vision and credibility to the vision caster

❏ *Stories:* bring relationships to the vision

❏ *Challenge:* brings stretching to the vision

❏ *Passion:* brings fuel to the vision

❏ *Modeling:* brings accountability to the vision

❏ *Strategy:* brings process to the vision

The next time you prepare to communicate vision to your people, use this checklist. Make sure you include each component, and I believe your team members will find the vision more accessible and will more readily buy into it. And if they do, you will see that they have greater direction and confidence.

8

THE LAW OF THE BAD APPLE

Rotten Attitudes Ruin a Team

Growing up, I loved basketball. It all started for me in the fourth grade when I saw a high school basketball game for the first time. I was captivated. Soon after that my dad poured a cement driveway along the side of our house and put a goal up on the garage for me. From that day until I went to college, I could usually be found practicing my shooting and playing pickup games on that small home court.

By the time I got to high school, I had become a pretty good player. I started on the junior varsity team as a freshman, and when I was a sophomore, our JV team had a 15-3 record, which was better than that of the varsity. We were proud of that—maybe a little too proud. I say that because of something that happened during my sophomore year.

One of the traditions on the team was that our coach, Don Neff, would give Ohio State basketball tickets to some of the players who

107

had performed especially well during the season. Those players were almost always seniors, and they were always on the varsity. But that year I was one of the players offered Buckeye tickets. What was my response? Was I grateful and humbled by Coach Neff's recognition? No, I told him I thought he should let the JV play the varsity for *all* the tickets. Needless to say, he never allowed that game to be played.

The next year, critics who followed high school basketball in Ohio thought our team had a chance to win the state championship in our division. I guess they looked at the players who would return as seniors from the previous year's varsity team and saw the talent that would be moving up from the JV, and they figured we would be a powerhouse. And we did have a lot of talent. How many high school teams in the late 1960s could say that all but a couple of players on the team could dunk the ball? But the season turned out far different from everyone's expectations.

FROM BAD TO WORSE

From the beginning of the season, the team suffered problems. There were two of us juniors on the varsity who had the talent to start for the team: John Thomas, who was the team's best rebounder, and me, the best shooting guard. We thought playing time should be based strictly on ability, and we figured we deserved our place on the team. The seniors, who had taken a backseat to the previous year's seniors, thought we should be made to pay our dues and wait.

What began as a rivalry between the JV and varsity the year before turned into a war between the juniors and the seniors. When we scrimmaged at practice, it was the juniors against the seniors. In games the seniors wouldn't pass to the juniors and vice versa. We judged our success not by whether the team won or lost, but by whether the juniors' stats were better than those of the seniors. If we outshot, outpassed, and outrebounded the seniors, then we thought we had "won" the game, regardless of the outcome against our opponent.

The battles became so fierce that before long, the juniors and the seniors wouldn't even work together on the court during games. Coach Neff had to platoon us. The seniors would start, and when a substitution became necessary, he'd put not one but *five* juniors in the game. We became two teams on one roster.

I don't remember exactly who started the rivalry that split our team, but I do remember that John Thomas and I embraced it early on. I've always been a leader, and I did my share of influencing other team members. Unfortunately, I have to confess that I led the juniors in the wrong direction.

What started as a bad attitude in one or two players made a mess of the situation for everyone. By the time we were in the thick of our schedule, even the players who didn't want to take part in the rivalry were affected. The season was a disaster. In the end, we finished with a mediocre record and never came close to reaching our potential. It just goes to show you, *rotten attitudes ruin a team.* That's the Law of the Bad Apple.

TALENT IS NOT ENOUGH

From my high school basketball experience I learned that talent is not enough to bring success to a team. Of course, you need talent. My friend Lou Holtz, the outstanding college football coach, observed, "You've got to have great athletes to win . . . You can't win without good athletes, but you can lose with them." But it also takes

> *Good attitudes among players do not guarantee a team's success, but bad attitudes guarantee its failure.*

much more than talented people to win.

My high school teammates were loaded with talent, and if that were enough, we could have been state champions. But we were also loaded with rotten attitudes. You know which won the battle between talent and attitude in the end. Perhaps that is why to this day I understand the importance of a positive attitude and have placed such a strong emphasis on it for myself, for my children as they were growing up, and for the teams I lead.

Years ago I wrote something about attitude for *The Winning Attitude*. I'd like to share it with you:

Attitude . . .

It is the "advance man" of our true selves.

Its roots are inward but its fruit is outward.

It is our best friend or our worst enemy.

It is more honest and more consistent than our words.

It is an outward look based on past experiences.

It is a thing which draws people to us or repels them.

It is never content until it is expressed.

It is the librarian of our past.

It is the speaker of our present.

It is the prophet of our future.[1]

Good attitudes among players do not guarantee a team's success, but bad attitudes guarantee its failure.

The following five truths about attitudes clarify how they affect a team and teamwork.

1. Attitudes Have the Power to Lift Up or Tear Down a Team

In *The Winner's Edge* Denis Waitley stated, "The real leaders in business, in the professional community, in education, in government, and in the home also seem to draw upon a special cutting edge that separates them from the rest of society. The winner's edge is not in a gifted birth, in a high IQ, or in talent. The winner's edge is in the attitude, not aptitude."

Unfortunately, I think too many people resist that notion. They want to believe that talent alone (or talent with experience) is enough. But plenty of talented teams out there never amount to anything because of the attitudes of their players.

Various attitudes may impact a team made up of highly talented players:

Abilities	+	Attitudes	=	Result
Great Talent	+	Rotten Attitudes	=	Bad Team
Great Talent	+	Bad Attitudes	=	Average Team
Great Talent	+	Average Attitudes	=	Good Team
Great Talent	+	Good Attitudes	=	Great Team

If you want outstanding results, you need good people with great talent and awesome attitudes. When attitudes go up, so does the potential of the team. When attitudes go down, the potential of the team goes with it.

2. An Attitude Compounds When Exposed to Others

Several things on a team are not contagious. Talent. Experience. Willingness to practice. But you can be sure of one thing: Attitude is catching. When someone on the team is teachable and his humility is rewarded by improvement, others are more likely to display similar characteristics. When a leader is upbeat in the face of discouraging circumstances, others admire that quality and want to be like her. When a team member displays a strong work ethic and begins to have a positive impact, others imitate him. People become inspired by their peers. People have a tendency to adopt the attitudes of those they spend time with—to pick up on their mind-set, beliefs, and approaches to challenges.

The story of Roger Bannister is an inspiring example of the way attitudes often "compound." During the first half of the twentieth century, many sports experts believed that no runner could run a mile in less than four minutes. And for a long time they were right. But then on May 6, 1954, British runner and university student Roger Bannister ran a mile in 3 minutes 59.4 seconds during a meet in Oxford. Less than two months later, another runner, Australian John Landy, also broke the four-minute barrier. Then suddenly dozens and then hundreds of others broke it. Why? Because the best runners' attitudes changed. They began to adopt the mind-set and beliefs of their peers.

Bannister's attitude and actions compounded when exposed to others. His attitude spread. Today, every world-class runner who competes at that distance can run a mile in less than four minutes. Attitudes are contagious!

3. Bad Attitudes Compound Faster Than Good Ones

There's only one thing more contagious than a good attitude—and that's a bad attitude. For some reason many people think it's chic to be negative. I suspect that they think it makes them appear smart or important. But the truth is that a negative attitude hurts rather than helps the person who has it. And it also hurts the people around him.

A wise baseball manager once remarked that he never allowed the positive players to room with the negative ones on the road.

When he created the team's room assignments, he always put the negative ones together so that they couldn't poison anyone else.

To see how quickly and easily an attitude or mind-set can spread, just think about this story from Norman Cousins. Once during a football game, a doctor at the first aid station treated five people for what he suspected might be food poisoning. Since their symptoms were similar, he tried to track down what they had in common. He soon discovered that all five people had bought drinks from a particular concession stand at the stadium.

> *There's only one thing more contagious than a good attitude—and that's a bad attitude.*

The physician wanted to do the responsible thing, so he requested that the game's announcer advise people in the stadium to avoid buying drinks from the particular vendor because of the possibility of food poisoning. Before long, more than two hundred people complained of food poisoning symptoms. Nearly half the people's symptoms were so severe that they were taken to the hospital.

The story doesn't end there, however. After a little more detective work, it was discovered that the five original victims had eaten tainted potato salad from one particular deli on the way to the game. When the other "sufferers" found out that the drinks in the stadium were safe, they experienced miraculous recoveries. That just goes to show you, an attitude spreads very quickly.

4. Attitudes Are Subjective, So Identifying a Wrong One Can Be Difficult

Have you ever interacted with someone for the first time and suspected that his attitude was poor, yet you were unable to put your finger on exactly what was wrong? I believe many people have that experience.

The reason people doubt their observations about others' attitudes is that attitudes are subjective. Someone with a bad attitude may not do anything illegal or unethical. Yet his attitude may be ruining the team just the same.

People always project on the outside how they feel on the inside. Attitude is really about how a person is. That overflows into how he acts. Allow me to share with you common rotten attitudes that ruin a team so that you can recognize them for what they are when you see them.

An inability to admit wrongdoing. Have you ever spent time with people who *never* admit they're wrong? It's painful. Nobody's perfect, but someone who thinks he is does not make an ideal teammate. His wrong attitude will always create conflict.

Failing to forgive. It's said that Clara Barton, the founder of modern nursing, was once encouraged to bemoan a cruel act inflicted on her years earlier, but Barton wouldn't take the bait.

"Don't you remember the wrong that was done to you?" the friend goaded.

"No," answered Barton, "I distinctly remember forgetting that."

Holding a grudge is never positive or appropriate. And when unforgiveness occurs between teammates, it's certain to hurt the team.

Petty jealousy. An attitude that really works against people is the desire for equality that feeds petty jealousy. For some reason the people with this attitude believe that every person deserves equal treatment, regardless of talent, performance, or impact. Yet nothing could be farther from the truth. Each of us is created uniquely and performs differently, and as a result, we should be treated as such.

The disease of me. In his book *The Winner Within*, highly successful NBA coach Pat Riley writes about the "disease of me." He says of team members who have it, "They develop an overpowering belief in their own importance. Their actions virtually shout the claim,

'I'm the one.'" Riley asserts that the disease always has the same inevitable result: "The Defeat of Us."[2]

A critical spirit. Fred and Martha were driving home after a church service. "Fred," Martha asked, "did you notice that the pastor's sermon was kind of weak today?"

"No, not really," answered Fred.

"Well, did you hear that the choir was flat?"

"No, I didn't," he responded.

"Well, you certainly must have noticed that young couple and their children right in front of us, with all the noise and commotion they made the whole service!"

"I'm sorry, dear, but no, I didn't"

Finally in disgust Martha said, "Honestly, Fred, I don't know why you even bother to go to church."

When someone on the team has a critical spirit, everybody knows it because everyone on the team can do no right.

A desire to hog all the credit. Another bad attitude that hurts the team is similar to the "disease of me." But where the person with that disease may simmer in the background and create dissension, the credit hog continually steps into the spotlight to take a bow—whether he has earned it or not. His attitude is opposite that of NBA Hall of Fame center Bill Russell, who said of his time on the court, "The most important measure of how good a game I played was how much better I'd made my teammates play."

> *Most bad attitudes are the result of selfishness.*

Certainly there are other negative attitudes that I haven't named, but my intention isn't to list every bad attitude—just some of the most common ones. In a word, most bad attitudes are the result of selfishness. If one of your teammates puts others down, sabotages teamwork, or makes himself out to be more important than the team, then you can be sure that you've encountered someone with a bad attitude.

5. Rotten Attitudes, Left Alone, Ruin Everything

Bad attitudes must be addressed. You can be sure that they will always cause dissension, resentment, combativeness, and division on a team. And they will never go away on their own if they are left unaddressed. They will simply fester and ruin a team—along with its chances of reaching its potential.

Because people with bad attitudes are so difficult to deal with and because attitudes seem so subjective, you may doubt your gut reaction when you encounter a bad apple. After all, if it's only your *opinion* that he has a rotten attitude, then you have no right to address it, right? Not if you care about the team. *Rotten attitudes ruin a team.* That is always true. If you leave a bad apple in a barrel of good apples, you will always end up with a barrel of rotten apples.

President Thomas Jefferson remarked, "Nothing can stop the man with the right mental attitude from achieving his goal; nothing on earth can help the man with the wrong mental attitude." If you care about your team and you are committed to helping all of the players, you can't ignore a bad attitude. If you do, you will find out the hard way about the Law of the Bad Apple.

YOUR BEST FRIEND OR WORST ENEMY

Attitude colors everything someone does. It determines how an individual sees the world and interacts with other people. A person's attitude—positively if it's good, negatively if it's not—always impacts his performance, regardless of talent, track record, or circumstances.

One of the most remarkable stories I've ever read that illustrates the Law of the Bad Apple came out of the San Francisco Bay area. Evidently the principal of a school called in three teachers to inform them of an experiment that the district would be conducting.

"Because you are the finest teachers in the system," she said, "we're going to give you ninety selected high-IQ students. We're going to let you move these students through this next year at their pace and see how much they can learn."

The faculty and students were delighted. During the next year, they had a wonderful experience. By the end of the last semester, the students had achieved 20 to 30 percent more than any other group of students in the area.

After the year was completed, the principal called in the teachers and told them, "I have a confession to make. I have to confess that you did not have ninety of the most intellectually prominent students. They were run-of-the-mill students. We took ninety students at random from the system and gave them to you."

The teachers were pleased. If the students were only average, that showed that the teachers had displayed exceptional skill and expertise.

"I have another confession," the principal continued. "You're not the brightest of the teachers. Your names were the first three names drawn out of a hat."

If the students and the teachers had been picked at random, then what had enabled them to make greater progress than any other group in the system? It was the attitudes of the people involved. Because the teachers and students expected to succeed, they increased their potential for success. Attitude had made all the difference.

If you want to give your team the best chance for success, then practice the Law of the Bad Apple. Trade your bad apples for good ones and you have a chance, because *rotten apples ruin a team.*

TEAMWORK THOUGHT

Your attitude determines the team's attitude.

BECOMING A BETTER TEAM MEMBER

The first place to start when it comes to attitude is yourself. How are you doing? For example, do you . . .

❑ Think the team wouldn't be able to get along without you?

❑ Secretly (or not so secretly) believe that recent team successes are really attributable to your personal efforts, not the work of the whole team?

❑ Keep score when it comes to the praise and perks handed out to other team members?

❑ Have a hard time admitting when you make a mistake? (If you believe you're not making mistakes, you need to check this!)

❑ Bring up past wrongs from your teammates?

❑ Believe that you are being grossly underpaid?

If you could place a check next to any of them, then you need to check your attitude.

Talk to your teammates, and find out if your attitude is doing damage to the team. Talk to your leader. And if you really think your pay is inequitable, you need to talk it out with your employer and find out where you stand. Anytime a relationship is unequal, it cannot last—whether you are giving more than you get or getting more than you deserve. In either case, the relationship will break down.

> *Anytime a relationship is unequal, it cannot last—whether you are giving more than you get or getting more than you deserve.*

Warning! I have one word of caution: If you leave your position because you believe you are undervalued, and you don't succeed in your new situation, then you most likely overestimated your value or underestimated what the organization was doing to help you succeed.

BECOMING A BETTER TEAM LEADER

If you think you have a bad apple on your team, you need to take the person aside and discuss the situation with him. Doing it the right way is important. Take the high road: As you approach him, share what you have observed, but give him the benefit of the doubt. Assume that your perception might be wrong and you want clarification. (If you have several people with bad attitudes, start with the ringleader.) If it truly is your perception and the team is not being hurt, then you haven't done any damage, and you have smoothed the relationship between you and the other person.

However, if it turns out that your perception was correct and the person's attitude is the problem, give him clear expectations and an opportunity to change. Then hold him accountable. If he changes, it's a win for the team. If he doesn't, remove him from the team. You cannot allow him to remain because you can be sure his *rotten attitude will ruin the team.*

9

THE LAW OF COUNTABILITY

Teammates Must Be Able to Count on Each Other When It Counts

One of the many strong points of Atlanta, Georgia, where I moved my family and my companies in 1997, is that it's a sports town. I don't get the chance to go to a lot of games, but there are few things I like better than attending a sporting event with all of the energy and excitement. Watching a team with a friend or two is a joy, whether it's the Braves (baseball), the Hawks (basketball), the Falcons (football), or the Thrashers (hockey).

When the announcement was made that Atlanta would be getting a hockey team, plans were set in motion to build the team a new arena. The old Omni, where the Hawks had played since the early 1970s, was slated to be demolished and replaced on the same site by the Philips Arena. It would be an 18,000-seat state-of-the-art entertainment complex with box seating, which could host not only hockey and basketball but also concerts and other events.

Tearing down the Omni wasn't going to be a routine process. First, it needed to be done quickly so that construction could begin on the new arena. Second, because the old structure had a cantilevered roof, taking the building apart in opposite order from the way it was constructed was out of the question. It would be far too dangerous for the demolition crews. That left only one choice: blowing it up.

EXPLOSIVE FAMILY BUSINESS

When demolition crews need help blowing up a building—or more accurately imploding a building—they inevitably turn to the Loizeaux family, the people who pioneered the safe demolition of buildings using explosives. They are owners and founders of Controlled Demolition Incorporated (CDI). The company was founded by Jack Loizeaux who had started a company in the 1940s removing tree stumps with dynamite. In 1957, he blasted his first building. And in the 1960s, he began CDI. Since that first demolition—an apartment building in Washington, D.C., his company has demolished more than seven thousand structures worldwide.

CDI is a family operation. Jack and his wife, Freddie, ran the business in the beginning. It wasn't long before they were joined by their sons, Mark and Doug. When Jack retired in 1976, his sons took over the operation. Today, they are joined by several of Mark's children, including his daughter Stacey, in her early thirties, who has worked in the field since age fifteen and is already an expert in her own right.

Like Threading a Needle

When the Loizeauxs were contacted for the job, they quickly discovered that the demolition wouldn't be easy because of the Omni's proximity to other buildings. On one side was the World Congress Center, which is used for conventions. On another side was a station for MARTA (Atlanta's mass-transit rail system). On the third was the CNN Center from which cable and radio programming broadcasts twenty-four hours a day. And CNN Plaza was a mere thirteen feet away from the Omni! A mistake could damage the MARTA line and shut it down at one of its busiest stations. Or it could put CNN news service temporarily out of business. And of course in a worst-case scenario, the Omni could topple in the wrong direction and take down the CNN building itself. It would take every bit of the Loizeauxs' expertise and fifty years of experience to do the task right.

Using explosives to take down a building is always a dangerous undertaking. Each project is different and requires a custom-made strategy. Holes are drilled in strategic places in many parts of the structure, such as in columns, and filled with appropriate amounts of explosive material. Then those blast points are often wrapped in chain-link fence (to catch the big pieces upon detonation) and wrapped in a special fabric that helps contain the explosion. "It allows the concrete to move, but it keeps the concrete from flying," says Stacey Loizeaux. "We also sometimes put up a curtain around the entire floor, to catch stuff that gets through these first two layers. That's really where your liability is."[1] Often, earthen berms are also erected around the building to protect nearby people and structures.

Obviously there is risk anytime someone works with explosives. But the greatest danger comes in the way explosives are rigged to go off. To get the building to fall in on itself, the Loizeauxs and their crew have to precisely sequence the charges, often using delays that differ from one another by the tiniest fractions of a second. That was the case for the Omni, where first the roof needed to fall straight down, then three of the walls would need to fall inward, and then the fourth wall outward. And on July 26, 1997, at 6:53 A.M., that's exactly the way it happened. The demolition took ten seconds.

When it comes to blowing up a building the way the Loizeauxs do, everything has to go right—from analyzing the building, to planning the demolition, to transporting the explosives, to rigging the devices, to preparing the building for the safety of the sur-rounding area. If anyone on the crew fails to get his part right and lets the other members of the team down, not only does the CDI team fail in its objective, but it also puts a lot of people and prop-erty in danger. *Teammates must be able to count on each other when it counts.* That's the Law of Countability.

HOLDING EACH OTHER ACCOUNTABLE

The importance of the Law of Countability is clearest when the stakes are high. But you don't have to be in an explosive situation for the law to come into play. The person running a business who is trying to get out a product on schedule depends on her vendors to deliver on their promises during crunch time. The waiter trying to please his customer counts on the kitchen staff to prepare the food properly. The mom getting ready for a job interview has to know that her baby-sitter will show up as promised. If there is a breakdown in countability, then the account is lost, the customer goes away unhappy, and the job goes to some other candidate. *Teammates must be able to count on each other when it counts.*

I was reminded of how often we encounter examples of the Law of Countability, even in small things, when I was on a trip to South Africa. I was there to teach at a confer-ence sponsored by EQUIP, my nonprofit organization. I was waiting in the hotel lobby for my ride to the conference, and I was having some trouble with a cough. That's usually no big deal, but when you're preparing to speak for five or six hours straight, it's not a great way to start the day. As the conference team and I got

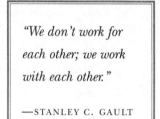

"We don't work for each other; we work with each other."

—STANLEY C. GAULT

under way, Erick Moon, a member of the team, pulled a Ricola cough drop (my brand) out of his pocket and handed it to me. When he saw my surprise, he said simply, "We're all carrying them for you, just in case."

Stanley C. Gault asserted, "We don't work for each other; we work with each other." That is the essence of countability—it's the ability and desire for teammates to work together toward common goals. But that doesn't happen on its own. Nor is countability a given. It has to be earned. Team members who can depend on each other only during the easy times have not developed countability.

THE FORMULA FOR COUNTABILITY

I believe that there is a formula for countability. It's not compli-cated, but its impact is powerful. Here it is:

Character + Competence + Commitment +
Consistency + Cohesion =
Countability

When every team member embraces each of these five qualities, within himself and with others, the team can achieve the countability that is necessary to succeed.

1. Character

In *The 21 Irrefutable Laws of Leadership*, I wrote about the Law of Solid Ground, which says that trust is the foundation of leadership. That law is really about character. In the book I state, "Character makes trust possible. Trust makes leadership possible. That is the Law of Solid Ground."[2]

> *"There is no substitute for character. You can buy brains, but you cannot buy character."*
>
> —ROBERT A. COOK

In a similar way, countability begins with character because it is based on trust, which is the foundation for all interaction with people. If you cannot trust someone, you will not count on him. As Robert A. Cook remarked, "There is no substitute for character. You can buy brains, but you cannot buy character."

Anytime you desire to build a team, you have to begin by building character in the individuals who make up the team. For example, my friend Lou Holtz, who coaches football at the University of South Carolina, introduces the players on his team to a list of twelve covenants at the beginning of the season to help them understand the team culture he is trying to create. Here are the covenants:

USC—12 Covenants

1. We will accomplish what we do together. We share our success, and we never let any one of us fail alone.

2. We are all fully grown adults. We will act as such, and expect the same from the people around us.

3. We will not keep secrets. Information that affects us all will be shared by all of us, and we will quickly and openly work to separate fact from fiction.

4. We will not lie to ourselves or to each other. None of us will tolerate any of us doing so. We will depend on each other for the truth.

5. We will keep our word. We will say what we mean, and do what we say. We trust the word of others to be good as well.

6. We will keep our head. We will not panic in the face of tough times. We will always choose to roll up our sleeves rather than wring our hands.

7. We will develop our abilities and take pride in them. We will set our own standards higher than our most challenging opponent, and we will please our fans by pleasing ourselves.

8. We will treat our locker room like home and our teammates like friends. We spend too much time together to allow these things to go bad.

9. We will be unselfish and expect that everyone else will exhibit this same quality. We will care about each other without expectations.

10. We will look out for each other. We truly believe that we are our brother's keeper.

11. We are students at USC, and as such we will strive to graduate. We take pride in our grade point average and expect our teammates to do the same.

12. Losing cannot and will not be tolerated in anything we do. Losing to us is to be shamed, embarrassed, and humiliated. There is no excuse for losing a football game at USC.

When you read through the twelve points, did you notice anything? Most of them touch on issues of character. Holtz knows that if he doesn't lay a solid foundation of character within the young men on his team, he can't build anything of value on top of it.

> *"Write and publish what you want, but the only missions, values, and ethics that count in your company are those that manifest themselves in the behavior of all the people, all the time."*
>
> —BARRY GIBBONS

Barry Gibbons, in his book *This Indecision Is Final*, asserted, "Write and publish what you want, but the only missions, values, and ethics that count in your company are those that manifest themselves in the behavior of all the people, all the time."[3]

2. Competence

I spent over twenty-five years as a pastor, so I know the church world very well, and I have seen people in the religious community who act as if character is the only thing that matters. I don't think that's true. What you do is also important, as Scripture makes clear.[4] Character is the most important thing, but it's not the only thing.

If you have any doubts about that, consider this. If you had to go into surgery because of a life-threatening illness, would you be happier having a good surgeon who was a bad person or a good person who was a bad surgeon? That puts it in perspective, doesn't it? Competence matters. And if the person is going to be on the same team with you, you want competence *and* character.

3. Commitment

Having fair-weather team members doesn't make for a very pleasant team experience. When times are tough, you want to know that you can count on your teammates. You don't want to be wondering whether they're going to hang in there with you.

Dan Reiland, who is a vice president at The INJOY Group, shared with me the table on the next page that indicates the commitment of various team members.

Teams succeed or fail based on teammates' commitment to one another and the team. My friend Randy Watts, who pastors a church in Virginia, sent me a note after a conference where I taught the Law of Countability. He wrote:

> Years ago, a friend of mine attended the Virginia Military Institute, known for its rugged physical, mental, and emotional training. He told me that all the incoming freshmen are separated into companies. One of their training obstacles is to race up House Mountain, which is very steep and more than a challenge. The motivation for climbing: If you finish last, you run again. Not you, but your whole company! This makes for team commitment. If a person in your company twists an ankle or breaks a leg, other members of his company carry him! It is not enough to be the first man on top of the mountain; everyone on the team has to make it.

Real teamwork requires that kind of commitment. When teammates can't make it, you carry them the rest of the way for the sake of the team.

Level	Type of Teammate	Description
1. Green Beret Colonel	Committed Team Leader	*Dedicated to the cause. Focused on the big picture. Has a whatever-it-takes attitude.*
2. First Lieutenant	Team Achiever	*Buys into the spirit and culture of the organization. Is self-motivated and productive.*
3. OCS Graduates	Genuine Team Player	*Has passion and enthusiasm. Arrives early and stays late. Is not yet a proven leader.*
4. Private	Formal Team Member	*Enjoys being on the team. Wants to stay. Serves out of duty. Not yet a high achiever.*
5. Boot Camp Recruit	Begrudging Follower	*Will work, but only with a kick in the seat of the pants.*
6. Deserter	Nonfollower	*Won't do anything. Needs to be court-martialed.*
7. Sniper	Dangerous Follower	*Works, but makes life difficult for team. Will shoot teammates if given the chance.*

4. Consistency

Every once in a while somebody comes along who defines consistency for the rest of his teammates. In the case of the Atlanta Braves, I believe that person is Greg Maddux. If you follow baseball, then you probably know about him. Maddux is a first-rate pitcher, and he has the awards—and statistics—to prove it. He has won more than 200 games, including 176 games in the 1990s, the most of any pitcher in major-league baseball. He is the only pitcher besides Cy Young and Gaylord Perry to have won 15 or more games in 13 consecutive seasons. He is the only pitcher in baseball's history to have won the Cy Young Award four years in a row (1992–95).

For all of Maddux's awards for pitching and noteworthy stats, do you know what has been his most remarkable honor? He has been recognized as the National League's best fielder in his position by receiving a Gold Glove *ten years in a row!*

Many great pitchers are not known for their fielding. When a difficult ball is hit to a pitcher, or when the pitcher has to cover first base on a tough play to the right side of the infield, many times the other players on the team hold their collective breath. If anyone on the field is likely to make a fielding mistake, it's the pitcher. But not Maddux. He works at his fielding with the same fantastic work ethic that has made him an outstanding pitcher. The result is a career that has seen only fourteen errors in fifteen years (with two seasons of error-free fielding).

If you want your teammates to have confidence in you, to know they can count on you day in and day out, then use someone like Maddux as your example. Consistency is key.

5. Cohesion

Teammates need to develop cohesion. That's the ability to hold together, no matter how difficult the circumstances become. Navy SEAL John Roat describes cohesion this way:

> Unit cohesion is one of those terms that everyone thinks they understand. In truth, most people don't have a clue. It is definitely

not about everybody liking each other or being nice. It means you have a pride in the ability of your group to function at a higher level than possible for the individual. The unit doesn't shine because you're a member, you shine because you're good enough to be a member.[5]

There's an old saying when it comes to teams: Either we're pulling together or we're pulling apart. Without cohesion people aren't really a team because they're not pulling together. They're merely a group of individuals working for the same organization.

> *There's an old saying when it comes to teams: Either we're pulling together or we're pulling apart.*

Novelist and civil rights activist James Baldwin asserted, "The moment we break faith with one another, the sea engulfs us and the light goes out." When it comes down to it, countability is being able to have faith in your teammates, no matter what happens. When the chips are down, you can turn to the people on your team. Let's face it: You can't do anything that counts unless you have countability. *Teammates must be able to count on each other when it really counts.*

BROKEN TRUST

When you see a major example of broken trust that destroys countability on a team, you know it instantly. When parents run out on their children, a spouse is guilty of infidelity, or children callously deceive their parents, it is a violation of countability in the family. When employees embezzle money, or leaders abuse the power entrusted to them by people in their organization, it undermines countability in a business. And when an officer in a government agency is guilty of espionage, it not only hurts his teammates; it breaks trust with the people in an entire nation.

When the news broke in early 2001 that an FBI agent had been caught passing highly classified national security information to Russia and the former Soviet Union, the first thing I thought of was the Law of Countability. The man in this case was Robert Philip Hanssen, a counterintelligence agent who had made a career with the FBI.

Hanssen is suspected of having given the KGB (and the organization that replaced it called the SVR) sensitive information on more than twenty occasions. That information totaled more than six thousand pages of material, including counterintelligence investigative techniques, sources, methods, and operations.[6] And just as in the case of Aldridge Ames, the CIA counterintelligence officer convicted of espionage in 1994, the information illegally passed by Hanssen is believed to have precipitated the deaths of field agents working for the U.S. government.[7]

Nobody likes a traitor. In fact, in America, the name Benedict Arnold is still associated with treachery and betrayal, even though his actions occurred more than two hundred years ago. (And few remember that Arnold was a brilliant military leader.) But what makes Hanssen's case especially distasteful is that the betrayer was a member of a team that maintains high standards of conduct because of the trust given to it by the people. The FBI identifies its core values as "rigorous obedience to the Constitution of the United States; respect for the dignity of all those we protect; compassion; fairness; and uncompromising personal and institutional integrity."[8] FBI Director Louis J. Freeh said of Hanssen:

A betrayal of trust by an FBI agent, who is not only sworn to enforce the law but specifically to help protect our nation's security, is particularly abhorrent. This kind of criminal conduct represents the most traitorous action imaginable . . . It also strikes at the heart of everything the FBI represents—the commitment of over 28,000 honest and dedicated men and women in the FBI who work diligently to earn the trust and confidence of the American people every day.[9]

In other words, *teammates must be able to count on each other when it counts.* Robert Hanssen broke the trust that makes countability possible. And it may be decades before we find out how much damage he did to the country. That's a terrible thought, but that's the price that sometimes has to be paid when someone breaks the Law of Countability.

TEAMWORK THOUGHT

The greatest compliment you can receive is being counted on.

BECOMING A BETTER TEAM MEMBER

People often say that imitation is a compliment. In regard to teamwork I believe the highest compliment you can receive is trust from your teammates when it really counts.

How do your teammates feel about you? In Chapter 6 we talked about how catalysts step up to a higher level of play when crunch time comes. You may or may not be the type of player who can make things happen and then some when the game is on the line. That's okay. But can you be depended on to do *your* part, whatever that is, when your teammates need you? Do you perform and follow through in such a way that the team considers you someone they can count on? How are you doing in each of the areas examined in the chapter?

- Is your integrity unquestioned (character)?
- Do you perform your work with excellence (competence)?
- Are you dedicated to the team's success (commitment)?
- Can you be depended on every time (consistency)?
- Do your actions bring the team together (cohesion)?

If you are weak in any of these areas, talk to a mentor or trusted friend to get suggestions concerning how you can grow in that area.

BECOMING A BETTER TEAM LEADER

Developing countability and cohesion among team members is not always an easy task. And it takes time. If you are responsible for leading your team, use the suggestions of William A. Cohen in *The Art of the Leader* for building a team that is able to count on each member when it counts:

1. Develop pride in group membership.

2. Convince your group that they are the best.

3. Give recognition whenever possible.

4. Encourage organizational mottos, names, symbols, and slogans.

5. Establish your group's worth by examining and promoting its history and values.

6. Focus on the common purpose.

7. Encourage your people to participate in activities together outside of work.[10]

The more of these activities you embrace, the greater countability you will develop.

THE LAW OF THE PRICE TAG

The Team Fails to Reach Its Potential When It Fails to Pay the Price

O n December 28, 2000, one of the nation's oldest retailers, Montgomery Ward and Company, announced that it would be filing Chapter 7 bankruptcy and closing its doors forever. That announcement saddened the people of Chicago, for Ward had been an institution in that city for more than a century. What's even sadder is that the company's failure might have been avoided if leaders had learned and practiced the Law of the Price Tag before it was too late.

The retailing chain's early history is really quite remarkable. The company was founded in 1872 by Aaron Montgomery Ward, a young salesman who had worked for various dry goods merchants throughout the Midwest and South. While he was working in rural areas far from cities or large towns, he discovered that many consumers in remote areas were at the mercy of local merchants who often overcharged them for merchandise. That gave him an idea. Railroads and mail service were improving by that time. What if he bought dry goods directly from manufacturers for cash and sold them for cash via mail order to rural consumers, thus eliminating the middlemen who were gouging those customers?

PAYING THE FIRST PRICE

In 1871, Ward saved enough money from his work as a salesman to purchase some merchandise and print a one-page price list that he planned to mail out to a bunch of farmers who belonged to a fraternal organization. But before he could follow through with his plan, the devastating Chicago fire of 1871 destroyed his stock and price sheets. The setback didn't stop Ward. He convinced two sales colleagues to join him as partners, began rebuilding his stock, and reprinted the price sheet, which would become the world's first general merchandise mail-order catalog. And in 1872, at age twenty-eight, Ward opened for business.

At first, Ward was only moderately successful. In fact, a year into the business, his two partners got cold feet and asked to be bought out. Ward paid them off, then took his friend George Thorne into the business as a full partner. Together they worked hard, taking orders and shipping out merchandise by rail. Meanwhile, in 1875, Ward and Thorne came up with a novel idea. They decided to include a new credo in their catalog. It said, "Satisfaction Guaranteed or Your Money Back." And the business took off.

Ward's tenacity and willingness to pay the price twice for starting his own business came to fruition less than a decade later. The company that had begun with $1,600 of capital in 1872 had sales of

$300,000 in 1878. Nine years after that, the company's sales rose to $1 million. By the turn of the century, Montgomery Ward and Company's catalog, which would come to be known as the "Wish Book," grew to five hundred pages and was being mailed to more than a million people every year. And the company's headquarters was a new building on Michigan Avenue in Chicago—the biggest skyscraper west of New York City.[1]

STOPPING PAYMENT

Then in 1901, Montgomery Ward retired in order to spend the final years of his life working to make Chicago a better place. During the first two decades of the new century, the company continued to thrive. But in the late 1910s, things began to change. Ward's success had prompted the start of another Chicago-based company in 1886: Sears, Roebuck, and Co. It, like Montgomery Ward and Company, was a catalog-based merchant that catered to rural customers. Back when both companies began business, most of the U.S. population lived in rural areas. But the country was changing. Cities were filling up. When the 1920 census was completed, it showed that for the first time in the nation's history, the majority of the population lived in urban centers—and shopping habits were changing as a result.

Robert E. Wood, a former army quartermaster general, was brought in to run Montgomery Ward in 1919, and he saw the coming boom in retail sales. He wanted to begin opening stores in cities where people could shop in person, but the owners were unwilling to go along with the idea.[2] They simply would not pay the price to make the change.

PASSED BY

Knowing where the future lay in the business, Wood left Ward. In 1924, he went on staff at Sears as vice president. He convinced the people who ran Sears to take a chance on retail store sales. They agreed to open one store in Chicago as a test the following year. It was an immediate success. Two years later, Sears had opened 27 stores. By 1929, the company had built more than 300. Even during the depression, Sears continued to expand, and in 1931, Sears retail store sales surpassed catalog sales.[3] Wood became the company's chairman, a position he held until 1954, and Sears became the most successful department store chain in the country.

Montgomery Ward and Company never really recovered from that early error. It opened some retail stores, but it wasn't aggressive enough to overtake Sears. *The team fails to reach its potential when it fails to pay the price.* Time after time, Ward failed to pay the price. During the depression, the company hoarded cash and stopped expansion while Sears gained more ground. After World War II when other stores began moving to the suburbs, Ward failed to seize the opportunity to try to get back on top. Each time the market changed, the company's leaders didn't pay the price necessary to win a market. For the last twenty-five years of the twentieth century, they struggled to keep their doors open. Finally, after 128 years in business, Montgomery Ward closed. That's what can happen when people violate the Law of the Price Tag.

PRICE POINTS

If a team doesn't reach its potential, seldom is ability the issue. It's rarely a matter of resources either. It's almost always a payment issue. Montgomery Ward and Company had plenty of resources, and it had the talent it needed, including the leader who could move the team forward. The problem was that the company's owners were unwilling to get out of their comfort zone, take a risk, and try to break new ground.

One of the reasons teams fail to pay the price to reach their potential is that they misunderstand the Law of the Price Tag. They honestly don't know how it works. Allow me to give you four truths about this law that will help to clarify it in your mind.

1. The Price Must Be Paid by Everyone

In *Straight Talk for Monday Morning*, Allan Cox observed:

> You have to give up something to be a member of a team. It may be a phony role you've assigned to yourself, such as the guy who talks too much, the woman who remains silent, the know-it-all, the know-nothing, the hoarder of talented subordinates, the non-sharer of some resource such as management information systems (MIS), or whatever. You give up something, to be sure, such as some petty corner of privilege, but gain authenticity in return. The team, moreover, doesn't quash individual accomplishment; rather it empowers personal contributions.[4]

> *If everyone doesn't pay the price to win, then everyone will pay the price by losing.*

People who've never had the experience of being on a winning team often fail to realize that *every* team member must pay a price. I think some of them think that if others work hard, they can coast to their potential. But that is never true. If everyone doesn't pay the price to win, then everyone will pay the price by losing.

2. The Price Must Be Paid All the Time

Many people have what I call destination disease. I describe it in my book *The 21 Indispensable Qualities of a Leader*:

> Some people mistakenly believe that if they can accomplish a particular goal, they no longer have to grow. It can happen with almost anything: earning a degree, reaching a desired position, receiving a particular award, or achieving a financial goal.
>
> But effective leaders cannot afford to think that way. The day they stop growing is the day they forfeit their potential—and the potential of their organization. Remember the words of Ray Kroc: "As long as you're green, you're growing. As soon as you're ripe, you start to rot."[5]

Destination disease is as dangerous for a team as it is for any individual. It makes us believe that we can stop working, stop striving, stop paying the price—yet still reach our potential. But as Earl Blaik, former football coach at the United States Military Academy, observed, "There is no substitute for work. It is the price of success." That truth never goes away. That's why President Dwight D. Eisenhower remarked, "There are no victories at bargain prices." If you want to reach your potential, you can never let up.

> *"There are no victories at bargain prices."*
>
> —DWIGHT D.
> EISENHOWER

3. The Price Increases If the Team Wants to Improve, Change, or Keep Winning

As I mentioned in the introduction of this book, there are few back-to-back champions in sports. And few companies stay at the top of *Forbes* magazine's lists for a decade. Becoming a champion has a high price. But remaining on top costs even more. And improving upon your best is even more costly. The higher you are, the more you have to pay to make even small improvements. World champion sprinters improve their times not by seconds, but by hundredths of a second.

No one can move closer to his potential without paying in some way to get there. If you want to change professions, you have to get more education, additional work experience, or both. If you want to run a race at a faster pace, you must pay by training harder and smarter. If you want to increase earnings from your investments, you put in more money or take greater risks. The same principle applies to teams. To improve, change, or keep winning, as a group the team must pay a price, and so must the individuals on it.

4. The Price Never Decreases

Most people who quit don't give up at the bottom of the mountain; they stop halfway up it. Nobody sets out with the purpose of losing. The problem is often a mistaken belief that a time will come when success will suddenly get cheaper. But life rarely works that way.

Maybe that kind of thinking was the problem with Montgomery Ward and Company. In 1919, when the decision

> *Most people who quit don't give up at the bottom of the mountain; they stop halfway up it.*

makers had the chance to make Ward one of the first big companies to open a chain of retail stores, they probably evaluated what it would cost them—in terms of time, money, effort, change—and they thought that it was too great a price to pay. So they passed on the opportunity.

A few years later when Sears began to breeze past Ward, the cost to compete was even higher. The company paid to get into retail store sales, yet it was still behind. That price continued to go up year after year, especially as Sears beat Ward in securing prime locations. Even as late as the 1970s and 1980s, Ward paid more and more to improve, yet fell farther and farther behind. The company dabbled in various niches, trying to compete against Wal-Mart, Target, and Circuit City, but it kept getting clobbered. The leaders thought the price would be less the next time—but it kept going up and up.

> *When it comes to the Law of the Price Tag, I believe there are really only two kinds of teams who violate it: those who don't realize the price of success, and those who know the price but are not willing to pay it.*

When it comes to the Law of the Price Tag, I believe there are really only two kinds of teams who violate it: those who don't realize the price of success, and those who know the price but are not willing to pay it. No one can force a team member to have the will to succeed. Each person must decide in his own heart whether the goal is worth the price that must be paid. But every person ought to know what to expect to pay in order for a team to succeed.

THE PRICE OF TEAMWORK

For that reason, I offer the following observations about the cost of being part of a winning team. To become team players, you and your teammates will have at least the following required of you:

Sacrifice

There can be no success without sacrifice. James Allen observed, "He who would accomplish little must sacrifice little; he who would achieve much must sacrifice much." When you become part of a team, you may be aware of some of the things you will have to give up. But you can be sure that no matter how much you expect to give for the team, at some point you will be required to give more. That's the nature of teamwork. The team gets to the top only through the sweat, blood, and sacrifice of its team members.

Time Commitment

Teamwork does not come cheaply. It costs you time—that means you pay for it with your life. It takes time to get to know people, to build relationships with them, to learn how you and they work together. Teamwork can't be developed in microwave time. Teams grow strong in a Crock-Pot environment.

Personal Development

Your team will reach its potential only if you reach your potential. That means today's ability is not enough. Or to put it the way leadership expert Max DePree did: "We cannot become what we need to be by remaining what we are." That desire to keep striving,

> *Your team will reach its potential only if you reach your potential.*

to keep getting better, is a key to your ability, but it is also crucial for the betterment of the team. That is why UCLA's John Wooden, a marvelous team leader and the greatest college basketball coach of all time, said, "It's what you learn after you know it all that counts."

Unselfishness

People naturally look out for themselves. The question "What's in it for me?" is never far from their thoughts. But if a team is to reach its potential, its players must put the team's agenda ahead of

> *"When you give your best to the world, the world returns the favor."*
>
> —H. JACKSON BROWN

their own. Some people see the big picture more easily than others do and realize that they will receive more if they give more. For others, that is more difficult—especially if they already have a track record of high achievement. But H. Jackson Brown's Boomerang Theory is true: "When you give your best to the world, the world returns the favor." And if you give your best to the team, it will return more to you than you give, and together you will achieve more than you can on your own.

Certainly there are other prices individuals must pay to be part of a team. You can probably list several specific ones you've paid to be on a team. The point is that people can choose to stand on the sidelines of life and try to do everything solo. Or they can get into the game by being part of a team. It's a trade-off between independence and interdependence. The rewards of teamwork can be great, but there is always a cost. You always have to give up to go up.

About a month ago I was teaching the 17 Laws of Teamwork to a group of businesspeople in Atlanta, and after I taught the Law of the Price Tag, Virgil Berry came up to me and slipped me a note. It said, "John, the price tag for failure is greater than the price of success. The price for accepting failure is poverty, depression, dejection, and a downtrodden spirit." The people at Montgomery Ward know that all too well. *The team fails to reach its potential when it fails to pay the price.*

WHAT PRICE FOR A NATION?

Paying a high price does not always guarantee victory. Many teams sacrifice dearly, only to fall short of their goals. But sometimes great sacrifice is rewarded with great results. That was the case for the Revolutionary Army of the newly formed United States and its commander, George Washington, during the winter of 1777 in Valley Forge, Pennsylvania.

The year 1777 was not a particularly successful one for General Washington and his troops. Following defeats at Brandywine, Paoli, and Germantown and the loss of Philadelphia to the British, Washington and eleven thousand soldiers straggled into Valley Forge on December 19 of that year. The troops were demoralized, and they were facing the prospect of a bitter winter with minimal shelter and comforts.

What those men probably wanted most was to go home and forget about the war for freedom. But if they did, the cost would be high. Positioned as they were, they could keep an eye on the British troops under General Howe in Philadelphia. More important, they were in a place where they could defend York, Pennsylvania, to which the Continental Congress had fled when the capital fell to the British. If the men at Valley Forge didn't pay the price, the government would fall, the army would be disbanded, and the Revolutionary War would be lost.

Conditions were horrible. The men were ill-equipped and poorly supplied. A few days after their arrival, Washington wrote to the Continental Congress, saying, "2,898 men were unfit for duty because they were barefoot or otherwise naked [insufficiently clothed for the harsh weather]." Things were so bad that sentries had to stand on their hats to ward off frostbite in their feet. By February 1, 1778, only 5,000 men were available for service.[6]

PAYING THE PRICE—AND THEN SOME

Miraculously, the troops didn't give up. They bore the brunt of the difficult winter. But they did more than just hang on and survive. They took the time to become better soldiers. Prior to their stay at Valley Forge, they were disorganized and untrained. To remedy that, General Washington employed the talents of a former officer in the Prussian army, Baron von Steuben.

First, von Steuben imposed organization on the camp and introduced improved sanitation. Then, under his instruction, one company of men was transformed into a crack team of soldiers. They in turn helped to train the other companies of men. Von Steuben also standardized the military maneuvers throughout the army so that the men could work better as a team, no matter which officers commanded them. By the time the army mobilized in June of 1778, it was a match for any group of soldiers, even the British, who were considered by some to be the best in the world.

Washington's army went on to win battles against a British army with far superior numbers. And his soldiers fought in the Battle of Yorktown, the decisive battle that turned the war in favor of the newly formed country. Those of us who live in the United States are grateful to them, for the price they paid more than two hundred years ago paved the way for us to live in a country of great freedom and opportunity. While it's true that *the team fails to reach its potential when it fails to pay the price,* it's also true that when the price *is* paid, the rewards can be abundant. That's the blessing of the Law of the Price Tag.

TEAMWORK THOUGHT

You seldom get more than you pay for.

BECOMING A BETTER TEAM MEMBER

If you are an achiever, then you probably have lots of dreams and goals. Write down some of the things you desire to accomplish in the next one to five years:

1. _____

2. _____

3. _____

4. _____

5. _____

6. _____

7. _____

8. _____

9. _____

10. _____

Now, which of them are you willing to give up? You always need to be ready to ask yourself that question when you are part of a team. When your personal goals conflict with the greater goals of your team, you have three choices:

1. *Put down the goal* (because the team is more important).

2. *Put off the goal* (because it's not the right time).

3. *Part with the team* (because it's better for everyone).

The one thing you have no right to do is to expect the team to sacrifice its collective goals for yours.

Becoming a Better Team Leader

If you lead a team, then you must convince your teammates to sacrifice for the good of the group. The more talented the team members, the more difficult it may be to convince them to put the team first.

Begin by modeling sacrifice. Show the team that you are . . .

- Willing to make financial sacrifices for the team.
- Willing to keep growing for the sake of the team.
- Willing to empower others for the sake of the team.
- Willing to make difficult decisions for the sake of the team.

Once you have modeled the willingness to pay a price for the potential of the team, you have the credibility to ask others to do the same. Then when you recognize sacrifices that teammates must make for the team, show them why and how to do it. Then praise their sacrifices to their teammates.

THE LAW OF THE SCOREBOARD

The Team Can Make Adjustments When It Knows Where It Stands

I n the previous chapter, you read about Montgomery Ward and Company, an American business that fell on hard times because it failed to heed the Law of the Price Tag. For a couple of decades, it looked as if another American institution was headed for a similar disaster: Walt Disney Productions.

THE MOUSE THAT ROARED

The company was founded by Walt Disney and his brother, Roy, in the 1920s. They began doing silent animation shorts and grew the company into one of the most loved and respected entertainment companies in the world. They continually broke new ground. They produced the first talking cartoon and the first color cartoon, both featuring Mickey Mouse, who has since become an American icon. *Snow White,* the first feature-length animated movie ever, was a radically innovative idea. While it was being made, many called it "Disney's folly." When it was released in 1937, it became the most successful film ever made up to that time. (Some say it's the most successful of all time!)

During the next two decades, Walt Disney Productions made wonderful movies that became classics. It expanded into television production. And it opened the world's first theme park. The name Disney became synonymous with creative family entertainment.

THE COMPANY THAT WHIMPERED

But after Walt died in 1966, the company started down a very bumpy road. Where Walt Disney Productions had once stood for innovation, it came to be marked by imitation—of its own past successes. Don Bluth, who left Disney in 1979, commented, "We felt like we were animating the same picture over and over again, with the faces changed a little."[1]

Instead of trying to look forward and break ground, Card Walker, who oversaw movie production, always asked himself, "What would Walt have done?" People at the studio began to joke morbidly, "We're working for a dead man."[2] The company cranked out more formula movies that didn't make a profit, and revenues continued to shrink. In 1981 the film division had an income of $34.6 million. In 1982 its income had fallen to $19.6 million. In 1983 it incurred a loss of $33.3 million. And the value of Disney stock was plummeting.

During that period, many American corporations were becoming victims of hostile takeovers, where Wall Street raiders would gain control of the company, cut it into pieces, and sell off its parts at a profit for themselves and their backers. Since Disney's stock value was down and it carried little debt, it became ripe for a hostile takeover.

In 1984, Disney narrowly avoided one takeover attempt and was facing the threat of yet another when its board of directors finally took a realistic look at where Disney stood. They decided that if the company was to survive, it would require radical changes, including something it had never done in its history—bringing in someone from outside Disney to run the company.

GETTING BACK INTO THE GAME

The people selected to turn around Disney were Michael Eisner as chairman and CEO and Frank Wells as president and COO. Concerning their challenging task, Eisner remarked,

> Our job wasn't to create something new, but to bring back the magic, to dress Disney up in more stylish clothes and expand its reach, to remind people why they loved the company in the first place . . . A brand is a living entity, and it is enriched or undermined cumulatively over time, the product of a thousand small gestures.[3]

Eisner was writing about his work on the Disney brand, but his remarks describe the approach he and Wells took to revitalizing the entire company. That involved a variety of strategies.

For one thing, they changed the name of the organization from Walt Disney Productions to the Walt Disney Company, reflecting the diversity of its interests. They brought together all of the organization's corporate executives and division heads for a weekly lunch to promote cohesiveness and to share ideas across divisions. They also hired key leaders, such as Jeffrey Katzenberg, to run their movie and television operations.

GOAL!

In a matter of a few years, Disney once again became a vital player in the entertainment industry. The almost-dead television division produced hits such as *The Golden Girls* and *Home Improvement*. The movie division, which had recently produced few movies and lost so much money, produced more movies in greater volume, with twenty-seven of its first thirty-three turning a profit. Before long, the company had four movie divisions: Disney, Touchstone, Hollywood Pictures, and Miramax. In late 1987, Disney became the number one studio at the box office for the first time in its history. And the animation division once again set the pace for the industry by creating films such as *The Little Mermaid, Beauty and the Beast, Aladdin,* and *The Lion King.*

Eisner and Wells expanded the company's efforts into new areas. They increased land development and built numerous new hotels at Walt Disney World. In 1987 they also opened retail stores in malls for the first time. Four years later, Disney owned 125 stores, which were generating $300 million in annual revenue. And of course, they improved the theme parks through expansion, innovation, and strategic partnerships with people such as George Lucas and Steven Spielberg. When they took over the company in 1984, the parks generated income of $250 million. By 1990, their income reached $800 million.

In 2000, the Walt Disney Company had revenues of $25.4 billion with $2.9 billion in net income (more than double the figures from 1984).[4] Disney has done more than just turn itself around. It has become an entertainment giant and one of the most powerful corporations in the world. For many of the years when the company was struggling, its team members looked at its history and the memory of its dead founder to gauge what to do. What they needed to do was to look at the scoreboard. *The team can make adjustments when it knows where it stands.* Eisner and Wells brought that ability to the company. They understood and implemented the Law of the Scoreboard.

UNDERSCORING THE SCOREBOARD

Every "game" has its own rules and its own definition of what it means to win. Some teams measure their success in points scored; others in profits. Still others may look at the number of people they serve. But no matter what the game is, there is always a scoreboard. And if a team is to accomplish its goals, it has to know where it stands. It has to look at itself in light of the scoreboard.

> *If a team is to accomplish its goals, it has to know where it stands.*

Why is that so important? Because teams that succeed make adjustments to continually improve themselves and their situations. For example, think about how a football team approaches a game. Before the competition starts, the team spends a tremendous amount of time planning. Players study hours of game film. They spend days figuring out what their opponent is likely to do, and they decide the best way to win. They come up with a detailed game plan.

As the game begins, the game plan is very important, and the scoreboard means nothing. But as the game goes on, the game plan means less and less, and the scoreboard becomes more and more significant. Why? Because the game is constantly changing. You see, the game plan tells what you *want* to happen. But the scoreboard tells what *is* happening.

Why the Scoreboard?

No team can ignore the reality of its situation and win. For years, Disney clung tenaciously to an out-of-date game plan while the world and the entertainment industry kept changing around it. The Disney team never really gave a hard look at the scoreboard. As a result they kept losing. That's what happens when you ignore the Law of the Scoreboard.

For any kind of team, the scoreboard is essential in the following ways:

1. The Scoreboard Is Essential to Understanding

In sports, players, coaches, and fans understand the importance of the scoreboard. That's why it is so visible at every stadium, arena, and ball field. The scoreboard provides a snapshot of the game at any given time. Even if you arrive at a game halfway into it, you can look at the scoreboard and assess the situation well.

> *The scoreboard provides a snapshot of the game at any given time.*

I'm often surprised by how many people outside sports try to succeed without a scoreboard. Some families operate their households without budgets, yet wonder why they are in debt. Some small-business owners go year after year without tracking sales or creating a balance sheet and wonder why they can't grow the business. Some pastors busy themselves with worthy activities, but never stop to measure whether they are reaching people or performing according to biblical standards.

2. The Scoreboard Is Essential to Evaluating

I believe that personal growth is a key to success. That's why I've taught lessons on growth at conferences and in books for more than twenty years. A key principle I teach is this:

$$Growth = Change$$

This sounds overly simple, doesn't it? But people sometimes lose sight of the fact that they cannot grow and remain the same at the same time. Most people are in a position that could be described by something Coach Lou Holtz once said: "We aren't where we want to be; we aren't where we ought to be; but thank goodness we aren't where we used to be."

But when it comes to growth, change alone is not enough. If you want to become better, you have to change in the right direction. You can do that only if you are able to evaluate yourself and your teammates. That is another reason for the scoreboard. It gives you continual feedback. Competing without a scoreboard is like bowling without pins. You may be working hard, but you don't really know how you're doing.

3. The Scoreboard Is Essential to Decision Making

Once you've evaluated your situation, you're ready to make decisions. In football, the quarterback uses information from the scoreboard to decide what play to call. In baseball, the scoreboard helps the manager know when to bring in a relief pitcher. In basketball, it can be used to determine whether to call a timeout.

That was the case at Disney. First Eisner looked at the company to understand its overall position. Then he evaluated individual areas for their effectiveness. Only then was he able to make sound decisions concerning how to get Disney back into the game.

4. The Scoreboard Is Essential to Adjusting

The higher the level on which you and your team are competing, the smaller the adjustments become to achieve your best. But making key adjustments is the secret to winning, and the scoreboard helps you to see where the adjustments need to be made.

One of the people on my staff is employing a unique scoreboard to help him make the adjustments required to go to the next level. That person is Kevin Small, the president of INJOY. Kevin is a real go-getter with high energy and enthusiasm. Being a young leader, he also has weak areas he needs to work on. To help him with that, he has engaged a personal coach to advise him, to help him read the scoreboard in his life, and to hold him accountable for growth. And it's really helping him. The small adjustments Kevin is making are taking him to another level and moving him closer to fulfilling his already tremendous potential.

5. The Scoreboard Is Essential to Winning

In the end, nobody can win without the scoreboard. How do you know when the game is on the line without the scoreboard? How do you know when time is running out unless you check the scoreboard? How will you know if it's cruise time or crunch time unless you have the scoreboard as a measuring device? If your desire is to take a leisurely drive with some friends, then you don't need to worry about a thing. But if you're trying to win the Indy 500, then you and your team *must* know how you're doing!

Some organizations view the scoreboard as a necessary evil. Others try to ignore it—something they cannot do for long and still do well in their profession. And some organizations make checking the scoreboard such an integral part of their culture that they are continually able to recognize and seize opportunities leading to huge success.

HIGH TOUCH IN A HIGH-TECH WORLD

That is certainly the case for eBay. I'm not a technical person. I don't have a computer—I don't even know how to use one—so I have not used eBay. I first heard about it from friends who are collectors. They talked about being able to find things they wanted through auctions held on the Internet. They seemed to be having fun with it, but to tell the truth I didn't pay much attention. Then I started seeing articles about eBay in the financial pages, and I read about the company's president and CEO, Meg Whitman.

Ebay is an e-commerce company that specializes in connecting buyers and sellers of goods on-line. It was founded by Pierre Omidyar in his San Jose, California, living room in September of 1995 with the idea of helping people find used, rare, or collectible items. The idea took off and became so successful that Omidyar soon recognized that he was in over his head. That's when he hired Meg Whitman, who had an MBA from Harvard and tremendous leadership experience as a general manager at Hasbro, president and CEO of FTD, and senior vice president of the Walt Disney Company.

An article in *Time* magazine explains eBay's success this way:

> As an online middleman between buyers and sellers, eBay is building an empire that bricks and mortar could not have touched. "If Buy.com goes down, you can still go to Circuit City," says Meg Whitman, . . . CEO of eBay. But if eBay crashes, there's nowhere else to go. And because eBay's job is connecting people—not selling them things—it isn't lumbered with a traditional retailing cost structure . . . "Ebay is the only e-tailer that really fulfills the promise of the Web," says Faye Landes, an e-commerce analyst at Sanford C. Bernstein & Co.[5]

The real genius of eBay is its mastery of the Law of the Scoreboard. It constantly makes adjustments because it knows where it stands, and that is what keeps it ahead. In the case of eBay, the scoreboard is the desires and interests of its customers—and potential customers. Sensing that many people are uneasy with conducting monetary transactions on the Internet, eBay made trust, safety, and privacy hallmarks of the company. Knowing that people wanted to get specific feedback on the individuals selling merchandise on the site, eBay created a unique rating system that allows subscribers to exchange information. The company even created a special Consumer Insights Group to track what people want.

LEARNING FROM THE CUSTOMER

Over the last three years, eBay has learned everything it can about its users and what they want while keeping its finger on the pulse of larger consumer trends. The company has expanded from being a place to trade Beanie Babies to a multifaceted auction service that offers among other services:

- Special local trading for difficult-to-ship items

- Global auction service that covers 150 countries (including a strong presence in Europe)

- A business-to-business exchange for products and services

- An automobile auction site

- Real estate services

And in 2000, when eBay saw that a new start-up company called Half.com was thriving by selling used CDs, books, movies, and video games at set prices, eBay bought the company and added it to its holdings.[6]

The result is that eBay has received highly favorable recognition and hundreds of awards, including *Business Week* Entrepreneur of the Year, E-Retailer of the Year Award from *E-Retailer*, and a place on the list of *Forbes* magazine's one hundred most dynamic companies in America. In 2000, it had 22.5 million registered users, controlled 80 percent of the on-line auction market, and had revenues of $430 million (up 92 percent from 1999).

While other Internet-based companies are struggling to survive and searching for ways to finally make a profit, eBay seems poised to keep growing—and winning. Why? Because the eBay team always has an eye on the scoreboard. And *the team can make adjustments when it knows where it stands.* That's the Law of the Scoreboard.

❦

Teamwork Thought

When you know what to do, then you can do what you know.

Becoming a Better Team Member

What is the scoreboard in your business or field? How do you measure your progress? Is it the bottom line? Is it the number of people you reach? Is it the level of excellence or innovation with which you do your work? How do you keep score?

> *When you know what to do, then you can do what you know.*

Take some time to identify how your team keeps score. Write the criteria here:

_____

_____

_____

_____

Now think about how you should be measuring yourself individually. What should you be keeping track of to make sure you are doing your best? Write the criteria here:

_____

_____

_____

_____

BECOMING A BETTER TEAM LEADER

If you lead the team, you have primary responsibility for checking the scoreboard and communicating the team's situation to its members. That doesn't necessarily mean you have to do it all by yourself. But you do need to make sure that team members continually evaluate, adjust, and make decisions as quickly as possible. That's the key to winning.

Do you have a system to make sure that happens? Or do you generally rely on your intuition? Using intuition is fine—as long as you have some fail-safe backups to make sure you don't let the team down.

Evaluate how consistently and effectively you consult your scoreboard. If you're not doing it as well as you should, then create a system that helps you to do it or empowers the leaders on your team to share the responsibility.

12

THE LAW OF THE BENCH

Great Teams Have Great Depth

Have you ever heard the expression "It's not over until the fat lady sings," or Yogi Berra's famous comment, "It ain't over till it's over"? Would you be surprised to know that sometimes it *is* over before it's over—and you can know when that is if you know the Law of the Bench?

Let me give you an example. One Saturday in September of 2000, I went to a football game with some friends: Kevin Small, the president of INJOY; Chris Goede, who used to play professional ball; and Steve Miller, my wonderful son-in-law. We were looking forward to an exciting game between the Georgia Tech Yellow Jackets and the Florida State Seminoles, even though FSU was a very strong favorite. There's an intense rivalry between all Georgia and Florida college teams, so the teams can get pretty pumped up.

And on that day, we weren't disappointed. The teams were battling, and the score was close. Tech was playing its heart out.

ONLY A MATTER OF TIME

But as the third quarter came to a close, I said, "Come on, guys. This one is over." I sometimes leave games early because I hate to be stuck in traffic. Of course, if a game is really close or is likely to have some historic significance (such as a no-hitter in baseball), I stay to the end. On that day, the guys were surprised by my desire to leave, especially since the game was close and Tech had finally pulled ahead, 15 to 12.

"You don't want to see the end of the game?" asked Chris, a little curious.

"No, this game is over," I said. "Let's go to the car."

On our way back, we talked about it. It's true that Tech was hanging in there against FSU, especially when it came to the way the Yellow Jackets were playing defense.

> *A great starter alone is simply not enough if a team wants to go to the highest level.*

That was no easy task because the Seminoles had a powerful offense. But I had noticed throughout the course of the game that while Tech's starters were still in the game, FSU had been substituting many players from the bench—and the team's level of play had not been negatively affected. Because of that, I knew it was only a matter of time before Tech's players would be worn down by the powerful bench of FSU. And sure enough, the final score was 26 to 21 with FSU on top. That's the impact of the Law of the Bench. *Great teams have great depth.*

THE ROLE OF THE BENCH

It's not difficult to see the importance of having well-trained, capable reserve players who sit on the bench in sports. In major-league baseball, the teams who win championships do so because they have more than just a good pitching rotation and solid fielding. They possess a bull pen with strong players who can substitute or pinch-hit off the bench. In the NBA, players and fans have long recognized the impact of the bench by talking about the all-important sixth man, the person who makes a significant contribution to the team's success yet isn't one of the five starters on the basketball court. And today's professional football coaches express the need to have two highly skilled quarterbacks capable of winning games on their teams. A great starter alone is simply not enough if a team wants to go to the highest level.

Any team that wants to excel must have good substitutes as well as starters. That's true in any field, not just sports. You may be able to do some wonderful things with a handful of top people, but if you want your team to do well over the long haul, you've got to build your bench. A great team with no bench eventually collapses.

DEFINING THE BENCH

In sports, it's easy to define which people are the starters and which make up the bench. But how do you define them in other fields? I want to suggest the following definitions:

Starters are frontline people who directly add value to the organization or who directly influence its course.

The bench is made up of the people who indirectly add value to the organization or who support the starters.

A team's starters are the people most often in the spotlight, and as a result, they get most of the credit, and the people on the bench are liable to be neglected or overlooked. In fact, the people most likely to discount or discredit the contribution of the bench may be the starters. Some key players enjoy reminding the substitutes that they are "riding the pine." But any starter who minimizes the contribution of the bench is self-centered, underestimates what it takes for a team to be a success, and doesn't understand that *great teams have great depth*.

A leader who truly understood the Law of the Bench was UCLA's John Wooden, the "Wizard of Westwood," whose teams won ten college basketball national championships. Coach Wooden valued every person on his teams and the contribution that each person made. No coach did a better job of keeping his teams playing at the highest level over the long haul than Wooden. He observed, "Unselfishness is a trait I always insisted upon. I believed that every basketball team is a unit, and I didn't separate my players as to starters and subs. I tried to make it clear that every man plays a role, including the coach, the assistants, the trainer and the managers."[1]

THE BENCH IS INDISPENSABLE

Every human being has value, and every player on a team adds value to the team in some way. These truths alone should be enough to make team members care about the bench players. But there are also more specific reasons to honor and develop the players who may not be considered starters. Here are several:

1. Today's Bench Players May Be Tomorrow's Stars

Rare are the people who begin their careers as stars. And those who do sometimes find that their success is like that of some child actors. After a brief flash in the pan, they are never able to recapture the attention they got early on.

Most successful people go through an apprenticeship or period of seasoning. Look at someone like quarterback Joe Montana, who was inducted into the NFL Hall of Fame in 2000. He spent two years on the bench as a backup before being named the San Francisco 49ers starter. And as he was breaking records and leading his team to numerous Super Bowls, the person who sat on the bench as a backup to him was Steve Young, another top-notch quarterback.

> *Every human being has value, and every player on a team adds value to the team in some way.*

Some talented team members are recognized early for their positive potential and are groomed to succeed. Others labor in obscurity for years, learning, growing, and gaining experience. Then after a decade of hard work, they become "overnight successes." With the way people like to move from job to job today—and even from career to career—good leaders should always keep their eyes open for emerging talent. Never be in a hurry to pigeonhole anyone on your team as a nonstarter. Given the right encouragement, training, and opportunities, nearly anyone who has the desire has the potential to emerge someday as an effective player.

2. The Success of a Supporting Player Can Multiply the Success of a Starter

When every team member fulfills the role that best suits his talents, gifts, and experience and excels in that role, then the team really hums. The achievement of the whole team makes the starters flourish, and the achievement of the starters makes the team flourish. The whole team really is greater than the sum of its parts. Or to put it the way John Wooden did: "The main ingredient of stardom is the rest of the team."

> "The main ingredient of stardom is the rest of the team."
>
> —JOHN WOODEN

You have probably seen teams led by people who don't understand this truth. For example, they have million-dollar salespeople spending half of their time bogged down in paperwork rather than making calls on potential clients. If the organization would hire someone who enjoyed administrative tasks, not only would the salespeople be happier and more productive, but the gains in sales would more than make up for the cost of that support person.

We follow this rule at ISS, my company that provides consulting to churches for fund-raising. We employ consultants whose skills and backgrounds are truly one in a million. They work with hundreds of individual churches out in the field every year, and that is where they need to be to use their strengths. However, each consulting job requires numerous letters, instruction manuals, and other printed materials. And to accomplish that, ISS employs a team of talented support people who do a fabulous job with that work. When each person is allowed to work in an area of strength, the entire team wins.

3. There Are More Bench Players Than Starters

If you read through the roster of any successful team, you will see that the starters are always outnumbered by the other players on the team. In professional basketball, twelve people are on the team, but only five start. Major-league baseball teams start nine but carry forty players. In pro football, twenty-two people start on offense and defense, but each team is allowed to have fifty-three players in all. (College teams often have more than one hundred!)

You find similar situations in every field. In the entertainment industry, the actors are often known, but the hundreds of crew members necessary to make a movie aren't. In ministry, everyone recognizes the people up front during a worship service, but it takes scores of people working behind the scenes to bring that service together. For any politician or corporate executive or big-name fashion designer that you know about, there are hundreds of people toiling quietly in the background to make the person's work possible. Nobody can neglect the majority of the team and hope to be successful.

4. A Bench Player Placed Correctly Will at Times Be More Valuable Than a Starter

I think if you asked most people how they would classify administrative assistants as team members, they would tell you that they consider them to be bench players since their primary role is support. I would agree with that—although in some cases, administrative people have direct influence on an organization.

Take, for example, my assistant, Linda Eggers. Over the years, Linda has done just about everything at INJOY. She has been the company's bookkeeper. She used to run our conferences. She did marketing and product development. She is a very talented person. I think Linda is capable of doing just about anything. But she has chosen to take a supporting role as my assistant. And in that position, she makes a huge impact. Today my company has more than two hundred employees. I respect and value all of them. But if I lost everything tomorrow and I could keep only five or six people with whom to start over from scratch, Linda would be one of the people I would fight to keep. Her value as a support person makes her a starter.

5. A Strong Bench Gives the Leader More Options

When a team has no bench, the only option of its leader is moving the starters around to maximize their effectiveness. If a starter can't perform, the team is out of luck. When a team has a weak bench, the leader has a few options, but they are often not very good. But when a team has a great bench, the options are almost endless.

> When a team has a great bench, the options are almost endless.

That's why someone like Bobby Bowden, the coach at FSU, was able to wear down Georgia Tech. If one of his players got hurt, he had someone to replace him. If his opponent changed defenses, he had offensive players in reserve to overcome the challenge. No matter what kind of situation he faced, with a strong bench he had options that would give the team a chance to win.

6. The Bench Is Usually Called Upon at Critical Times for the Team

When an army is in trouble, what does it do? It calls up the reserves. That's the way it is in every area of life. You don't need the bench when things are going well; you need it when things aren't going well. When the starter gets hurt and the game is in jeopardy, a substitute steps in. That person's effectiveness often determines the team's success.

If your team is experiencing a tough time, then you know the importance of having a good bench. But if you are experiencing a smooth period, then now is the time to develop your backup players. Build the bench today for the crisis you will face tomorrow.

TODAY'S ACTIONS BUILD TOMORROW'S TEAM

As you think about the starters and the bench players on your team, recognize that the future of your team can be predicted by three things:

1. Recruitment: Who Is Joining the Team?

Adlai E. Stevenson offered this advice: "There are only three rules of sound administration: Pick good men, tell them not to cut corners, and back them to the limit; and picking good men is the most important." You cannot build a winning team without good players.

When it comes to recruiting, there are really only two kinds: You find the player for the position, or you find the position for the player. In the first situation, you have a position open, and you look for someone to fill that position. That is the typical way most recruiting works. But sometimes even when you don't have a position open, you find a potential player who is so good that you simply cannot pass up the opportunity to get him on the team.

I was in the second situation last year. When I discovered that John Hull might be interested in coming to work for The INJOY Group, I didn't have a specific position for him. But he is such a high-impact player that I brought him aboard. And in a matter of a few months, he became the president of EQUIP, the nonprofit organization I founded, when its original president, Ron McManus, desired to lead another department for me. If I hadn't asked John to come aboard when I did, the team might have missed out on a wonderful leader.

2. Training: Are You Developing the Team?

You cannot solve tomorrow's problems with today's solutions. If

> You cannot solve tomorrow's problems with today's solutions.

you want the team to succeed as it meets new challenges, you have to prepare it. That means helping starters to maximize their potential and training the people on the bench to become starters when their time comes.

If you have leadership responsibility for your team, then take the initiative to make sure everyone on the team is growing and improving.

3. Losses: Who Is Leaving the Team?

The only place that never loses people is the cemetery. Losing team members is inevitable. But the good news is that you can choose the members you lose. If you keep nonproductive people, the productive ones become frustrated and leave. If you remove the people who don't add value, then the whole team gets better. It's just like trimming trees: If you don't cut the deadwood, eventually the whole tree falls. But if you remove the deadwood, the tree becomes healthier, the healthy branches produce more, and there's room for productive new branches on the tree.

The best way to describe how to grow and improve the team

and its bench is what I call the revolving door principle. Here's the way it works: A team will always have gains and losses. People are constantly coming into an organization while others leave it. The key to its future success is gaining a more effective person with each loss.

Let's say, for example, that you can rate every person's effectiveness on a scale of 1 to 10, with 10 as the highest. As the revolving door turns, if your team is losing 4s but gaining 8s, then your future looks bright. If you're losing 8s and gaining 4s, then the future looks bleak. And if you're losing 4s and gaining other 4s, then you're wearing your team out with activity but making no progress.

PHASES OF AN ORGANIZATION AND ITS REVOLVING DOOR

Any team that is avoiding stagnation by trying to improve will go through changes, and as the revolving door moves, different kinds of people will come and go during various phases. For example, when an organization is new and just getting started, it recruits strongly. It has no one to lose and is glad to gain anyone. The good news is that as people come on board, a team is being formed. The bad news is that the people the team is gaining are not always good.

When a team asks for commitment, some team members leave the team. But that's good. Commitment drives away the uncommitted, while it makes those who stay even stronger in the commitment they already possess.

Once the team has a committed core and begins to grow, it again gains people. The people who join the team are often attracted to it because of the level of commitment they see in existing players. That

Type of Team	Gain or Loss	Nature of Loss or Gain
New Team	More Gains Than Losses	Gains Are Not Always Positive
Committed Team	More Losses Than Gains	Losses Are Positive
Growing Team	More Gains Than Losses	Gains Are Positive
Successful Team	More Losses Than Gains	Losses Are Not Positive
Legacy Team	More Gains Than Losses	Gains Are Positive

builds the team's ability and drives it to achieve—and leads to its success.

However, once a team becomes successful, some members will want to leave to try to find greater success on their own. That's a critical time for a team. If you can give people intriguing challenges and share both responsibilities and rewards with them, you may be able to persuade them to stay. (If you can't, you'll probably have to rely on your backup players, and then you'll find out what kind of bench you've built!)

If you can sustain growth in the midst of success and repeat the process while continually building your bench, then you can create a legacy team. That's what organizations such as General Electric, Disney, and Home Depot have done. Their sustained growth and reputations for success continue to draw good people to them.

Who Is Your MVP?

The key to making the most of the Law of the Bench is to continually improve the team. As you bring on better players, first improve your starters. Then build your bench. Do that long enough and you will build a great team because *great teams have great depth.* That's the Law of the Bench.

Building a great team is a process that takes a tremendous amount of work, and the bigger the organization gets, the harder the task becomes. I'm acutely aware of that because in the last three and a half years, The INJOY Group has grown from less than fifty people to more than two hundred! When you're experiencing that kind of explosive growth, your HR person may be your MVP.

Let me tell you about the person most responsible for keeping the revolving door moving in the right direction in my company. Her name is Stacy Buchanan. Two and a half years ago, an acquaintance of hers who was a headhunter directed her to The INJOY Group. At the time, we were looking for a senior accountant, and Stacy had an exten-

> *The key to making the most of the Law of the Bench is to continually improve the team.*

sive background in accounting, having done much of the groundwork to become a CPA. She had also worked for six years at an internationally known nonprofit organization and spent several years teaching.

Bold Move

Stacy believed with all her heart that she belonged at The INJOY Group, and she really wanted to work with us. So she came in and interviewed with us. But the last thing in the world she wanted to do was go back into accounting. Christine Johnson, a longtime INJOY employee who was functioning as our HR manager at the time, was interviewing Stacy. Christine could tell that she was an "eagle" and didn't want her to get away. So she introduced Stacy to the COO, Dick Peterson. As they talked, he, too, could tell she was a tremendous catch. Finally he asked her, "What do you want to do?"

Stacy gathered her courage and replied, "To tell you the truth, Dick, I want Christine's job: recruiting."

That was music to Christine's ears. She was dutifully recruiting new employees, but she didn't really enjoy it—nor did it utilize her greatest strengths. She and Dick were happy to create a position for Stacy as a recruiter, thus freeing Christine to focus on administration and management. In the thirty months since then, Stacy has hired nearly two hundred people for the company— both starters and bench players. And she does a fantastic job.

"I know I am going to sound like a preacher with my six Ps," says Stacy, "but this will give you an idea of how I place people. I analyze the following areas:

1. *Personality:* I use the DISC test, a diagnostic tool that indicates whether someone's personality is driving, influencing, supporting, or calculating.

2. *Passion:* I find out what motivates them—results, relationships, money, recognition, affirmation, impact, or security.

3. *Pattern:* I look for patterns in their successes and their failures. I figure out whether they work best alone or on a team.

4. *Potential:* I try to see what they might accomplish given the

right direction, motivation, coaching, and leadership. I particularly gauge whether they are maintainers or builders.

5. *Profile:* I gauge whether they will fit our culture and whether they are really INJOY material.

6. *Placement:* Finally I try to measure where they fit—which team will both benefit from them and add value to them.

Stacy has done a wonderful job of building our team through recruiting. And now she has expanded her role into the area of training. She has played an instrumental role in starting the nine mentoring groups that are currently in place at The INJOY Group. Stacy summarizes her work by saying, "My desire is to see people play the music that is contained in their souls."

If you want your team to become the very best it can be, then you need to concentrate on the people you're gaining, the ones you're losing, and the ones you're developing. That's the only way to build a great team. It has to be solid at every level. And never lose sight of the Law of the Bench. Remember, *great teams have great depth.*

TEAMWORK THOUGHT

Better players make you a better player.

BECOMING A BETTER TEAM MEMBER

How would you define yourself: a bench player or a starter? If you are on the bench, then your job is to do two things: Help the starters to shine, and prepare yourself to be a starter in the future. You can do that by cultivating an attitude of service and teachability, and by doing whatever you can to learn and grow.

If you are a starter, then you should perform at your best for the sake of the team, and you should honor the people on the bench. You do that by acknowledging the value of their contribution and by helping prepare them to start someday. If you are not already mentoring a teammate on the bench, start doing so right away.

BECOMING A BETTER TEAM LEADER

If you lead your team, you are responsible for making sure the revolving door moves in such a way that the players who are joining the team are better than those who are leaving. One way you can facilitate that is to place high value on the good people already on the team.

Every team has three groups of players. In this chapter I described the *starters*, who directly add value to the organization or who directly influence its course, and the *bench players*, who indirectly add value to the organization or who support the starters. The third group is a core group within the starters that I call the *inner-circle members*. Without these people the team would fall apart. Your job is to make sure each group is continually developed so that bench players are able to step up to become starters, and starters are able to step up to become inner-circle members.

If you're not sure who the inner-circle members are on your team, then try this exercise: Write the names of the people on your team who are starters. Now determine the people you could most easily do without. One by one, check off the names of the people whose loss would hurt the team least if they left. At some point you will end up with a smaller group of people without whom the team would be dead. That's your inner circle. (You can even rank the remaining people in order of importance.)

It's a good exercise to remind you of the value of people on the team. And by the way, if your treatment of those people doesn't match their value, you run the risk of losing them and having your revolving door work against you.

13

THE LAW OF IDENTITY

Shared Values Define the Team

At least one day a year, I try to bring together everyone in my organization. Early in INJOY's history, that was easy. Back in 1985 when we founded the company, Dick Peterson, who is now the company's COO, and I could get together on a moment's notice with his mother-in-law, Erma (our only employee), and the four or five volunteers who helped us (two of whom were our wives). Even ten years later we were still a fairly small outfit. The entire company could meet around one large conference table.

Today things are different. Now we have to rent a hall to accommodate all of our employees, but we still make the effort to get together. In fact, it's more important for us to do that now than it ever was before. Because of our size and the diversity of operations, the people on our team have a tendency to get disconnected from one another. And it becomes increasingly difficult for the leaders in the organization to maintain a personal connection with everyone.

DEFINING THE TEAM

Maybe you've experienced the disconnectedness that often accompanies rapid growth in an organization. Granted, with slightly more than two hundred employees, ours is not a large company, but it is big enough to experience growing pains. Where the team was once defined almost entirely through relationships, it now needs something more to keep it together. That's where the Law of Identity comes into play: *Shared values define the team.* Even if some members of a team don't share common experiences or have a personal relationship with one another, they can possess a cohesiveness that defies the size of the team. What it takes is a common vision (the Law of the Compass) and shared values. If everyone embraces the same values, team members can still have a connection to one another and to the larger team.

> *Just as personal values influence and guide an individual's behavior, organizational values influence and guide the team's behavior.*

We've all seen teams that have a common goal yet lack common values. Everyone on the team has different ideas about what's important. The result is chaos. Eventually the team breaks down if everyone tries to do things his own way. That's why team members need to be on the same page. Just as personal values influence and guide an individual's behavior, organizational values influence and guide the team's behavior.

THE VALUE OF VALUES

Values can help a team to become more connected and more effective. Shared values are like . . .

Glue

When difficult times come—and they do for every team—values hold people together. Look at a marriage, for example. It's easy for a couple to stay together when they are feeling the flush of love and everything is going smoothly. But eventually the passion that drew them together fades. And adversity comes. What keeps the people who stay married together? It's their values. Their values are more important than their feelings. They value their marriage so highly that they are willing to fight *for* the relationship. If two people don't have that mind-set going into the wedding, then their chances of staying together are pretty slim.

The same is true for any other team. If the players don't know what their values are—and live them out—their chances of working as a unit and reaching their potential are very small.

A Foundation

All teams need stability to perform well and to grow. Values provide a stable foundation that makes those things possible. This is true for just about any kind of relationship to grow. For example, if you are trying to build a relationship with someone from another culture, you begin by looking for the things you have in common. If you are trying to make a sale with a new customer, you look for common ground. The same is true when it comes to team building. You need something to build on, and values make the strongest foundation.

A Ruler

Values also help set the standard for a team's performance. In the corporate world, the values are often expressed in a mission statement or set of guidelines for doing business. But sometimes a company's stated values and its real values don't match up.

Author and management expert Ken Blanchard emphasizes, "Lots of companies claim they have a set of core values, but what they mean is a list of generic business beliefs that everyone would agree with, such as having integrity, making a profit, and responding to customers. Such values have meaning only when they are further defined in terms of how people actually behave and are rank-ordered to reveal priority." And they function as a measure of expectations and performance when they are genuinely embraced.

> *Values help set the standard for a team's performance.*

A Compass

Do you remember the television show *Dallas* from the 1980s? The main character was J. R. Ewing, a notoriously dishonest businessman. His character code for living can be summarized by something he said in an episode of the show: "Once you give up your ethics, the rest is a piece of cake." To a person with no values, anything goes.

I think we live in a time when people are searching for standards to live by. When individuals embrace strong values, they possess a moral compass that helps them make decisions. The same is true for people in an organization. When the team identifies and embraces a set of values, then in a month, a year, or a decade, no matter how much circumstances change or what challenges present themselves, people on the team still know it's moving in the right direction and make good decisions.

A Magnet

A team's values attract people with like values to the team. Think about some of the teams we've examined in previous chapters. What kinds of people are drawn to Habitat for Humanity? People who want to see substandard housing eliminated. What kinds of people are attracted to Enron? People who value innovation and organizational flexibility.

In *The 21 Irrefutable Laws of Leadership*, the Law of Magnetism states, "Who you are is who you attract." That law is as true for teams as it is for leaders. People attract other like-minded people.

An Identity

Values define the team and give it a unique identity—to team members, potential recruits, clients, and the public. What you believe identifies who you are.

THE VALUES OF THE INJOY GROUP

When I brought together all of the employees of The INJOY Group for our annual meeting this year, I wanted to emphasize our values. I think our team members see them acted out every day, but I wanted to give everyone a common language for the values to help ensure our alignment with them. To do that, I taught a lesson on those values.

Communication of the team's values is the place to start with the Law of Identity. A team cannot share values if the values have not been shared with the team. Allow me to acquaint you with the six core values that I shared with The INJOY Group so that you have a sense of what I mean.

1. The Personal Growth of Each Team Member

I am a strong believer in potential. Every day I work to develop my own, and I encourage everyone in my sphere of influence to do the same. How do people work to develop their potential? They start by making personal growth a priority.

Personal growth has been a major theme of my life. When I was a kid, my father used to pay me and my siblings to read books that would improve us. He also sent us to conferences. As I got older, reading books, listening to instructional tapes, and attending conferences became regular practices for me. Later, as I sought the key to organizational growth, I discovered another reason to promote personal growth because I found that the way to grow any organization is to grow the people in that organization.

> *A team cannot share values if the values have not been shared with the team.*

To promote personal growth in my organization, we encourage people to become members of a mentoring group. We also send people to our own conferences and to other types of training. We provide books, tapes, and other personal-growth tools. And I personally spend time every month mentoring and developing the top leaders of the organization. When we or an employee discovers that the person would flourish in a different position or division of the company, we encourage him to explore new possibilities and make a change. You can't stand in the way of your employees' growth and still hope to grow your organization.

2. The Priority of Adding Value to Others

The INJOY Group exists to add value to people. That is our primary mission. First, we do that with the people in our own organization. But we also do it for our customers and clients. It's the reason we develop and provide consulting, training, and resources to organizations and individuals across the country and around the world. The day we can't add value to people is the day we close our doors.

3. The Power of Partnership

One of my favorite quotes comes from Mother Teresa, who observed, "You can do what I cannot do. I can do what you cannot do. Together we can do great things." That's a succinct way to describe partnership.

> *"You can do what I cannot do. I can do what you cannot do. Together we can do great things."*
>
> —MOTHER TERESA

It took me almost forty years to discover that I can't do everything. (You probably learned that sooner than I did; my high energy, low IQ, and endless optimism got the better of me for years!) That's when I realized the power of partnership. Over the years, our organization has learned more and more about working with others. Now partnership is the way we choose to accomplish our mission. Dave Sutherland, the CEO of The INJOY Group, likes to remind everyone, "Partnership begins the moment that a leader realizes we add value to him, and it ends when his vision is accomplished."

In recent years, we have expanded our partnership to include strategic alliances with other organizations. These partnerships have enabled The INJOY Group to train thousands of leaders in nearly a dozen countries overseas and to give away tens of thousands of books every year to people in developing countries.

I've come up with an acronym that describes what partnership means to me. As your partner, we promise to . . .

Put your needs first in every situation.

Add value to your personal leadership.

Recognize we serve a common goal.

Tailor our services to meet your need.

Never take for granted the trust placed in us.

Embody excellence in everything we do.

Respect everyone's uniqueness.

As individuals and as an organization, we can be good partners if we can remember each element.

4. The Practice of Raising Up and Developing Leaders

Everything rises and falls on leadership. That's why I have dedicated the past twenty years of my life to teaching leadership. That's also why I spend so much time finding and developing leaders. The single greatest way to impact an organization is to focus on leadership development. There is almost no limit to the potential of an organization that recruits good people, raises them up as leaders, and continually develops them.

> *The single greatest way to impact an organization is to focus on leadership development.*

5. The Proper Stewardship of the Organization

Any organization that wants to continue fulfilling its mission must learn to be a good steward of its resources. There are three primary ways we do that in our company: managing our assets to get the most out of them, placing our people strategically so they can give and receive as much as possible, and giving of ourselves to worthy causes. If we can do all three of these things, then we are maximizing the use of all the resources we have.

6. The Purpose of Glorifying God

The INJOY Group is an organization made up primarily of Christians, and our roots are in helping churches and pastors to reach their potential. Because of our heritage and our strong convictions, we believe that everything we do should honor God.

Undoubtedly the values of your organization will be different from ours. And that's as it should be. Your values should reflect the people on the team and their leader. What's important is that you go through the discovery process and embrace the team's values. Once you do, you will better understand your team, its mission, and its potential. Never forget that *shared values define the team.* That's the Law of Identity.

VALUES ADD VALUE TO YOUR TEAM

If you've never really thought about how your team's values can reveal its identity and increase its potential, go through the following process with your team:

- *Articulate the values.* Spend some think time or bring together a group of key team members to articulate the team's values. Then put them on paper.

- *Compare values with practices.* Then watch the team in action. You want to make sure the values you identify match the ones you're living. The alignment of the stated values and the behavior of team members boosts the team's energy and effectiveness. But if they are out of alignment, then the team will suffer.

- *Teach the values.* Once you settle what the right values are, you need to teach them to everyone on the team. Do it clearly, creatively, and continually.

- *Practice the values.* Values have no value if you don't put them into practice. If you discover teammates whose actions don't match the team's values, help them to make the changes necessary to align themselves with the rest of the team.

- *Institutionalize the values.* Weave the team's values into the fabric of the team. For example, my friend Bill Hybels, senior pastor of Willow Creek Community Church, identifies "community" as one of the core values of his church. To reinforce that value, the first third of every leadership meeting—whether it is staff, elders, or the board—is dedicated to building and maintaining the personal relationships among the members of that group.

- *Publicly praise the values.* The most fundamental management truth I've ever learned is that what gets rewarded gets done. If you praise and honor the people who epitomize the values of the team, those values get embraced and upheld by other members of the team. There is no better reinforcement.

If you are the leader of your team, it is especially important that you take your team through this process. Left to themselves, with no help to embrace the values you know to be fundamental, team members will create an identity of their choosing. For better or worse, the values of the most influential people on the team will become the team's values. However, by implementing each of the steps I outlined and continuing to repeat them over time, you will find that the culture of your organization will begin to change, and your people will embrace a new identity that you help them find. And once they develop a common team identity, they will work together better, even as the organization grows and changes.

> *The most fundamental management truth I've ever learned is that what gets rewarded gets done.*

No Place Like Home

When I moved to Atlanta, I became acquainted with an organization that has developed its unique identity and fosters a strong sense of teamwork despite being a huge company. That organization is Home Depot.

Now, I am not a do-it-yourselfer. What's the opposite of handy? Handless? Manually challenged? Whatever it is, that describes me. Then there's my son, Joel Porter. He never met a tool he didn't like, and if a thing can be fixed, he will find a way to do it. When he was thirteen years old, we let him create a workshop in a room adjacent to our garage. He put in a workbench, installed fixtures, and wired the room. A friend of ours who used to be a contractor said Joel had put enough power in that small room to light up an entire house!

After our arrival in Atlanta, Joel found himself a job at Home Depot, and he couldn't have been happier. Every day he would come home and tell us about the company, what he did that day, and the values the company held dear.

Intrigued, I did some research of my own. I discovered that the company was founded by Bernie Marcus and Arthur Blank. They opened their first store in Atlanta in June of 1979 after both men had been fired fourteen months earlier from Handy Dan, a home improvement chain located in the western part of the United States. For years, Marcus, a man with considerable retail experience and leadership talent, had possessed a vision for a national chain of huge one-stop home improvement stores. His idea was to offer the widest selection of products at the lowest prices with the best customer service possible.

BUILDING HOME DEPOT

Getting the company off the ground required the two men to keep plugging away, slowly expanding the business, opening more stores, and attracting first-rate people. Marcus said, "We are only as good as our people—especially the men and women working in our stores every day . . . That's why we believe a sure way of growing this company is to clearly state our values and instill them in our associates."[1]

The right leaders with the right values have attracted the right people to make the company a blockbuster. In 1979, they started with four stores. In 1999, Home Depot had 775 stores, 160,000 employees, and $38.4 billion in annual sales.[2]

Values truly are at the heart of Home Depot's success. Marcus explained,

A set of eight values has been our bedrock for the past twenty years. Although they were not put in writing until 1995, these values—the basis for the way we run the company—enabled us to explode across the North American landscape and will be the vehicle for reaching our ambitious goals in the international marketplace . . .

- *Excellent customer service.* Doing whatever it takes to build customer loyalty.

- *Taking care of our people.* The most important reason for The Home Depot's success.

- *Developing entrepreneurial spirit.* We think of our organizational structure as an inverted pyramid: Stores and customers are at the top and senior management is on the bottom.

- *Respect for all people.* Talent and good people are everywhere, and we can't afford to overlook any source of good people.

- *Building strong relationships with associates, customers, vendors and communities.*

- *Doing the right thing, not just doing things right.*

- *Giving back to our communities as an integral part of doing business.*

- *Shareholder return.* Investors in The Home Depot will benefit from the money they've given us to grow our business.[3]

These values have made the company a great place for people to work. For example, from the day Home Depot opened, the company has offered employees stock options rather than bonuses. That kind of treatment has made more than one thousand of its employees millionaires!

Joel Porter has since left his job at Home Depot. He now works for The INJOY Group in a technical capacity as our studio production manager. But he will always have a heart for Home Depot. Why? Because the company has an identity he respects. It has *shared values, and the values define the team.* That's the impact their organization had on him, and that's the impact the Law of Identity can have on you and your team.

TEAMWORK THOUGHT

If your values are the same as the team's, you become
more valuable to the team.

BECOMING A BETTER TEAM MEMBER

If you want to add value to your team and help it reach its potential, then you need to share in its values. First, make sure that you know what they are. Then, examine your values and goals in comparison to them. If you can wholeheartedly buy into the team's values, commit yourself to aligning yourself with them. If you can't, then your misalignment will be a constant source of frustration to you and your teammates. And you might want to think about finding a different team.

BECOMING A BETTER TEAM LEADER

As the leader of an organization, you have responsibilities when it comes to the team's values. I recommend that you proceed by following these steps:

- Know the values that the team should embrace.

- Live the values.

- Communicate the values to the team.

- Obtain buy-in of the values through aligned behavior among teammates.

Remember, the process takes time. Getting your people to buy in can be especially difficult. But the better leader you are, the more quickly they will buy into you. And the more quickly they buy into you, the more rapidly they will buy into the values you communicate. (To explore this leadership concept in more depth, read the Law of Buy-In in *The 21 Irrefutable Laws of Leadership*.)

THE LAW OF COMMUNICATION

Interaction Fuels Action

When Gordon Bethune took over Continental Airlines in 1994, the company was a mess. It had suffered through ten changes in leadership in ten years. It had gone through bankruptcy proceedings twice. Its stock value was at a pitiful $3.25 a share. It had not made a profit in a decade. Customers were flocking away from the airline, and those who did use Continental were rarely happy because in the words of Bethune, their planes "came and went as they happened to" with no predictability. That's not what business travelers and vacationers are looking for in an airline!

TRYING TIMES FOR THE TEAM

In his book, *From Worst to First*, Bethune described the state of Continental when he arrived:

In the years leading up to 1994, Continental was simply the worst among the nation's 10 biggest airlines . . . For example, DOT [the Department of Transportation] measures those 10 largest airlines in on-time percentage . . . *Continental was dead last.* It measures the number of mishandled-baggage reports filed per 1,000 passengers. *Continental was worst.* It measures the number of complaints it receives per 100,000 passengers on each airline. Continental was last. And not just last—in 1994, *Continental got almost three times as many complaints as the industry average* and more than 30 percent more complaints than the ninth-best airline, the runner-up in lousy service. We had a real lock on last place in that category . . . We weren't just the worst big airline. *We lapped the field.*[1]

When a company is that bad, the employees can't help being affected. Morale at Continental was abysmal. Cooperation was non-existent. Communication was at an all-time low. Employees had been lied to so often and so thoroughly that they didn't believe anything they were told. According to Bethune, they had learned one survival strategy: Duck. "That's what I joined in 1994," commented Bethune, "a company with a lousy product, angry employees, low wages, a history of ineffective management, and, I soon learned, an incipient bankruptcy, our third, which would probably kill us."[2]

Trying to Turn Around the Team

Bethune's goal was to save Continental, but he knew that to do it, he would have to change the culture of the company. The key would be communication. He knew that positive interaction could turn the company around. If he could win the communication battle, he believed he could get the employees to work together again for the good of the team, the customers, and the stockholders.

His first step was to open up the executive offices to the rest of the team. When he began working for Continental, the twentieth-floor suite occupied by top management in Houston was like a fortress. Its doors were locked, the area was surveyed by lots of security cameras, and nobody could enter the area without a proper ID. It wasn't exactly inviting. Bethune literally propped open the doors and hosted open houses for employees to break down the intimidation factor between leaders and the rest of the team.

The next thing he did was to work to break the old bureaucracy that had developed over the years. At Continental, rules and manuals had taken the place of communication and the use of judgment. The chief symptom of that mind-set was the nine-inch-thick book of rules for employees that had come to be known as the "Thou Shalt Not" book. It was so detailed that it dictated what color pencil an agent was supposed to use on a boarding pass. In a significant gesture, CEO Bethune, along with Continental President Greg Brenneman, gathered employees in the parking lot, dropped the manual in a trash can, doused it with gasoline, and burned it![3] The message was clear. Everything at Continental was going to change.

COMMUNICATION CULTURE

Continental didn't change overnight. In fact, as Bethune and Brenneman laid out their "Go Forward Plan," employees were skeptical. But the leaders kept meeting with the people, committed themselves to being honest with them, and maintained their patience. If the news was good, they told the people. If the news was bad, they still told them. They put up bulletin boards in every employee area that showed two things: (1) their ratings for the last year according to the Department of Transportation rating guidelines; and (2) daily news updates from the company. They created a weekly voice-mail message to everyone on the team. They also put lots of communication in writing, using a monthly employee newsletter called *Continental Times and Continental Quarterly*, which they mailed to every employee's home. They put news wire–style LED displays by every coffee and soda machine. They even created 800-number hot lines for questions and information that could be accessed by any employee from anywhere in the world.

> *Bethune's communi-*
> *cation policy was—*
> *and is—simple:*
> *"Unless it's dangerous*
> *or illegal for us to*
> *share it, we share it."*

A company that had been characterized by distrust and lack of cooperation became a place where communication was pervasive. Bethune's communication policy was—and is—simple: "Unless it's dangerous or illegal for us to share it, we share it."[4] It took time, but eventually the company began to turn. Employees started to trust their leaders. They began to work with and trust one another. And for the first time in more than a decade, the employees of Continental functioned as a team.

Today, Continental's service is among the best in its industry. Employee morale is high. And the company is profitable. In 1994, the year Bethune took over, the company *lost* $204 million. In 1995, it made a *profit* of $202 million. The next year it doubled. As of April 2001, Continental had posted twenty-four consecutive profitable quarters in an industry where many of its competitors are struggling to stay in the black. The company's stock has split twice, and each share is worth more than ten times the value it had in 1994.

WHAT'S IN A WORD?

Communication wasn't the entire reason for Continental's success. But without good communication, the company most likely would have continued on autopilot right into its third (and final) bankruptcy. Creating positive change in an organization requires communication. *Interaction fuels action.* That is the power of the Law of Communication.

Only with good communication can a team succeed—it doesn't matter whether that team is a family, a company, a ministry,

> *Effective teams have teammates who are constantly talking to one another.*

or a ball club. Effective teams have teammates who are constantly talking to one another. Communication increases commitment and connection; they in turn fuel action. If you want your team to *perform* at the highest level, the people on it need to be able to talk to and listen to one another.

COMMUNICATION MATTERS

When people don't communicate effectively, the result can often be comical. Years ago, I came across the following illustration that conveys what I mean. It is made up of a series of memos on a college campus:

President to Academic V.P.: Next Thursday Halley's Comet will appear over this area. This is an event which occurs only once every 75 years. Call the Division Heads and have them assemble their professors and students on the athletic field and explain this phenomenon to them. If it rains, then cancel the observation and have the classes meet in the gym to see a film about the comet.

Academic V.P. to Division Chairmen: By order of the President, next Thursday Halley's Comet will appear over the athletic field. If it rains, then cancel classes and report to the gym with your professors and students where you will be shown films, a phenomenal event which occurs only once every 75 years.

Division Chairman to Professors: By order of the Phenomenal President, next Thursday Halley's Comet will appear in the gym. In case of rain over the athletic field the President will give another order, something which occurs every 75 years.

Professor to Students: Next Thursday the President will appear in our gym with Halley's Comet, something which occurs every 75 years. If it rains the President will cancel the comet and order us all out to our phenomenal athletic field.

Student Writing Home to Parents: When it rains next Thursday over the school athletic field, the phenomenal 75-year-old President will cancel all classes and appear before the whole school in the gym accompanied by Bill Halley and the Comets.

Scott Adams, the creator of the Dilbert comic strip, has masterfully described an organization where everyone does his best to undermine communication. The boss sends an employee to work for a year on a project that has been canceled, then later demotes the person for wasting so much time. Members of the marketing department continually think up harebrained products and promote them to the public; then they ask the engineers to produce them on an impossible timetable. The higher up in the organization people are, the more clueless they are. Thinkers are punished, the lazy are rewarded, and every decision is arbitrary. The comic strip is hilarious. What's sad is that too many American workers identify with it.

If you've ever been on a team where teammates never let one another know what's going on, then you know how frustrating poor communication can be. The team gets stuck because nobody knows what the real agenda is. Important tasks remain uncompleted because each of two team members believes the other one is taking care of it—or people duplicate others' work. Departments within the organization fight because each believes it is being sabotaged by the other.

In the book *Empowered Teams*, authors Richard Wellins, William Byham, and Jeanne Wilson state, "Communication refers to the style and extent of interactions both among members and between members and those outside the team. It also refers to the way that members handle conflict, decision making, and day-to-day interactions."

A DIFFERENT PICTURE OF COMMUNICATION

An excellent example of the complexity—and importance—of good communication can be seen by watching a professional football team in the half minute prior to a play. When one play ends, the offensive team has only forty seconds to get itself ready for the next play. In that time, the quarterback first decides if there is enough time for the team to huddle. If there is, he calls the team members together and gives them the play. If there isn't, he communicates that he will call the play using a code at the line of scrimmage.

For many plays at the professional level, the team will line up with players in one formation and then move them around before the play to try to confuse the defense. If time is short, the quarterback will communicate to the players that they should skip the extra steps and just line up in the formation that will be used to run the play.

As the eleven offensive players approach the line, each is doing two things: assessing what the defense is doing, and paying attention to teammates for communication cues. The linemen who will be blocking pay attention to what kinds of players the other team has in the game and where they are positioned. The center, who hikes the ball to the quarterback, is usually responsible for calling out the blocking scheme to his teammates based on the defense.

Meanwhile, the quarterback is assessing the defense. If he thinks the play he has called in the huddle will fail against the defense, he is likely to use a few words to call an alternate play at the line of scrimmage. If the defense is lined up in such a way that the original play will work, but the blocking scheme of the running backs behind him is likely to fail, then he can change their blocking assignments.

At the same time, the quarterback, the running backs, and the receivers are watching the defense to see if they are about to do anything unusual, such as sending extra players after the quarterback to tackle him in a blitz. If the offensive players do see a blitz coming, then, without a word, the receivers and running backs change their assignments to a predetermined Plan B for that play, and they hope that everyone on the team made the same assessment.

Football is an extremely complex sport. The casual observer has no idea so much communication is going on before every play.

Sometimes it's subtle. Players call out things in code. They use hand signals. One player may simply point and communicate a lot of information to another teammate. And sometimes a quarterback and a receiver will just give each other a look and communicate enough information to make it possible for them to score on the play.

COMMUNICATION ON YOUR TEAM

Communication on your team may not look anything like what happens on a football field. But the success of your team and the ability of your team members to work together are just as dependent on good communication. Allow me to give you some guidelines that will help your team to improve in this area. Every team has to learn how to develop good communication in four areas.

> "If I had to name a single all-purpose instrument of leadership, it would be communication."
>
> —JOHN W. GARDNER

1. From Leader to Teammates

John W. Gardner observed, "If I had to name a single all-purpose instrument of leadership, it would be communication." Perhaps you are familiar with my books on leadership; then you know that I believe everything rises and falls on leadership. What I haven't mentioned before is that leadership rises and falls on communication. You must be able to communicate to lead others effectively.

If you lead your team, give yourself these standards to live by as you communicate to your people:

- *Be consistent.* Nothing frustrates team members more than leaders who can't make up their minds. One of the things that won the team over to Gordon Bethune was the consistency of his communication. His employees always knew they could depend on him and what he said.

- *Be clear.* Your team cannot execute if the members don't know what you want. Don't try to dazzle anyone with your intelligence; impress people with your straightforwardness.

- *Be courteous.* Everyone deserves to be shown respect, no matter what the position or what kind of history you might have with him. By being courteous to your people, you set the tone for the entire organization.

Never forget that because you are the leader, your communication sets the tone for the interaction among your people. Teams always reflect their leaders. And never forget that good communication is never one-way. It should not be top-down or dictatorial. The best leaders listen, invite, and then encourage participation.

2. From Teammates to Leader

Good team leaders never want yes-men. They want direct and honest communication from their people. Even autocratic movie mogul Sam Goldwyn quipped, "I want my people to speak up and be honest, even if it costs them their jobs."

I have always encouraged people on my team to speak openly and directly with me. When we hold meetings, they are often brainstorming sessions where the best idea wins. Often, a team member's remarks or observations really help the team. Sometimes we disagree. That's okay because we've developed strong enough relationships that we can survive conflict. Getting everything out on the table always improves the team. I never want to hear a teammate say, "I could have told you that wouldn't work." If you know it beforehand, that's the time to say it.

Besides directness, the other quality team members need to display when communicating with their leaders is respect. Leading a team isn't easy. It takes hard work. It demands personal sacrifice. It requires making tough and sometimes unpopular decisions. We should respect the person who has agreed to take on that role and show him loyalty.

3. Among Teammates

Author Charlie Brower remarked, "Few people are successful unless a lot of other people want them to be." In a team that desires to experience success, all team members must communicate for the common good. That means exhibiting the following qualities:

- *Being supportive.* Former NBA player Earvin "Magic" Johnson summed up support by paraphrasing President John F. Kennedy: "Ask not what your teammates can do for you. Ask what you can do for your teammates." Communication that is focused on giving rather than getting takes the team to a whole new level.

> "Ask not what your teammates can do for you. Ask what you can do for your teammates."
>
> —EARVIN "MAGIC" JOHNSON

- *Staying current.* Teammates who rehash old problems and continually open old wounds don't work together. And if they don't work together, they're sunk. As Babe Ruth remarked, "You may have the greatest bunch of individual stars in the world, but if they don't play together, the club won't be worth a dime."

• *Being vulnerable.* Teams are like little communities, and they develop only when the people in them don't posture with one another. In his book *The Different Drum*, psychiatrist M. Scott Peck observes, "If we are to use the word *community* meaningfully, we must restrict it to a group of individuals who have learned how to communicate honestly with each other, whose relationships go deeper than their masks of composure."

Teams succeed or fail based on the way that team members communicate with one another. Martin Luther King Jr. declared, "We must learn to live together as brothers or perish together as fools." If the interaction is strong, then the action teams take can be strong. *Interaction fuels action.* That's the essence of the Law of Communication.

4. Between the Team and the Public

For most teams, communication within the team isn't the only kind that's important. Most teams interact with outsiders in some way, whether the people are clients, customers, or the concerned public. When approached by people from outside the group, team members must remember three Rs; they need to be *receptive, responsive,* and *realistic.* If they receive communication from others gracefully, always respond in a timely fashion, and are realistic about setting and receiving expectations, they will do just fine. Outsiders will perceive that their concerns are being well received.

On the other hand, when it comes to communicating to people who are not on the team, the most important quality a team can display is unity. The more independent team members are, the more difficult that can be; it's not easy to get eagles to fly in formation. Yet the power of unity is incredible.

An old story that I heard when I lived in the Midwest was about a horse-pull at a country fair. That's an event where various horses compete to see which one can pull a sled with the greatest weight. One year, the champion horse pulled 4,500 pounds. The runner-up pulled 4,400. Wondering what the two stout horses might be able to pull together, a group of men yoked them together. They pulled more than 12,000 pounds—an increase of more than 33 percent over their individual efforts.

There's tremendous power in unity. One of the principles I always tell my team is that when we are brainstorming and planning, I want all the ideas and criticisms out on the table. We need an opportunity to hash things out. But once we leave the room, we must be united— even if we face opposition or criticism. We remain a strong team.

When it comes down to it, you spell cooperation "w-e." Working together means winning together. But no team works together unless it's communicating. It takes *interaction to fuel action.* That's just the way it works. That's the Law of Communication.

> *Working together means winning together.*

HANG TOGETHER OR HANG SEPARATELY

One of the most remarkable stories of communication and teamwork I've ever encountered occurred among the U.S. prisoners of war (POWs) who were detained in Vietnam. As American involvement in the war in Vietnam increased, so did the number of U.S. servicemen who were captured. Ultimately 772 servicemen, mostly pilots, were captured and imprisoned.

Most of the prisoners were held at the Hoa Lo prison, which the men called the Hanoi Hilton. There they suffered unspeakable torture and inhumane conditions. Most of them wasted away. It wasn't unusual for someone over six feet tall to weigh 120 pounds. But the worst part for most of the men was the forced solitude. Former POW Ron Bliss explained, "You get isolated. That's when the trouble begins. You have to communicate at virtually any cost. If you get caught and tortured for a little while, that's just the overhead. But you do it anyway."

The North Vietnamese captors at the Hanoi Hilton tried to defeat the POWs by breaking them physically, crushing their spirits, and keeping them isolated. If a man thought of himself as an abandoned individual, then he would give up hope. Jerry Driscoll, a POW who originally thought he might be released after a few months, was told by a fellow prisoner that it might be two years: "When I finally came to that realization that, my God, that's going to be a long time . . . it just kind of hit me all at once. And I just took my blanket and kind of balled it up and I . . . screamed with all this anguish that it's going to be that long. Two years. And when I was finished, I felt, *Oh, okay. I can do that. I can do two years.* Of course, as it turned out, it was two years, and it was two years after that, and two years after that, until it was about seven years in my case."

TAPS FOR THE PRISONERS

Communication and connection with the other prisoners became necessary for the men to endure and survive. To make that communication possible, the prisoners devised an ingenious system. When four POWs—Carlyle Harris, Phillip Butler, Robert Peel, and Robert Shumaker—were held in the same cell for a time, they devised a tapping code that they could use to spell out words. When they were split up, they used it to communicate, and they taught the code to every prisoner they could. In a matter of months, nearly all of the prisoners knew the code and were using it. "The building sounded like a den of runaway woodpeckers," recalled former POW Ron Bliss.

The men would tap on the walls between cells or push a wire through a wall and tug on it using the code. They would sweep or shovel rhythmically, sending each other messages. They also developed hand signals and other ways of communicating. Ex-POW Thomas McNish observed, "We passed the equivalent of *War and Peace* several times over through different methods of communication."[5]

Even though the prisoners were kept separate from one another—and many men who "talked" all the time never saw the others' faces until they were released—they became a team. They worked together. They shared information. They supported one another. They became such a solid unit that they determined none of them would accept release until all of them could obtain it. The one person who did leave early, Seaman Douglas Hegdahl, accepted release only because he was given a direct order by Lt. Commander Al Stafford to accept it. And he was given the order for one reason: Hegdahl had memorized the 256 names of fellow prisoners, which the men wanted communicated to authorities back home.

Finally in January of 1973, a cease-fire was signed in Paris that made provision for the release of American POWs. They began coming home on February 12, and on March 29, the last prisoners left the

Hanoi Hilton. In all, 462 prisoners were released. That number might have been far fewer if they had not found—and fought for—a way to communicate with one another. But *interaction fuels action*. And their connection with one another fueled their ability to endure and to hold together as a team. That's the value of the Law of Communication.

TEAMWORK THOUGHT

Communication increases connection.

BECOMING A BETTER TEAM MEMBER

How committed are you to communicating with the other members of your team? Are you supportive of everyone, even the people who aren't your friends? Are you open and vulnerable, even if it's not pleasant? Are you holding a grudge against anyone on the team? If you are, you need to clear the air. If there are *any* barriers to good communication standing between you and another team member, you need to remove them. That is your responsibility.

BECOMING A BETTER TEAM LEADER

As the leader of an organization, you set the tone for communication. In this chapter, I mention that a leader's communication must be consistent, clear, and courteous. But leaders must also be good listeners. When leaders don't listen . . .

- They stop gaining wisdom.

- They stop "hearing" what isn't being said.

- Team members stop communicating.

- Their indifference spreads to other areas.

Ultimately, poor listening leads to hostility, miscommunication, and a breakdown of team cohesion.

Give yourself a 360-degree review. Ask for feedback concerning your listening skills from your boss or mentor, your colleagues, and your subordinates. If you don't get high marks from all of them, then quiet down, listen up, and work to become a better communicator.

THE LAW OF THE EDGE

The Difference Between Two Equally Talented Teams Is Leadership

Teams are always looking for an edge. I'm sure you've seen it. A ball team recruits new talent or develops new plays to beat a tough opponent—or even develops a whole new system to turn around a legacy of losing. Businesses invest in the latest technology, hoping to improve their productivity. Companies fire their ad agencies and hire new ones to launch a campaign, desiring to make gains on major competitors. Corporations cycle through the latest management fads like channel surfers through television reruns. Everyone is seeking the magic formula that will lead to success. The more competitive the field, the more relentless the search.

What is the key to success? Is it talent? Hard work? Technology? Efficiency? To be successful, a team needs all of these things, but it still needs something more. It needs leadership.

- *Personnel* determine the potential of the team.

- *Vision* determines the direction of the team.

- *Work ethic* determines the preparation of the team.

- *Leadership* determines the success of the team.

Everything rises and falls on leadership. If a team has great leadership, then it can gain everything else it needs to go to the highest level.

FINDING THE EDGE

Look at any team that has achieved great success, and you will find that it has strong leadership. What enabled General Electric to gain the respect of the corporate world? The leadership edge of Jack Welch. What sealed the victory of the United States in the Persian Gulf War? The leadership edge of Generals Norman Schwarzkopf and Colin Powell. What powered the Chicago Bulls to win six NBA championships? The leadership edge of Phil Jackson and Michael Jordan. That's why I say *the difference between two equally talented teams is leadership.* That's the Law of the Edge.

> *Look at any team that has achieved great success, and you will find that it has strong leadership.*

To get a clearer picture of the difference that leadership can make, think of the same players on the same team with different leadership. The Los Angeles Lakers are a notable example. During the late 1990s, they struggled despite having a very talented group of players, including Kobe Bryant, who many hoped would be the next Michael Jordan, and Shaquille O'Neal, the best center in the game. Both players were acquired in 1996, yet they continued to have major problems and never clicked as a team. In 1999, teammate Eddie Jones remarked, "Something isn't right with this team. We're all struggling to keep it together and with a team that has that much talent, this shouldn't be going on."[1]

The next year, the team brought in Phil Jackson, the man who had led the Chicago Bulls to six championships, to coach the Lakers. He kept the same team intact with few changes because he knew talent was not the issue. Of his three key players, O'Neal, Bryant, and Glen Rice, Jackson remarked,

> I think we have three of maybe the most talented players since the time of Kareem and Worthy and Magic. However, Baylor, West and Chamberlain [on the 1968–71 Lakers] outshone even those people. They were three of the greatest scorers in the game, and yet they couldn't win a championship. So yeah, we got the talent, we got the show, we got everything else—but how do you make all the pieces complement each other? That's really what my specialty is as a coach, to try to bring that to bear. And this team is learning that.[2]

Leadership is all about understanding players, bringing them together, and getting them to work together as a team to reach their potential. And Jackson provided it. In only one season, the team came together. In 2000, the Lakers won the NBA championship that everyone had believed they had the potential to win. They did it in the same city working under the same conditions and with the same players they'd had in previous years. The only thing that had changed was the leadership. That gave them the edge. *The difference between two equally talented teams is leadership.* That is the Law of the Edge.

Need a Lift?

With good leadership, everything improves. Leaders are lifters. They push the thinking of their teammates beyond old boundaries of creativity. They elevate others' performance, making them better than they've ever been before. They improve their confidence in themselves and each other. And they raise the expectations of everyone on the team. While managers are often able to maintain a team at its current level, leaders are able to lift it to a higher level than it has ever reached before. The key to that is working with people and bringing out the best in them.

- *Leaders transfer ownership for work to those who execute the work.* For a team to succeed, responsibility must go down deep into the organization, down to the roots. Getting that to happen requires a leader who will delegate responsibility and authority to the team. Stephen Covey remarked, "People and organizations don't grow much without delegation and completed staff work, because they are confined to the capacities of the boss and reflect both personal strengths and weaknesses." Good leaders seldom restrict their teams; they release them.

- *Leaders create an environment where each team member wants to be responsible.* Different people require different kinds of motivation to be their best. One needs encouragement. Another needs to be pushed. Another will rise to a big challenge. Good leaders know how to read people and find the key that will make them take responsibility for their part on the team. They also remember that they are responsible *to* their people, not *for* them.

- *Leaders coach the development of personal capabilities.* The team can reach its potential only if each individual on the team reaches his potential. Effective leaders help each player do that. For example, Phil Jackson is well known for giving his players books to read that will help them improve themselves, not just as basketball players, but as people.

- *Leaders learn quickly and encourage others to learn rapidly.* Leaders lift themselves to a higher level first; then they lift the others around them. Modeling comes first, then leadership. If everyone is improving, then the team is improving.

If you want to give a team a lift, then provide it with better leadership. The Law of the Edge works every time.

THE LAWS OF LEADERSHIP IMPACT THE TEAM

Leadership can improve a team and give it an edge in many ways, and the 21 laws from my book on leadership provide a useful summary. Good leaders . . .

1. Do not limit an organization as others do. (The Law of the Lid)

2. Have greater influence than others do. (The Law of Influence)

3. Value the process of developing people more than others do. (The Law of Process)

4. Prepare the team for the journey better than others do.
   (The Law of Navigation)

5. Communicate more effectively than others do.
   (The Law of E. F. Hutton)

6. Create momentum and lift the team to a higher level than others do. (The Law of the Big Mo)

7. Stand on a foundation of trust that is more solid than others' is. (The Law of Solid Ground)

8. Command greater respect than others do.
   (The Law of Respect)

9. Work on leadership issues earlier than others do.
   (The Law of Intuition)

10. Draw more leaders to themselves than others do.
    (The Law of Magnetism)

11. Connect with people better than others do.
    (The Law of Connection)

12. Bring stronger key people around them than others do.
    (The Law of the Inner Circle)

13. Reproduce more leaders than others do.
    (The Law of Reproduction)

14. Empower team members more than others do.
    (The Law of Empowerment)

15. Win with teams more than others do. (The Law of Victory)

16. Sell themselves and their vision to a greater degree than others do. (The Law of Buy-In)

17. Establish priorities more effectively than others do.
    (The Law of Priorities)

18. Understand and use timing more effectively than others do.
    (The Law of Timing)

19. Give up their personal agendas more than others do.
    (The Law of Sacrifice)

20. Grow leaders and organizations faster than others do.
    (The Law of Explosive Growth)

21. Leave a legacy that lasts longer than others do.
    (The Law of Legacy)

Good leaders do things just a little bit better than others do. The result is usually victory. That's the Law of the Edge.

TURNING THE TABLE ON THE TABLES

Leadership is the key to the Law of the Edge, but I don't want you to get the idea that the responsibility for leadership always falls on one person. Although most teams have a designated leader who is ultimately responsible for the oversight of the team, the actual leadership of the team is usually shared.

I find that when it comes to leadership, many people tend to see it in one of two ways. The first I call *the myth of the head table*. It's the notion that on a particular team, one person is always in charge in every situation. It's the idea that this particular individual permanently occupies the "head table" in the organization and that everyone else always takes a subordinate role to him. For example, here is an illustration that might have been written by someone who sub-scribes to the myth of the head table:

> As everyone knows, an executive has practically nothing to do except . . .
> To decide what is to be done;
> To tell somebody to do it;
> To listen to reasons why it should not be done, why it should be done by somebody else, or why it should be done in a different way;
> To follow up to see if the thing has been done, only to discover that it has not;
> To inquire why;
> To listen to excuses from the person who should have done it;
> To follow up again to see if the thing has been done, only to discover that it has been done incorrectly;
> To point out how it should have been done;
> To conclude that as long as it has been done, it may as well be left where it is;
> To wonder if it is not time to get rid of a person who cannot do a thing right;
> To reflect that the person probably has a spouse and large family, and that certainly any successor would be just as bad—or maybe worse;
> To consider how much simpler and better the thing would have been done if one had done it oneself in the first place;
> To reflect sadly that one could have done it right in twenty min-utes, and as things turned out, one has had to spend two days to find out why it has taken three weeks for somebody else to do it wrong.

The idea that one person is always doing all the leading is false. The same person should not always lead the team in every situation. The challenge of the moment often determines the leader for that challenge because every person on the team has strengths that come into play. Let me illustrate this point. Even though I lead The INJOY Group as its founder, I don't always lead the team. Other people on the team have gifts, skills, and abilities that I do not possess. When we moved our offices—along with the employees, their equipment, our supplies and computers, our information and communication systems—the job required sophisticated navigating and incredible planning skills.

The most obvious person to lead the team was Frank Hartman, a logistical thinker, exceptional planner, and detailed administrator. Frank created the plan for the move. He had the authority and responsibility of managing the process—and of leading all of the people, including the CEO and other officers of the organization. And he did a wonderful job. We didn't lose a single day of productivity at the office during the move. Nobody else on our team could have pulled it off as effectively. I handed the ball off to Frank, and he successfully led us—and fulfilled the Law of the Edge.

> *Everyone is important, but everyone isn't equal.*

The other misconception about leadership takes the opposite extreme. I call it the *myth of the roundtable.* It's the belief that everyone on the team is equal, all opinions count the same, and a team can function without leadership. That isn't true either. A team that tries to function like a democracy never gets anything done.

Everyone is important, but everyone isn't equal. The person with greater experience, skill, and productivity in a given area is more important to the team in that area. GE CEO Jack Welch's opinion carries more weight than the person who packs boxes on the assembly line. The NBA's Michael Jordan is worth more money than the guard who sits on the bench. That's the way it is. That doesn't mean that Jack and Michael have more value as *human beings*. In the eyes of God, everyone is loved equally. But when it comes to leading the team, somebody needs to step forward.

Giving the Team a Head Start

In essence, leadership is like a running head start for the team. Leaders see farther than their teammates. They see things more quickly than their teammates. They know what's going to happen and can anticipate it. As a result, they get the team moving in the right direction ahead of time, and for that reason, the team is in a position to win. Even an average runner can win a 100-meter race against a world-class sprinter if he has a 50-meter head start.

The greater the challenge, the greater the need for the many advantages that leadership provides. And the more leaders a team develops, the greater the edge from leadership. If you want to win and keep winning for a long time, train players on the team to become better leaders.

The edge gained from good leadership is quite evident in sports, but the power of leadership carries over into every field. The business that is run by a top-notch leader often finds its market niche first and outperforms its rivals, even if the rivals possess greater talent. The nonprofit organization headed by strong leaders recruits more players, equips them to lead, and serves a greater number of people as a result. Even in a technical area such as engineering or construction, leadership is invaluable in ensuring the team is successful.

GOLDEN OPPORTUNITY

The Law of the Edge was at work in one of the most extraordinary feats of engineering in the world: the Golden Gate Bridge. Completed in 1937, the bridge had the longest main span of any suspension bridge in the world until the construction of the Verrazano Narrows Bridge was finished in New York City in 1964. If you've been to San Francisco, then you've seen how beautiful and impressive the Golden Gate Bridge is. But the story of its construction is even more impressive.

The concept of a bridge spanning the Golden Gate—the opening to San Francisco's bay—was proposed as early as 1872, although nobody thought it was really possible. The idea wasn't brought up again and taken seriously until 1916. The reason people wanted a bridge was simple: San Francisco's growth and expansion were being hindered by its location since it was surrounded on three sides by water. Plenty of open land lay to the north, but getting to it was hard. Even though Marin County lay only about a mile north across the strait, getting there required a circuitous drive of one hundred miles around San Francisco's huge bay area. The only other alternative was to take a ferry across the gap, but at peak times, drivers had to wait in line for hours to catch the ferry.

Building a bridge across the Golden Gate Strait looked as if it would never happen. The physical and technological challenges of the project were overwhelming. The entrance of the bay experienced strong ocean currents and battering winds. The depth of the channel, which reached more than three hundred feet at points, would make construction very difficult. On top of that, any bridge that would be built had to be high enough to allow large ships to navigate beneath it. Engineers from around the country estimated that a bridge would cost as much as $250 million. (At that time, the value of every piece of property in the entire city of San Francisco totaled only $375 million!)

ENTER A LEADER

Then along came Joseph B. Strauss. He was the owner of an engineering firm that had built more than four hundred bridges. But more important than his experience were his astonishing vision and powerful leadership. He believed he could build a bridge spanning the Golden Gate for $25 million. In 1921, Strauss put together preliminary designs for a bridge and began to gather support for the project among the leaders of the counties adjoining San Francisco. He promoted the bridge tirelessly. In the beginning, his influence was unofficial. But in time, after the formation of the Golden Gate Bridge and Highway District, he was named chief engineer of the proposed project.

If it hadn't been for a leader like Strauss, the bridge never would have been built. For twelve years, he fought every imaginable obstacle and opponent to the project. When the San Francisco political machine (including the city's chief engineer, Michael O'Shaughnessy) opposed him, he met with leaders and citizens in every county to raise grassroots support. When the Army Corps of Engineers and the War Department (which controlled the land on both sides of the strait) threatened to withdraw approval, Strauss went to Washington and persuaded the secretary of war to guarantee the government's cooperation. When the Golden Gate Bridge and Highway District experienced a severe cash flow problem, Strauss met with Amadeo P. Giannini, founder of Bank of America. In just a few hours he was able to persuade Giannini to buy bonds immediately to keep the project going—

and commit to buy more the next time they were offered. Strauss overcame powerful special interest groups, environmentalists, labor problems, and the ravages of the Great Depression, which hit in the middle of the process. His energy and influence were astounding.

A LEADER WHO DIDN'T GET IN HIS OWN WAY

One of Strauss's greatest strengths was his ability to attract good leaders and engineers. To make the project successful, he brought in the best bridge designers in the world. When he realized that his original design for the bridge was inadequate and could endanger the project, he abandoned it and relied on his leaders to create something better. "Strauss had an unusual ability," remarked author John Van der Zee, "to locate and draw to him men of greater abilities than his own, men who would accept his leadership."[3]

Strauss was a leader's leader, and no matter what difficulty was thrown at him, he handled it. He was a natural leader who understood how to influence others. Van der Zee observed, "Strauss was, if anything, stronger at marketing and promoting ideas than he was at conceiving them. He seemed to know instinctively whom to reach, whom to get to and persuade, who were the decision makers, the people who mattered in any given situation."[4]

FINALLY BREAKING GROUND

In 1933, construction finally began on the bridge. Again, Strauss hired the best engineers he could find to oversee construction.

That was no small task. The team who built the bridge put in 25 million hours of work on it.[5] But the actual construction of the bridge seemed almost easy by comparison to what had been necessary before the process could begin. When the bridge was completed, Strauss remarked that it had taken him two decades to convince people that the bridge was feasible, but only four years to actually build it! And he completed it just in time. He died at age sixty-eight—the year after the bridge was finished.

Look behind the scenes of any major undertaking, and you will always find a strong leader. If Joseph Strauss hadn't taken personal responsibility for the creation of the Golden Gate Bridge—and dedicated himself to it wholeheartedly—then it wouldn't have been built. That's the reality of the Law of the Edge. It takes a leader if a team wants to realize its potential and reach its goals. That's why I say that *the difference between two equally talented teams is leadership.*

❧

TEAMWORK THOUGHT

Everything rises and falls on leadership.

BECOMING A BETTER TEAM MEMBER

You don't have to be *the* leader to be *a* leader on your team. Begin the process of improving your leadership skills today. Do the following:

- Acknowledge the value of leadership.
- Take personal responsibility for your leadership growth.

• Put yourself on a leadership development program.

• Find a leadership mentor.

Once you have added value to yourself, you will be able to add value to—and influence—others to help your team.

BECOMING A BETTER TEAM LEADER

If you are *the* leader of your team, then the best thing you can do for your teammates is to follow the example of Joseph Strauss. Add other leaders to the team.

You can do that in two ways. First, attract the best leaders you can—people whose talent and potential are greater than your own. Second, develop the people already on the team. The stronger the leadership of the team, the greater the team's potential for success. Never forget: Everything rises and falls on leadership.

16

THE LAW OF HIGH MORALE

When You're Winning, Nothing Hurts

It's an image most Americans will never forget: gymnast Kerri Strug being carried in the arms of Coach Bela Karolyi to the podium to receive her gold medal along with her six teammates in the 1996 Summer Olympic Games in Atlanta. It was a landmark moment. It was the first time the women's gymnastics team from the United States had won the gold medal, but that isn't why people will remember it. Although it was a stick-in-your-mind image—the tiny eighty-seven-pound Strug being cradled by a big bear of a man who is considered the greatest gymnastics coach in history—it will be remembered primarily because it is the perfect picture of the Law of High Morale.

A First for the Team

Even if you didn't see it on television as I did, you probably know the story. In a sport dominated by the Russian and Romanian teams, the United States team was actually ahead during the Olympic Games. The Russians had opened strong, but after the first rotation of events, the Americans were in first place. As the athletes competed in each event, the U.S. team's lead continued to grow—not by a lot but steadily. As the teams went into the final event—the floor exercise for the Russians and the vault for the Americans—all the U.S. team had to do was to finish solidly, and the gold medal would be theirs.

The second to last vaulter for the U.S. was Dominique Moceanu, usually a smooth performer. Much to everyone's surprise, on her first attempt she landed on her bottom instead of her feet, which gave her a very low score. Fortunately, in women's vault, each athlete gets a second attempt, and only the better of the two scores counts. But, unbelievably, Moceanu missed her second attempt with the same results.

Although Moceanu's performance was unexpected, the situation wasn't desperate. The U.S. still had one athlete left: Kerri Strug, who had received the highest scores in the vault during U.S. Olympic trials. One good vault from her, and the gold medal would belong to the team. When Strug tried to land her first vault, however, her feet weren't positioned quite right. She, too, slipped and fell. Worse yet, she injured herself, and she still needed to complete another vault for the team.

The situation was desperate. After the fact, some commentators remarked that the U.S. could have won without Strug's second vault. But at that moment, Russian gymnast Rozalia Galiyeva was still to compete in the floor exercise. U.S. coach Bela Karolyi was concerned that a high score by the Russian would cost the Americans their hard-fought victory.

Strug knew what she had to do. She needed to land her vault—the final attempt of the final event of the women's team competition. "Give me one last vault," Karolyi encouraged her. "Give me one last good vault."

NOT A FIRST FOR STRUG

Every athlete who makes it to the highest levels knows what it means to play through pain. Kerri Strug was no different. Besides all the normal strains, sprains, and bruises, in the past she had recovered from a torn stomach muscle and a serious back injury received in a fall on the uneven parallel bars. Karolyi said of her, "She is just a little girl who was never the roughest girl . . . always a little shy, always standing behind someone else. But sometimes this is the person with the biggest ggrrrrr."[1]

A gymnast has only thirty seconds to complete her second vault after the scores from the first one have been tabulated. In those moments, Strug focused herself. She later remembered, "I knew something was wrong with me. I heard something snap. I kept telling myself not to fall on the vault or the gold would slip away and all that hard work and effort would fall apart in a few seconds. I just said a little prayer and asked God to help me out."[2]

PAIN OR GAIN?

What Strug didn't know then was that two ligaments in her left ankle had torn during her first vault. But that didn't matter. She flew down the runway, hit the beat-board, sprang off the vault with her hands, and went flying through the air. Miraculously, she landed solidly on both feet. Then, she felt excruciating pain. Standing on one foot, she quickly saluted the judges, then crumpled to the floor. She landed her vault, she got her score, and the entire team received its gold medal.

After that, the girl who had always been in the background, who had never been the star of her gym, became the star of the Olympic team. Everyone seemed to appreciate the sacrifice she made. Sports journalist E. M. Swift wrote,

> All she knew, beyond the certainty of the gold medal, was that she had injured herself too badly to compete in the individual all-around competition two days later, a goal she'd clung to for the past four years. This was her moment of greatest triumph, also her moment of greatest disappointment. Her will had found a way to block out the pain for a few crucial seconds, but it had exacted a punishing price. She had literally sacrificed herself for the team.[3]

Strug's own words were direct and simple: "When you do well, you think it's worth it. When you sacrifice so much and you finally do well, it feels really good."[4] In other words, *when you're winning, nothing hurts*. That is the Law of High Morale.

TAKING THE TEAM HIGHER

The Law of High Morale may ring a bell with you because the phrasing of the law was inspired by the words of Joe Namath, the quarterback who helped the New York Jets win the Super Bowl in 1969.

Like any champion, he understood that there is an exhilaration that comes from winning. That feeling can be so strong that it sustains you through the discipline, pain, and sacrifice required to perform at the highest level.

That's what Kerri Strug felt. As she faced that final vault, she knew that her performance would help her team win. And that knowledge empowered her to come through for the team when it mattered most. Perhaps that's why George Allen, who coached the Washington Redskins in the early 1970s, said, "Every time you win, you're reborn; when you lose, you die a little." It's ironic, but if you play hurt, you can put the team in the position to win. And if you win, nothing hurts.

> *It's ironic, but if you play hurt, you can put the team in the position to win. And if you win, nothing hurts.*

Really high morale helps the team to perform at its best. High morale can be a crucial difference maker. When a team has high morale, it doesn't just have to deal with whatever circumstances get thrown at it. It creates its own circumstances.

- The *fund-raiser* knows that under the right circumstances, people love to give.

- The *teacher* knows that under the right circumstances, students love to grow.

- The *leader* knows that under the right circumstances, people love to follow.

- The *coach* knows that under the right circumstances, players are able to win.

High morale is one of the essentials to creating the right circumstances for any team to perform at the highest level.

HIGH MORALE IS GREAT . . .

If the team is winning, then morale is high. And if morale is high, then the team is in a position to win. So which comes first: high morale or winning? I believe that high morale usually comes first. Why? Because high morale magnifies everything positive that is happening for a team.

1. High Morale Is the Great Exaggerator

When an entire team is positive and all the players feel good about themselves, *everything* seems good. Preparation seems to proceed more smoothly. Every break seems to go your way. The small victories seem sweet, and the big ones make you feel almost invincible. The stars of the team deliver at crunch time, and even the bench players seem to be playing beyond their usual capabilities.

Some people call such a time a winning streak or a stretch of good luck. But it's really just high morale. In sports, during times of high morale, everybody jumps onto the bandwagon as a fan. In big business, people buy the company's stock. In entertainment, magazines and television networks ask for interviews—and producers pay top dollar for the team's services. Has the team changed from talentless to talented overnight? Is the team really as good as its press? Probably not. The team is enjoying the great exaggerator at work.

2. High Morale Is the Great Elevator

When a team possesses high morale, the performance of its people goes to a whole new level. The team focuses on its potential, not its problems. Team members become more committed. And everyone finds it easier to be unselfish. Team members are confident, and that confidence helps them to perform at a higher level.

When a team is losing, the opposite effect occurs. Players focus on their problems. Everyone's level of commitment goes down. The team repels others rather than attracts them. And everyone starts to look out for himself rather than his teammates. When you're losing, everything hurts.

3. High Morale Is the Great Energizer

High morale gives a team energy. Players become like the Energizer bunny: They keep going and going. No mountain seems too high. No project seems too difficult. No race seems too long. Their enthusiasm builds along with their energy, and the team develops a momentum that is almost unstoppable.

4. High Morale Is the Great Eliminator

Because of the momentum and energy that come with it, high morale also becomes the great eliminator. While a team that is losing and experiencing poor morale can be hurt by even the most minor problem, a team with high morale will keep right on going even when faced with a huge obstacle or otherwise disabling setback. Problems just seem to disappear—no matter how big they are.

5. High Morale Is the Great Emancipator

Something else that high morale does for a team is to free it up. Winning creates breathing room. A good team with high morale will use that breathing room to take risks and try out new ideas, new moves, new concepts that it otherwise wouldn't. It stops to ask questions that it otherwise might not. And doing these things yields creativity and innovation. In the end, high morale releases the team to reach its potential.

THE FOUR STAGES OF MORALE

You may be saying, "Okay, I agree. *When you're winning, nothing hurts.* High morale is great for the team. How in the world do we get it?" Let me tell you. If you are a player, then you need to have a good attitude, always give your best, and support the people on the team—players and leaders alike. If you have little influence, then exert what influence you have by modeling excellence.

However, if you're one of the team's leaders, then you have more extensive responsibilities. You need to model excellence, but you also need to do more. You need to help the people you lead to develop morale and momentum to create a winning team. The key to knowing what to do can be found in the four stages of morale.

Stage 1: Poor Morale–The Leader Must Do Everything

Nothing is more unpleasant than being on a team when nobody wants to be there. When that is the case, the team is usually negative, feels lethargic, or has no hope. That is often the atmosphere found in a team that is losing.

If you are in that situation, then do the following:

- *Investigate the situation.* Start by addressing what the team is doing wrong. Begin by fixing what's broken. That alone won't give the team high morale, but it will stop giving players reasons to have poor morale.

- *Initiate belief.* A team will change only when people believe in themselves. As the leader, you must initiate that belief. Show people you believe in yourself and them.

- *Create energy.* The desire to change without the energy to change just frustrates people. To bring a greater level of energy to the team, you need to be energetic. Work with energy long enough, and someone on the team will eventually come alongside you and join you. Then another person will. Eventually the energy will spread.

- *Communicate hope.* The deepest need of players at this stage is hope. As Napoleon Bonaparte said, "Leaders are dealers in hope." Help them to see the potential of the team.

> *"Leaders are dealers in hope."*
>
> —NAPOLEON BONAPARTE

In stage one, the only way to get the ball rolling is to start pushing it yourself. As the leader, you can't wait for anyone else to do it.

Stage 2: Low Morale—The Leader Must Do Productive Things

In the beginning, any movement is a noteworthy victory. But to create positive morale, you need to pick up some speed. You need to be productive. After all, you can't steer a parked car! Get the team moving.

- *Model behavior that has a high return.* People do what people see. The best way for them to learn what you expect of them is to model it yourself.

- *Develop relationships with people of potential.* To get any team going in the right direction, you need players who can produce. At this stage, your team may have some producers. If it does, develop relationships with them. If it doesn't, then find the people who have the potential to be productive, and start with them. Don't ask too much of them too soon. Leaders touch a heart before they ask for a hand. That's why you want to begin by building relationships.

- *Set up small victories and talk teammates through them.* Nothing helps people grow in skill and confidence like having some wins under their belts. That's what you want to give the people on your team. Once again, begin with the people who have the most potential. Their small victories will help less talented team members to gain confidence and succeed.

- *Communicate vision.* As I've already explained in the Law of the Compass, vision gives team members direction and confidence. Keep the vision before your team continually.

Once you've got the team really moving, then you can begin to steer.

Stage 3: Moderate Morale—The Leader Must Do Difficult Things

Do you remember what it was like when you first got your driver's license? Maybe before you received it, you enjoyed just sitting in the driver's seat of a car and imagining what it would be like to drive. Later, when you had your license and you were allowed to take out the car, just going for a drive was probably a thrill. It didn't really matter where you went. But as you got older, just driving wasn't enough. Having a destination became significant.

The same is true with a team. Getting the team together and moving add up to an accomplishment. But where you're going matters. To change from simply *moving the team* to *moving the team in the right direction*, you must do the difficult things that help the team to improve and develop high morale. You need to . . .

- *Make changes that make the team better.* You already understand the Law of the Chain. Just remember that leaders are responsible for minimizing the damage any team member can do because of weakness or attitude, and for maximizing the effectiveness of all team members by placing them in their proper niches. Often these actions require tough decisions.

- *Receive the buy-in of team members.* It's one thing to cast vision to the team. It's another to get your teammates to buy in. Yet to build higher morale, you must do that. The teammates must buy into you as a leader, embrace the values and mission of the team, and align themselves with your expectations. If you can do all of that, you will be able to take the team where it needs to go.

- *Communicate commitment.* Part of the process of getting people to buy in comes from showing them your commitment. The Law of Buy-In from *The 21 Irrefutable Laws of Leadership* says that people buy into the leader, then the vision. If you have consistently demonstrated high competence, good character, and strong commitment, you have laid the foundation for your people to buy in.

- *Develop and equip members for success.* Nothing builds morale like success. Most people are not capable of achieving success on their own. They need help, and that is one of the primary reasons for anyone to lead them. If you invest in your teammates, then you help them and the team succeed.

The two toughest stages in the life of the team are the first stage, when you are trying to create movement in a team that's going nowhere, and the third stage, when you must become a change agent. These are the times when leadership is most needed. And stage three is the make-or-break time for a leader. If you can succeed in stage three, then you will be able to create high morale on your team.

Stage 4: High Morale–The Leader Must Do Little Things

In stage four, your job as a leader is to help the team maintain high morale and momentum.

- *Keep the team focused and on course.* High morale leads to winning, and winning maintains morale. That's why it's important to keep team members focused. If they lose focus or get off course, then they'll stop winning. And remember, the farther you intend to go, the greater the impact of an error in direction. If you want to cross a street, being a degree or two off course doesn't hurt you. If you want to cross the ocean, miscalculating by a few degrees can get you into a lot of trouble.

- *Communicate successes.* Knowing what they're doing right helps people stay on track. You can indicate that by communicating the team's successes. Nothing boosts morale like winning and then celebrating it.

- *Remove morale mashers.* Once the team is rolling in the right direction, keep it rolling. The Law of the Big Mo from *The 21*

Irrefutable Laws of Leadership says that momentum is a leader's best friend. Leaders see before others do, so they need to protect the team from the things that will hurt the team.

• *Allow other leaders to lead.* A leader who prepares other team members to lead and then turns them loose to do it accomplishes two things. First, he uses the momentum the team already has to create new leaders for the team. It's easier to make new leaders successful if they are part of a successful team. Second, he increases the leadership of the team. And that makes the team even more successful. A leader who continually does that can create a cycle of success that feeds the team's high morale.

The process of building high morale takes strong leadership, and it takes time. When I think of someone who was a master at that process, I think of Ronald Reagan. When he took office as president of the United States in 1981, morale in the country was at the lowest it had been since the Great Depression. People had lost faith in the American government following Watergate. The threat of nuclear war with the Soviet Union was never far from people's thinking. Inflation was out of control. Oil prices were up. And interest rates were off the charts. People could not have been more discouraged.

Ronald Reagan helped people to

Four Stages of Morale:
1. Poor Morale—
The leader must do everything.
2. Low Morale—
The leader must do productive things.
3. Moderate Morale—
The leader must do difficult things.
4. High Morale—
The leader must do little things.

believe in the country again. Under his presidency, the economy revived, the cold war ended, the Berlin Wall fell, and people believed in themselves and their country again.

High Morale at Home

You don't need to have the power of a president or the ability of an Olympic athlete to practice the Law of High Morale. You can apply the principle to your business, your volunteer service, or even your

> *When the Law of High Morale is working at its best, the leader boosts the morale of the team, and the team boosts the morale of the leader.*

family. In fact, when the Law of High Morale is working at its best, the leader boosts the morale of the team, and the team boosts the morale of the leader. That's the way it should be. *When you're winning, nothing hurts.*

Let me tell you about a team where the members continually inspire one another and build up one another to such an extent that their morale is high and they keep winning despite the pain they feel. They are the father-and-son team of Dick and Rick Hoyt.

When Rick Hoyt was born in 1962, his parents possessed the typical excited expectations of first-time parents. But then they discovered that during Rick's birth, his umbilical cord had been wrapped around his neck, cutting off the oxygen to his brain. Later, Rick was diagnosed with cerebral palsy. "When he was eight months old," his father, Dick, remembers, "the doctors told us we should put him away—he'd be a vegetable all his life."[5] But Rick's parents wouldn't do that. They were determined to raise him like any other kid.

An Uphill Battle

Sometimes that was tough. Rick is a quadriplegic who cannot speak because he has limited control of his tongue. But Rick's parents worked with him, teaching him everything they could and including him in family activities. When Rick was ten, his life changed; engineers from Tufts University created a device that enabled him to communicate via computer. The first words he slowly and painstakingly punched out were, "Go Bruins." That's when the family, who had been following the NHL's Boston Bruins in the play-offs, found out Rick was a sports fan.

In 1975, after a long battle, the family was finally able to get Rick into public school, where he excelled despite his physical limitations. Rick's world was changing. It changed even more two years later. When Rick found out that a fund-raising 5K race (3.1 miles) was being put on to help a young athlete who had been paralyzed in an accident, he told his father that he wanted to participate.

Dick, a lieutenant colonel in the Air National Guard (who has since retired), was in his late thirties and out of shape. But he agreed to run and push his son in a modified wheelchair. When they crossed the finish line (second to last), Dick recalls, Rick flashed "the biggest smile you ever saw in your life." After the race, Rick wrote out this simple message: "Dad, I felt like I wasn't handicapped." After that day, their lives would never be the same again.

Working Together

What does a father do when his son, who has never been out of a wheelchair, says that he loves to race? He becomes his boy's hands and feet. That's the day "Team Hoyt" was born. Dick got Rick a more sophisticated racing chair. Then the quadriplegic teenager and the out-of-shape dad began running together—and not casually. Before long, they were training seriously, and in 1981, they ran in their first Boston Marathon together. Since then, they haven't missed a Boston Marathon in twenty years.

After four years of running marathons, the two decided that they were ready for another challenge: triathlons, which combine swimming, cycling, and running. That was no small challenge, especially since Dick would have to learn how to swim! But he did. Dick explained, "He's the one who has motivated me because if it wasn't for him, I wouldn't be out there competing. What I'm doing is loaning Rick my arms and legs so he can be out there competing like everybody else."[6]

Of all the races in the world, one is considered the toughest—the Ironman Triathlon in Hawaii. The race consists of three back-to-back legs: a 2.4-mile swim, a 112-mile bike race, and a full marathon run of 26.2 miles. It's an excruciating test of stamina for any individual. In 1989, Dick and Rick competed in the race together. For the swimming portion, Dick towed a small boat with Rick in it. Then he biked for the 112 miles with Rick in a seat on his bicycle's handlebars. By the time they got to the running leg, Dick was exhausted.

But it's in such situations that the Law of High Morale kicks in. All Dick had to do was to think of the words of his son:

> When I'm running, my disability seems to disappear. It is the only place where truly I feel as an equal. Due to all the positive feedback, I do not feel handicapped at all. Rather, I feel that I am the intelligent person that I am with no limits.[7]

When you're winning, nothing hurts. By continuing to run, Dick would be winning for his son, and that's what makes all the training and pain worthwhile. Dick loaded Rick into his running chair, and off they went to finish the Ironman. The pair finished the race in a little over thirteen hours and forty-three minutes—a very strong time.

Since then, Rick has earned his college degree, and he works at Boston University helping to design computer systems for people with disabilities. And of course, he still competes with his father, who is now more than sixty years old. As of March 2001, Team Hoyt had completed a total of 731 races. They had run 53 marathons and 135 triathlons, including 4 races at Ironman distances. And they will keep running. "There is nothing in the world that the both of us can't conquer together," says Dick.[8] He should know. For almost twenty-five years, he and his teammate have been reaping the rewards of the Law of High Morale.

TEAMWORK THOUGHT

When you do good, you feel good—when you feel good, you do good.

BECOMING A BETTER TEAM MEMBER

If you want to reap the rewards of the Law of High Morale, you can't wait until your morale is high to begin performing. You need to act your way into feeling, not feel your way into acting. Begin by performing at a level of excellence appropriate for someone who is experiencing a winning season. Your dedication and enthusiasm will help your performance—and will inspire some of your teammates.

BECOMING A BETTER TEAM LEADER

If you are a leader on your team, then you need to figure out what kind of morale your team is currently experiencing:

- *Poor morale:* The team is dead in the water and negative.
- *Low morale:* The team is making some progress, but it is not cohesive and confident.
- *Moderate morale:* The team is experiencing some wins and beginning to believe in itself, but some hard decisions need to be made to take it to the next level.
- *High morale:* The team is performing close to its potential, it's winning, and it just needs to be kept on track.

Once you've determined the stage of your team, then apply the guidelines in the chapter so that you can take the team (or your area of it) to the next stage.

THE LAW OF DIVIDENDS

Investing in the Team Compounds Over Time

He's one of the greatest team builders in all of sports, yet you've probably never heard of him. Here is a list of these impressive accomplishments:

- Forty consecutive basketball seasons with at least twenty wins

- Five national championships

- Number one ranking in his region in twenty of the last thirty-three years

- Lifetime winning percentage of .870

His name is Morgan Wootten. And why have most people never heard of him? Because he is a *high school* basketball coach!

When asked to name the greatest basketball coach of all time, most people would respond with one of two names: Red Auerbach or John Wooden. But do you know what John Wooden, the UCLA coach called the Wizard of Westwood, had to say about Morgan Wootten? He was emphatic in his appraisal: "People say Morgan Wootten is the best high school coach in the country. I disagree. I know of no finer coach at any level—high school, college or pro. I've said it elsewhere and I'll say it here: I stand in awe of him."[1]

That's a pretty strong recommendation from the man who won ten NCAA national championships and coached some of the most talented players in the game, including Kareem Abdul-Jabbar. (By the way, when Kareem was in high school at Power Memorial Academy, his team lost only one game—to Morgan Wootten's team!)

No Plan to Be a Team Builder

Morgan Wootten never planned to coach a team. He was a decent athlete in high school, but nothing special. However, he was an excellent talker. When he was growing up, his ambition was to be an attorney. But when he was a nineteen-year-old college student, a friend tricked him into accepting a job coaching baseball, a game he knew little about, to kids from an orphanage. The team had no uniforms and no equipment. And despite working hard, the boys lost all sixteen of their games.

During that first season, Wootten fell in love with those kids. When they asked him to come back and coach football, he couldn't refuse them. Besides, he had played football in high school, so he knew something about it. The orphanage team went undefeated and won the Washington, D.C., Catholic Youth Organization (CYO) championship. But more important, Wootten began to realize that he wanted to invest his time in children, not in court cases.

Even that first year he made a difference in the lives of kids. He remembers one boy in particular who had started stealing and kept being brought back to the orphanage by the police. He described the boy as having "two and a half strikes against him already." Wootten let the boy know he was headed for trouble. But he also took the boy under his wing. Wootten recalled,

> We started spending some time together. I took him to my house and he'd enjoy Mom's meals. He spent weekends with us. He became friends with my brother and sisters. He's still in Washington today and doing quite well and known to a lot of people. Anyone would be proud to call him their son. He was bound for a life of crime and jail, however, and maybe a lot worse, until someone gave him the greatest gift a parent can give a child—his time.

Giving of himself to the people on his teams is something Wootten has done every year since then. NCAA basketball coach Marty Fletcher, a former player and assistant under Wooten, summarized his talent this way: "His secret is that he makes whomever he is with feel like the most important person in the world."[2]

CREATING A DYNASTY

It wasn't long before Wootten was invited to become an assistant coach at a local powerhouse high school. Then with a couple of years' experience under his belt, he became head coach at DeMatha High School.

When he started at the school in 1956, Wootten was taking over a bunch of losing teams. He called together all of the students who wanted to play sports at DeMatha, and he told them:

> Fellas, things are going to change. I know how bad DeMatha's teams have been during these last few years, but that's over with. We're going to win at DeMatha and we're going to build a *tradition* of winning. Starting right now . . . But let me tell you how we're going to do it. We're going to outwork every team we ever play . . . With a lot of hard work and discipline and dedication, people are going to hear about us and respect us, because DeMatha will be a winner.[3]

That year, the football team won half of its games, which was quite an accomplishment. In basketball and baseball, they were division champions. His teams have been winning ever since. DeMatha has long been considered a dynasty.

On October 13, 2000, Wootten was inducted into the Naismith Basketball Hall of Fame in Springfield, Massachusetts. At that time, his teams had amassed a record of 1,210–183. Over the years, more than 250 of his players have won college scholarships. Twelve players from his high school teams went on to play in the NBA.[4]

IT'S NOT ABOUT BASKETBALL

But winning games and honors isn't what excites Wootten most. It's investing in the kids. Wooten says,

> Coaches at every level have a tendency to lose sight of their purpose at times, especially after success arrives. They start to put the cart

before the horse by working harder and harder to develop their teams, using their boys or girls to do it, gradually forgetting that their real purpose should be to develop the kids, using their teams to do it.[5]

Wootten's attitude reaps rewards not only for the team, but also for the individuals on the team. For example, for a twenty-six-year stretch, every single one of Wootten's seniors earned college scholarships—not just starters but bench players too. Penn State assistant coach Chuck Swenson observed, "Even if you know a kid isn't a great player, if he's a DeMatha player, he'll help your program. With Morgan, you know you're getting a quality kid, who will make good grades and work hard for you."[6] Gary Williams, head coach of the University of Maryland, agreed about the quality of the players: "His players are so fundamentally sound, do so many things right, that they may not improve as much as kids in another program who haven't been as well coached . . . These aren't raw talents: They're refined ones."[7] What's remarkable is that these comments describe *high school* students, not college players or pros.

Investing in the team compounds over time. Morgan Wootten invests in his players because it is the right thing to do, because he cares about them. That practice has made his players good, his teams successful, and his career remarkable. He is the first basketball coach to have won 1,200 games at any level. Developing people pays off in every way. That is the power of the Law of Dividends.

GREAT INVESTORS

Throughout the chapters of this book, you've read about people who have dedicated themselves to investing in the people on their teams. And those investments pay all kinds of rich dividends. Gordon Bethune's investment of trust has paid off by keeping Continental in business and saving the jobs of its fourteen thousand employees. The investment of Bernie Marcus and Arthur Blank is paying dividends to the employees who own Home Depot stock, including one thousand employee-millionaires. The investment of Jeff Skilling at Enron is paying dividends in the formation of new industry initiatives by leaders in the company. And Lilly Tartikoff's investment in people is paying dividends in cancer research. Usually the time, money, and effort required to develop team members don't change the team overnight, but developing them always pays off. *Investing in the team compounds over time.*

> *The time, money, and effort required to develop team members don't change the team overnight, but developing them always pays off.*

HOW TO INVEST IN YOUR TEAM

I believe that most people recognize that investing in a team brings benefits to everyone on the team. The question for most people isn't *why*, but *how*. Allow me to share with you ten steps you can take to invest in your team. You can implement these practices whether you are a player or coach, employee or employer, follower or leader. There is always someone on the team who can benefit from what you have to offer. And when everyone on the team is investing, then the benefits are like those of compound interest. They multiply.

Here is how to get started:

1. Make the Decision to Build a Team . . . This Starts the Investment in the Team

It's said that every journey begins with the first step. Deciding that people on the team are worth developing is the first step in building a better team. That requires *commitment*.

> *Deciding that people on the team are worth developing is the first step in building a better team.*

2. Gather the Best Team Possible . . . This Elevates the Potential of the Team

As I've previously mentioned, the better the people on the team, the greater the potential. There's only one kind of team that you may be a part of where you *shouldn't* go out and find the best players available, and that's family. You need to stick with those teammates through thick and thin. But every other kind of team can benefit from the recruitment of the very best people available.

3. Pay the Price to Develop the Team . . . This Ensures the Growth of the Team

When Morgan Wootten extended himself to benefit the kid who had two-and-a-half strikes against him, he and his family had to pay a price to help that boy. It wasn't convenient or comfortable. It cost them in energy, money, and time.

It will cost you to develop your team. You will have to dedicate time that could be used for personal productivity. You will have to spend money that could be used for personal benefit. And sometimes you will have to set aside your personal agenda. But the benefit to the individuals—and the team—is worth the price. Everything you give is an investment.

4. Do Things Together as a Team . . . This Provides
Community for the Team

I once read the statement, "Even when you've played the game of your life, it's the feeling of teamwork that you'll remember. You'll forget the plays, the shots, and the scores, but you'll never forget your teammates." That is describing the community that develops among teammates who spend time doing things together.

> *Even when you've played the game of your life, it's the feeling of teamwork that you'll remember.*

The only way to develop community and cohesiveness among your teammates is to get them together, not just in a professional setting but in personal ones as well. There are lots of ways to get yourself connected with your teammates, and to connect them with one another. Many families who want to bond find that camping does the trick. Business colleagues can socialize outside work (in an appropriate way). The *where* and *when* are not as important as the fact that team members share common experiences.

5. Empower Team Members with Responsibility and
Authority . . . This Raises Up Leaders for the Team

The greatest growth for people often occurs as a result of the trial and error of personal experience. Any team that wants people to step up to a higher level of performance—and to higher levels of leadership—must give team members authority as well as responsibility. If you are a leader on your team, don't protect your position or hoard your power. Give it away. That's the only way to empower your team.

6. Give Credit for Success to the Team . . . This Lifts the Morale of the Team

Mark Twain said, "I can live for two months on one good compliment." That's the way most people feel. They are willing to work hard if they receive recognition for their efforts. That's why Napoleon Bonaparte observed, "A soldier will fight long and hard for a bit of colored ribbon." Compliment your teammates. Talk up their accomplishments. And if you're the leader, take the blame but never the credit. Do that and your team will always fight for you.

> *"I can live for two months on one good compliment."*
>
> —MARK TWAIN

7. Watch to See That the Investment in the Team Is Paying Off . . . This Brings Accountability to the Team

If you put money into an investment, you expect a return—maybe not right away, but certainly over time. How will you know whether you are gaining or losing ground on that investment? You have to pay attention to it and measure its progress.

The same is true of an investment in people. You need to observe whether you are getting a return for the time, energy, and resources you are putting into them. Some people develop quickly. Others are slower to respond, and that's okay. The main outcome you want to see is progress.

8. Stop Your Investment in Players Who Do Not Grow . . . This Eliminates Greater Losses for the Team

One of the most difficult experiences for any team member is leaving a teammate behind. Yet that is what you must do if someone on your team refuses to grow or change for the benefit of teammates. As I mentioned in the Law of the Chain, that doesn't mean that you love the person less. It just means you stop spending your time trying to invest in someone who won't or can't make the team better.

9. Create New Opportunities for the Team . . . This Allows the Team to Stretch

There is no greater investment you can make in a team than giving it new opportunities. When a team has the possibility of taking new ground or facing new challenges, it has to stretch to meet them. That process not only gives the team a chance to grow, but it also benefits every individual. Everyone has the opportunity to grow toward his or her potential.

10. Give the Team the Best Possible Chance to Succeed . . . This Guarantees the Team a High Return

James E. Hunton says, "Coming together is a beginning. Keeping together is progress. Working together is success." One of the most essential tasks you can undertake is to clear obstacles so that the team has the best possible chance to work toward success. If you are a team member, that may mean making a personal sacrifice or helping others to work together better. If you are a leader, that means creating an energized environment for the team and giving each person what he needs at any given time to ensure success.

Where there's a will there's a way; where there's a team, there's more than one way.

Investing in a team almost guarantees a high return for the effort because a team can do so much more than individuals. Or as Rex Murphy, one of my conference attendees, told me: "Where there's a will there's a way; where there's a team, there's more than one way."

MY PERSONAL INVESTMENT—AND RETURN

Once you have experienced what it means to invest in your team, you will never be able to stop. Thinking about my team—about how the teammates add value to me as I add value to them—brings me abundant joy. And just like my investment and their return, my joy continues to compound.

I value everyone on my team, and if I could, I would tell you about every person. But since that isn't possible, I want to at least acquaint you with key players in my inner circle:

- Larry Maxwell (fifty-four years). He loves me unconditionally. He has taken The INJOY Group to a whole new level. Asks great questions. Keeps our team focused. Protects me. He's my big brother!

- Margaret Maxwell (thirty-seven years). My wife. She knows me so well, loves me so much. Her partnership has allowed me to go to a higher level. Our journey together is my greatest joy.

- Dan Reiland (nineteen years). He was my executive pastor for many years. Now as a consultant, he helps pastors with my heart and experience plus his wisdom and perspective. He is a pastor's best friend and mine!

- Dick Peterson (eighteen years). He follows up on all the details of my company. I open the door, and he closes it. I start a sentence, and he finishes it!

- Tim Elmore (fifteen years). He teaches my leadership material better than I do. He gives me leadership material better than my own.

- Linda Eggers (fourteen years). She knows my strengths and weaknesses. Represents me so well. Answers the team's questions better than I would and much more quickly.

- Charlie Wetzel (eight years). He shapes the lives of more people than anyone else on my team. He takes my ideas, lessons, and outlines and turns them into books. From there, they multiply.

- Dave Johnson (seven years). He stewards The INJOY Group's resources to extend its impact around the globe. He is a financial wizard who loves and understands me.

- Kevin Small (seven years). He has unlimited energy and unlimited potential. Sees an opportunity a mile away. I love pouring myself into him. The return is huge!

- Dave Sutherland (seven years). He is my number one guy. He's the man. A great thinker. He can grow the company without me. When I give him the ball, it's always a touchdown.

- Kirk Nowery (five years). He represents me so well and loves pastors and local churches. Every night he tells the story of how we can add value through ISS. Every night we get that opportunity.

- Doug Carter (five years). He loves to share the mission of EQUIP (my nonprofit organization) with others. He helps businesspeople go from success to significance. He has taken me to a whole new level.

At this stage of my life, everything I do is a team effort. When I first started teaching seminars, I did everything. Certainly there were other people pitching in, but I was just as likely to pack and ship a box as I was to speak. Now, I show up and teach. My wonderful team takes care of everything else. Even the book you're reading was a team effort.

My team is my joy. I would do anything for the people on my team because they do everything for me:

> My team makes me better than I am.
>
> My team multiplies my value to others.
>
> My team enables me to do what I do best.
>
> My team gives me more time.
>
> My team represents me where I cannot go.
>
> My team provides community for our enjoyment.
>
> My team fulfills the desires of my heart.

If your current team experiences are not as positive as you would like, then it's time to increase your level of investment. Building a team for the future is just like developing a financial nest egg. It may start slowly, but what you put in brings a high return— similar to the way that compound interest works with finances. Try it and you will find that the Law of Dividends really works. *Investing in the team compounds over time.*

TEAMWORK THOUGHT

Is the team's investment in you paying off?

BECOMING A BETTER TEAM MEMBER

Are you giving a good return for what your teammates are investing in you? Think about the opportunities you have received and the positive learning experiences to which you've been exposed. Have you seized all of them enthusiastically, or have you allowed many of them to slip by?

If you've been lackadaisical about pursuing growth opportunities, then change your attitude today. Grow all you can, and determine to give the team a good return on its investment in you.

BECOMING A BETTER TEAM LEADER

As a leader, you, more than anyone else, determine the environment of your organization and whether your people are investing in others. Begin by institutionalizing investment and making it a part of your organization's culture. Encourage growth. Set aside time and money for investment in the team. And take on the responsibility for investing in your core leaders. The more leaders you have on the team and the further developed they are, the greater the dividends.

AFTERWORD

A lot of people talk about team chemistry. You hear it often in sports. Analysts will say, "That team certainly had the talent, but they weren't able to develop the chemistry. That's why they didn't perform the way everyone expected."

You may have noticed that there is no Law of Chemistry in this book, and that may have been a disappointment to you. But let me tell you why that concept isn't one of the 17 Indisputable Laws of Teamwork.

Chemistry isn't something you can create with one skill or implementation of a single technique. Chemistry develops when you are able to implement *all* of the Laws of Teamwork. The more laws you put into practice, the greater the chemistry your team will develop. Each time a player finds his niche on the team, it helps to create positive chemistry. Each time a weak link is replaced by a better player from the bench, it creates better chemistry. When a catalyst steps up to the plate and makes something happen for the first time, or when a leader finds a way to help the team perform at a higher level, it creates good chemistry. When players finally count on one another, it makes the chemistry better. Every time another law comes to life for the team, the chemistry gets that much better—and the team gets that much stronger.

I hope you have enjoyed learning about the Laws of Teamwork. More important, I hope they will help you develop the team of your dreams. Embrace them and you will empower your team. That is my promise to you!

NOTES

Chapter 1

1. Brandon Tartikoff and Charles Leerhsen, *The Last Great Ride* (New York: Turtle Bay Books, 1992), 60.
2. "OncoLink: An Interview with Lilly Tartikoff," <www.oncolink.upenn.edu>.

Chapter 2

1. Frye Gaillard, *If I Were a Carpenter: Twenty Years of Habitat for Humanity* (Winston-Salem, NC: John F. Blair, 1995).
2. "The History of Habitat," <www.habitat.org>.

Chapter 3

1. "Bush Nominates Powell as Secretary of State," 17 December 2000.
2. Colin Powell with Joseph E. Persico, *My American Journey* (New York: Random House, 1995), 28.

3. Michael Hirsh and John Barry, "Leader of the Pack," *Newsweek* <www.newsweek.com>, 25 December 2000.

4. "Town Hall Meeting: January 25, 2001," <www.state.gov>.

5. "Packing Parachutes," audiotape excerpt, <www.charlieplumb.com>.

6. "Charlie Plumb's Speech Content," <www.charlieplumb.com>.

Chapter 4

1. "Mount Everest History/Facts," <www.mnteverest.com>.

2. James Ramsey Ullman, *Man of Everest: The Autobiography of Tenzing* (London: George G. Harrap and Co., 1955), 178.

3. Ibid., 250.

4. Ibid., 255.

5. Jim Lovell and Jeffrey Kluger, *Lost Moon: The Perilous Voyage of Apollo 13* (Boston: Houghton Mifflin, 1994), 159–60.

6. W. David Compton, *Where No Man Has Gone Before: A History of Apollo Lunar Exploration Missions* (Washington DC: NASA SP-4214, 1989).

7. Ullman, *Man of Everest*, 227.

Chapter 5

1. "Quick Answers to the Most Frequently Asked Questions," <www.oilspill.state.ak.us/history>.

2. "Exxon's Appeal of the Valdez Oil Spill $5 Billion in Punitive Judgement," <www.exxon.mobil.com>.

3. Danny Cox with John Hoover, *Leadership When the Heat's On* (New York: McGraw-Hill, 1992), 69–70.

4. John Carl Roat, *Class-29: The Making of U.S. Navy SEALs* (New York: Ballantine Books, 1998), 192.

5. Ibid., 7.

6. Ibid., 223.

Chapter 6

1. "The President Suits Up for Practice,"
   <www.cbs.sportsline.com>.

2. "The History of the 'I Have a Dream' Program,"
   <www.ihad.org>.

Chapter 7

1. Greg Farrell, "Building a New Big Blue," <www.usatoday.com>,
   23 November 1999.

2. "IBM Wants Business Partners to Focus on Growth,"
   <www.findarticles.com>, 2 March 1999.

3. Farrell, "Building a New Big Blue."

4. Michelle Marchetti, "IBM's Marketing Visionary," *Sales and
   Marketing Management,* September 2000, 55.

5. Proverbs 29:18 KJV.

6. Howard Schultz and Dori Jones Yang, *Pour Your Heart into It:
   How Starbucks Built a Company One Cup at a Time,* (New York:
   Hyperion, 1997), 36-37.

7. Ibid., 3-4.

8. Ibid., 102.

9. Ibid., 101.

10. Alex Frew McMillan, "Starbucks' Schultz on Being Big in
    Japan," <www.cnn.com>, 10 October 2001.

11. "Howard Schultz," *BusinessWeek,* <www.businessweek.com>, 14
    January 2002.

12. Schultz and Jones Yang, 200.

Chapter 8

1. John C. Maxwell, *The Winning Attitude* (Nashville: Thomas Nelson, 1993), 24.

2. Pat Riley, *The Winner Within* (New York: Berkley Publishing Group, 1994), 41, 52.

Chapter 9

1. "Interview with Stacey Loizeaux."

2. John C. Maxwell, *The 21 Irrefutable Laws of Leadership: Follow Them and People Will Follow You* (Nashville: Thomas Nelson, 1998), 58.

3. Barry J. Gibbons, *This Indecision Is Final: 32 Management Secrets of Albert Einstein, Billie Holiday, and a Bunch of Other People Who Never Worked 9 to 5* (Chicago: Irwin Professional Publishing, 1996).

4. Colossians 3:23–24.

5. Roat, *Class-29: The Making of U.S. Navy SEALs*, 135–36.

6. "Statement of FBI Director Louis J. Freeh on the Arrest of FBI Special Agent Robert Philip Hanssen," <www.fbi.gov>, 20 February 2001.

7. Walter Pincus and Brooke A. Masters, "U.S. May Seek Death Penalty Against Accused Spy Hanssen," <www.washingtonpost.com>, 28 March 2001.

8. "Core Values," <www.fbi.gov>, 30 March 2001.

9. "Statement of FBI Director Louis J. Freeh on the Arrest of FBI Special Agent Robert Philip Hanssen."

10. William A. Cohen, *The Art of the Leader* (Englewood Cliffs, NJ: Prentice Hall, 1994).

Chapter 10

1. Stephen Franklin, "Founder a Force in Retail, Civic Affairs," <www.chicagotribune.com>, 29 December 2000.

2. "End of the Line," <www.nytimes.com>, 29 December 2000.

3. "Historical Chronology—1925: Opening Retail Stores," <www.sears.com>, 15 March 2001.

4. Allan Cox, *Straight Talk for Monday Morning* (New York: John Wiley & Sons, 1990).

5. John C. Maxwell, *The 21 Indispensable Qualities of a Leader: Becoming the Person Others Will Want to Follow* (Nashville: Thomas Nelson, 1999), 144–45.

6. Robert Newall, "History Comes Alive in Valley Forge," <www.vaportrails.com>, 11 March 2001.

Chapter 11

1. Michael D. Eisner with Tony Schwartz, *Work in Progress* (New York: Random House, 1998), 171.

2. John Taylor, *Storming the Magic Kingdom: Wall Street Raiders and the Battle for Disney* (New York: Knopf, 1987), 14.

3. Eisner, *Work in Progress*, 235.

4. "The Walt Disney Company Annual Report 2000: Financial Review," <www.disney.go.com>, 28 March 2001.

5. Adam Cohen, "eBay's Bid to Conquer All," *Time*, 5 February 2001, 48.

6. "Company Overview," <pages.ebay.com>, 12 March 2001.

Chapter 12

1. John Wooden with Jack Tobin, *They Call Me Coach* (Chicago: Contemporary Books, 1988), 104.

Chapter 13

1. Bernie Marcus and Arthur Blank with Bob Andelman, *Built from Scratch: How a Couple of Regular Guys Grew The Home Depot*

from Nothing to $30 Billion (New York: Times Business, 1999), xvi–xvii.

2. "Company Information," <www.homedepot.com>, 11 April 2001.

3. Marcus and Blank, *Built from Scratch*, xvii.

Chapter 14

1. Gordon Bethune with Scott Huler, *From Worst to First: Behind the Scenes of Continental's Remarkable Comeback* (New York: John Wiley and Sons, 1998), 4.

2. Ibid., 6.

3. Thomas A. Stewart, "Just Think: No Permission Needed," *Fortune*, 8 January 2001, <www.fortune.com>.

4. Bethune, *From Worst to First*, 211.

5. "Return with Honor," *The American Experience*, <www.pbs.org>, 22 February 2001.

Chapter 15

1. Mike Kahn, "Harris' Deletion No Surprise," <www.cbs.sportsline.com>, 24 February 1999.

2. Mike Rowland, *Los Angeles Magazine*, June 2000, <www.findarticles.com>.

3. John Van der Zee, *The Gate: The True Story of the Design and Construction of the Golden Gate Bridge* (Lincoln, NE: Backinprint.com, 2000), 50.

4. Ibid., 42.

5. Craig A. Doherty and Katherine M. Doherty, *The Golden Gate Bridge* (Woodbridge, CT: Blackbirch Press, 1995), 17.

Chapter 16

1. Johnette Howard, "True Grit," <sportsillustrated.cnn.com>, 24 July 1996.
2. Ibid.
3. E. M. Swift, "Carried Away with Emotion," <sportsillustrated.cnn.com>, 8 December 1996.
4. "Not Just the Wink of an Eye," <www.strug.com>, 30 March 2001.
5. David Tereshchuk, "Racing Towards Inclusion," <www.teamhoyt.com>, 14 March 2001.
6. "Father-Son Duo Are World Class Competitors, Despite Odds," <www.cnn.com>, 29 November 1999.
7. Ibid.
8. Ibid.

Chapter 17

1. Don Banks, "Teacher First, Seldom Second, Wootten has Built Monument to Excellence at Maryland's DeMatha High," *St. Petersburg Times*, 3 April 1987, <www.dematha.org>.
2. John Feinstein, "A Down-to-Earth Coach Brings DeMatha to New Heights," *Washington Post*, 27 February 1984, <www.dematha.org>.
3. Morgan Wootten and Bill Gilbert, *From Orphans to Champions: The Story of DeMatha's Morgan Wootten* (New York: Atheneum, 1979), 24–25.
4. William Plummer, "Wooten's Way," *People*, 20 November 2000, 166.
5. Wootten and Gilbert, *From Orphans to Champions*, 12–13.
6. Feinstein, "A Down-to-Earth Coach Brings DeMatha to New Heights."
7. Ibid.

WINNING
WITH
PEOPLE

DISCOVER the PEOPLE PRINCIPLES
THAT WORK for YOU EVERY TIME

Winning with People is dedicated to
Hannah Elisabeth Maxwell,
our second grandchild.

Her sparkling personality
has already won the hearts of her grandparents.
It is our prayer that as she grows older,
she will always be able to win with people.

INTRODUCTION

What does it take to win with people? Does an individual have to be born with an outgoing personality or a great sense of intuition to succeed relationally? When it comes to people skills, are there haves and have-nots, and we just have to accept whatever abilities God has given us? Can someone who is good at building relationships become even better?

Most of us can tell instantly when we're in the presence of a real "people person." Individuals with excellent people skills connect with us easily, make us feel good about ourselves, and lift us to a higher level. Our interaction with them creates a positive experience that makes us want to spend time with them.

Some people are so skilled at working with people that they ought to be in a relationship hall of fame. People such as Dale Carnegie, John Wooden, Ronald Reagan, and Norman Vincent Peale easily come to mind. Likewise, there are people whose relational abilities could make them candidates for a relational hall of *shame*. Leona Helmsley, Henry Ford (Sr.), Frank Lorenzo, and Dennis Rodman have such reputations.

But you don't have to read the paper or study history to find examples of relational extremes. You have to deal with them in your own life every day: on the street, at church, (perhaps at home,) and certainly at work. Take a look at the following statements that people put on job applications that reveal their deficiency when dealing with people:

- It's best for employers if I don't work with people.

- The company made me a scapegoat, just like my previous employers.

- Note: Please don't misconstrue my fourteen jobs as job-hopping. I have never quit a job.

- References: None. I've left a path of destruction behind me.

You may find yourself thinking that some of those applicants are now working at *your* place of employment!

SOME KNOW THE SECRET

What kind of price would you put on good people skills? Ask the successful CEOs of major corporations what characteristic is most needed for success in leadership positions, and they'll tell you it's the ability to work with people. Interview entrepreneurs to find out what separates the successes from the failures, and they'll tell you it is skill with people. Talk to top salespeople and they'll tell you that people knowledge is much more important than mere product knowledge. Sit down with teachers and tradesmen, shop foremen and small business owners, pastors and parents, and they'll tell you that people skills make the difference between those who excel and those who don't. People skills are invaluable. It doesn't matter what you want to do. If you can win with people, you can win!

Many people fall into the trap of taking relationships for granted. That's not good because our ability to build and maintain healthy relationships is the single most important factor in how we get along in every area of life. Our people skills determine our potential success. Robert W. Woodruff, the man whose leadership transformed the Coca-Cola Company from a small, regional beverage producer to a global organization and financial powerhouse, understood the people factor when it came to achievement. In his book *Top Performance*, relationship expert Zig Ziglar quotes the former CEO of the Coca-Cola Company. Zig says that Woodruff used to hand out a little pamphlet he had created that read:

> Life is pretty much a selling job. Whether we succeed or fail is largely a matter of how well we motivate the human beings with whom we deal to buy us and what we have to offer.
>
> *Success or failure* in this job *is essentially a matter of human relationships.* It is a matter of the kind of reaction to us by our family members, customers, employees, employers, and fellow workers and associates. *If this reaction is favorable we are quite likely to succeed. If the reaction is unfavorable we are doomed.*
>
> The deadly sin in our relationship with people is that we take them for granted. We do not make an active or continuous effort to do and say things that will make them like us, and believe us, and that will create in them the desire to work with us in the attainment of our desires and purposes.
>
> Again and again, we see both *individuals and organizations perform only to a small degree of their potential success, or fail entirely, simply because of their neglect of the human element in business and life.*
>
> They take people and their actions for granted. Yet it is these people and their responses that make or break them.[1]

IT ALL STARTS WITH PEOPLE

All of life's successes come from initiating relationships with the right people and then strengthening those relationships by using good people skills. Likewise, life's failures can usually be traced back to people. Sometimes the impact is obvious. Becoming entangled with an abusive spouse, a crooked partner, or a codependent family member is going to cause great damage. Other times the trouble is less dramatic, such as alienating a coworker that you must interact with every day, failing to build a positive relationship with an important client, or missing key opportunities to encourage an insecure child. The bottom line is this:

people can usually trace their successes and failures to the relationships in their lives.

When I think about my personal failures, I can trace most of them to specific individuals in my life. I once picked the wrong person for financial advice and went into an oil deal with him. It cost me $10,000, which it had taken my wife, Margaret, and me a long time to save. Another time I started a business and asked a friend to take charge of it, thinking he could make it go. But my judgment was poor, and after just a couple of years, the business was more than $150,000 in the red.

I'm not playing victim and blaming my failures on others. Rather, I'm saying that my interaction with others is a huge part of the process. In a similar way, I can't take credit for my successes. None of them was a solo endeavor. My interaction with others helped me to be successful. For every achievement, I can look back and see a relationship that made it possible. Without the help of people like Elmer Towns, Peter Wagner, and Jack Hayford, my career never would have gotten this far. Without the help of a whole slew of people at Thomas Nelson and at my company, the INJOY group, my book *The 21 Irrefutable Laws of Leadership* never would have been a million seller. And most of my financial blessings can be credited to the help and advice of my brother, Larry Maxwell, and my friend Tom Phillippe.

As important as relationships are professionally, they're even more critical personally. My spiritual life can be traced back to my relationship with my father, Melvin Maxwell. The reason I feel fulfilled every day can be attributed to my relationship with my wife, Margaret; she helps me enjoy our successes. And I must give credit for life itself to my relationships with others. If I hadn't met cardiologist John Bright Cage, I wouldn't be writing this right now. The heart attack I suffered in December 1998 probably would have killed me.

MORE THAN AN ADD-ON

Have you ever found yourself dealing with someone difficult and thought, *She's talented, but she sure is hard to work with*, or *He's brilliant*, *but he doesn't seem to get along with anybody?* Such people never reach their full potential because they are able to accomplish only a fraction of what they could if they knew how to win with people. They don't understand that good relationships are more than just the icing on the cake in life. They *are* the cake—the very substance we need to live a successful and fulfilling life.

So what are people to do if they don't possess great relational skills? I must admit, relationship building comes naturally to me. I was born a people person. But I've also worked hard to improve my skills. I've learned a lot of things about others and myself in half a century. And I've translated those ideas into twenty-five People Principles that *anyone* can learn. The most introverted individual can learn them and become more of a people person. And someone with a knack for people can become a master relationship builder.

I say that because these People Principles work every time. They apply whether you are young or old, sanguine or melancholic, male or female, employed or retired. I've practiced them for decades, and I've seen them work

> Good relationships are more than just the icing on the cake in life. They *are* the cake.

as I've traveled to dozens of countries on six continents. By following these principles, I've optimized my chance for success with others, and I've built positive, healthy relationships that have brought me professional success and personal satisfaction.

As you read and learn these People Principles, you will see that some of them are common sense. Others may surprise you. Perhaps you may question a few as a bit too optimistic. But I can tell you from experience, they really do work. One People Principle does not a relationship guru make. But practicing all of these principles will improve your life. (And you can be sure that you will never be nominated for Relational Hall of Shame!)

That doesn't mean you will have a successful relationship with every person you meet. You can't control another person's response to you. All you can do is make yourself the kind of person others want to know and with whom they can build a relationship.

In life, the skills you use and the people you choose will make or break you. I've divided the People Principles in this book according to five critical questions we must ask ourselves if we want to win with people.

1. Readiness: Are we prepared for relationships?

2. Connection: Are we willing to focus on others?

3. Trust: Can we build mutual trust?

4. Investment: Are we willing to invest in others?

5. Synergy: Can we create a win-win relationship?

Learn and practice the People Principles, and you will be able to answer each of these questions in a positive way. That will make you relationally successful. You will be able to build healthy, effective, and fulfilling relationships. And you have a chance to become the kind of person who makes others successful too. What could be better than that?

THE READINESS QUESTION:
ARE WE PREPARED
FOR RELATIONSHIPS?

The most useful person in the world today is the
man or woman who knows how to get along with other people.
Human relations is the most important science in living.

—STANLEY C. ALLYN

I spent the first twenty-six years of my career as a pastor. I know of no other profession as demanding or intense when it comes to working with people. Individuals in ministry are called upon to lead, teach, coach, counsel, and comfort people at every age and stage of life, from the cradle to the grave. We're with them during many of the most joyful moments of their lives, such as the day they marry or christen a baby. And we're called upon during their darkest hours, such as when they try to save a marriage from a painful divorce, experience a child's tragic death, or look for answers as they face their own imminent deaths.

Over the years, I learned quickly to recognize people who were struggling relationally. They came in all ages, shapes, and sizes. Sometimes when I was counseling an unmarried person who just couldn't seem to get a relationship to work, he would lament about being alone and how much he wanted to get married. The sad thing was that instead of focusing on getting married, some people should be working on their emotional readiness—the basic ability to build a healthy relationship.

Let's face it. Not everyone has the skills to initiate, build, and sustain good, healthy relationships. Many people grow up in dysfunctional households and never have positive relationships modeled for them. Some people are so focused on themselves and their needs that others might as well not even exist. Still others have been hurt so badly in the past that they see the whole world through the filter of their pain. And because of huge relational blind spots, they don't know themselves or how to relate to people in a healthy way.

It takes relationally healthy people to build great relationships. It all starts there. I believe there are fundamental building blocks that make people ready for relationships. They answer the readiness question. The essential components are contained in the following five People Principles:

The Lens Principle: Who we are determines how we see others.

The Mirror Principle: The first person we must examine is ourselves.

The Pain Principle: Hurting people hurt people and are easily hurt by them.

The Hammer Principle: Never use a hammer to swat a fly off someone's head.

The Elevator Principle: We can lift people up or take people down in our relationships.

Anyone missing any of these essential components will not be prepared for relationships. And as a result, he will have recurring problems working with others.

If you or someone you know just can't seem to build the kind of positive relationships that all human beings desire, then the reason may be a readiness issue. By learning these five People Principles, you will prepare yourself for the creation of positive, healthy relationships.

THE LENS PRINCIPLE

WHO WE ARE
DETERMINES HOW
WE SEE OTHERS

*I wouldn't want to belong to any club
that would accept me as a member.*

—GROUCHO MARX

THE QUESTION I MUST ASK MYSELF:
WHAT IS MY PERCEPTION OF OTHERS?

H ave you ever started in a new job and had someone with experience in the organization tell you to watch out for this person or steer clear of that person? That's happened to me a number of times. When I took my first professional leadership position, my predecessor told me to watch out for two people: Audrey and Claude. "They'll cause you a lot of problems," I was told. So I went into my job expecting trouble from them.

First, I watched Audrey. She was a strong woman—and she had a strong personality. (It takes one to know one!) To my surprise, working with her ended up being a wonderful experience. She was confident and competent, and she got things done. We had a good working relationship, and she became a family friend. And Claude turned out to be an old farmer who loved the church. True, he was the greatest influencer in the organization. (More than thirty-five years later he still is.) But that didn't hurt my feelings. Why should I have expected a man twice my age who had been in that church all his life to follow me just because I had a leadership position and title? I made it my goal to work with Claude, and he and I got along well.

When I accepted a position at my second church, once again my predecessor warned me: "Watch out for Jim. He'll battle you on everything." So the first week I was there, I met with Jim. We had a difficult conversation, but Jim let me know that he loved God, loved the church, and was with me. He ended up being my number one guy during the years I was there. He went to battle all right—as my strongest supporter. I couldn't have asked for a better team member.

After I had accepted the position at my third church, the leader who preceded me offered to sit down with me and give me a heads-up on those who might cause me problems. As had been the case with the predecessors in the previous two positions, his heart was to help me. But I respectfully declined his offer. By then I'd been in leadership long enough to realize that his problem people wouldn't be mine—and vice versa. I would have no connection with some people he relied on, and others who left him cold would probably become key players for me. Why? Because who we are determines how we view others.

YOU ARE YOUR LENS

A classic example of the impact of perspective occurred to me when I was in college. I was asked to be the best man in the wedding of my friend Ralph Beadle. I stayed with him the night before the ceremony, and early on the morning of his wedding day, Ralph wanted to go squirrel hunting. (I guess there's nothing like shooting small animals to calm a guy's nerves.) Ralph lent me one of his shotguns, and out we went into the woods. We walked around for a while, but I couldn't see any squirrels.

"Where are the squirrels?" I kept asking Ralph as I tramped around, making noise.

After I asked the question a half dozen times, Ralph finally said, "John, you stay on this side of the woods, and I'll go over to the other side."

> Who you are determines the way you see everything.

Ralph hadn't been gone two minutes when I started to hear *bam, bam*. I still didn't see any squirrels, so I sat down and rested. I started to wish I had brought a book with me. I began to watch the chipmunks frolicking. Meanwhile, every now and then I'd hear gunshots. And I kept wondering, *What is he shooting at?*

A few minutes later Ralph strolled up. He had bagged his limit, and I had never even *seen* a squirrel.

"How come all the squirrels were on *your* side?" I asked.

Ralph just shook his head and laughed.

Who you are determines the way you see everything. You cannot separate your identity from your perspective. All that you are and every experience you've had color how you see things. It is your lens. Here's what I mean:

WHO YOU ARE DETERMINES *WHAT YOU SEE*

A Coloradan moved to Texas and built a house with a large picture window from which he could view hundreds of miles of rangeland. When asked how he enjoyed the view, he responded, "The only problem is that there's nothing to see." About the same time, a Texan moved to Colorado and built a house with a large picture window overlooking the Rockies. When asked how he liked it, he said, "The only problem with this place is that you can't see anything because all those mountains are in the way."

The story may be a little exaggerated, but it points out a truth just the same. What people see is influenced by who they are. People in the same room will look at the same things and see everything totally differently. That's always true with my wife, Margaret, and me. We'll be at a party chatting with people, and she'll come up and ask, "What was the guy in the blue sweater talking to you about?" I won't have a clue who she means. Margaret has great style and fashion sense. I don't. When I look at people, I don't see what they're wearing. It's all just clothes to me.

Each of us has his or her own bent, and that colors our view of everything. What is around us doesn't determine what we see. What is within us does.

WHO YOU ARE DETERMINES *HOW YOU SEE OTHERS*

A traveler nearing a great city asked an old man seated by the road, "What are the people like in this city?"

"What were they like where you came from?" the man asked.

"Horrible," the traveler reported. "Mean, untrustworthy, detestable in all respects."

"Ah," said the old man, "you will find them the same in the city ahead."

Scarcely had the first traveler gone on his way when another stopped to inquire about the people in the city before him. Again the old man asked about the people in the place the traveler has just left.

"They were fine people: honest, industrious, and generous to a fault," declared the second traveler. "I was sorry to leave."

The old man responded, "That's exactly how you'll find the people here."

The way people see others is a reflection of themselves.

If I am a trusting person, I will see others as trustworthy.

If I am a critical person, I will see others as critical.

If I am a caring person, I will see others as compassionate.

Your personality comes through when you talk about others and interact with them. Someone who doesn't know you would be able to tell a lot about who you are based on simple observation.

Who You Are Determines *How You View Life*

Here's an old story I used to tell in conferences. A grandfather was sleeping on the couch one day when his young grandchildren decided to play a trick on him. They went to the refrigerator and pulled out a bit of extra smelly Limburger cheese. They took the cheese and quietly rubbed a little into their grandpa's mustache. Then they hid around the corner to see what would happen.

After a few moments, the old man's nose began to twitch. Then his head started to toss. And finally Grandpa sat bolt upright on the couch with a sour look and said, "Something in here stinks!"

He got up, shuffled into the kitchen, took a deep sniff, and said, "It stinks in here too."

At that point, he decided to go outside to get a breath of fresh air, but when he took a deep breath, there was the foul smell again. "The whole world stinks!" he lamented.

The moral of the story? To a person with Limburger cheese under his nose, everything stinks! The good news for Grandpa is that he can remove the foul stuff from his mustache with soap and water, and things will seem sweet again. But a person who has foul stuff on the inside has a more difficult task. The only way to change how you view life is to change who you are on the inside.

We all have a personal frame of reference that consists of our attitudes, assumptions, and expectations concerning ourselves, other people, and life. These factors determine whether we're optimistic or pessimistic, cheerful or gloomy, trusting or suspicious, friendly or reserved, brave or timid. And they color not only how we see life, but also how we let people treat us. Eleanor Roosevelt said, "No one can make you feel inferior without your consent." Or to put it another way, in the words of psychologist and author Phil McGraw, "You teach people how to treat you." What you teach comes from how you see life. And how you see life comes from who you are.

A few years ago, I had the opportunity to teach leadership to the NFL's St. Louis Rams. The team invited me to attend one of their games afterward, and I was allowed to sit with the spouses of the coaches and players. I sat next to Kim Matsko, wife of associate head coach/offensive line coach of the St. Louis Rams, John Matsko. As we chatted, I asked her of all the cities where she had lived, what was her favorite? (She had lived in many states: Ohio, North Carolina, Arizona, California, New York, and Missouri.) Her response: "Where I am living right now."

"Oh, so you like St. Louis the best?" I said.

"No, I didn't say that. I like the place I'm currently living best," she answered. "It's a choice." What a great attitude! If you can maintain a perspective like that, you will always view life in a positive light.

WHO YOU ARE DETERMINES WHAT YOU DO

In *Animals, Inc.*, Kenneth A. Tucker and Vandana Allman of the Gallup organization tell a story of barnyard characters that's meant to point out how companies mismanage their people. Believing that anyone can be trained to do anything, those in charge of the farm ask the workhorse to operate the computer. A shy sheep is encouraged to make sales calls. And here's my favorite: the scarecrow is sent into the henhouse to lay eggs. He works at it all day. Physically, he exhibits perfect form. With hens all around cranking out eggs, he tries and tries. But by the end of the day, exhausted, he has failed to produce a single egg.

You may be thinking, *Of course, he doesn't produce an egg.* It's pretty obvious that hens lay eggs, horses pull plows, and sheep produce wool. It's easy to see that natural ability affects what we do. But our thinking and our attitudes are as much parts of us as our talents and abilities. They also determine what we do. We cannot separate them, and if we expect results different from our makeup, we're in for disappointment.

FIVE THINGS THAT DETERMINE WHO WE ARE

What factors come into play in determining who you are? Obviously there are many, but here are what I consider to be the top five:

1. Genetics

When Margaret and I were young and naive, we believed that genetics played only a small role in a person's makeup. We thought environment was 98 percent responsible for who a person was. Raise your children to be like you, and they'll turn out like you. Then we adopted our children, Elizabeth and Joel Porter. We discovered that upbringing, character development, education, and spiritual instruction play important roles, but some things are hardwired into people that are going to be there no matter what their environment.

Your genetic makeup is probably good news and bad news. There are some qualities and characteristics you got when you were created that are awesome. That's true for every person on the planet. But there are also things you don't like. You may just have to learn to live with them. When it comes to character issues, work on your weaknesses. When it comes to talents, go with your strengths.

You don't have a choice on this one. You can't change your genes. However, of the top five factors that determine who you are, it is the only one you cannot change by making choices. The other four are, at least to some extent, up to you.

---

2. Self-Image

Poet T. S. Eliot observed, "Half of the harm that is done in this world is due to people who want to feel important. They do not mean to do harm. They are absorbed in the endless struggle to think well of themselves." People are like water: they find their own level. A person with a negative self-image will expect the worst, damage relationships, and find others who are similarly negative. Those with a positive self-image will expect the best for themselves. And those who have a self-image that is both *positive* and *accurate* are likely to be highly successful, see others as potentially successful, and gravitate to other successful people. As psychologist Nathaniel Branden said, "We tend to feel most comfortable, most 'at home' with persons whose self-esteem level resembles our own. Opposites may attract about some issues, but not this one."

It's said that Oliver Wendell Holmes was walking down a street one day, and a little girl joined him. When the girl started to turn back home, the famed jurist said, "When your mother asks you where you've been, tell her you've been walking with Oliver Wendell Holmes."

"Okay," said the girl confidently, "and when your folks ask you where you've been, tell them you were walking with Mary Susanna Brown." Now, that's someone with a positive self-image.

3. Experiences in Life

Once upon a time a group of villagers instructed their young shepherd, "When you see a wolf, cry *wolf* and we'll come with guns and pitchforks."

The next day the boy was tending his sheep when he saw a lion in the distance. He cried out, "Lion, lion!" But no one came. The lion killed several sheep. The shepherd boy was distraught.

"Why didn't you come when I called?" he asked the villagers.

"There are no lions in this part of the country," the older men replied. "The wolves are what you have to look out for."

The young shepherd learned a valuable lesson: people respond to what they are prepared to believe. And what prepares them for what they believe is their experience.

Hasn't that been true for you? Think about some of your childhood experiences. If you had great success in sports, they probably became an important part of your life. If you made friends easily, you probably enjoy being around people. If you were neglected or abused, that has made another kind of impact on you. Everything you've experienced has contributed to who you are.

We don't choose *all* of our life experiences; that was especially true when we were children. But we *do* choose many of the ones we have now. We choose who we marry. We choose our jobs. We choose where to take a vacation, whether to exercise, and what we learn. And people who have a particularly difficult background decide whether to pursue experiences that will improve how they live and think. We can't undo our past experiences, but we can reprogram ourselves using new ones.

4. Attitude and Choices About Those Experiences

Even more important than choosing our experiences is deciding what our attitudes will be about the experiences we have. As I already mentioned, we have only limited control over what we experience. However, we have complete control over our attitudes. Whether our outlook is up or down, expectant or reluctant, open or closed is completely our choice. I may not be able to change the world I see around me, but I can change what I see within me.

> I may not be able to change the world I see around me, but I can change what I see within me.

I believe that attitude is the second most important decision anyone can make. (The most important is faith.) Your attitude will make or unmake you. It's not the result of your birth, your circumstances, or your bank account. It's all a choice. (If you find this to be a difficult issue, you may want to look at two other books I've written: *Failing Forward* or *The Winning Attitude*.)

5. Friends

In a *Peanuts* strip by Charles Schulz, Charlie Brown rests his head in his hands while leaning on the wall, looking miserable. His friend Lucy approaches.

"Discouraged again, eh, Charlie Brown?"

Charlie Brown does not even answer.

"You know what your trouble is?" Lucy asks. Without waiting for a response, she announces, "The whole trouble with you is that you are you!"

Charlie Brown says, "Well, what in the world can I do about that?"

"I don't pretend to be able to give advice," Lucy replies. "I merely point out the trouble!"

If Charlie Brown wanted to improve himself, perhaps a place to start would be to find a new friend.

One of the most important things you will ever do is to choose your friends. As parents, Margaret and I carefully watched the friends our children chose. We knew that positive people with good character would help to lift our children up. Negative people with poor character would pull them down. We always made our home a place where our kids and their friends would want to spend time so that we could see who was influencing them.

The people you are closest to—and that especially includes your spouse—will shape who you are. Haven't you seen a child who has been good begin to have problems after he hangs out with kids who get into trouble? And haven't you watched a friend or colleague take off professionally after he began spending time with people who stretched his mind and challenged him to grow? The people you choose to spend time with will change who you are. The words of author and speaker Charlie "Tremendous" Jones really are true: the difference between who you are today and who you will be in five years will be the people you spend time with and the books you read.

The way you view others is determined by who you are. You cannot get away from that truth. If you don't like people, that really is a statement about you and the way you look at people. Your viewpoint is the problem. If that's the case, don't try to change others. Don't even focus on others; focus on yourself. If you change yourself and become the kind of person you desire to be, you will begin to view others in a whole new light. And that will change the way you interact in all of your relationships.

LENS PRINCIPLE DISCUSSION QUESTIONS

1. If asked to write a statement describing human nature and people in general, what would you say? (Take some time to do that now.) Would you describe your philosophy as optimistic, skeptical, tentative, detached, etc.? What does your personal philosophy concerning others say about you?

2. Would you describe your attitude as generally positive or negative? (Don't cop out and call yourself a realist. Which way do you lean?) Do you see your attitude as an asset or a liability? What could you do to improve your attitude?

3. Think back to your childhood. What experiences have especially marked you as an individual? Did they inspire you to trust or mistrust people? How has that outlook colored your relationships as an adult? If it has negatively affected your relationships, what positive experiences can you pursue to create a new, more positive history?

4. Do you agree with the statement that the difference between who you are today and who you will be in five years will be the people you spend time with and the books you read? What other factors do you believe to be equally (or more) important?

5. Think about the personal qualities you would like to cultivate. List them. Now create a plan for growth to develop those qualities. First, dedicate time on your calendar with people who possess the qualities you desire. Second, select a book a month to read to help you grow.

THE MIRROR PRINCIPLE

THE FIRST PERSON
WE MUST EXAMINE
IS OURSELVES

Coping with difficult people is always a problem,
especially if the difficult person happens to be you.

THE QUESTION I MUST ASK MYSELF:
HAVE I EXAMINED MYSELF AND
TAKEN RESPONSIBILITY FOR WHO I AM?

Have you ever known someone who was his own worst enemy, who always managed to short-circuit himself when success was within reach, or who could not seem to hold down a job? Some of these people possess great potential but keep blowing themselves up. But not everyone with these kinds of issues is a person who can't get ahead in life. Sometimes people who are their own worst enemies achieve big things while slowly chipping away at themselves and their relationships with others. I believe Pete Rose is one such person.

A ROSE BY ANY OTHER NAME

When it comes to playing baseball, few people compare to Pete Rose. Here are just a few of his major-league baseball records:

- Most career hits (4,256)

- Most games played (3,562)

- Most at bats (14,053)

- Most total bases by a switch-hitter (5,752)

- Most seasons of 200 or more hits (10)

- Most seasons with 600 or more at bats (17)

- National League record for most career runs (2,165)

- National League record for most years played (24)[1]

Rose, who was a Gold Glove outfielder for two seasons, also has received numerous awards: he was named the National League Rookie of the Year (1963), the National League Most Valuable Player (1973), and the World Series MVP (1975).[2]

But while Pete Rose was succeeding on the baseball field, he was failing in other areas of his life. Specifically, the thing that was causing chaos in his personal life and that would eventually end his baseball career was gambling.

Ever since the World Series betting scandal in the early 1900s, major-league baseball has worked to keep gambling out of the sport. In every major-league baseball clubhouse in the United States, Rule 21(d) is posted where players and coaches can see it. The rule states:

> Any player, umpire or club or league official or employee, who shall bet any sum whatsoever upon any baseball game in connection with which the bettor has no duty to perform, shall be declared ineligible for one year.
>
> Any player, umpire or club or league official or employee, who shall bet any sum whatsoever upon any baseball game in connection with which the bettor has a duty to perform shall be declared permanently ineligible.[3]

Pete Rose must have walked past that posted rule at least 3,562 times as a player, because that's how many games he played in. He saw it at least an additional 554 times as a manager.[4] Yet he still bet on baseball. And in January 2004, after denying it for fourteen years, Rose finally admitted to betting on baseball, including making bets on his own team, the Cincinnati Reds.

BLIND SPOT

When Pete Rose began betting on baseball in 1987, he said he "didn't even consider the consequences."[5] Perhaps it was just a natural next step in his progression as a compulsive gambler—a label that Rose vehemently says does not describe him.[6] But what else would you call a person who bet year-round on various sporting activities, but who apparently could not stop gambling even when it might cost him his livelihood, and who spent mind-boggling sums on bets? Bookmaker Ron Peters testified that he took more than $1 million in bets from Rose. Just on baseball. Just in one season![7]

How could Rose not see what was happening to him? Why didn't he keep himself from gambling on baseball? How could he continue to lie about what he'd done for more than a decade? How could he say that his only real problem was the friends he picked? How could he continue to say that he didn't have a problem? I believe the answer is that he was focused so intently on baseball that he never really looked in the mirror and examined himself.

TAKE A GOOD LOOK

Rose realized he was different from other players, but he rarely stopped to reflect on whether that was a positive or a negative thing. He says, "Joe Morgan [Rose's former teammate who is now in the Hall of Fame] used to say that he felt sorry for me because when baseball was all over, I would have nothing else in my life to occupy my time. I never understood Joe's way of thinking. I always thought he was somehow less committed than me, that he didn't love the game as much as I did. Who in his right mind could ever put anything in life ahead of baseball?"[8]

While Rose was playing, his refusal to examine himself didn't hurt his career, although it did damage his personal relationships. But once his playing days were over, it caught up with him. Rose states:

> In hindsight I should have taken some time to reflect on my life, on where I'd been and where I was headed. If I had been a book reader, I could have read up on how other famous folks handled retirement . . . I could have called Dick Butkus and asked how he felt about retiring from the NFL after achieving godlike status as a player. I could have called Terry Bradshaw . . . But I didn't find

out how any of them dealt with retirement because I never talked
to them. I never talked to anybody. It wasn't my style.[9]

In one of his rare moments of reflection and genuine self-assessment,
Rose sums up the way he handled himself: "I was aware of my records
and my place in baseball history. But I was never aware of boundaries or
able to control that part of my life. And admitting that I was out of
control has been next to impossible for me. I was aware of my privileges,
but not my responsibilities."[10] In my opinion, he's still struggling to
figure out what his responsibilities are. That's very hard to do when you
don't like looking in the mirror.

THE MIRROR TEST

People unaware of who they are and what they do often damage rela-
tionships with others. The way to change that is to look in the mirror.
It's something all of us must do. It's what I call taking the mirror test.
Consider these truths that we must learn about ourselves:

The First Person I Must Know Is Myself— Self-Awareness

Human nature seems to endow people with the ability to size up
everybody in the world but themselves. Pete Rose does not have a
clear image of himself. He tends to
think of himself as a victim. Rose
has described himself as a kid from
the wrong side of the tracks and as
someone who got by with only average
athletic talent. And he thinks that
the punishment he has received
(being banned from baseball) does not fit his crime.[11]

> Human nature seems to endow people with the ability to size up everybody in the world but themselves.

Some people are endowed with natural self-awareness. Thomas
Armstrong, author of *7 Kinds of Smart*, points out that these kinds of people

possess intrapersonal intelligence. However, becoming self-aware does not come easily for most people. It is a process—sometimes a slow one—that requires intentionality.

The First Person I Must Get Along with Is Myself— Self-Image

Author Sydney J. Harris observed, "If you're not comfortable with yourself you can't be comfortable with others." I would take that one step further. If you do not believe in yourself, you will sabotage relationships.

For years I have taught a concept called the Law of the Lid, which is found in *The 21 Irrefutable Laws of Leadership*. It states, "Leadership ability determines a person's level of effectiveness." Here's what I mean by that: no matter how hard you work, you can only go so far professionally if you are a poor leader. A company, department, or team will always be held back by a weak leader.[12]

When it comes to relationships, self-image works in a similar way. It is the relational lid. Your image of yourself restricts your ability to build healthy relationships. A negative self-image will even keep a person from being successful. And even when a person with a poor self-image does somehow achieve success, it won't last because he will eventually bring himself down to the level of his own expectations. In a backward sort of way, it's a tribute to Pete Rose's self-confidence that his lack of self-awareness didn't catch up with him sooner.

> "I always say that the most important relationship you will ever have is with yourself. You've got to be your own best friend first."
> —PHIL McGRAW

Psychologist and *New York Times* bestselling author Phil McGraw states, "I always say that the most important relationship you will ever have is with yourself. You've got to be your own best friend first."[13] How can you be "best friends" with someone you don't know or don't like? You can't. That's why it's so important to find out who you are and work to become someone you like and respect.

The First Person to Cause Me Problems Is Myself—
Self-Honesty

Comedian Jack Parr quipped, "Looking back, my life seems like one big obstacle race, with me being the chief obstacle." He was making a joke, but what he says is still true for most of us. Pete Rose isn't alone in his ability to cause problems for himself. That's an issue for me. And it is for you too. If we could kick the person responsible for most of our troubles, we wouldn't be able to sit down for weeks. What can save us is the willingness to look in the mirror and get honest about our short-comings, faults, and problems.

A couple of years after I graduated from college, I had lunch with a friend who had been a fellow student. Like me, he was in his first job as the pastor of a small church. As we ate, he began talking to me about the people in his congregation. He said he had a problem with this ding-a-ling on his church board and with that ding-a-ling in committee meetings and with another ding-a-ling he was counseling. After about the fifth ding-a-ling, I was getting irritated. *How can you lead people when you don't like or respect them?* I thought.

"Fred, do you want to know why you have so many ding-a-lings in your church?" I asked.

He stopped eating and said with great interest, "Yeah, I really would."

"It's because you're the biggest ding-a-ling of them all."

He was shocked.

Perhaps that was not my finest hour relationally because Fred wasn't much interested in my explanation after I said that. But it was obvious to an outsider that Fred was the problem. It wasn't long afterward that he left his church and went to another one. And it didn't take long for him to think that his new church was filled with ding-a-lings too.

Ralph Stayer, CEO and owner of Johnsonville Foods, acknowledges, "[This is the insight] I realized early and return to often. In most situations, I am the problem. My mentalities, my pictures, my expectations, form the biggest obstacles to my success." If you want to keep from becoming your own worst enemy, you have to look at yourself realistically.

The First Person I Must Change Is Myself—
Self-Improvement

A danger of teaching conferences or writing books like this one is that people start to assume you're an expert who has mastered everything you teach. Don't believe it. Like you, I'm still working on my relational and leadership skills. There are principles in this book that I don't do well, so I'm still working to improve myself. And that will always be true for me. If I ever think I've finished growing, then I'm in trouble.

In the crypts of Westminster Abbey, the following words were written on the tomb of an Anglican bishop who lived in the eleventh century:

> When I was young and free my imagination had no limits, I dreamed of changing the world. As I grew older and wiser, I discovered the world would not change, so I shortened my sights somewhat and decided to change only my country. But it, too, seemed immovable. As I grew in my twilight years, in one last desperate attempt, I settled for changing only my family, those closest to me, but alas, they would have none of it. And now as I lie on my deathbed, I suddenly realized: If I had only changed my self first, then by example I would have changed my family. From their inspiration and encouragement, I would then have been able to better my country and, who knows, I may have even changed my world.

People who often experience relational difficulties are tempted to look at everyone but themselves to explain the problem. But we must always begin by examining ourselves and being willing to change whatever deficiencies we have. Critic Samuel Johnson advised that "he who has so little knowledge of human nature as to seek happiness by changing anything but his own disposition will waste his life in fruitless efforts and multiply the grief which he purposes to remove."

The First Person That Can Make a Difference Is Myself— Self-Responsibility

In *The 17 Indisputable Laws of Teamwork*, I wrote about the Law of Significance: "One is too small a number to achieve greatness." I truly believe that no significant accomplishments can be achieved by individual effort. However, I also believe that every significant accomplishment begins with the vision of one individual. That person not only possesses the vision but also takes responsibility for carrying it to others. If you want to make a difference in this world, you must take responsibility for yourself.

TAKING A LOOK IN THE MIRROR

A few years ago when I traveled to New Zealand to do a conference, I stayed in a hotel in Christchurch. One evening I was thirsty and started looking for a Coke machine. When I couldn't find one and I saw a door marked "Staff," I figured I'd go in and see if anyone in there could help me. I didn't find a hotel worker or a drink machine there, but I did observe something interesting. As I approached the door to go back out into the hall, I found that the door had a full-length mirror with the following words: "Take a good look at yourself. This is what the customer sees." The hotel's management was reminding employees that to fulfill their purpose, they needed to take a look at themselves.

And that's true for us too. Psychotherapist Sheldon Kopp believes "all the significant battles are waged within the self." As we examine ourselves, we discover what those battles are. And then we have two choices. The first is to be like the man who visited his doctor and found out he had serious health issues. When the doctor showed him his X-rays and suggested a painful and expensive surgery, the man asked, "Okay, but how much would you charge to just touch up the X-rays?"

The second choice is to stop blaming others, look at ourselves, and do the hard work of resolving the issues that are causing us problems. If you want to have better relationships with others, then stop, look in the mirror, and start working on yourself.

MIRROR PRINCIPLE DISCUSSION QUESTIONS

1. If you were to ask family members, friends, and colleagues which of your practices and habits are causing you more harm than good, what would they say? (If you have the courage, really ask them this question.) How do those factors affect your relationships?

2. Where does personal reflection fit into the Mirror Principle? How likely are people in our culture to set aside time for self-examination? Explain your answer. When, where, how long, and how often do you examine your character, review your habits, and critique your practices? How can you improve in this area?

3. How would you describe yourself? List your strengths and weaknesses. Overall, have you experienced more wins or losses in life? What do you expect the future to hold? How has your past colored your perspective?

4. One of the knocks against the current "self-worth" movement is that it encourages people to think highly of themselves regardless of character or performance. Why is it important to be sure self-image is grounded in truth? How can one guard against false pride and still have confidence in himself?

5. In what area do you need the greatest growth? How have you taken responsibility for it? What is your plan to improve in this area? Have you dedicated resources to it and put it on your calendar? If not, why not? How can you improve in this area?

THE PAIN PRINCIPLE

HURTING PEOPLE HURT PEOPLE AND ARE EASILY HURT BY THEM

*"Be yourself" is about the
worst advice you can give some people!*

THE QUESTION I MUST ASK MYSELF:
DO I HURT PEOPLE, OR AM I
TOO EASILY HURT BY THEM?

E arly in my career, I accepted an invitation to lead a church. It was a wonderful opportunity, and it was in a nice town. It was an exciting time for Margaret and me.

My New Pen Pal

I had been at the church only ten days when I received a piece of mail from Tom, a member of the congregation. I opened it up, began reading, and soon discovered that it was a typed transcript of the sermon I had delivered on my first Sunday. I was amazed—and flattered—that someone had taken the time to capture every word I had said. And then I looked more carefully. The pages were covered with comments. Tom had red-penned every grammatical mistake, corrected every misspoken word, and pointed out anything he thought was a factual error.

I thought it was odd, but I didn't worry too much about it. I know I'm not perfect, and I'm aware that I sometimes make mistakes when I speak. But I have a healthy self-image, so I didn't let it bother me. But then the next week, another envelope arrived in the mail from Tom. Once again, the message I had preached the previous Sunday had been transcribed. And once again, every tiny mistake was marked in red ink. That's when I figured I'd better meet Tom and find out what was bothering him.

The next Sunday after delivering the sermon message, I asked someone to point out Tom to me. I walked over to him, stuck out my hand, and said, "Hi, I'm John Maxwell."

At first Tom just stared at me. Finally he said, "Hello, *Pastor*." And that's when I realized he wasn't going to shake my hand. Then he turned on his heel and walked away.

Sure enough, a couple of days later, guess what I received in the mail? Another envelope from Tom. I started calling them his "love letters." I got one every week with his in-depth critique. Would you care to guess how long I received Tom's love letters? Seven years! During that time, he never voluntarily shook my hand. I tried to connect with him, but he wanted little to do with me. In only one subject could I get him to engage in conversation with me. Our kids were adopted, and so were his, so he'd talk to me about them. But he wouldn't warm up.

WHAT LIES BENEATH

Then one day I had lunch with a veteran pastor. I told him about Tom, the weekly love letters I received, and my inability to win Tom over. My pastor friend looked at me and said, "You know, John, hurting people hurt people." That statement really connected for me. "Whenever someone says or does something hurtful," he continued, "you need to go beneath the surface."

I looked at Tom in a new way after that. I began searching for the cause of his pain, and I tried again to connect with him. Finally one day when I was trying to get him to engage, he made a statement that more than hinted at the problem. He said, "Never trust a pastor." I later came to find out that Tom had once served as a board member at a church and had been mistreated by the pastor. He decided from then on that pastors were bad news and couldn't be trusted.

After I understood the problem, I was able to work on winning Tom's trust. It took a lot of effort, but by the time I left Lancaster to accept another leadership position, Tom had gotten over his mistrust of me. We became friends. And not only was he willing to shake my hand, but he'd give me a great big bear hug. By then, he had long since given up sending me love letters.

SOME PAIN, NO GAIN

To really understand the Pain Principle and have it help you in dealing with others, you need to keep in mind four truths:

1. There Are Many Hurting People

It doesn't take a psychiatrist to see that many people are hurting today. Columnist Ann Landers asserted that one in four Americans is imbalanced. (She added that we should look at our three closest friends, and if they seem okay, it means we're the one!)

Of course, the fact that many people are hurting is not a new phenomenon. In the nineteenth century, philosopher Arthur Schopenhauer compared the human race to porcupines huddled together on a bitter cold winter night:

> The colder it gets outside, the more we huddle together for warmth; but the closer we get to one another, the more we hurt one another with our sharp quills. And in the lonely night of earth's winter eventually we begin to drift apart and wander out on our own and freeze to death in our loneliness.

Schopenhauer was quite a pessimist. Unlike him, I believe there is hope for everyone. But at the same time we can't be naive about people. A tremendous number of individuals are nursing deep hurts.

2. Those Hurting People Often Hurt People

German poet Herman Hesse wrote, "If you hate a person, you hate something in him that is part of yourself. What isn't part of ourselves doesn't disturb us." I agree with his viewpoint. When hurting people lash out, it is in response to what's happening inside them more than what's happening around them. They feel or believe something negative within themselves. The problem is that people who don't believe in themselves will never succeed, and they will also keep those around them from succeeding.

Early in my pastoral career, I did a lot of counseling, a responsibility I eventually gave to staff members because I didn't have the temperament for it. But over the years I counseled enough hurting couples to observe that their interaction usually followed a pattern. Emotionally one spouse would "throw up," and then the other one would clean up. I saw it happen again and again. And always the individual in the most pain did the most damage to the other person.

3. Those Hurting People Are Often Hurt by People

Not only do hurting people hurt others, but they are also easily hurt by others. My friend Kevin Myers illustrates it this way. If someone has a splinter in his finger and he allows it to remain there, his finger becomes swollen and infected. Then if another person barely brushes against it, the individual howls with pain and says, "You hurt me!" But the reality is that the problem isn't with the person who innocently bumped the finger. It's with the person who has the splinter but has neglected to address the injury.

Emotional pain works in a similar way. Hurting people overreact, overexaggerate, and overprotect. They also overinfluence. By that I mean they control the relationship. That was the case with Tom. The old wound was his unresolved conflict with a previous pastor. He had never removed the "splinter" so that it could heal. And because he was hurting, he prevented our relationship from growing for seven years. That's always the way: relationships are held back by the less healthy person.

As you interact with others, remember this: anytime a person's response is larger than the issue at hand, the response is almost always about something else.

4. Those Hurting People Often Hurt Themselves

In an old comedy routine, a know-it-all is fond of lecturing his friend at the station where they wait to take the commuter train each morning. And every time the know-it-all talks, he pokes his friend in the chest with his finger. That, of course, doesn't sit well with the other man. So he finally determines that he's going to put a stop to it.

The next day on the way to the station, he meets a third friend and says, "I'm so tired of that know-it-all lecturing me and poking me in the chest. Today I'm going to get 'im."

"How are you going to do that?" his buddy asks.

The first man opens his coat to reveal three sticks of dynamite strapped to his chest. "Today when he pokes me," he says with a smile, "he's going to blow his hand off."

> "He who cannot forgive others breaks the bridge over which he must pass himself."
> —GEORGE HERBERT

Hurting people are often like that. They may hurt others, but the ones they hurt deepest and most often are themselves. Poet George Herbert declared, "He who cannot forgive others breaks the bridge over which he must pass himself."

DEALING WITH HURTING PEOPLE

Author Glenn Clark advises, "If you wish to travel far and fast, travel light. Take off all your envies, jealousies, unforgiveness, selfishness, and tears." People who have not gotten past their hurt have a hard time doing that. As a result, they act and react differently from healthy people.

Healthy people are . . .	*Hurting people are . . .*
more willing to change.	less willing to change.
more willing to admit failure.	less willing to admit failure.
more willing to discuss issues.	less willing to discuss issues.
more willing to learn from others.	less willing to learn from others.
more willing to do something about the problem.	less willing to do something about the problem.
able to travel light.	carrying a lot of baggage.

If you find yourself dealing with a hurting person, which we all must do from time to time, then I advise that you do the following:

Don't Take It Personally

Hurting people are going to find offense when none is given. When you know that you've done nothing wrong, remember that it's not what others say about you; it's what you believe about yourself. You can apologize for their pain and feel compassion for their state, but you should try not to take it personally. That can be difficult—even for a person with a healthy self-image—but it's worth the effort.

Look Beyond the Person for the Problem

Just as I did with Tom, you would do well to try to look past the person and his hurtful actions and try to see what's causing him pain. Even if you can't discover the source of the problem, this plan will help you to approach the person with greater compassion.

Look Beyond the Situation

Have you ever had to make a bad-news phone call and dreaded it, not so much because of the news you had to deliver but because you were dreading the response from the person on the other end of the line? Just last week, my wife and I had to make such a call. The weekend had been planned, but at the last minute things changed. We had to call a friend who would be negatively affected by the change. We hated to make the call, not because the news was that bad, but because the person is not always emotionally strong and would react badly.

In such cases, try not to focus on the situation. Just remember that it's not what happens *to* you; it's what happens *in* you that matters. Try to rise above the emotional turmoil that the other person may create.

Do Not Add to Their Hurt

The natural inclination for many people is to meet fire with fire, pain with pain. But striking back at a hurting person is like kicking a man while he's down. Statesman Sir Francis Bacon said, "This is certain, that a man that studieth revenge keeps his wounds green, which otherwise would heal and do well." If someone lashes out at you, the best thing to do is to forgive him and move on.

Help Them Find Help

The kindest thing you can do for hurting people is to try to get them help. Some people don't want to deal with their issues, and you certainly can't force them to receive help. But you can always choose to extend your hand. It may take a long time, as it did with Tom, but even very bitter people have been known to come around.

WHAT IF YOU'RE THE ONE WHO'S HURTING?

At the beginning of this chapter, the question was asked: *Do I hurt people, or am I too easily hurt by them?* If you answered yes, then you need to answer a second question: *Am I prepared to work through my issues and get beyond my pain?* Here's the key. Most people just want a quick fix, something to give them some relief in the moment. That's why some choose to lash out; it makes them feel better temporarily. Others use alcohol, food, sex, or something else to lessen the pain. But as my friend Kevin Myers says, "If you want to become well, you need more than a fix. You need to become fit."

People who seek emotional fitness don't look for momentary relief. They search for what's right. How can you tell what kind of person you are? People searching for a fix stop working at resolving a problem as soon as the pain or pressure is relieved. People seeking fitness continue doing what's right and improving themselves even when the discomfort goes away.

Delving into your old hurts and emotional issues often takes the help of a professional counselor and can be a messy proposition, but it's worth it. I recently read a story that provides a good analogy for what it's like. In March 1995, the New England Pipe Cleaning Company of Watertown, Connecticut, was working under the streets of Revere, Massachusetts, to clean out a ten-inch sewer line. The workers found many of the usual items that clog those kinds of pipes. However, they also discovered many other things: sixty-one rings, vintage coins, and silverware. The bad news is that the workers had to do an unpleasant job. The good news is that they were allowed to keep the valuable things they discovered in the process.

If your relational capacity is all "clogged up," you, too, may have to do some digging to make things right. And you may have to deal with some pretty nasty stuff. But the reward is

> "If you want to become well, you need more than a fix. You need to become fit."
> —KEVIN MYERS

that you may discover some treasures that you didn't know existed. And at the end of your hard work, you can develop a healthy capacity for relationships.

PAIN PRINCIPLE DISCUSSION QUESTIONS

1. What is your reaction to Schopenhauer's porcupine analogy? Do you think it accurately represents how we respond to one another? Do you have a better description or analogy?

2. Do you agree that we are most likely to react negatively to something in another person that we dislike about ourselves? Explain.

3. Do you find it difficult to separate the person or situation from the pain he causes? Explain. What strategies can one use to do that effectively?

4. In general, are you more likely to be someone who unintentionally hurts others or who is hurt by others who are hurting? Explain.

5. How do you maintain compassion for hurting people without encouraging them to wallow in their pain or dump on you? Where can a hurting person get help? Explain sensitive yet effective ways that might assist a hurting person to get help.

THE HAMMER PRINCIPLE

NEVER USE A HAMMER TO SWAT A FLY OFF SOMEONE'S HEAD

If you would win the world, melt it, do not hammer it.

—ALEXANDER MACLAREN

THE QUESTION I MUST ASK MYSELF:
WOULD OTHERS SAY I OVERREACT
TO SMALL THINGS IN A RELATIONSHIP?

My wife, Margaret, and I were married in June 1969, and like most couples, we naively believed that nothing but smooth sailing lay ahead of us. Of course, it didn't take long for us to find ourselves in the kinds of minor disagreements that all couples experience, especially when they're first adjusting to married life.

Like most people, I thought I was right nearly all of the time, and I let Margaret know about it. I've always been a good talker, and I can be pretty persuasive, so I used my skills to win our arguments. We never yelled or screamed at each other. It was always very rational and controlled, but I always made sure I won. The problem was that with my approach, Margaret always had to lose.

We did a lot of things right during those first two years of marriage, but this wasn't one of them. Unknowingly I was slowly but surely beating Margaret down emotionally. We'd disagree, I'd overreact, and I'd unwittingly lay another brick in the wall that was building between us. I didn't realize that winning at all costs could eventually jeopardize our marriage. Then one day Margaret sat me down, shared how she felt when we argued, and explained what it was doing to our relationship. It was the first time I understood I was putting winning the arguments ahead of winning the relationship.

From that day I decided to change. Realizing that having the right attitude was more important than having the right answers, I softened my approach, listened more, and stopped making a big deal out of little things. In time, the wall that had begun to form came down, and we began building bridges. And since that time, I've made a conscious effort to initiate connection anytime I'm in conflict with someone I care about.

IF I HAD A HAMMER . . .

Let's face it. Because of their personalities, some people are inclined to use a hammer, even when something gentler will do. They're like Calvin in this comic strip.

I must admit I am sometimes more like Calvin than I would like. When tempted to use overkill, I try to temper my behavior using the following four Ts. You may want to embrace them when you find yourself in a similar situation.

1. Total Picture

A middle-aged man entered a cocktail lounge and walked directly to the bar. "Do you have anything that will cure hiccups?" he asked the bartender. Without a word, the bartender reached down under the bar, picked up a wet bar rag, and slapped the man across the face with it.

"Hey! What's the idea?" the astonished man said.

The bartender smiled. "Well, you don't have hiccups anymore, do you?" he asked.

"I never did," the man replied. "I wanted something to cure my wife. She's out in the car."

Do you come to conclusions long before the problem has been laid out before you? That is a common occurrence for most of us who have strong personalities. That's why I have trained myself to follow a process to keep me from hammering people with answers before they've finished asking the question. When someone is sharing his point of view with me, I try to . . .

listen,

ask questions,

listen again,

ask more questions,

listen some more,

then

respond.

I find that if I slow myself down, I am more likely to respond patiently and appropriately.

2. Timing

I recently read a quote attributed to author Dan Zadra that said, "It's what you do, not when you do it, that counts." That's not always true. If the general doesn't order the attack at the right time, the battle is lost. If the parent doesn't get the injured child to the hospital quickly enough, her life might be lost. If you don't apologize to someone when you've wronged him, the relationship might be lost.

When you act is as important as taking the right action. Even knowing when not to act can be important. Noted hostess and writer Lady Dorothy Nevill observed, "The real art of conversation is not only to say the right thing in the right place, but to leave unsaid the wrong thing at the tempting moment."

Today Kevin McHale is the general manager of the Minnesota Timberwolves. Prior to that, he was an outstanding player for the Boston Celtics during their championship years. He has this to say about his Celtics coach, K. C. Jones:

> After every loss, or whenever somebody had taken a bad shot at the end of the game, he'd be the first one to walk over, pat the

guy on the back and say, "Don't worry, we'll get 'em next time."
But he'd never come up to you after you'd do something great.
So, I asked him about it one night, and he said, "Kevin, after
you've made the winning basket, you've got 15,000 people
cheering for you, TV stations come at you, and everybody giving
you high-fives. You don't need me then. When you need a real
friend is when you feel that nobody likes you."

It seems to me that the most common cause of bad timing in
relationships is selfish motives. (If you have small children, think about
their timing. It's often poor, but that's
because they usually think only of
themselves.) For that reason, when
little things bother us, our number one
objective must be putting our personal
agendas aside and building the relationship. If you have examined your
motives, and you can be certain

> "The real art of conversation
> is not only to say the right thing
> in the right place, but to leave
> unsaid the wrong thing at
> the tempting moment."
> —LADY DOROTHY NEVILL

they're good, then you need to ask yourself two timing questions. First,
am I ready to confront? That's a pretty easy question to answer, because
that's really a matter of whether you've done your homework. The
second is harder: *Is the other person ready to hear?* If you've laid a
relational foundation and the two of you are not in the "heat of battle,"
then the answer may be yes.

3. Tone

There was once a single mom with two children, ages five and three,
who was constantly battling their bad language. She tried everything to
get them to stop swearing, including taking them to a child psychologist.
After months of frustration, she thought to herself, *The M&M's didn't
work, and neither has ignoring their behavior. Now they're swearing even
more. So I'm going to treat these guys the way my mom treated my brothers
when they were swearing.*

The next morning the five-year-old got up, and he went into the kitchen. The mom said, "Honey, what would you like for breakfast this morning?"

He looked up and said, "Just gimme some of those @#*&%! old Wheaties."

With that she swatted the kid, and across the kitchen he flew. His three-year-old brother, who was watching, was amazed. He had never seen anything like it. Then his mother looked over at him and said, "And what do you want for breakfast?"

He looked at her with wide eyes and said, "Well, you can bet your #@*& I don't want any of those @#*&%! Wheaties!"

People often respond to our attitudes and actions more than to our words. Many petty conflicts occur because people use the wrong tone of voice. The writer of Proverbs stated, "A soft answer turns away wrath, but a harsh word stirs up anger."[1] Haven't you found that to be true? If not, try this experiment. The next time someone says something to you in anger, respond with gentleness and kindness. When you do that, the person who spoke harshly is likely to tone down, if not soften, his attitude.

4. Temperature

As tempers flare, people are prone to dropping bombs when using a slingshot will do. And that can cause a lot of trouble because the size of a problem often changes based on how it is handled. In general . . .

> If the reaction is worse than the action, the problem usually increases.

> If the reaction is less than the action, the problem usually decreases.

That's why I try to follow a self-imposed guideline that I call the Reprimand Rule: "Take thirty seconds to share feelings—and then it's over." Anytime we let a little thing create a big reaction (one that lasts longer than thirty seconds), then we're using a hammer.

My wife, Margaret, and I continually help each other with this issue.

When our two children were younger and still living at home, we used a strategy whenever we needed to confront them. She and I would sit side by side on the couch and hold hands as we talked to the kids. And if one of us started to get too heated or to overreact, the other would gently squeeze the hand as a warning. Over the years it often kept us from verbally "hammering" on the kids when a gentler approach was more appropriate. It did, however, make for some sore, bruised hands!

TRADE IN YOUR HAMMER FOR A VELVET GLOVE

Some people seem to think that a hammer is good for anything and everything. I guess you could say they take a hammering approach to life. I've observed this attitude most often among high achievers. When they give something their attention, they go at it full bore. That's usually a good approach to tasks. It's a terrible way to treat people, however. As psychologist Abraham Maslow observed, "If the only tool you have is a hammer, you tend to see every problem as a nail." People require more judicious treatment than that.

If you desire to develop a softer touch with people, take the following advice to heart:

Let the Past Stay in the Past

Two men were complaining about their wives. "When we quarrel," said the first man, "my wife becomes historical."

His friend replied, "Don't you mean hysterical?"

"No," the first responded, "I mean historical. She reminds me of everything I ever did wrong."

Resolve an issue when it occurs. And once you've done that, don't bring it up again. If you do, you're treating someone as a nail.

Ask Yourself, *Is My Reaction Part of the Problem?*

As I mentioned in the Pain Principle, when a person's response is greater than the issue, the response is about something else. Don't make things worse by overreacting.

Remember That Actions Are Remembered Long After Words Are Forgotten

If you have a high school diploma or college degree, can you recall the message the commencement speaker delivered at your graduation? Or if you're married, can you recite your wedding vows from memory? I'm guessing the answer to both questions is no. But I bet you do remember getting married and receiving your diploma. The way you *treat* people will stay with them a lot longer than the words you choose. Act accordingly.

Never Let the Situation Mean More Than the Relationship

I believe that if I hadn't made my relationship with Margaret a higher priority than always being right, we might not be married today. Relationships are based on bonding. The more important the relationship, the greater the bond. There will be more about this in the Situation Principle.

Treat Loved Ones with Unconditional Love

Because ours is a society with lots of broken and dysfunctional individuals, many people have never had good models of unconditional love. In *The Flight*, John Whit gave his perspective on where we fall short in our treatment of the important people in our lives: "We gossip because we fail to love. When we love people, we don't criticize them. If we love them, their failures hurt. We don't advertise the sins of people we love any more than we advertise our own."

Admit Wrongs and Ask Forgiveness

Chicago mobster Al Capone reportedly said, "You can get farther with a kind word and a gun than you can with a kind word alone." Despite the humor, I can tell you this: forgiveness is better. Admitting you're wrong and asking for forgiveness can cover a multitude of sins. That approach is also one of the best ways to try to make things right when you find that you've used the hammer instead of the velvet glove.

As you've read this chapter, a friend or colleague may have come to mind, and you may be thinking, *I know somebody who needs this.* Before you try to take the hammer out of his hand, stop for a moment. The first thing you ought to do is to look at yourself.

The problem with most individuals who use the hammer all the time is that they may not know that they do it. A recent article by executive coach Marshall Goldsmith told about a man named Mike who was a top-performing investment banker. Goldsmith was asked to help him because he was a hammer wielder. Mike saw himself as "a warrior on Wall Street but a pussycat at home." Goldsmith instructed Mike to call his wife to confirm his self-assessment, and much to his surprise, she said that he was a jerk at home too. When his children confirmed her assessment, Mike finally began to see himself as others did.

> "You can get farther with a kind word and a gun than you can with a kind word alone."
> —AL CAPONE

Goldsmith's advice is this: "Let your colleagues hold the mirror and tell you what they see. If you don't believe them, do the same with your loved ones and friends."[2] If you do that, you will find out whether you treat others as people or as nails. If you do the latter, then you need to make a change.

Hammer Principle Discussion Questions

1. In what situations are you most tempted to use the hammer instead of the velvet glove? Why is that? How can you anticipate when that is about to happen and change it?

2. Some people are naturally inclined to look at the total picture; others are prone to focus on details. Which are you? What can you do to improve your ability to see things in context and make you less likely to jump to conclusions?

3. Think of someone who is a master at using the velvet glove. What makes him or her so good with people? What can you learn from this individual?

4. How would you define *unconditional love*? What gets in the way of loving others unconditionally? How can one love others unconditionally and still maintain high personal and professional standards?

5. What happens inside you when another person admits wrongdoing and apologizes? How does that affect the relationship in the future? If it has such a positive effect, then why are we so reluctant to do it? How can we get over that reluctance?

THE ELEVATOR PRINCIPLE

WE CAN LIFT PEOPLE UP OR TAKE PEOPLE DOWN IN OUR RELATIONSHIPS

People can be the wind beneath our wings or the anchor on our boat.

THE QUESTION I MUST ASK MYSELF:
WOULD OTHERS SAY THAT I
LIFT THEM UP OR TAKE THEM DOWN?

In the 1920s, physician, consultant, and psychologist George W. Crane began teaching social psychology at Northwestern University in Chicago. Though he was new to teaching, he was an astute student of human nature, and he believed strongly in making the study of psychology practical to his students.

One of the first classes he taught contained evening students who were older than the average college student. The young men and women worked in the department stores, offices, and factories of Chicago by day and were trying to improve themselves by attending classes at night.

After class one evening a young woman named Lois, who had moved to Chicago from a small town in Wisconsin to take a civil service job, confided in Crane that she felt isolated and lonely. "I don't know anybody, except a few girls at the office," she lamented. "At night I go to my room and write letters home. The only thing that keeps me living from day to day is the hope of receiving a letter from my friends in Wisconsin."

A New Kind of Club

It was largely in response to Lois's problem that Crane came up with what he called the Compliment Club, which he announced to his class the following week. It was to be the first of several practical assignments he would give them that term.

"You are to use your psychology every day either at home or at work or on the streetcars and buses," Crane told them. "For the first month, your written assignment will be the *Compliment Club*. Every day you are to pay an honest compliment to each of three different persons.

You can increase that number if you wish, but to qualify for a class grade, you must have complimented at least three people every day for thirty days . . .

"Then, at the end of the thirty-day experiment, I want you to write a theme or paper on your experiences," he continued. "Include the changes you have noted in the people around you, as well as your own altered outlook on life."[1]

Some of Crane's students resisted this assignment. Some complained that they wouldn't know what to say. Others were afraid of being rejected. And a few thought it would be dishonest to compliment someone they didn't like. "Suppose you meet somebody you dislike?" one man asked. "Wouldn't it be insincere to praise your enemy?"

"No, it is not insincerity when you compliment your enemy," Crane responded, "for the compliment is an honest statement of praise for some objective trait or merit that deserves commendation. You will find that nobody is entirely devoid of merit or virtue . . . Your praise may buoy up the morale of lonely souls who are almost ready to give up the struggle to do good deeds. You never know when your casual compliment may catch a boy or girl, or man or woman, at the critical point when he would otherwise toss in the sponge."[2]

Crane's students discovered that their sincere compliments had a positive impact on the people around them. And the experience made an even greater impact on the students themselves. Lois blossomed into a real people person who lit up a room when she entered it. And another student, who was ready to quit her job as a legal secretary because of an especially difficult boss, began complimenting him, even though at first she did so through clenched teeth. Eventually not only did his surliness toward her change, but so did her exasperation with him. They wound up taking a genuine liking to each other and were married.

George Crane's Compliment Club probably sounds a little bit corny to us today. But the principles behind it are just as sound now as they were in the 1920s. The bottom line is that Crane was teaching what I call the Elevator Principle: we can lift people up or take people down in our relationships. He was trying to teach his students to be proactive.

Crane said, "The world is starving for appreciation. It is hungry for compliments. But somebody must start the ball rolling by speaking first and saying a nice thing to his companion."[3] He embraced the sentiment of Benjamin Franklin, who believed, "As we must account for every idle word—so we must for every idle silence."

What Kind of Person Are You?

For years psychologists have attempted to divide people into various categories. Sometimes an observant poet can do a better job. Ella Wheeler Wilcox did so in the poem "Which Are You?"

There are two kinds of people on earth today;
Just two kinds of people, no more, I say.

Not the sinner and saint, for it's well understood,
That the good are half-bad and the bad half-good.

Not the rich and the poor, for to rate a man's wealth,
You must first know the state of his conscience and health.

Not the humble and proud, for in life's little span,
Who puts on vain airs, is not counted a man.

Not the happy and sad, for the swift flying years
Bring each man his laughter and each man his tears.

No; the two kinds of people on earth I mean,
Are the people who lift, and the people who lean.

Wherever you go, you will find the earth's masses,
Are always divided in just these two classes.

And oddly enough, you will find too, I ween,
There's only one lifter to twenty who lean.

In which class are you? Are you easing the load,
Of overtaxed lifters, who toil down the road?
Or are you a leaner, who lets others share
Your portion of labor, and worry and care?[4]

These are good questions we must ask ourselves because our answers
will have a huge impact on our relationships. I think Wilcox was on the
right track. People do tend to add value to others, lessening their load
and lifting them up, or they take away value from others, thinking only
of themselves and taking people down in the process. But I would take
that one step farther. I believe the intensity with which we lift or lower
others can determine that there are really *four* kinds of people when it
comes to relationships:

1. Some People *Add* Something to Life—We Enjoy Them

Many people in this world desire to help others. These people are adders.
They make the lives of others more pleasant and enjoyable. They're the
lifters Wilcox wrote about. Evangelist D. L. Moody advised people to . . .

do all the good you can,
to all the people you can,
in all the ways you can,
as long as ever you can.

Moody was an adder.

People who add value to others almost always do so *intentionally*. I
say that because adding value to others requires a person to give of
himself, and that rarely occurs by accident. I have endeavored to become
an adder. I like people and I want to help them. I make it my goal to be
a friend.

Recently the CEO of a large corporation invited me to speak on
leadership for his organization. After teaching his executives and conducting sessions for his managers, I had gained enough credibility with
him that he wanted to do something nice for me.

"John, I like what you've done for us," he said as we sat one day in his office. "Now, what can I do for you?"

"Nothing," I replied. "You don't need to do anything for me." The corporation had, of course, paid me for the times I had spoken, and I had really enjoyed the experience. His people were sharp and eager to learn.

"Oh, come on," he said. "Everybody wants *something*. What do you want?"

"Look, doesn't everybody need an easy friend? Somebody who doesn't want anything?" I answered, looking him in the eye. "I just want to be an easy friend."

He chuckled and said, "Okay, you'll be my easy friend." And that's who I have endeavored to be. Author Frank Tyger says, "Friendship consists of a willing ear, an understanding heart and a helping hand." That's what I'm trying to give my friend.

> "Friendship consists of a willing ear, an understanding heart and a helping hand."
> —FRANK TYGER

Years ago, my nephew, Troy, came to live with our family after he finished college and went to work at a mortgage company. Troy was smart, he was a hard worker, and he wanted to be successful. And we wanted to help him. So I gave him some advice as we went off to his new job. I suggested that he do these things:

- *Go early and stay late—do more than is expected.* I advised him to arrive at work thirty minutes early, eat lunch in half the time allotted, and work thirty minutes after quitting time.

- *Do something every day to help the people around him.* I suggested that he add value to the team by adding value to his coworkers.

- *Offer to go the extra mile for the boss.* I told him to make an appointment with his boss and let him know that if he needed anything extra done—no matter how menial—he was available to help. And that meant after hours or on the weekend.

What I was doing was giving Troy a lesson in becoming an adder. And Troy added value to the people around him and to the company— so much so that he was promoted very quickly and was rising high in the organization before his thirtieth birthday.

2. Some People *Subtract* Something from Life— We Tolerate Them

In *Julius Caesar*, playwright William Shakespeare's Cassius asserts, "A friend should bear his friend's infirmities, / But Brutus makes mine greater than they are." That's what subtracters do. They do not bear our burdens, and they make heavier the ones we already have. The sad thing about subtracters is that what they do is usually unintentional. If you don't know how to add to others, then you probably subtract by default.

In relationships, receiving is easy. Giving is much more difficult. It's similar to the difference between building something and tearing it down. It takes a skilled craftsman much time and energy to build a beautiful chair. It takes no skill whatsoever to smash that chair in a matter of moments.

3. Some People *Multiply* Something in Life— We Value Them

Anyone who wants to can become an adder. It takes only a desire to lift people up and the intentionality to follow through. That is what George Crane was trying to teach his students. But to go to another level in relationships—to become a multiplier—one must be intentional, strategic, and skilled. The greater the talent and resources a person possesses, the greater his potential to become a multiplier.

I am fortunate. I have a lot of multipliers in my life, highly gifted people who want to see me succeed, people such as Todd Duncan, Rick Goad, and Tom Mullins. Each of these men has a servant's heart. They are tops in their fields. They value partnership. They're always generating great ideas. And they're passionate about making a difference. They help me to sharpen my vision and maximize my strengths.

You probably have people like that in your life, people who live to help you succeed and have the skills to help you along the way. If you can think of people who have played the role of multiplier in your life, stop and take some time to call or write them and let them know what they've meant in your life.

4. Some People *Divide* Something in Life— We Avoid Them

R. G. LeTourneau, inventor of numerous kinds of heavy earthmoving equipment, says that his company used to make a scraper that was known as Model G. One day a customer asked a salesman what the G stood for. The salesman, like many people in his profession, was quick on his feet, and he replied, "The G stands for gossip because like a talebearer, this machine moves a lot of dirt and moves it fast!"

Dividers are people who will really "take you to the basement," meaning they'll take you down as low as they can, as often as they can. They're like the company president who sent his personnel director a memo saying, "Search the organization for an alert, aggressive young man who could step into my shoes—and when you find him, fire him."

> A friend should bear his friend's infirmities, not make them greater than they are.

Dividers are so damaging because unlike subtracters, their negative actions are usually intentional. They are hurtful people who make themselves look or feel better by trying to make someone else do worse than they do. As a result, they damage relationships and create havoc in people's lives.

TAKE OTHERS TO A HIGHER LEVEL

I believe that deep down everyone—even the most negative person— wants to be a lifter. We all want to be a positive influence in the lives of others. And we can be. If you want to lift people up and add value to their lives, keep the following in mind:

Lifters Commit Themselves to Daily Encouragement

Roman philosopher Lucius Annaeus Seneca observed, "Wherever there is a human being, there is an opportunity for kindness." If you want to lift people up, take George Crane's advice. Encourage others and do it daily.

Lifters Know the Little Difference That Separates Hurting and Helping

The little things you do every day have a greater impact on others than you might think. A smile, rather than a frown, can make someone's day. A kind word instead of criticism lifts an individual's spirits rather than dragging him down.

You hold the power to make another person's life better or worse by the things you do today. Those closest to you—your spouse, children, or parents—are most affected by what you say and do. Use that power wisely.

Lifters Initiate the Positive in a Negative Environment

It's one thing to be positive in a positive or neutral environment. It's another to be an instrument of change in a negative environment. Yet that's what lifters try to do. Sometimes that requires a kind word, other times it takes a servant's action, and occasionally it calls for creativity.

American revolutionary Ben Franklin told in his autobiography about asking a favor to create a positive connection in a negative environment. In 1736, Franklin was being considered for a position as clerk of the general assembly. Only one person stood in the way of his nomination, a powerful man who did not like Franklin.

Franklin wrote, "Having heard that he had in his library a certain very scarce book, I wrote a note to him, expressing my desire of perusing that book and requesting he would do me the favor of lending it to me." The man was flattered and delighted by the request. He loaned Franklin the book, and the two became lifelong friends.

Lifters Understand Life Is Not a Dress Rehearsal

Here's a quote I've always loved: "I expect to pass through this world but once. Any good therefore that I can do, or any kindness that I can show to any fellow creature, let me do it now. Let me not defer or neglect it, for I shall not pass this way again."[5] People who lift others don't wait until tomorrow or some other "better" day to help people. They act now!

Everyone is capable of becoming a person who lifts up others. You don't have to be rich. You don't have to be a genius. You don't have to have it all together. You do have to care about people and initiate lifting activities. Don't let another day go by without lifting up the people in your life. Doing that will positively change the relationships you already have and open you up to many more.

ELEVATOR PRINCIPLE DISCUSSION QUESTIONS

1. Do people who don't intentionally work at adding value to others automatically become subtracters? Why? What is the main difference between adders and subtracters? Explain.

2. Why do people become dividers? Is unforgiveness ever an issue? (George Herbert says, "He who cannot forgive others breaks the bridge over which he must pass himself.") Is the choice to become a divider permanent? What actions at work or home have you engaged in that could be seen as divisive? How can you be sure to avoid such behavior in the future?

3. Do you agree that the small things a person does can easily lift or lower others? How do small things affect a child? Are parents responsible for lifting up their children or toughening them up? Explain. If you are a parent, do you find yourself more often encouraging your children or disciplining them? If change would be beneficial, what things might you do to improve?

4. How can a person lift or lower others without saying a word? How might a person's facial expressions either encourage or discourage others? How would you describe your natural facial expression? How would others describe it? How can you make it more open and encouraging?

5. What is the main difference between adders and multipliers? Can anyone become a multiplier? Explain. How often have you multiplied value in another person's life? What must you do to become a better multiplier?

Before moving on, let's review the People Principles that relate to the issue of readiness . . .

The Lens Principle: Who we are determines how we see others.

The Mirror Principle: The first person we must examine is ourselves.

The Pain Principle: Hurting people hurt people and are easily hurt by them.

The Hammer Principle: Never use a hammer to swat a fly off someone's head.

The Elevator Principle: We can lift people up or take people down in our relationships.

THE CONNECTION
QUESTION:
ARE WE WILLING
TO FOCUS ON OTHERS?

Strangers are what friends are made of.

—CULLEN HIGHTOWER

All human beings possess a desire to connect with other people. It doesn't matter how young or old, introverted or extroverted, rich or poor, learned or uneducated they happen to be. The need for connection is sometimes motivated by the desire for love, but it can just as easily be prompted by feelings of loneliness, the need for acceptance, the quest for fulfillment, or the desire to achieve in business.

How can we fulfill our desire for relationships? What is the best way to get started? In other words, how can we connect? The answer is that we must stop thinking about ourselves and begin focusing on the people with whom we desire to build relationships. That's why the

Connection Question asks, "Are we willing to focus on others?"

To increase your chances of connecting with another person, you need to understand and learn the following six People Principles:

The Big Picture Principle: The entire population of the world—with one minor exception—is composed of others.

The Exchange Principle: Instead of putting others in their place, we must put ourselves in their place.

The Learning Principle: Each person we meet has the potential to teach us something.

The Charisma Principle: People are interested in the person who is interested in them.

The Number 10 Principle: Believing the best in people usually brings the best out of people.

The Confrontation Principle: Caring for people should precede confronting people.

When you stop worrying so much about yourself and start looking at others and what they desire, you build a bridge to other people, and you become the kind of person others want to be around. These are the keys to connecting.

THE BIG PICTURE
PRINCIPLE

THE ENTIRE POPULATION
OF THE WORLD—
WITH ONE MINOR EXCEPTION—
IS COMPOSED OF OTHERS

A person first starts to live when he can live outside himself.

—ALBERT EINSTEIN

THE QUESTION I MUST ASK MYSELF:
DO I HAVE A HARD TIME
PUTTING OTHERS FIRST?

W hat does it take to change people's perspective and help them see the big picture for the first time in their lives? Sometimes it's getting married. Other times it's getting divorced. Or having a child. The bottom line is that people need to understand that everything is not about them.

READING BETWEEN THE LINES

I recently read an article about actress Angelina Jolie. The catalyst for her change in perspective was a script. Jolie, who won an Oscar in 1999 for her role in *Girl, Interrupted*, could have been the poster girl for a life adrift. The child of actors Jon Voight and Marcheline Bertrand, she had grown up in Hollywood and indulged in many of its excesses. She was called a "wild child." And she was well known for drug usage, outrageous behavior, and sometimes self-destructive actions. She was convinced she would die young.

"There was a time where I never had a sense of purpose, never felt useful as a person," says Jolie. "I think a lot of people have that feeling— wanting to kill yourself or take drugs or numb yourself out because you can't shut it off or you just feel bad and you don't know what it's from."[1]

Success in movies did little to help her. "I felt so off balance all the time," admits Jolie. "I remember one of the most upsetting times in my life was after I had attained success, financial stability and I was in love, and I thought, 'I have everything that they say you should have to be happy and I'm not happy.'"[2]

But then she read the script for *Beyond Borders*, the story of a woman living a life of privilege who discovers the plight of refugees and orphans around the world. Jolie recalls, "Something in me really wanted to understand what the film was about, these people in the world, all these displaced people and war and famine and refugees."[3] For a year she traveled around the world with UN workers. "I got my greatest life education and changed drastically," she observes. She visited camps in Sierra Leone, Tanzania, Côte d'Ivoire, Cambodia, Pakistan, Namibia, and Thailand. Her entire perspective changed. She realized that the entire world was made up of other people, many of whom were in dire circumstances, many of whom she could help.

When the United Nations High Commissioner for Refugees asked her to become a goodwill ambassador in 2001, she was happy to do it. She also began donating money to help refugees and orphans, including $3 million to the UN's refugee program. (She says she makes a "stupid amount of money" to act in movies.)[4] And she adopted a Cambodian orphan, Maddox. Recently *Worth* magazine listed her as one of the twenty-five most influential philanthropists in the world. She estimates that she gives almost a third of her income to charity.[5]

Jolie puts it all into perspective: "You could die tomorrow and you've done a few movies, won some awards—that doesn't mean anything. But if you've built schools or raised a child or done something to make things better for other people, then it just feels better. Life is better."[6] Why does she feel that way? Because she finally gets the big picture. She stopped focusing on herself and began putting other people ahead of herself.

FROM HERE EVERYTHING LOOKS DIFFERENT

When it comes to winning with people, everything begins with the ability to think about people other than ourselves. That is the most basic principle in building relationships. I know that may sound like common sense, yet not everyone gets the big picture or practices unselfishness. Instead, too many people act more like toddlers do. Their perspective may be best expressed by something that's been making the rounds via email:

If I like it, it's mine.

If I can take it away from you, it's mine.

If I had it a while ago, it's mine.

If I say it is mine, it's mine.

If it looks like mine, it's mine.

If I saw it first, it's mine.

If you're having fun with it, it's definitely mine.

If you lay it down, it's mine.

If it is broken, it's yours.[7]

People who remain self-centered and self-serving will always have a hard time getting along with others. To help them break that pattern of living, they need the big picture, which requires three things:

1. Perspective

People who lack perspective are like Lucy in the *Peanuts* comic strip by Charles Schulz. In one strip, while Lucy swings on the playground, Charlie Brown reads to her, "It says here that the world revolves around the sun once a year."

Lucy stops abruptly and responds, "The world revolves around the sun? Are you sure? I thought it revolved around me."

Of course, lack of perspective is usually much more subtle than that. I know it was for me. Early in my career as a pastor, as I led others, the question I continually asked myself was, *How can these people help* me? I wanted to use people to help me accomplish my goals. It took me a couple of years to realize that I had everything backward and should have been asking, *How can I help these people?* When I did, not only was I able to help others, but I was also helped. I learned what author and management expert William B. Given Jr. meant when he observed, "Whenever you are too selfishly looking out for your own interest, you have only one person working for you—yourself. When you help a dozen other people with their problems, you have a dozen people working with you."

Most of the time, what we worry about is small in the big scheme of things. Many years ago John McKay, former head football coach of USC, wanted to help his team recover after being humiliated 51–0 by Notre

Dame. McKay went into the locker room and saw a group of beaten, worn-out, and thoroughly depressed young football players who were not accustomed to losing. He stood up on a bench and said, "Men, let's keep this in perspective. There are 800 million Chinese people who don't even know this game was played."

The entire world—with one minor exception—is composed of others. And most of the people in the world don't know you and never will. Most of the ones you do know probably have greater needs and problems than you do. You can choose to ignore them and focus on yourself, or you can get over yourself and learn to put other people first.

2. Maturity

My granddaughters, Hannah and Maddie, are three years old as I write this. I just spent a wonderful Thanksgiving with them. It was a joy watching them play and doing things for them. But I have to say one thing about them. In all the time we were together, they never once asked, "What can I do for you, Papa?" That's okay for a three-year-old. It's not okay at age thirty!

We often expect maturity to come with age, but the truth is, sometimes age comes alone. An attitude that says, "Save time—see it my way," can be lifelong unless a person chooses to fight against it.

Several years ago, author and consultant Bob Buford wrote an excellent book titled *Halftime*. Its thesis is that as they approach middle age, many people reach a time of uneasiness that comes from wanting greater meaning in their lives. He defines that as *halftime*. He says that most people try to do in the second half of their lives what they did in the first half—only more so. Instead, the key to a successful halftime is to take stock, focus on your area of strength, and make giving to others your goal.

Here is how Bob describes the difference in attitude between people before and after halftime:

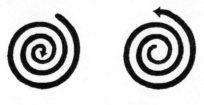

While the first-half self is small, the second-half self is large. The first-half self winds inward, wrapping tighter and tighter around itself. The second-half winds outward, unraveling itself from the paralysis of a tightly-wound spring.

The small self contains only you. It is basically alienated, alone, and pathologically individualistic. The larger self is whole because it is bonded with something transcendent. Self-transcendence has legs; it goes the distance and completes the race.[8]

Bob is describing real maturity. It is knowing that the world does not revolve around you. It is the ability to see the big picture.

3. Responsibility

You may have observed that marriage has a way of magnifying an irresponsible person's lack of responsibility. Unmarried people without children have much more freedom than people who are married or are parents. Anyone who goes into marriage expecting to maintain the same level of freedom he had when he was single is going to put his marriage at risk. To make a marriage work, both partners must be responsible. Marriage relationships mature when each partner stops asking, *What can my spouse do for* me? and starts taking the responsibility to ask, *What can I do for my spouse?*

Leadership puts similar demands on people. Accepting leadership responsibilities for the first time exposes an individual's level of maturity and sense of responsibility. Irresponsible leaders have a "me first" attitude and use their position for personal benefit. Responsible leaders have an "others first" attitude and use their position for serving people, taking responsibility, being an example, giving others credit, and mending relationships. Good leaders understand that for the team to succeed, they must put others first.

OPENING YOUR EYES TO THE BIG PICTURE

If you would like to improve your ability to see the big picture and put others first, then do the following:

Get out of Your "Own Little World"

When I was a kid growing up in Ohio, I didn't know much about the world. And that led me to have a rather narrow view of life when I was a young man. I remember thinking that anyone, regardless of circumstances, could get ahead through hard work. Then I took a trip to a developing country, and I saw people who worked much harder than I did but were unable to escape poverty. My thinking began to change as my world enlarged.

To change focus, people need to get out of their own little world. If you have a narrow view of people, go places you have never gone, meet the kind of people you do not know, and do things you have not done before. It will change your perspective, as it has done mine.

Check Your Ego at the Door

Have you ever spent much time talking to someone with a big ego? The good news is that such people never talk much about others. (Maybe that is because they're always "me-deep" in conversation!) The bad news is that if you don't want to hear about them, you're going to be bored very quickly.

An egotist can be described *not* as a person who thinks too much of himself, but as someone who thinks too little of other people. That's a good description.

We often mistakenly believe that the opposite of love is hate. But I believe that's incorrect. The opposite of loving others is being self-centered. If your focus is always on yourself, you'll never be able to build positive relationships.

> An egotist can be described not as a person who thinks too much of himself, but as someone who thinks too little of other people.

Understand What Brings Fulfillment

Ultimately the things that bring fulfillment involve others. A person who is entirely self-focused will always feel restless and hungry.

Antislavery reformer Henry Ward Beecher said, "No man is more cheated than the selfish man." That is true because he separates himself from what's most important in life: people.

If you want to live a fulfilling life, you need healthy relationships. And to build those kinds of relationships, you need to get over yourself. Embrace the Big Picture Principle and remind yourself that the entire population of the world—with one minor exception—is composed of others.

BIG PICTURE PRINCIPLE DISCUSSION QUESTIONS

1. At what phase of life do many people begin learning to think about others? What events often prompt people to start putting others first? What happens when a person tries to skip the life lessons that inspire other-mindedness? What happens to people whose focus, time, and energy are spent entirely on themselves, even in their later years?

2. What is the main difference between people with big egos and those with great confidence? Why is a big ego undesirable? Why is confidence desirable? Do you think ego and lack of confidence are related? Explain.

3. Describe your experiences with traveling. Which destinations have been similar to your own environment? Have you traveled to places with cultures very different from your own? Which specific destinations made you most uncomfortable? Why? Did you learn anything from traveling there? Where would you like to travel in the future? Why?

4. How would you define *fulfillment?* Can a person with no meaningful relationships be fulfilled? Explain your opinion. How does your opinion affect the effort you put into relationship building?

5. Think about the most important relationships in your life. Have you always displayed appropriate maturity and responsibility in them? If not, how can you work to make things right? What should you change about yourself so that your behavior is appropriate in the future?

THE EXCHANGE
PRINCIPLE

INSTEAD OF PUTTING
OTHERS IN THEIR PLACE,
WE MUST PUT OURSELVES
IN THEIR PLACE

*Sometimes when you give someone
a piece of your mind, you lose your own peace of mind.*

> THE QUESTION I MUST ASK MYSELF:
> DO I TRY TO SEE THINGS FROM
> OTHERS' POINTS OF VIEW?

Since 1996 I have been teaching leadership internationally to Christian leaders through a nonprofit organization I founded called EQUIP. It is one of my greatest joys, and I believe that its accomplishments will be a major part of my legacy. Everyone on the EQUIP team is working hard to achieve the goal of raising up and equipping one million leaders by 2008.

One place where my messages have been received well is the Philippines. When I first began teaching there, I was teaching leadership almost exclusively to Filipino pastors and other Christian leaders. However, my books and other materials started to spread beyond the Christian community into the business world. That didn't come as a big surprise because a similar thing had already happened in the United States and in several African countries. What surprised me was that the Philippine government became interested in my leadership teachings.

The country's secretary of the interior contacted me to say that the government wanted to send a copy of *The 21 Irrefutable Laws of Leadership* to every mayor in the Philippines. Then later he let me know that they also wanted to send a copy to every town council member in the country. It was very humbling to think that ideas I had put into writing might be shared with so many people of influence. I was glad to give my permission.

A VISIT WITH THE PRESIDENT

In January 2003, I was invited to meet with the president of the Philippines, Gloria Macapagal-Arroyo. It was a great honor. I found the president to be very sharp, very warm, and very intelligent. (She has a

Ph.D. in economics.) We talked about leadership, and to my surprise and delight, she pulled out a well-worn copy of *The 21 Irrefutable Laws of Leadership*. She told me she was using it to mentor her cabinet. For a while she asked me questions about leadership, and we discussed various points from the book. It was a totally enjoyable experience.

As our time came to a close, I decided to talk to her about something that had made an impression on me. In my travels around the world, I had observed that in developing countries, many leaders take advantage of their people. Those with power take advantage of the powerless. That trend is at its worst in countries with dictators, but it seems to happen everywhere at every level of leadership: the poorer the country, the greater the abuse.

I shared my observation with the president and said that I saw many leaders using their positions to add value to themselves instead of adding value to others. And I added, "You seem to be a leader who really wants to add value to others."

"Oh, yes," she answered, "my only agenda is to help the people of my country. I am considering serving only one term in office so that I can focus on service instead of politics." From what I have seen and read, she is adding value and serving well.

THE POWER OF PERSPECTIVE

Success can bring many things: power, privilege, fame, wealth. But no matter what else it brings, with success come options. How we use those options reveals our character. Wealthy people can use their resources to benefit others or only themselves. Famous people can use their notoriety to model good character or to selfishly serve themselves. Leaders can make decisions that affect others positively or negatively. It's up to them.

At the heart of the matter is whether people desire to use their power to put others in their place or to put themselves in others' place. I believe that President Macapagal-Arroyo tries to see things from the perspective of her people and acts accordingly.

Educator and agricultural chemist George Washington Carver made an incredible observation: "How far you go in life depends on your being tender with the young, compassionate with the aged, sympathetic with the striving and tolerant of the weak and strong. Because someday in life you will have been all of these." Our treatment of others results from our perspective of them. The problem is that seeing things from another person's point of view doesn't come naturally to everyone. Here's what I have discovered about the Exchange Principle:

We Naturally Do Not See Ourselves and Others from the Same Perspective

National Baseball Hall of Fame member Hank Greenberg worked as the general manager of the Cleveland Indians after his playing days were over with the Detroit Tigers. One off-season, contracts were sent out to all the players on the team for their signatures. Several weeks later Greenberg received an unsigned contract from one player. He sent a telegram to the player: "In your haste to accept the terms, you forgot to sign the contract." A telegram from the player arrived the next day. It read, "In your haste to give me a raise, you put in the wrong figures."

We do not look at ourselves and others in the same way. People naturally see themselves in the light of their intentions, but they measure others according to their actions. Or to put it the way poet Henry Wadsworth Longfellow did: "We judge ourselves by what we feel capable of doing, while others judge us by what we have already done."

We naturally try to see ourselves in the most positive light. And that's okay as long as we're being honest with ourselves. But we really ought to give others the same benefit of the doubt that we give ourselves.

When We Fail to See Things from the Perspective of Others, We Fail in Our Relationships

Much of the conflict we experience in relationships comes from our failure to see things from the other person's perspective, as the following joke illustrates. A man in a hot air balloon realized he was lost. He reduced altitude and spotted a woman below. He descended a bit more and shouted, "Excuse me, can you help me? I promised a friend I would meet him an hour ago, but I don't know where I am." The woman below replied, "You're in a hot air balloon hovering approximately 30 feet above the ground. You're between 40 and 41 degrees north latitude and between 59 and 60 degrees west longitude."

"You must be an engineer," said the balloonist.

"I am," replied the woman. "How did you know?"

"Well," answered the balloonist, "everything you told me is technically correct, but I've no idea what to make of your information, and the fact is, I'm still lost. Frankly, you've not been much help at all. If anything, you've delayed my trip."

The woman below responded, "You must be in management."

"I am," replied the balloonist, "but how did you know?"

"Well," said the woman, "you don't know where you are or where you're going. You have risen to where you are due to a large quantity of hot air. You made a promise, which you've no idea how to keep, and you expect people beneath you to solve your problems. The fact is, you are in exactly the same position you were in before we met, but now, somehow, you've managed to make it my fault."

How often have you found yourself in conflict with another person because you see things one way and he sees them another? Think about it. If you're married, don't you continually face potential conflict because of the way men and women naturally see things differently? If you have children, doesn't a lot of the friction occur because they don't see things the way you do? Even in a really positive working environment, people don't see everything eye to eye. (Just remember this: before you have an argument with your boss, take a good look at both sides—his side and the outside.) Seriously, though, I believe that if people made the effort to see things from others' points of view, 80 percent of our relational conflict would disappear.

Learning to See Things from Others' Perspectives Helps Us Succeed in Our Relationships

I read this saying in a sales journal: "If you would sell John Smith what John Smith buys, then you must see John Smith through John Smith's eyes." The concept is so simple that we think it's too obvious. Yet many people don't practice it. They're so busy putting others in their place that they don't make the effort to put themselves in someone else's place.

HOW TO MAKE THE EXCHANGE

How do you become better at making the exchange, at seeing things from another person's perspective? Start by doing these four things:

1. Leave "Your Place" and Visit "Their Place"

The best way to keep from stepping on other people's toes is to put yourself in their shoes. In the 1930s, American Airways, which later became American Airlines, had a tremendous problem with complaints from passengers about lost luggage. LaMotte Cohn, general manager of the airline at that time, tried to get his station managers to overcome this issue, but he saw little progress. Finally he came upon an idea to help the airline's personnel to see things from their customers' points of view. Cohn asked all of the station managers from across the country to fly to company headquarters for a meeting. Then he made sure that every manager's luggage was lost in transit. Afterward, the airline suddenly made a huge leap of efficiency in that area.

> The best way to keep from stepping on other people's toes is to put yourself in their shoes.

How do you put yourself in someone else's place? Master salesman Art Mortell offers insight on that:

> I love playing chess. Whenever I'm losing at chess, I consistently get up and stand behind my opponent and see the board from his side. Then I start to discover the stupid moves I've made because I can see it from his viewpoint. The salesperson's challenge is to see the world from the prospect's viewpoint.[1]

Do whatever you can to change your perspective. Listen to people's concerns. Study their culture or profession. Read in their areas of interest.

Or literally visit their place—their home, office, neighborhood, or region. You may be surprised by how it alters your thinking. You may find out, as President Harry Truman did, that "when we understand the other fellow's viewpoint . . . understand what he is trying to do . . . nine times out of ten he is trying to do right."

2. Acknowledge That the Other Person Has a Valid Viewpoint

People's belief systems and personal experiences are diverse and complex. And even if you do work to see things from another person's point of view, there will still be differences of opinion. That's all right. My viewpoint isn't right just because it's mine. If I work to find the legitimacy of another person's point of view, it will stretch my thinking. And as jurist Oliver Wendell Holmes said, "Once a mind has been stretched by a new idea, it never returns to its original shape."

3. Check Your Attitude

When it comes to seeing things from another person's point of view, attitude is huge. It is always easy to see both sides of an issue that you are not particularly concerned about. It becomes much harder when you have a vested interest in it. When that's the case, you are often more concerned with getting your way than making a way to connect with others. At the core of that is whether or not you are willing to change. When you don't want to change, you look for differences in others. When you are willing to change, you look for similarities.

4. Ask Others What They Would Do in Your Situation

The key to the Exchange Principle is empathy. And when you have empathy with others' points of view, it becomes much easier to connect with them. Why? Because they know that you care. Sometimes the easiest way to do that is to simply ask.

I read a hilarious story that shows what can happen when you don't do something as obvious as asking. Three sons left home to make their fortunes and did very well. One day, the three competitive brothers got back together to discuss the gifts that they were giving their elderly mother.

The first said, "I built a big house for Mother."

The second said, "I got her a Mercedes with a driver."

"I've got you both beat," said the third. "You know how Mom enjoys the Bible, and you know she can't see very well. I sent her a brown parrot that can recite the entire Bible. It took twenty monks in a monastery twelve years to teach him. I had to pledge to contribute $100,000 a year for ten years for them to train him, but it was worth it. Mom just has to name the chapter and verse, and the parrot will recite it."

Soon thereafter, their mother sent out her letters of thanks. To the first son, she wrote, "Milton, the house you built is so huge. I live in only one room, but I have to clean the whole house."

To the second son, she wrote, "Marty, I am too old to travel. I stay home all the time, so I never use the Mercedes. And the driver is so rude!"

To the third son, her message was softer: "Dearest Melvin, you were the only son to have the good sense to know what your mother likes. The chicken was delicious."

If you put yourself in the place of others instead of putting others in their place, it changes the way you see life, and it changes the way you live it. Author and speaker Dan Clark recalls that when he was a teenager, he and his father once stood in line to buy tickets for the circus. As they waited, they noticed the family immediately in front of them. The parents were holding hands, and they had eight children in tow, all well behaved and all probably under the age of twelve. Based on their clean but simple clothing, he suspected that they didn't have a lot of money. The kids jabbered about the exciting things they expected to see, and he could tell that the circus was going to be a new adventure for them.

As the couple approached the counter, the attendant asked how many tickets they wanted. The man proudly responded, "Please let me buy eight children's tickets and two adult tickets so I can take my family to the circus."

When the attendant quoted the price, the man's wife let go of his hand, and her head drooped. The man leaned a little closer and asked, "How much did you say?" The attendant again quoted the price. The man obviously didn't have enough money. He looked crushed.

Clark says that his father watched all of this, put his hand in his pocket, pulled out a twenty-dollar bill, and dropped it on the ground. His father then reached down, picked up the bill, tapped the man on the shoulder, and said, "Excuse me, sir, this fell out of your pocket."

The man knew exactly what was going on. He looked straight into Clark's father's eyes, took his hand, shook it, and with a tear streaming down his cheek, replied, "Thank you, thank you, sir. This really means a lot to me and my family."

Clark and his father went back to their car and drove home. They didn't have enough money to go to the circus that night, but it didn't matter. Because they had put themselves in the place of others, they had done something more important.

EXCHANGE PRINCIPLE DISCUSSION QUESTIONS

1. What kinds of positive things can happen to people's perspectives of others when they travel to foreign places and become exposed to other cultures? What kinds of changes might occur? How can preconceptions work against those positive changes?

2. What issues prevent people from wanting to "get outside themselves" and see things from another person's point of view? What obstacles do you face? What have you done in the past to overcome them? What might you do in the future to increase your ability to see things from others' points of view?

3. How would you describe your general attitude toward people? Do you automatically assume that others have a valid point of view, or do you always believe you are right? Explain. If you need to do better about giving people the benefit of the doubt, how will you work to improve?

4. What happens in relationships when someone puts others "in their place"? How can someone repair a relationship that has experienced that dynamic?

5. How good are you at focusing on others? How often do you ask people to share their perspective on an issue? How frequently do you ask others what they desire? Are you generally focused on your agenda, or is seeing things from others' perspectives a high priority in your life? Would those closest to you agree with your assessment?

THE LEARNING PRINCIPLE

EACH PERSON WE MEET HAS THE POTENTIAL TO TEACH US SOMETHING

There are some people that if they don't know, you can't tell them.

—LOUIS ARMSTRONG

THE QUESTION I MUST ASK MYSELF:
DO I APPROACH PEOPLE WITH
A DESIRE TO LEARN FROM THEM?

You would recognize him if you saw him. A well-known character actor, he has appeared in dozens of movies and on numerous television shows. He appeared as Guido the pimp in *Risky Business*. He was Tommy Lee Jones's sidekick in *The Fugitive*. He portrayed the traitor Cypher in *The Matrix*. And he played Ralphie on *The Sopranos*. To his friends, he's known as Joey Pants. His real name is Joe Pantoliano.

Joe was born and grew up in Hoboken, New Jersey. It was a tough area. He says his role models were the local wiseguys—the gangsters who worked with the Mafia. His parents moved a lot; both were gamblers and, as a result, not very good at paying their bills. When Joe was nine or ten, his mother was working as a bookie to earn money, and she used Joe as her runner. Joey Pants seemed to be destined for a life of crime

WISEGUY AT HOME

That fate was seemingly sealed when a distant cousin, Florio Isabella, got out of prison and moved into the Pantoliano household when Joe was thirteen. Florie, as he was called, was a career criminal. As a boy growing up in Little Italy in New York City, Florie delivered the heroin that his parents prepared in their one-room apartment. By age twelve, he was selling the narcotic. He had spent twenty-one years of his life in prison. Besides drug trafficking, he had committed armed robbery and other serious crimes, including hijacking the Hoboken Ferry.

Joe recalls, "He immediately violated his parole by getting back into the life [of crime] with some gangsters called the Paradise Brothers. I remember he made $50,000 in cash."[1] But after one of the Paradise Brothers was killed gangland style, Florie got to thinking. The fork in the road for Florie became a fork in the road for Joe, though he didn't recognize it at the time. Florie could have taken on Joe as his criminal protégé. That's the way many criminals get started. But the old gangster did something different. Joe remembers, "He always said, 'Every move I made was always the wrong one. And that ain't going to be you.' He was the only one who had faith in me and encouraged me to follow my heart."[2]

Joe's heart was set on acting. But when he summoned the courage to tell people about it, friends and family alike ridiculed him. "Who do you think you are," his mother told him, "you wanna be an actor? People like us don't become actors. People like us don't go to college. People like us don't get ahead. Don't shake the boat, Joey."[3]

But Florie—the most unlikely person in his life—taught him to be different from the rest of his family and the friends he grew up with. Florie got him connected to his first acting teacher. When Joe was ready to leave home and move to New York City, Florie not only encouraged him but also gave him money. He drove Joe to work the day he played in his first movie—as an extra in *The Valachi Papers*. Most important, Florie kept him away from the life of crime that could have brought Joe easy money the first seven years he struggled as an actor. "Had not Florio Isabella, my other father, my honorary stepfather and third cousin to my mother, stepped on to the scene in time," says Joe, "[my] return address would be Attica, New York," meaning the prison.[4]

"In the end," observes Joe, "I am left with the tragic fact that the one person in my life who made me feel I could be something did some very terrible things. Florie would, by some standards, be considered a horrible person, who may have tried to rectify his deeds through helping encourage my confidence and success with his unconditional love. He was the sweetest wiseguy I ever knew."[5]

WHAT'S YOUR ATTITUDE?

The truth is that all of us, like Joe Pantoliano, can learn things in unlikely places—and from unlikely people. Everybody has something to share, something to teach us. But that's true only if we have the right attitude.

What kind of attitude do you have when it comes to learning from others? All people fall into one of the categories described by the following statements:

No One Can Teach Me Anything—Arrogant Attitude

I think we sometimes assume that ignorance is the greatest enemy of teachability. However, that really has little to do with teachability. Haven't you known some highly educated and highly successful people who do not want to hear the suggestions or opinions of anyone else? Some people think they know it all! A person who creates a large, successful organization may think he can't learn from people who run a smaller one. A person who receives a doctorate can become unreceptive to instruction from anyone else because she is now considered an expert. Another person who is the most experienced in a company or department may not listen to the ideas of someone younger.

Such people don't realize how much they are hurting themselves. The reality is that no one is too old, too smart, or too successful to learn something new. The only thing that can come between a person and the ability to learn and improve is a bad attitude.

Someone Can Teach Me Everything—Naive Attitude

People who realize that they have room to grow often seek a mentor. That's usually a good thing. However, it's naive for individuals to think they can learn everything they need to know from just one person. People don't need *a* mentor—they need *many* mentors. I've learned so much from so many people. Les Stobbe taught me how to write. My brother Larry is my business mentor. I've learned a lot about communication from Andy Stanley. Tom Mullins models relationships for me. If I tried to include all the people who have taught me over the years, I'd fill page after page with names.

Everyone Can Teach Me Something—Teachable Attitude

The people who learn the most aren't necessarily the ones who spend time with the smartest people. They are the ones with a teachable attitude. Every person has something to share—a lesson learned, an observation, a life experience. We just need to be willing to listen. In fact, often people teach us things when they don't intend to do so. Ask any parents and you will find out that they learned things from their children—even when their kids were infants incapable of communicating a single word. The only time people can't teach us things is when we are unwilling to learn.

I'm not saying that every person you meet *will* teach you something. All I'm saying is that people have the potential to do so—if you'll let them.

HOW TO LEARN FROM OTHERS

If you have a teachable attitude—or you are willing to adopt one—you will be positioned well to learn from others. Then all you will need to do is to take the following five steps:

1. Make Learning Your Passion

Management expert Philip B. Crosby notes, "There is a theory of human behavior that says people subconsciously retard their own intellectual growth. They come to rely on cliches and habits. Once they reach the age of their own personal comfort with the world, they stop learning and their mind runs on idle for the rest of their days. They may progress organizationally, they may be ambitious and eager, and they may even work night and day. But they learn no more."[6]

That's sometimes the problem with people who received the *positions* they dreamed of or reached the *goals* they set for their organizations or earned the *degrees* they strived for. In their minds, they have reached their destinations. They get comfortable.

> "When the pupil is ready, the teacher will appear."
> —PLATO

If you desire to keep growing, you cannot sit back in a comfort zone. You need to make learning your goal. Do that and you will never run out of gas mentally, and your motivation will be strong. And don't worry about having people to teach you.

Greek philosopher Plato said, "When the pupil is ready, the teacher will appear."

2. Value People

In 1976, I had been in my career for seven years, and I felt successful. In those days, churches were often judged by the success of their Sunday school programs, and the church I led had the fastest-growing program in the state of Ohio. And by then my church had grown to be the largest in my denomination. But I still wanted to learn. That year I signed up to attend a conference. There were three speakers that I wanted to hear. They were older, more successful, and more experienced than I.

During the conference, one of the sessions was an idea exchange where anybody could talk. I figured it would be a waste of time, and I was going to skip it, but my curiosity got the best of me. It turned out to be a real eye-opener. Person after person shared what was working in his organization, and I sat there scribbling notes and jotting down ideas. It turned out that I learned more during that session than in all the others combined.

That surprised me, and later I realized why. Before that conference, I thought only older, more successful people could teach me anything. I had walked into that room placing very little value on the other people there. And that was a wrong attitude. People don't learn from people they don't value. I determined to change my thinking from that day forward.

3. Develop Relationships with Growth Potential

It's true that everyone has *something* to teach us, but that doesn't mean anyone can teach us *everything* we want to learn. We need to find people who are especially likely to help us grow—experts in our field, creative thinkers who will stretch us mentally, achievers who will inspire us to go to the next level. Learning is often the reward for spending time with remarkable people. Who they are and what they know rub off. As Donald Clifton and Paula Nelson, authors of *Soar with Your Strengths*, observe, "Relationships help us define who we are and what we become."

4. Identify People's Uniqueness and Strengths

Philosopher-poet Ralph Waldo Emerson remarked, "I have never met a man who was not my superior in some particular." People grow best in their areas of strength—and can learn the most from another person's area of strength. For that reason, you can't be indiscriminate in choosing the people you seek out to teach you.

In the mid-1970s, I identified the top ten church leaders in the nation, and I tried to get an appointment for lunch with each of them. I even offered them one hundred dollars for an hour of their time—that was a half week's pay back then. Some were willing to meet me. Others weren't. I was extremely grateful to the ones who did.

My wife and I didn't have much money then, and these leaders lived all over the country, so we planned our vacations for several years around these visits. Why would I go to such lengths to meet these people? Because I was dying to learn the unique skills and strengths they possessed. The meetings made a huge difference in my life. And do you know what? Connection with great men and women continues to affect my life. Every month I try to meet with someone I admire and from whom I want to learn.

5. Ask Questions

The first year I was in college, I took a part-time job at a locker plant in Circleville, Ohio. It was a place where cows were slaughtered and the meat was stored in giant refrigerated lockers. My job was to haul freshly processed meat to the refrigeration areas and to retrieve orders of meat for customers.

Anytime I'm exposed to something new—and this was a new area for me—I try to learn about it. And the best way to learn is to watch and ask questions. I had been working for about two weeks when Pense, an old guy who had worked there for years, pulled me aside and said, "Son, let me tell you something. You ask too many questions. I've been working here for a long time. I kill cows. That's all I do—and that's all I'm gonna do. The more you know, the more they expect you to do." I had a hard time understanding why anybody *wouldn't* want to learn and grow. But obviously he was committed not to change.

Writer Johann Wolfgang von Goethe believed that "one ought, every day at least, to hear a little song, read a good poem, see a fine picture, and, if it were possible, to speak a few reasonable words." I would add that one ought to also ask questions to learn something new each day. The person who asks the right questions learns the most.

Learning begins with listening. But it doesn't end there. Theology professor Hans Küng asserted, "Understanding someone properly involves learning from him, and learning from someone properly involves changing oneself." Change is always the goal of learning. You cannot have growth without change.

This chapter has focused on the importance of learning from others. But you never know who might be listening and learning from you. I found that out one day recently when Margaret answered the phone. She talked on the phone for a moment, looked at me with her hand over the mouthpiece, and asked, "Do you know a Dick Vermeil?"

I practically knocked her down trying to get to the phone.

Vermeil is a coaching legend. He started as a high school coach in 1959 and has coached football at every level. He's been named Coach of the Year on four levels: high school, junior college, NCAA Division I, and the NFL. In the 1990s, he came out of retirement to coach the St. Louis Rams, and in 1999, he won the Super Bowl with them. Was it really Dick Vermeil? And why in the world would he be calling me?

It really was Dick Vermeil. He was calling me because of something I had taught for Maximum Impact, the CD lesson that more than fifteen thousand subscribers

> Change is always
> the goal of learning.
> You cannot have growth
> without change.

receive from me every month. I had mentioned that when I read an excellent book and I take away a lot from it, I jot a note to the author to say thank you and let him or her know what the work meant to me. All teachers want to hear that their work is making a difference.

Vermeil was calling to let me know that he's been reading my books and receiving my CDs for six years. He listens to the lesson in his car to and from practice, and he sometimes shares the principles with his coaches and players. He just wanted to let me know.

It was a real privilege to chat with him. That kind of encouragement can energize a person for a month! But it also does something else: it proves the Learning Principle. If someone like Dick Vermeil—a guy who has won the Super Bowl—can learn something from me, then it's true that each person we meet has the potential to teach us something.

LEARNING PRINCIPLE DISCUSSION QUESTIONS

1. How open are most people to learning from others? What kind of attitude do most people possess? Do you think most people quickly prejudge whether they can learn something from another individual? If so, do you think it's done intentionally or unintentionally? Explain. What factors come into play (such as appearance, position, income, race, age, etc.) concerning whether a person has something to offer? What prejudices do you think *you* might possess? How can you change them?

2. Two kinds of learning are mentioned in the chapter: one has to do with being *open* to learning from anyone at any time; the other has to do with being *strategic* about how we learn and from whom. What kinds of benefits are you likely to receive from each? What are the greatest challenges you may face for each? Which one is more appealing to you personally?

3. What is your philosophy concerning learning and personal growth? Had you previously given it much thought? How would you say it differs from the ideas stated in the chapter? What new ideas can you easily adopt and make your own?

4. What kind of role have mentors played in your personal growth so far in your life? Describe a key person from your past who taught you something significant. Who currently helps you to grow? Have you sought out a single mentor to guide you, or do you try to connect with several people? Who in your current circle of acquaintances has expertise in an area that can help you? What can you do to enlist that help?

5. How are you when it comes to asking questions? When you meet people for the first time, do you ask questions to get to know them better? Do some of your questions prompt conversation that will teach you something? How about when you get ready to meet with a mentor or teacher: Do you prepare questions in advance to make the best use of the time?

THE CHARISMA
PRINCIPLE

PEOPLE ARE INTERESTED
IN THE PERSON WHO IS
INTERESTED IN THEM

You can make more friends in two months
by becoming interested in other people than you can
in two years by trying to get other people interested in you.

—DALE CARNEGIE

> THE QUESTION I MUST ASK MYSELF:
> DO I USUALLY FOCUS ON OTHERS AND
> THEIR INTERESTS OR ON MY OWN?

I n August 2003, Margaret and I were booked to go on a Seabourn cruise in the Mediterranean. When we arrived at the check-in area and were waiting to be helped, a woman who was just a little bit older than we are came up and introduced herself.

"Hi, I'm Phyllis," she said with a brilliant smile. "What are your names?" We introduced ourselves. "It's so nice to meet you," she said. "I'm looking forward to getting to know you better. I'll let you check in. See you tonight at dinner."

"What an engaging person," Margaret said as we checked in and found out where our stateroom was.

By the time we'd unpacked later that afternoon, I'd forgotten about Phyllis. But when we went down to dinner, there she was talking to people. When she saw us, she smiled and came over to say hello.

"John and Margaret," she said, "this is my husband, Stanley," and immediately she began to engage us in conversation. We ended up eating dinner together.

"What do you do?" she asked.

"I'm an author and conference speaker," I answered.

"That sounds so interesting. Tell me about it."

I told her about my background and some of my experiences as she asked questions. Then she engaged Margaret in conversation, and soon they were talking about art and antiques.

Over the next couple of days, I watched as Phyllis and Stanley introduced themselves to the 120 passengers on the ship and connected with them. I noticed the effort Phyllis put into making people feel good about themselves. She initiated conversation, and when someone wanted to talk about her, she quickly turned the conversation back to him.

Phyllis knew everybody's name and had something nice to say about each person. After a couple of days, people walked around the ship looking for her. She was the Pied Piper. Everybody fell in love with her. In one of our conversations, I found out from her that she and Stanley were retired, and they were spending their retirement time taking cruises and meeting people. They seemed to be having a wonderful time.

As the cruise wound down, I told Phyllis how much Margaret and I appreciated her and let her know we'd love to stay in touch with her. She reached into a pocket and pulled out a business card that read,

Phyllis and Stanley Hughes
Your Cruisin' Friends

and beneath it was the ship's logo along with the couple's home address and phone number. Since that cruise, Phyllis has written us and extended an invitation to visit her and Stanley in Florida.

Phyllis Hughes was as charismatic a person as I've ever met. She was a master at connecting with people. What was her secret? It's the same thing I was taught in 1963 when my father sent me to my first Dale Carnegie class: if you want to connect with others, focus on them, not on yourself.

SIX WAYS TO MAKE PEOPLE LIKE YOU (WITH THANKS TO DALE CARNEGIE)

Carnegie's teachings in the class and in *How to Win Friends and Influence People* made a profound impression on me as a teenager. They had such an impact that I've worked to pattern my people skills on much of what he taught. Here are the six things Carnegie suggested, along with my explanations:

1. Become Genuinely Interested in Other People

Someone once asked Perle Mesta, the greatest Washington hostess since Dolley Madison, the secret of her success in getting so many rich and famous people to attend her parties. "It's all in the greetings and good-byes," she claimed. As her guests arrived, she met them with, "At last you're here!" As each one departed, she expressed her regrets by saying, "I'm sorry you have to leave so soon!"

For nearly twenty years, I've used the following statement as a guideline and reminder for interacting with others: people don't care how much you know until they know how much you care. It doesn't matter how much power, education, or expertise you possess; people will respond to you more favorably if you first let them know that they matter to you as individuals.

2. Smile

Have you ever experienced one of those look-in-the-mirror realizations about yourself that changed the way you lived? I had one when I was in the third grade. It came when I was literally standing in front of the mirror one morning. I looked at my face, and for the first time I saw it as someone else might, and I thought, *John, you are not a handsome dude.* I wondered, *What can I do to change that?* Then I smiled. And I thought, *That helps!* I've been smiling ever since.

A smile is inviting. Charlie Wetzel, my writer, once worked educational trade shows where he sold classroom supplies to teachers. When he worked in the booth, he always made it a point to smile at everyone. Most of

> People don't care how much you know until they know how much you care.

the people walked down the aisles with their eyes focused on the various products each vendor had to offer. But Charlie says an interesting thing often happened. Many people walked down the aisle, but at the last second, when they were almost past the booth, they would look up at him for a moment. More than half of those people saw his smile, made a sudden U-turn, and came back to look at his products in the booth. It was almost as though a string was attached to them and drew them back.

Charlie is not unusually handsome, so looks weren't the reason for the sudden change. Nor were his products especially flashy or colorful. It was the smile. (He even experimented to verify this. When he made eye contact without smiling, people just kept walking.) If you want to draw others to you, light up your face with a smile.

3. Remember That a Person's Name Is to Him or Her the Sweetest and Most Important Sound

When I took that first Dale Carnegie course, the instructor's emphasis on learning names really made an impression on me. And from that day forward, it became a priority for me. Over the years, I've used all kinds of tricks to remember people's names. I'll find a distinguishing characteristic on a person's face and associate that with the name. I'll do a little trick with words to remind me of a name.

When I was the pastor of a large church, I even offered to memorize the names of people willing to have a Polaroid picture taken of themselves. At one point I had about five hundred photos to memorize. I used to punch a hole in the corner of them and keep them on big rings. I remember once on a plane I had pulled a couple of the rings out of my briefcase so that I could review them and work on the names.

A fellow sitting beside me asked, "What are you doing?"

"Looking at pictures of my family," I responded without missing a beat.

"That's a *big* family," he answered.

I kept flipping through the pictures and said, "Yeah, but just wait until we have grandchildren."

Of course, my efforts to remember names haven't always paid off. No matter how hard you try, you sometimes mess up. Once I was asked to speak at the national conference for Auntie Anne's Pretzels. For five minutes I praised the company's founder, telling the people what a wonderful leader she was, and I talked about the organization. I kept saying how great Aunt Annie's was. Then someone finally stopped me and sheepishly said, "Uh, John. It's 'Auntie Anne's,' not 'Aunt Annie's.'" I felt like a complete idiot. I'd had founders Anne and Jonas Beiler to my house for dinner, and I *still* messed up the name!

4. Be a Good Listener—Encourage Others to Talk About Themselves

Novelist George Eliot advised, "Try to care about something in this vast world besides the gratification of small selfish desires. Try to care for what is best in thought and action—something that is good apart from the accidents of your own lot. Look on other lives besides your own. See what their troubles are, and how they are borne."

How does one take that advice to heart? By listening! That was Phyllis Hughes's gift. She was one of the best listeners I've ever known. She reminded me a lot of my mother, Laura Maxwell. She is the best listener I've ever known. Not only has she always been there for me, but she's been a good listener for many people. Years ago when she was the librarian at Circleville Bible College, dozens of girls used to seek her out and confide in her because she cared about them and they knew she would always listen. Margaret says that ability made her a great mother-in-law.

Two great prime ministers in Great Britain's history are William Gladstone and Benjamin Disraeli. It's said that a young lady went to dinner with them on successive nights. When asked for her impressions of the two men, she said, "When I left the dining room after sitting next to Mr. Gladstone, I thought he was the cleverest man in England. But after sitting next to Mr. Disraeli, I thought I was the cleverest woman in England!"

5. Talk in Terms of the Other Person's Interests

A young married couple sat silently on a porch swing one warm June evening. The young wife looked over at her new husband and asked, "George, do you think my eyes are beautiful?"

"Yep," answered George. A minute went by.

"George, do you think my hair is attractive?"

Again George answered, "Yep." More time passed.

"George, would you say that I have a gorgeous figure?"

Once again George answered, "Yep."

"Oh, George," she gushed, "you say the nicest things."

Poor George loves his bride, but he hasn't learned how to talk to her yet. To win in relationships, a person needs to learn to talk in terms of the other person's interests. That's true when meeting somebody for the first time, and it's true when you're building a marriage.

One of the keys is what author Tony Allesandra calls the Platinum Rule. You probably know the Golden Rule: do unto others as you would have them do unto you. The Platinum Rule says, "Treat others the way *they* want to be treated." Do that, and you almost can't go wrong.

6. Make the Other Person Feel Important, and Do It Sincerely

The bottom line is that you need to make others feel important. Phyllis's charm wasn't a put-on. You could tell that she genuinely loved people. To her, everyone was important. And anyone can learn to value people and make them feel important.

> "Treat others the way they want to be treated."
> —TONY ALLESANDRA

Alan Zimmerman tells the story of Cavett Roberts, a successful lawyer, salesman, and founder of the National Speakers Association that I met and heard speak in the early 1970s. Zimmerman says,

> Roberts looked out his window one morning and saw a skinny twelve-year-old boy going door to door selling books. The boy was headed for his house. Roberts turned to his wife and said, "Just watch me teach this kid a lesson about selling. After all these years of writing books about communication, lecturing all over the country, I might as well share some of my wisdom with him. I don't want to hurt his feelings, but I'll get rid of him before he knows what's happened. I've used this technique for years, and it works every time. Then I'll go back and teach him how to deal with people like me."
>
> Mrs. Roberts watched as the twelve-year-old boy knocked on the door. Mr. Roberts opened the door and quickly explained that he was a very busy man. He had no interest in buying any books. But he said, "I'll give you one minute, but I have to leave then—have a plane to catch."
>
> The young salesman was not daunted by Roberts's brush-off. He simply stared at the tall, gray-haired, distinguished-looking man, a man that he knew was fairly well known and quite wealthy. The boy said, "Sir, could you be the famous Cavett Roberts?" To which Mr. Roberts replied, "Come on in, son."

Mr. Roberts bought several books from the youngster—books that he might never read. The boy had mastered the principle of making the other person feel important, and it worked. It's an approach that even the rich and famous or the big and strong can rarely resist.[1]

Authors Marcus Buckingham and Donald O. Clifton call this ability "Woo," which stands for winning over others. He believes that individuals who have "Woo" are drawn to people and "want to learn their names, ask them questions, and find some area of common interest so that [they] can strike up a conversation and build rapport."[2] In their view, "Woo" is a natural strength that you have or you don't. I believe that is true. But I also believe any person can develop people skills and learn to have charisma.

When talking about charisma, it all boils down to this: the person *without* charisma walks into a group and says, "Here I am." The person *with* charisma walks into a group and says, "There you are." Just about anybody can learn to do that.

FROM WOO TO YOU

Recently I bought Buckingham's and Clifton's book *Now, Discover Your Strengths*, and I took the Strengths Finder test. And I must confess that "Woo" was in my top five. I've always had the ability to win over others. But I didn't always have charisma, and I'll tell you why. As a young pastor just out of college, I made a mistake by trying to impress everybody. I played the expert, and I purposely taught over people's heads. I even wore glasses to try to look older and smarter. Today I'm embarrassed by how I behaved. But I learned my lesson. I didn't need to impress anybody. (It wasn't working or helping me anyway.) I just needed to let people know I cared about them and wanted to help them.

If you want to be the kind of person who makes others smile when they see you coming, get outside yourself, change your focus, and become interested in others. Doing these things will change your life.

CHARISMA PRINCIPLE DISCUSSION QUESTIONS

1. Why do people find it so difficult to become genuinely interested in others? Has that been a problem for you? Explain.

2. Can you think of someone you know personally who is charismatic and gifted at connecting with others? Describe that person. How does he or she make you feel? How much of that person's charm comes from natural talent and how much from learnable actions? What can you do to be more like that charismatic person?

3. How good are you at remembering people's names? Where does that skill fit on your priority list? What tricks, if any, have you used to help you?

4. Have you ever done "homework" to find out more about someone else's interests so that you could better connect with that person? Did you find the experience pleasurable or a chore? How did it ultimately affect the relationship? How can you quickly find out about another person's interests "on the fly" when it's impossible or inappropriate to do research? What kinds of questions should you ask? How can you use observation?

5. What can happen when one uses insincere flattery with another person to make him feel important? Do you find it difficult to make people feel important when you don't especially admire them? Explain. How can you find genuine ways to express appreciation in such situations? How can you work to change your attitude toward people you don't like?c

THE NUMBER 10 PRINCIPLE

BELIEVING THE BEST IN PEOPLE USUALLY BRINGS THE BEST OUT OF PEOPLE

Keep away from people who try to belittle your ambitions. Small people always do that, but the really great make you feel that you, too, can become great.

—MARK TWAIN

> THE QUESTION I MUST ASK MYSELF:
> DO I BELIEVE THE BEST OF OTHERS?

I n 1995, I saw the movie *Dangerous Minds*, an inspiring tale of a teacher who wanted to make a difference in the lives of her teenage students. I didn't know until recently that the story was based on a real person.

A FEW GOOD WOMEN

When LouAnne Johnson got out of high school, she discovered she didn't much care for college. She lasted forty-five days before dropping out and enlisting in the U.S. Navy. There she flourished. She served eight years, and along the way she earned a degree in psychology. Then she decided to join the U.S. Marines, completed officer candidate school, and served as a second lieutenant. But nine years into her military career, Johnson did some soul-searching and decided to leave the service. She wanted something more.

For a while she worked for the *New York Times* in sales, where she earned a good salary. But she didn't find it rewarding enough.

"I had been reading about kids graduating from school who couldn't read, couldn't write and didn't have the basic literacy skills," she recalled. "I thought it was criminal, if it was true." She moved to the West Coast, took a job as an executive assistant at Xerox, and returned to college to earn her master's degree. Her desire was to become a teacher. "I decided I would rather make $25,000 and do something that was really important."[1]

THE CLASS FROM HELL

When Johnson completed her degree, she took a position as an intern at Parkmont High School in Belmont, California, a town south of San

Francisco in San Mateo County. It was a lot like the class depicted in the movie.

"What they [administrators] didn't say was that this veteran teacher had been driven off by these kids," Johnson stated. "That first day they were just wild. They acted like I wasn't there." She came back the next day with great resolve. She continued, "I told them I was too young to retire and too mean to quit."[2]

She quickly developed strategies for connecting with the students. "I tried to use humor rather than threats," explained Johnson. "Sometimes I would get on my knees and say: 'Please don't make me beg. It's so unattractive.' You can't be a tough guy when you're smiling at the teacher."[3]

But more than anything else, her deep belief in her students won them over. A practice she developed for the first day of class—something she called her "card trick"—is typical of the kinds of things she did. She passed out index cards for students to supply name, address, phone number, and personal information. While they completed the cards, she walked the room with her roll sheet, glancing at their cards to see their names, which she secretly memorized.

As each teenager finished the information, she picked up each card and individually thanked each student. When she had all of the cards, she announced that the students were about to have their first test. The grumbling began, but she let them know that the test wasn't for them—it was for her. If she could name each student, she would win. If she missed even one name, every student would get an automatic A on the first test.

After she named every student (which she always succeeded in doing), many of the kids were impressed. And she told them, "I know your names because you are important people to me. When I look at you, I see you. I like you. And I care about you. That's why I'm here."[4]

Putting Her Money Where Her Mouth Is

Johnson's attitude wasn't restricted to parlor tricks, such as the one she did learning students' names. She lived it out every day. Once when a student named Raul was in debt for one hundred dollars to a street tough, Johnson lent him the money. But it was on one condition. Raul, who was a sophomore, could pay her back only on the day he graduated.

Raul's journal revealed the impact that Johnson's actions made on him:

> Last week, you told us to write in our journals about the nicest thing anybody ever did for us and I had to make something up because nobody never did nothing nice for me that I can remember before now. So I wrote you a lie . . . Anyway, what you did yesterday was the nicest thing and I think you did it because you think I am wonderful, honest, smart, and special! (That's what you always tell us anyway and I think you really believe it.) Anyway, I am going to work harder in school so I won't let you down because if you think I can make it then I can make it.[5]

Johnson believed in her students so much that they began to believe in themselves. Raul, whose father and mother had stopped going to school in third and second grades, hung in there and graduated. He was the first person in his family to earn a high school diploma.

"Our team held high expectations for our students," said Johnson, "too high, many people said. Don't ask for too much, they warned. Passing grades and graduation would be good enough. But we wanted more. We asked our students to come to school every single day, to stay away from drugs and alcohol, to change their bad habits, to complete every classroom and homework assignment, to resist the pressure to join gangs, to give up their bad attitudes and clean up their language. We asked for everything we could think of, and they gave us everything they had."[6]

"I think it's almost a political statement to be a teacher," Johnson explained. "What you're saying is that you believe in the children of this country and you're not giving up on them. It's almost like being a Peace Corps volunteer."[7] And that's why she wrote about her experience. "I wrote the book [My Posse Don't Do Homework] after working with at-risk teens because I was concerned about how easily adults give up on kids who have made mistakes. If we give up on them, they give up on themselves. BUT, if we believe they can overcome the challenges they face, they believe it, too."[8] In other words, Johnson is convinced that believing the best in people brings out the best in them.

YOU'RE A 10!

I embrace this principle with all of my heart. It's the reason I have taught people for more than thirty years. I am convinced that all people have potential. If people will only believe in themselves, they can reach their potential and become the individuals they were created to be. And here's how I think of it as I interact with people: I believe everyone I meet is a 10. That's why I call this the Number 10 Principle.

Back in 1983, I did a presentation at the Spokane Convention Center that has been broadcast often on Jim Dobson's *Focus on the Family* program. It probably best illustrates how I feel about people. It was called "Five Things I Know About People," and here is the essence of it:

1. Everybody Wants to Be Somebody

Author George M. Adams states, "There are high spots in all of our lives and most of them have come about through encouragement from someone else. I don't care how great, how famous or successful a man or woman may be, each hungers for applause." Don't you find that to be true? Everyone wants his life to matter. Everyone wants to feel significant. Don't you feel that way? Then you know it's true for everybody, even those who don't show it.

2. Nobody Cares How Much You Know Until He Knows How Much You Care

LouAnne Johnson worked with kids who had little interest in learning. The majority of students in their circumstances dropped out of school as soon as they could. She beat those odds by letting her students know that she cared about them—really cared. And once they understood that, they opened up to receive what she had to offer in the way of education. Too often we want to help people with what we know instead of caring for them because of who we are.

3. Everybody Needs Somebody

There isn't a person in the world who doesn't need other people. If we're honest, the issue often isn't *whether* we need others; the issue is, *How much* do we need others?

I recently received an e-mail from my friend Steve Babby. It told the story of a kid named Fred, who played on a summer basketball league team coached by Corky Calhoun, a former college player from the University of Pennsylvania. Fred's team had the best players in the league, and it was obvious that they were destined to win. But Corky could see that Fred had serious problems with his confidence and self-image. Corky challenged players to help Fred believe in himself. So every time Fred scored a basket, they praised him mightily.

By the end of the season, two things happened. The team won the championship, and Fred believed he was the best player on the team, which he had become. Fred wasn't the same after that, but he never could have done it on his own. It took the help and belief of other people.

4. Anybody That Helps Somebody Influences Lots of Bodies

When LouAnne Johnson won Raul's heart, she got the rest of his "posse" with him. Raul was a tiny kid—ninety-five pounds at age seventeen (a result of eating beans and rice nearly every meal of his life). Since grammar school, he had spent his time with three friends who always considered him to be the clown of the group. However, once he started studying hard, his role among his friends changed. At first, they resented it, but soon they started to see him as an example. Before long, all of them were studying and trying to improve themselves.

By helping Raul, Johnson had helped all four. And that's the way it often turns out. When you help one person, it overflows into the lives of others.

5. Somebody Today Will Rise Up and Become Somebody

When you believe in people—when you see each person as a 10—every day is a great day. Why? Because every morning brings a day in which someone's life can change. What a wonderful gift! LouAnne Johnson had no idea that her offer to lend a kid money would turn his life around when she got up that morning. But she looked at every day as an opportunity to make a difference. If you believe in people, each day can hold the same promise for you.

IT'S BETTER TO BELIEVE

Life holds that promise for me. I really believe in people and see the best in them. It is one of my greatest strengths. At times, it can also be a great weakness. I'm sometimes too trusting, and I desire to empower others before they're ready. Occasionally it gets me into trouble. But I'm willing to live with that risk because the rewards for others are so great.

If you currently are not someone who has a high belief in people, then think about this:

Our Disappointment in a Few People Should Not Stop Us from Believing in People

When I was a young leader, one of the first people I hired burned me. He didn't perform in the way he should have, and then he lied about it to cover his tracks. And I naively believed him. I came out of that interaction saying to myself, *I'll never let a staff member get close to me again*. But I couldn't sustain that mind-set. First of all, it was unfair to the other people I would lead in the future. Why should one person's failure affect how I treat another person? Second, I realized that if I kept people at a distance, they might not be able to hurt me, but they wouldn't be able to help me either.

If you've been hurt or disappointed in the past, please don't let that negatively color your attitude in the future. Most of the time, believing in people truly does bring out the best in people.

A Trusting Heart Is Emotionally Healthy

In his book *The Trusting Heart*, Dr. Redford Williams, director of the Behavioral Medicine Research Center at Duke University Medical Center, writes, "Those who have a trusting heart are more likely to remain healthy throughout most of their lives and to live long." He says that such a heart "believes in the basic goodness of humankind, that most people will be fair and kind in relationships with others." A soft heart is more likely to be a healthy one.

We Behave in Light of Our Beliefs

If you don't like people or don't believe in them, you won't be able to fake it. The students in LouAnne Johnson's class responded to her because they could tell her affection for them was real. It wasn't an act. It was action rooted in her belief in people. If you desire to add value to people, then you need to value them first.

A Healthy Marriage Is Built on High Expectations

If you are married, the most important person for you to believe in is your spouse. At a Living Leadership conference in 2003, Marcus Buckingham, senior vice president of the Gallup Organization and author of *Now, Discover Your Strengths*, said that the number one sign of a healthy marriage is that spouses see each other more positively than other people do. And anytime a partner esteems his or her spouse lower than outsiders do, it's a sign that there is trouble in the relationship.

My experience as a pastor counseling people bears this out. When I saw couples during premarital counseling, each person thought the other could do no wrong. And when I saw couples who were contemplating divorce, each person thought the other could do no right.

Each of us has to be realistic about his or her spouse. Nobody's perfect, and no person can make another person happy. But if you're married and you don't believe in your spouse and support him or her 100 percent, then get some help because your relationship could be headed for trouble.

Expressing Belief in People's Potential Encourages Them to Reach Their Potential

It's not enough just to believe in people, to think they are 10s. You need to express that belief. Philosopher-poet Johann Wolfgang von Goethe said, "Treat a man as he appears to be and you make him worse. But treat a man as if he already were what he potentially could be, and you make him what he should be."

One of the most skilled "believers in people" that I know is Dan Reiland, who used to work with me as an executive pastor and then later as a vice president of one of my companies. I've known Dan since he was an intern. When he first began his career, he believed in people, but I don't think he expressed it well. Now he has become a master at it. Not only does he do it every day, but every year since 1987, he's taken a handful of men with potential and personally mentored them. Time after time, he's seen people embrace their potential and blossom. That's something I believe each of us can do, at least to a modest degree, if we're willing to invest in people.

> "Treat a man as he appears to be and you make him worse. But treat a man as if he already were what he potentially could be, and you make him what he should be."
> —JOHANN WOLFGANG VON GOETHE

Think about the people who have made a difference in your life: the teacher who made you believe you could achieve; the boss who gave you a chance to show that you could do it; the counselor who let you know you had what it takes to change and have a better life; the man or woman who loved you enough to say, "I do." Not only were they *there* at pivotal times, in many cases they probably *created* those pivotal times in your life.

In almost every instance where the impact was positive, the person believed in you. He or she probably saw something in you that perhaps you didn't even see in yourself. Wouldn't you like to be that person to others? If the answer is yes, then try to love others and see them as 10s. If you have a family, start with your spouse and your kids. And then broaden the circle from there. Believe the best in others, and you will bring out their best.

NUMBER 10 PRINCIPLE DISCUSSION QUESTIONS

1. What characteristics does a person display who desires to go it alone in life? Name some things that may cause that attitude. Why is it often difficult to help someone who has that mind-set? If you have that mind-set, in what way does it make it difficult for you to help others?

2. In what ways—both positive and negative—does a person's desire to be "somebody" show itself? In general, has your desire for recognition or significance driven you in a positive or negative direction? How do you think that colors your reaction to others' desire for attention? Has it made you supportive or resentful?

3. Do you agree that having a trusting heart is emotionally healthy? Explain your answer.

4. Where do you find it easier to believe in people: at home or at work? Explain your answer. How do you desire to change? What positive steps could you take to change?

5. Name some ways a person can *express* belief in others. How would you rate your practice of expressing belief in others: poor, average, or excellent? Why? Would your family and colleagues agree with you? Which of the means of expression that were named could you adopt and use to better express yourself?

THE CONFRONTATION PRINCIPLE

CARING FOR PEOPLE
SHOULD PRECEDE
CONFRONTING PEOPLE

*Conflict is like cancer: early detection
increases the possibility of a healthy outcome.*

THE QUESTION I MUST ASK MYSELF:
DO I CARE ENOUGH TO
CONFRONT THE RIGHT WAY?

Years ago, when I arrived at Skyline Church in San Diego, California, to become its senior pastor, I was following the founding pastor, Orval Butcher. When I first learned that he was retiring and the position would soon be open, some people advised me not to consider taking it. In the church world, it can be very tough following a founding pastor, especially one like Pastor Butcher, who had served there for twenty-seven years and had done a wonderful job. Everybody loved Orval Butcher.

A QUESTION OF LOYALTY

Like many leaders or executives who come into an organization from the outside, I soon found that not everyone was immediately on board with the change. Fortunately, because the people were very gracious and Pastor Butcher had been a good leader, most accepted me. I quickly settled in and began building relationships.

One Sunday a few months after I had arrived there, I noticed that Sally Johnson was there without her husband, Joe. They had always been active in the church and were consistent in attendance. And it occurred to me that I hadn't seen Joe in a couple of weeks. So I asked Sally how he was doing.

"Well, to be honest," she said, "he's having a difficult time with the changes here at church, and he didn't want to come."

I immediately called Joe and asked if he was willing to meet with me.

A few days later, Joe sat down with me in my office, and I said, "Joe, how are you doing? Sally tells me you're having a hard time with the transition."

"I guess you could say that," answered Joe. "I just miss Pastor Butcher."

"Joe," I said, "would you do something for me?"

"What?" Joe asked a little suspiciously.

"Tell me what you love about Pastor Butcher."

Joe looked surprised by the request, but he was happy to comply.

"Well," Joe began, "Pastor Butcher was always there for us. He married every one of our kids. He buried my mom and my dad. He did my brother's funeral too." Joe went on to talk about how Orval Butcher had been at their side during the most important moments of their lives.

"It's no wonder that Pastor Butcher has such a special place in your heart," I said. Joe looked as though he was fighting back tears. "Joe, Pastor Butcher should always be your favorite. And let me tell you something. I'll never be offended if he is *always* number one. I give you my permission for him to always be your favorite pastor." Joe's eyes sparkled, and a weight seemed to have lifted from his shoulders. "And if you ever have any love left over, just throw a little bit my way."

Joe was back at church the next Sunday, and he was his old self again. Every now and then, he would sneak up on me and give me a great big hug, saying, "Pastor, I have a little love left over this month." He did that until the day he died.

THE TRUTH ABOUT CONFLICT

My interaction with Joe Johnson turned out well, but as you can imagine, not all of my conflicts have ended so positively. Like anyone else, I've had my share of confrontations that ended poorly. But most of the time they went well, and I'll tell you why. I went into them with the mind-set of caring about the other person and trying to help him.

I could have pushed Joe Johnson. I could have drawn a line in the sand and said, "You follow me or else." That's the way a lot of leaders handle it when they come into an organization. That's one reason there is often high turnover when a department or organization has a new leader. Or I could have simply given up on Joe. I could have said, "He was part of the old guard. He obviously doesn't care for me, so why bother?" Instead, I acknowledged him and validated his feelings. It wasn't about competition. It would have been foolish to think that I could replace Orval Butcher in his heart. And it would have been inappropriate to try. It would be like a new stepparent saying bad things about a child's biological parent and trying to steal the child's affection.

I believe that we instinctively know some things about relationships to be true:

Conflict Is Unavoidable

Perhaps we ought to add conflict to death and taxes as one of the things we can count on in this life. The only way to avoid conflict is to isolate ourselves from all other people on the planet. Although if you've seen the movie *Castaway* with Tom Hanks, where his character argues with a volleyball, you know that even people in isolation can find a way to create conflict.

Confrontation Is Difficult

In leadership conferences I used to teach an entire session on confrontation. It would often start with an informal poll to find out how many attendees were experiencing ongoing conflict with someone in their organization. Nearly everyone was. When asked how many of them had confronted that person, usually only about 5 percent raised their hands. Nobody likes confrontation, so everybody avoids it. (And those who do like it have their own psychological issues!)

> Perhaps we ought to add conflict to death and taxes as one of the things we can count on in this life.

Why is it difficult to confront? We fear being disliked, misunderstood, or rejected. We fear the unknown. We're not used to sharing our feelings. And we worry that we will just make things worse. Let's face it: few people have been taught healthy confrontation skills.

How We Handle Conflict Determines Our Success in Tough Situations

How do you handle conflict in your relationships? Did you know that conflict always compounds when confrontation is not done quickly and correctly? That's why your approach matters. Here's a sampling of harmful strategies that I see people using when they deal with conflict:

- *Win at all costs.* It's like a shootout at the OK Corral. It's quick, brutal, and destructive.

- *Pretend it doesn't exist.* If you hear no evil, see no evil, and speak no evil, evil will not cease to exist.

- *Whine about it.* Winners aren't whiners and whiners aren't winners. Playing the victim doesn't cure conflict. It just irritates everybody.

- *Keep score.* People who keep a record of wrongs can't ever start over fresh. And nobody can ever get "even."

- *Pull rank.* Using position never really resolves conflict. It merely postpones it.

- *White flag it.* Quitting is a permanent solution to a temporary problem.

None of these approaches will give the help a person needs to resolve conflict in a healthy way.

A ROAD MAP FOR HEALTHY CONFRONTATION

Conflict resolution isn't complicated. Intellectually it's simple. But emotionally it can be difficult. It requires honesty, humility, and dedication to the relationship. Here is a six-step plan to help you tackle the task of confrontation:

1. Confront a Person Only If You Care for That Person

In rare instances people must confront someone they don't care about, such as in legal trials or when abuse has occurred. But these are not typical relational conflicts. In nearly all relational situations, it is most productive to go into a confrontation keeping the other person's interests in mind.

In the past when you attempted to resolve conflict with another person, what has been your goal? Sympathy? Quick relief? Victory at all costs? Next time try to go into it with the goal of making it a win for both parties. And if you attempt to ensure that the other person wins first, then you know you have the most beneficial perspective.

Bo Schembechler, the former head football coach of the University of Michigan, said, "Deep down, your players must know you care about them. This is the most important thing. I could never get away with what I do if the players felt I didn't care. They know, in the long run, I'm in their corner." When you get ready to confront someone, he should have that same kind of sense from you.

2. Meet Together ASAP

Whenever conflict arises, we are tempted to avoid it, procrastinate dealing with it, or ask someone else to resolve it for us. But the truth is that anytime you let conflict go—for whatever reason—it only gets worse. If people are put in a position to start speculating about another person's motives or to figure out what might have really happened, they often think the worst. Putting off confrontation only causes the situation to fester.

Consultant Fred Smith, who was one of my mentors in leadership, spoke of his experience: "Whenever I am tempted not to act in a difficult personnel situation, I ask myself, *Am I holding back for my personal comfort or for the good of the organization?* If I am doing what makes me comfortable, I am embezzling. If doing what is good for the organization also happens to make me comfortable, that's wonderful. But if I am treating irresponsibility irresponsibly, I must remember that two wrongs do not make a right."

I have always taken that advice to heart. I tell my staff that if I ever experience a major problem that involves them, they will hear about it from me very quickly. I never "gunny sack" issues. It's never a good idea to save up a bunch of stuff and then give a person a history lesson during a confrontation. Instead meet together right away, face-to-face. If that's absolutely impossible, then consider a conversation by phone. But under no circumstances should you confront someone via e-mail.

3. First Seek Understanding, Not Necessarily Agreement

A significant hindrance to positive conflict resolution is having too many preconceived notions going into a confrontation. There's a saying that the person who gives an opinion before he understands is human, but the person who gives a judgment before he understands is a fool.

> The person who gives an opinion before he understands is human, but the person who gives a judgment before he understands is a fool.

President Abraham Lincoln was well known for his tremendous people skills. He remarked, "When I'm getting ready to reason with a man, I spend one-third of my time thinking about myself and what I am going to say—and two-thirds thinking about him and what he is going to say." That is a good rule of thumb. You cannot reach understanding if your focus is on yourself. As engineer Charles F. Kettering said, "There is a great difference between knowing and understanding; you can know a lot about something and not really understand it."

4. Outline the Issue

When it's your turn to speak and to make yourself understood, it's important that you take a positive approach. Here's what I suggest:

- *Describe your perceptions.* In the beginning, stay away from conclusions and/or statements about the other person's motives. Just tell what you think you see, and describe the problem you think it's causing.

- *Tell how this makes you feel.* If the other person's actions make you angry or frustrated or sad, express it clearly and without accusation.

- *Explain why this is important to you.* Many times when a person finds out that something is a priority to you, that is enough to make him want to change.

Engaging in this process without emotional heat or bitterness is essential. You don't have to turn off your emotions; you just need to make sure you don't verbally assault the person you're confronting.

5. Encourage a Response

Never confront others without letting them respond. If you care about people, you will want to listen. Besides, as politician Dean Rusk stated, "One of the best ways to persuade others is with your ears—by listening to them."

Sometimes simply having the discussion helps you to realize that your perceptions were wrong. I know that's happened to me. It's very humbling when I realize I am the problem. Other times you discover that you need to take extenuating circumstances into account. Encouraging a response helps you better understand the problem.

It also gives the other person a chance to process the issue emotionally. Most of the time when you confront people, they will have an emotional reaction. They may be shocked or get angry or feel guilty. They may want to share those feelings with you, or they may not. But no matter what, you should encourage them to give you a genuine response. Why? Because if they don't have their say, they won't be able to move toward a resolution to the problem. They will be so focused on their response that they can't hear anything else.

When confronting people, I've discovered the following:

50 percent of the time people don't realize there is a problem.

30 percent of them realized there was a problem, but didn't know how to solve it.

20 percent realized there was a problem, but didn't want to solve it.

The bad news is that one out of five people doesn't want to seek a positive resolution. The good news is that 80 percent of the time there is great potential to solve the conflict.

6. Agree to an Action Plan

Most people hate confrontation, but they love resolution. And the only way to achieve resolution is to take positive action. By developing and agreeing to an action plan, you place the focus on the future, not on the problems of the past. If the person you're confronting wants to change, he will gravitate toward the possibility of making things better.

A good action plan should include these points:

a) Clear identification of the issue

b) Agreement to solve the issue

c) Concrete steps that demonstrate the issue has been solved

d) An accountability structure, such as a time line and a responsible person

e) A deadline for completion

f) A commitment by both parties to put the issue in the past once resolved

If your confrontation is formal, such as in a work setting, then put the action plan in writing. Then you can always go back to that document if resolution doesn't go as planned.

Successful confrontation usually changes both people, not just one. Did you know that people begin to have similar opinions of one another over time? Some people call this the reciprocity rule. Positive change is the first measure of success when resolving conflict through confrontation. The second is the ongoing growth of the relationship. Any time you truly do resolve conflict in a

> Successful confrontation usually changes both people, not just one.

relationship, it doesn't hurt the relationship; it actually strengthens the bond between the people.

But it all starts with genuine concern for the other person. Abraham Lincoln summed it up when he said, "If you would win a man to your cause, first convince him that you are his sincere friend . . . Assume to dictate to his judgement, or to command his action, or to mark him as one to be shunned and despised, and he will retreat within himself . . . you shall no more be able to pierce him than to penetrate the hard shell of a tortoise with a rye straw."

CONFRONTATION PRINCIPLE DISCUSSION QUESTIONS

1. What happens when a confrontation doesn't go well? Have you been involved in a confrontation that went badly? Were you the confronter or the one being confronted? Explain what went wrong. What did it do to the relationship?

2. Would you say that most people have the other person's best interests at heart during a confrontation? What often motivates people to confront others? How about your motivations? Are they usually altruistic or self-defensive?

3. Consider the various ways people often react to potential conflict:

   Win at all costs.
   Walk away from it.
   Pretend it doesn't exist.
   Whine about it.
   Keep score.
   Pull rank.
   White flag it.

   In the past, which approach have you been most likely to take? Why? How would you like to handle conflict in the future? What steps must you take to improve in this area?

4. What happens when the person initiating the confrontation becomes overly emotional? How about when he doesn't? What can one do to remain emotionally even-tempered during a confrontation?

5. What often happens when no clear action plan has been created as part of a confrontation? Do you find it difficult to create such plans? What are some of the common roadblocks? What happens if the other person doesn't wish to participate? How do you come to resolution and closure in such cases?

Before moving on, let's review the People Principles related to the Connection Question . . .

The Big Picture Principle: The entire population of the world—with one minor exception—is composed of others.

The Exchange Principle: Instead of putting others in their place, we must put ourselves in their place.

The Learning Principle: Each person we meet has the potential to teach us something.

The Charisma Principle: People are interested in the person who is interested in them.

The Number 10 Principle: Believing the best in people usually brings the best out of people.

The Confrontation Principle: Caring for people should precede confronting people.

THE TRUST QUESTION:
CAN WE BUILD
MUTUAL TRUST?

The glory of friendship is not the outstretched hand,
not the kindly smile, nor the joy of companionship;
it is the spiritual inspiration that comes to one when
you discover that someone else believes in you
and is willing to trust you with a friendship.

—RALPH WALDO EMERSON

W hy do many relationships fall apart? Some marriages that begin with great passion come to a bitter end. Friendships that people hope will last for a lifetime falter and die. Business partnerships that began with promise come to a disastrous conclusion. The reasons for such breakdowns are many, but the cause that outweighs all others is broken trust.

How do you define trust? *Webster's New World Dictionary*, third edition, calls *trust* a "firm belief or confidence in the honesty, integrity, reliability, justice, etc. of another person." Kevin Myers says, "You may not know what trust is, but you know what it isn't." If people lie to you, steal from you, or physically harm you, then you know you can't trust them. That's obvious. But are there other ways that a person can break trust? Are there things people can do to make a relationship unworthy of trust? For that matter, what kind of person must *you* be in a relationship in order to be worthy of another person's trust?

These questions are at the heart of the next five chapters. And the People Principles contained in them will help you answer the question, Can we build mutual trust?

The Bedrock Principle: Trust is the foundation of any relationship.

The Situation Principle: Never let the situation mean more than the relationship.

The Bob Principle: When Bob has a problem with everyone, Bob is usually the problem.

The Approachability Principle: Being at ease with ourselves helps others be at ease with us.

The Foxhole Principle: When preparing for battle, dig a hole big enough for a friend.

THE BEDROCK PRINCIPLE

TRUST IS THE FOUNDATION OF ANY RELATIONSHIP

*It is a greater compliment
to be trusted than to be loved.*

—GEORGE MACDONALD

THE QUESTION I MUST ASK MYSELF:
AM I A TRUSTWORTHY PERSON?

He was a promising young journalist. He was energetic and hard-working. The principal of his high school remembered, "He was always into the newspaper business, even here. He had a wonderful, positive persistence about him that we all admired."[1] At the University of Maryland where he went to school, he was known as a productive and talented writer. That reputation won him a ten-week summer internship at the top newspaper in the country: the *New York Times*. There he was said to have done very well, having written nineteen articles and helped with many others.

That was in 1998. The next summer he returned to the *Times* for a job and was soon promoted to intermediate reporter. He did the kind of work an entry-level reporter is assigned, and he was successful, though he was warned about being too sloppy in his work. In January 2001, Jayson Blair became a full-time reporter.

Despite his progress, not everything was going smoothly with Blair. His editors continued to admonish him for sloppy work. Jonathan Landman, the paper's metropolitan editor, told Blair his correction rate was "extraordinarily high by the standards of the paper."[2] That didn't sit well with the editor. As he told his staff in an e-mail, "Accuracy is all we have. It's what we are and what we sell."[3] Because of Blair's talent and potential, editors checked up on him frequently and worked with him to help him improve his accuracy in reporting. Eventually he was transferred to the sports department.

Somehow along the way, he was rerouted from sports to the national desk and then sent to help report on the sniper case in Virginia. Reporting on national stories, he flourished and made a name for himself. He broke a huge story on the sniper case. He reported on the family of POW Jessica Lynch, who was taken prisoner in Iraq. And he wrote many other high-profile stories.

THE REST OF THE STORY

But then Jayson Blair got into trouble. Big trouble. Someone noticed that parts of a story he submitted from southern Texas about the mother of a slain American soldier were remarkably similar to a story by another reporter written several days before his. An editor from the *San Antonio Express-News*, who had published the original story, e-mailed the editors at the *Times* to alert them to the problem. That prompted the paper to look more closely at Blair's past work.

The *Times* staff found that one hundred of the more than six hundred articles Blair wrote for the *Times* had problems or needed significant corrections.[4] And nearly half of the articles he wrote for national reporting assignments had problems. But Blair was guilty of more than sloppy reporting. Former *New York Times* editor Howell Raines says an investigation revealed a "pathological pattern of misrepresentation, fabricating and deceiving."[5] Blair had lied to his bosses, pretending to go on assignment and then filing false "firsthand" stories. He had fabricated parts of stories using photos and other news sources. And he had plagiarized other reporters' work. He even filed false expense reports to try to cover his tracks.

When the story broke, its impact was huge. The credibility of the *New York Times* was at stake. 2Representatives at the *Times* called it a "huge black eye" and the "low point" in the paper's 152-year history.[6] *Times* writers commented, "Although the deceit of one *Times* reporter does not impugn the work of 375 others, experts and teachers of journalism say that The *Times* must repair the damage done to the public trust."[7]

Blair resigned in the wake of the revelations. His former bosses, colleagues, and friends no longer trusted him, and many expressed anger at him for his betrayal.[8] The reporter whose south Texas story he plagiarized—Macarena Hernandez, who ironically had served as a *New York Times* intern with Blair—says of him, "His story is that of a guy who disrespected his profession, cheated his readers, deceived his editors and stole from his peers. Period. Any other way of looking at it lets Jayson Blair off the hook."[9]

What was Blair doing all those times he was supposed to be on assignment? According to *New York Times* reporters, he was hiding out in his Brooklyn apartment, fabricating stories, and working on a book proposal on the sniper story. After the news of his deception broke, he changed tacks and wrote instead about his exploits at the *New York Times*. One writer who reviewed the resulting book, titled *Burning Down My Master's House*, called Blair a "world-class Pinocchio" and a "confessed serial liar."[10] The book's publisher evidently expected it to do well, having ordered a first printing of 250,000 copies. But *Time* magazine reported that after being available for nine days, it sold only 1,400 copies.[11] I guess that means nobody was buying what Jayson Blair had to say!

TRUST ME ON THIS

It is impossible to overestimate the importance of truth when it comes to trust. The article in the *New York Times* that outlined Blair's deceptions included the following statements: "Every newspaper, like every bank and every police department, trusts its employees to uphold central principles, and the inquiry found that Mr. Blair repeatedly violated the cardinal tenet of journalism, which is simply truth."[12]

If you boil relationships down to the most important element, it's always going to be trust—not leadership, value, partnership, or anything else. If you don't have trust, your relationship is in trouble. Here's why:

Trust Is the Foundation of Any Relationship

In *The 21 Irrefutable Laws of Leadership*, I wrote about the Law of Solid Ground: "Trust is the foundation of leadership."[13] In his book *On Becoming a Leader*, Warren Bennis says, "Integrity is the basis of trust, which is not so much an ingredient of leadership as it is a product. It is the one quality that cannot be acquired, but must be earned. It is given by coworkers and followers, and without it, the leader can't function."

That can be said not only of leaders and followers, but also of all relationships. Developing trust is like constructing a building. It takes time, and it must be done one piece at a time. As in construction, it's much quicker and easier to tear something down than it is to build it up. But if the foundation is strong, there is a good chance that what is built upon it will stand.

Trust Is the Frame of Any Relationship

A relationship can also be described as being like a painting. Trust is like the frame that surrounds it—and holds it together. It provides a context in which to view the work of art. Trust defines its boundaries. And trust secures it to the wall so that it can be enjoyed. Trust provides emotional structure.

> "Integrity is the basis of trust . . . It is the one quality that cannot be acquired, but must be earned. It is given by coworkers and followers, and without it, the leader can't function."
> —WARREN BENNIS

William M. Boast, author of *Masters of Change*, gives his perspective on how relationships are held together:

> Trust is . . . established when words and deeds are congruent. Trust also develops when people feel safe and secure. When thoughts and ideas are shot down and ridiculed, it doesn't take long to realize that the climate is neither safe nor conducive to making yourself vulnerable. Defensive climates can be diminished by providing descriptive rather than evaluative comments, expressing feelings of caring and involvement, and being willing to actively seek out, listen to, understand, and utilize other people's perspectives.[14]

If you want to enjoy the beauty of relationships, frame them with trust.

Trust Is the Height of Any Relationship

When two people trust each other completely, the relationship can grow to a level of friendship that is as rewarding as anything in life. It reaches the highest heights. Writer and chaplain to Queen Victoria, Charles Kingsley, said, "A blessed thing it is for any man or woman to have a friend, one human soul whom we can trust utterly, who knows the best and worst of us, and who loves us in spite of all our faults."

EARNING TRUST OF OTHERS

Psychologist and consultant Jack R. Gibb observed that "trust is the result of a risk successfully survived." What a wonderful description! When others trust us, they truly take a risk. But with each successive time people put their trust in us and we don't let them down, we reduce that risk and build the relationship. If you desire to build your trustworthiness—and as a result, your relationships—remember these three truths about trust:

1. Trust Begins with Yourself

Shakespeare wrote, "This above all: To thine own self be true, and it must follow, as the night the day, thou canst not then be false to any man." If you are not honest with yourself, you will not be capable of honesty with others. Self-deception is the enemy of relationships. It also undermines personal growth. If a person does not admit his shortcomings, he cannot improve them.

It all goes back to the Mirror Principle. The first person we must examine is ourselves. Take a good look at yourself. Are you honest with yourself about how you live your life? Is your character solid? Does your yes mean yes and your no mean no? Do you follow through with your commitments? Don't ask others to put their confidence in you if you believe you may betray it. Work on your character first, then your relationships.

2. Trust Cannot Be Compartmentalized

Cheryl Biehl, wife of friend and author Bobb Biehl, says, "One of the realities of life is that if you can't trust a person at all points, you can't truly trust him or her at any point." I believe that to be true. Unfortunately I think many people today try to compartmentalize their lives. They believe that they can cut corners or compromise their values in one area of life and it won't affect another area. But character doesn't work that way. And neither does trust.

In 2003, I wrote a book called *There's No Such Thing as "Business" Ethics*. The premise is that you can't have one set of ethics for your business life and another for your personal life. Character doesn't work that way. If someone asks you to help him in a lie, don't believe that he will avoid lying to you whenever it's convenient. What a person will do *with* you, he'll also do *to* you. An individual's character eventually bleeds into every aspect of his life.

3. Trust Works Like a Bank Account

Mike Abrashoff, author of *It's Your Ship*, states, "Trust is like a bank account—you have got to keep making deposits if you want it to grow. On occasion, things will go wrong, and you will have to make a withdrawal. Meanwhile, it is sitting in the bank earning interest."[15]

Mike learned that from his years as a naval officer. I learned the same thing as a pastor. For years at leadership conferences, I taught the idea of having "change" in your pocket relationally. When you first begin a relationship with someone, you start fresh with that person. If the person is trusting and generous, you may begin with a little bit of change. If he is suspicious or hurting, you probably begin with none. Each time you do something to build trust, you put relational change in your pocket. Each time you do something negative, you spend some of that change. Do enough negative things—due to lack of character or competence—and you're bankrupt. And that spells the end of that relationship.

This dynamic works in every area of your life. If you spend all of your change with your colleagues at work, they no longer willingly work with you. If you spend all of your change with your boss, you end up looking for another job. If you spend all of your change with your friends, you spend a lot of time alone. If you spend all of your change with your spouse, you end up in divorce court.

If this is a new concept to you, then you need to ask yourself some questions at the end of every day:

- *Am I making deposits?* Think about your most important relationships. Are you exhibiting trustworthy behavior that's putting relational "money in the bank"?

- *Am I making withdrawals?* Have you undermined trust in any of those important relationships? If so, you need to try to make things right. Don't wait another minute to take the appropriate action by doing the following:

  1. Apologize.

  2. Ask yourself why you broke trust.

  3. Correct the issue in your life.

  4. Recognize that it takes longer to restore trust than to lose it.

  5. Remember, trust is restored by deeds, not just words.

Doing these things won't *earn* you new change, but it may stop you from losing more. And you just might save the relationship.

- *Am I compounding my trust?* Mike Krzyzewski, head basketball coach at Duke University, offers this advice: "If you set up an atmosphere of communication and trust, it becomes a tradi-tion. Older team members will establish your credibility with newer ones. Even if they don't like everything about you, they'll still say, 'He's trustworthy, committed to us as a team.'" You can, as Mike Abrashoff says, develop so much trust that it actually builds without additional deposits. But it takes time and incredible consistency.

A FRIEND INDEED

In 1978, as I began to achieve some success as a speaker and consultant and reach a larger audience, my friend Tom Phillippe took me to lunch one day and said, "John, you're going to be successful. The higher you go, the more difficult it's going to be to discern the motives of others concerning your relationships. I just want you to know, I will be a trustworthy friend."

And he has been. When I stepped down from a position of national impact in the church world to once again become a local church pastor, Tom offered to take over the organization I started, and he kept it going for me until I was able to take it back. He has always given me wonderful advice, full of depth and wisdom. And he has been there as a friend during some of the toughest times my family has faced during the last twenty-five years.

The main reason for any success I have achieved has been due to people like Tom. And I'm blessed with many people of high caliber like him. I would trust any of the people in my inner circle with my life. They love me unconditionally, embrace my vision, embody my values, represent me well to others, look out for my best interests, speak the truth when I need to hear it, support me during the tough times, and defend me to my critics. I couldn't do the things I do without them— nor would I want to if I could.

WHAT IF YOU'RE RELUCTANT TO TRUST OTHERS?

I've given a lot of my attention in this chapter to the concept of *being* a trustworthy person. But I recognize that some trustworthy people have a difficult time trusting others. Perhaps people have broken trust with you. If so, attempt to take these three steps:

1. *Forgive them.* Because you are in the right, you have power over the other persons. Please don't abuse that power.

2. *Explain that the violation must* never *happen again.* Forgiving others doesn't mean allowing them to continue hurting you.

3. *Remember their better moments.* We all have our highs and lows. It takes maturity to treat people according to their best qualities.

There is great relief in forgiving others. If you desire to forgive and begin trusting again, then take to heart these words of Henry L. Simpson, former U.S. secretary of state: "The chief lesson I have learned in a long life is that the only way you can make a man trustworthy is by trusting him; and the surest way to make him untrustworthy is to distrust him and show your distrust." As I already mentioned, trusting others is a risk, but it's a risk worth taking. Without trust, you cannot build healthy, lasting relationships.

Take the plunge. I'm not saying you will never get hurt. You might. But I can say this: you'll never experience the joy that comes only from relationships unless you're willing to give trust a try.

BEDROCK PRINCIPLE DISCUSSION QUESTIONS

1. How does being reluctant to trust others affect someone's ability to connect? What can someone who doesn't easily trust others do to change that natural reluctance?

2. What happens to a relationship when one person exhibits untrustworthiness? Describe how relationships break down over time. Is a relationship ever beyond hope? If not, explain why. If so, describe how one would know. Is your answer the same for relationships in every area of life: with friends, colleagues, a spouse, children?

3. Think about someone with whom you have spent a lot of your relational change. Describe some things you did that damaged the relationship. What can you do to rebuild trust and "bank" some change? What is currently preventing you from doing these things?

4. Broken trust is not always a character issue. Sometimes it comes from lack of competence or lack of communication. Which issues erode trust most quickly? From which of these issues can a relationship recover more quickly? Explain.

5. What happens when someone's inner circle contains untrustworthy people? How does that affect his ability to achieve? How does that affect his character? How hard is it to change the kinds of people with whom one associates? What steps can one take to create a new inner circle?

THE SITUATION PRINCIPLE

NEVER LET THE SITUATION MEAN MORE THAN THE RELATIONSHIP

*It is more rewarding to resolve
a situation than to dissolve a relationship.*

THE QUESTION I MUST ASK MYSELF:
DO I SOMETIMES PUT SITUATIONS
AHEAD OF MY RELATIONSHIPS?

W hat would you do if you had the opportunity of a lifetime to fulfill your dreams, to rise up and take your place among the elite in your profession, to become a champion? And what if only one person stood between you and your goal? Would you make the best of the situation? Would you seize the moment? What if the one person in your way was your sister?

Sister Act

That's the situation Serena Williams faced. If you're a tennis fan, you know who I'm talking about. But even if you don't follow tennis, you have probably still heard of the Williams sisters or seen sports shoe commercials that feature them.

Venus and Serena Williams were tennis prodigies. Their father, Richard, says that when he saw the televised image of a women's tennis champion at the 1978 French Open receiving a large check, he decided that if he and his wife had any more children, they would become pro tennis players. Venus was born in 1980 and Serena in 1981. When Venus was four, Richard Williams began to teach her the game in a park in Compton, California. A year later Serena joined their sessions.

The girls showed promise early and dominated everywhere they played. In 1991, Venus was ranked number one among twelve-and-under girls in highly competitive Southern California, and Serena was ranked number one in the ten-and-under division. But instead of keeping them in junior tennis, which was considered the normal route to the pros, Richard pulled them out of it, moved the family to Florida, and enrolled the girls in a top tennis academy, where they trained for four years.

In 1994, Venus became eligible to turn pro, and Richard put her in her first competition. She won her first match, but lost her second to the number two–ranked woman in the world. When reporters asked Venus how the loss compared to previous defeats, the teenager explained that she didn't know—because she had never lost a match before! The next year Reebok signed Venus to a multimillion-dollar endorsement deal. By the end of 1997, she was ranked sixty-fourth in the world. Meanwhile, Serena was also making a name for herself. At age sixteen, she finished just outside the top one hundred.

Growing up, the girls had trained together, practiced together, and played together. And the older Venus always had the upper hand. But they had never played against each other in a professional tournament. Then in 1998, the inevitable happened. The two young women faced each other in the second round of the Australian Open. And as expected, Venus won.

"It wasn't fun eliminating my little sister, but I have to be tough," Venus said after defeating Serena. "After the match, I said, 'I'm sorry I had to take you out.' Since I'm older, I have the feeling I should win."[1]

The Williams sisters continued to live and train together. They played doubles together and won. And when they met in the finals of the Lipton Championships in March 1999, it was a big deal. It was the first time two sisters had competed against each other in a pro women's tennis title since the Watson sisters at Wimbledon in 1884. Venus said, "The way we were playing, it was inevitable we'd meet in the final. And it's inevitable we'll meet again."[2] And once again, Venus won.

QUEST FOR THE BEST

But that year Serena got a taste of major success when she won the U.S. Open—it was the first time either sister had won a Grand Slam event. She was ready to go to a new level. Serena said, "I'm tired of losing to people I should beat. Whatever my potential is, I want to reach it—now. And if I do, I see Venus as my biggest competition."[3]

Then in October 1999, less than a month after her eighteenth birthday, Serena finally did it. She defeated her sister for the first time, winning the Grand Slam Cup in Munich. She went on to defeat Venus many more times. In 2002, Serena became the number one–ranked player in the world, and in 2003, she signed the biggest endorsement contract ever for a female athlete: $40 million with Nike.

And what did all this competition do to their relationship? Did they develop bad blood and come to hate each other? The answer is no. Just as they had since they were kids, they remained best friends. They continued to room together on tour. And when Serena skipped the Australian Open in 2004, Venus talked about how much she missed Serena.

"Family comes first, no matter how many times we play each other," says Serena. "Nothing will come between me and my sister."[4] Not fame, not fortune, not professional rank. They don't let any situation mean more than their relationship.

DO YOU?

Venus and Serena didn't choose to be sisters. Most of us don't get to choose who's family. But we *do* choose how we *treat* our family. We choose whether we nurture or neglect our family relationships. And let's face it: every family has someone who stretches relationships. How we treat that person is still our choice.

Many people expect relationships to be smooth sailing. That's really very naive. Just think about the way wedding vows are written. Typically they read something like this:

> I take you to be my wedded wife, to have and to hold, from this day forward, for better or worse, for richer or poorer, in joy and sorrow, in sickness and in health, to love and to cherish, till death do us part, and hereto I pledge you my faithfulness.

Marriage vows assume that life is difficult and situations will occur that can cause separation: sorrow, poverty, sickness, and challenging times. The question is, When the tough times come, what will be more important to us: the situation or the relationship?

Take a moment to think about your relationships. Now look at the following lists and determine which words best describe them:

Volatile	or	Steady
Deceitful	or	Open
Selfish	or	Mature
Draining	or	Refreshing
Insecure	or	Secure
Manipulating	or	Accepting
Conditional	or	Unconditional
Breaking	or	Bonding

The column on the left describes interaction where the relationship fluctuates with the situation. The column on the right describes interaction where the relationship is rock solid regardless of the situation.

MAKE THE DECISION FIRST

In my book *Today Matters*, I assert that successful people make right decisions early and manage those decisions daily. That's true when it comes to values, priorities, finances, faith, health—and especially relationships. Keeping a relationship strong is a decision. One reason the divorce rate is so high is that many people go into marriage without a firm commitment on the front end of the relationship to never let some situation mean more than the relationship.

Having said that, let me clarify. There are some life-or-death situations where the relationship becomes secondary. When a partner is being abusive, the other person needs to be concerned for his or her safety. But abuse is not involved in most situations where there is a relational breakdown. When some people find themselves in a situation where the relationship requires hard work, they must make personal sacrifices, or they simply don't feel "happy" enough, they bail out.

Other people violate the Situation Principle in other ways. They may not abandon the relationship. Instead, they stay around and damage it. Once again, they pay more attention to the situation than to the relationship. I have been guilty of this. As a parent of teenagers, I sometimes let the situation become too important to me, and as a result, my insensitivity to my children puts a strain on our relationship. I also violated the Situation Principle in my marriage. I've already told you about how I won arguments but hurt my wife, Margaret, during our early years of marriage. I've also let circumstances cloud my judgment as a leader, and as a result, I've hurt my relationship with some of the people I led.

> Successful people make right decisions early and manage those decisions daily.

Anytime a person puts the situation ahead of the relationship, it happens for one reason: loss of perspective. That was true when I made mistakes with my family. It was the case as a leader. It will be the case for you if you violate the Situation Principle. People are always more important than mere things. Our property, our position or power, and our agenda are transitory.

How Can I Keep the Situation in Proper Perspective?

To keep your perspective and prevent you from allowing the situation to become more important than the relationship, you can ask yourself several questions. I suggest you start with these five:

1. Do I See the Big Picture—or Just the Bad Picture?

Whenever we experience a rough time in a relationship, we need to remind ourselves of why that relationship is significant to us in the first place. When a child comes home with a bad grade, when a spouse forgets to do something really important to us, or when a good friend lets us down, we may feel angry or disappointed. But what is that in the big scheme of things? What would you trade for your children? Your spouse? Your closest friends? Nothing is more important.

2. Do I Communicate the Big Picture Along with the Bad One?

When I was a kid, my parents were marvelous at communicating the big picture to me, even as I was creating a bad one that required correction and discipline. They might spank or punish me when I deserved it, but they always told me they loved me. And when I was old enough to understand, they often explained their reasons behind their actions. I didn't always appreciate it at the time, but I realized later in life that it made me very secure in my relationship with them. Thanks to their perspective, I never lost sight of the big picture, no matter how bad I had been.

3. Is This a One-Time Situation or an Oft-Repeated One?

There is a big difference between a situation that occurs once and one that occurs again and again. Both affect the relationship, and both require commitment. However, a recurring issue will need the commitment from all parties involved to sustain the relationship and ultimately change the situation.

For example, if one member of a married couple makes a one-time mistake that hurts them financially, it's relatively easy to overcome it and sustain the relationship. But if one person continually blows the budget and puts the couple into deeper and deeper debt, only with a commitment from both of them—to sustain the relationship and to change their actions—will their relationship survive.

4. Do I Make Too Many Situations a Life-or-Death Issue?

Dean Smith, the former head basketball coach at North Carolina, observed, "If you make every game a life-and-death proposition . . . you'll be dead a lot." In other words, we need to pick our battles.

If you are, or have been, the parent of teenagers, you know from experience that this is true. If you make every issue something worth fighting about, you'll be fighting your children so much that you will alienate them.

How do you know if you're making too many situations life-or-death issues? Answer these questions:

- How often are you tense and upset?
- How often do you raise your voice when talking to others?
- How frequently are you battling for your personal rights or for what's right?

If these issues occur day after day, your perspective may be off. Being in a constant state of agitation is not a healthy way to live, nor does it develop and maintain healthy relationships.

5. Do I Show My Unconditional Love During Difficult Situations?

My friend Tim Elmore told me the story of a girl named Deanna, a good high school student who usually earned high grades. As a college prep student, she enrolled in a chemistry class and worked hard. But for some reason, the subject just never clicked. And for the first time in her life, she failed a class.

Fortunately Deanna had an encouraging teacher. He believed in her and knew her poor performance was unusual. He was sure that she would succeed in college, but it bothered him to put an F on her report card. So what did he do? He couldn't in good conscience give her a passing grade. So in the margin next to the F, he wrote, "We cannot all be chemists— but, oh, how we would all love to be Deannas."

At some point, everyone faces difficult situations in close relationships. But not everyone handles those situations well. If you are able to communicate your love to those closest to you in the midst of pain or difficulty, you greatly increase the stability of the relationship.

No one in my life has been a better example of the Situation Principle than my mother, Laura Maxwell. She communicated unconditional love to me every day of my life, and I could talk to her, no matter what happened. When I was a kid, going through my orneriest phase, she would often say as I left for school, "John, I always want you to do what is right. But regardless of what you do, know that I still love you!"

I've always wished that I was more like my mother. Perhaps there is someone in your life you wish you were more like too. Make a decision to put your relationships ahead of the circumstances of life. If you do, you will develop deeper trust in your relationships, and they will go to a whole new level.

SITUATION PRINCIPLE DISCUSSION QUESTIONS

1. What pressures of life often cause people to place relationships as a lower priority than they should? How prone are you to allowing pressures to damage your relationships? What can you change to break unhealthy patterns?

2. Under what circumstance does a relationship legitimately become less important than the situation? What can happen if one does not reprioritize in such situations?

3. Have you ever known someone who made every little thing seem like a life-and-death situation? If so, what was the result? What was it like trying to develop a good relationship with him or her? Is it possible to sustain a healthy relationship with such a person? Explain.

4. Think about an important relationship in which you allowed a situation to sway you to act badly. What happened as a result? Have you been able to repair the relationship? Have you apologized? What could you do now to improve or restore that relationship?

5. Your relationships with your immediate family members are the most important ones in your life. What do those relationships mean to you? (If you've never expressed those ideas and feelings in writing, consider doing it now.) How can you use those thoughts to maintain the right perspective the next time you face a tough situation?

THE BOB PRINCIPLE

WHEN BOB HAS A PROBLEM WITH EVERYONE, BOB IS USUALLY THE PROBLEM

All seems infected that the infected spy,
As all looks yellow to the jaundiced eye.

—ALEXANDER POPE

THE QUESTION I MUST ASK MYSELF:
AM I BOB?

On June 23, 1988, Billy Martin was fired as manager of major-league baseball's New York Yankees. Baseball managers lose their jobs all the time, so that may not sound like news. What was different was that Martin was being fired from his job as Yankees manager for the *fifth* time!

New York, We Have a Problem

Have you ever known a person who had problems follow him wherever he went? That seemed to be the case with Billy Martin. When he got called up to the Yankees in 1950 as a second baseman, he was joining one of the best teams of all time. And Martin, only a .257 career hitter, held his own. He performed especially well during World Series games and was named the Series' MVP in 1953. While he was with the Yankees as a player (1950–57), the only year they did not win the pennant was 1954, the year Martin was in the army.

But despite his success, Martin's life was never smooth sailing. The problem was that he often seemed to have a hard time getting along with people. The reason he left the Yankees after seven seasons is that he was traded following a big fight in a nightclub involving other Yankees players. It wasn't his first fight, nor would it be his last.

After Martin left the Yankees, he played for six other teams in four years: the Athletics, Tigers, Indians, Reds, Braves, and Twins. He retired in 1961 and went on to coach. In 1969 he became a manager. But everywhere he went, trouble followed. He was legendary for the fistfights he started. The first one of note occurred in 1952, but there are too many of them to list. Tobias Seamon of *The Morning News* summarizes Martin this way:

> The fights and insobriety [from his playing days] continued into Martin's managerial career. In 1969 during his tenure as manager of the Minnesota Twins, he beat up his star pitcher Dave Boswell and was fired. In 1974 with the Texas Rangers, he popped the team's 64-year-old traveling secretary in a fight over a proposed club for the team's wives. Hired back as manager of the Yankees in 1977, he took the team to a world title, but was, at one point, seen battling with Reggie Jackson in the dugout during a nationally televised game, and was again relieved of his position. In 1979—again managing in Minnesota—he clobbered a marshmallow salesman.
>
> The early eighties were the usual for Martin. Hired, fired, and rehired again by the Yankees, Martin drank and brawled his way out of every job he ever had. His teams almost always won, but the price of living with Martin was too much. Yankee star Ron Guidry said of the manager, "If you approach Billy Martin right, he's okay. I avoid him altogether."[1]

Martin was continually ejected from games and often suspended for his treatment of umpires. And he didn't get along with the owners of the teams that employed him either. (He once demanded a five-year contract extension; instead he received a pink slip.) Pulitzer Prize-winning sports columnist Jim Murray said of Martin, "Some people have a chip on their shoulder. Billy has a whole lumberyard."[2]

HE LOOKS LIKE A BOB TO ME

Billy Martin is the perfect example of what I call the Bob Principle. It's a relational truth I discovered years ago: if Bob has problems with Bill, and Bob has problems with Fred, and Bob has problems with Sue, and Bob has problems with Jane, and Bob has problems with Sam, then Bob is usually the problem.

Billy Martin seemed to have problems with nearly everyone. He was involved in more fights than some professional boxers! Yet he never indicated that he saw a problem with how he conducted himself. Martin said, "I believe if God had ever managed, he would have been very aggressive, the way I manage."[3] And why did he think he was fired from so many teams? He explained, "I get fired because I'm not a yes-man. The world's full of yes-men."[4]

Not every Bob gets into fistfights the way Billy Martin did. (Nor does every Bob get fired five times from the same job!) Where someone who violates the Mirror Principle may be incapable of building good relationships, a Bob takes things to a whole new level. He doesn't just cause problems for himself. He causes problems for everybody with whom he comes in contact. So how do you know a Bob when you see him? Look for the following four characteristics:

1. Bob Is a Problem Carrier

The Bobs of the world carry around problems, and those problems affect others. I first became aware of this truth only a few years into my professional career. At a monthly board meeting, a board member would bring up an issue, saying that a member of the congregation was having a problem with something I was doing. Immediately three or four other board members would say that they had heard the same kinds of complaints. My first thought was to examine my actions. After reflecting, I still believed what I was doing was right, but if so many people had problems with it, I wondered if I needed to give it more consideration.

After this kind of thing happened several times, I made a decision. I talked to the board members, and we all agreed: if someone on the board heard a complaint, he needed to disclose who had made it.

The next time we met, one of the board members brought up a complaint he had heard. Several other board members confirmed that they had heard it too. When the first board member revealed the name of the person who complained, the others said, "That's the same person who complained to me."

I felt as if I were in the same situation as the old farmer who went to a restaurant owner to find out if he wanted to buy a million frog legs. When the proprietor asked where he could find so many frogs, the farmer replied, "I've got a pond at home just full of them. They drive me crazy night and day." After they made an agreement for several hundred frog legs, the farmer came back a week later with two scrawny sets of frog legs and a foolish look on his face. "I guess I was wrong," he stammered. "There were just two frogs in the pond, but they sure were making a lot of noise!"

That night I learned something. Not only did I find out that we had one very vocal person, but I discovered that problem carriers spread their poison far and wide. And guess what? The next several times a negative comment came up at a meeting, we discovered it was the same complainer again. If you're a leader and someone tells you there are "lots of complaints," then find out the source. It may turn out to be one person doing lots of complaining.

2. Bob Is a Problem Finder

Bob also likes to find problems and expose them to others. He subscribes to Chisholm's Second Law, which says, "Any time things appear to be going better, you have overlooked something."

Because some people have this tendency, I developed a rule for staff members. Anyone who brings me a problem must also bring three possible solutions to solve it. It doesn't take great talent to see a problem. In fact, if you look hard enough, people can find a problem in every situation. It takes greater talent to solve problems. Most Bobs have no interest in doing that.

3. Bob Is a Problem Creator

Bob always creates problems, and he usually involves others in what he's doing. He's like the guy in the corny joke who brags to some friends, "'Yes, there is a proud fighting tradition in my family! My great-great-grandfather stood his ground at Bunker Hill. My great-grandfather valiantly joined up with the troops to destroy the Germans. My grand-

father was at Pearl Harbor. And my father fought the North Koreans.'
'Mercy!' one of his friends remarked. 'Can't your family get along with
anyone?'"

I teach people in my organizations that
they have two choices every time they
encounter Bob or anyone else creating a
problem. Every problem starter is like a
fire lighter. And each of us is like a person
carrying two buckets. One is filled with

> "Any time things appear
> to be going better, you have
> overlooked something."
> —CHISHOLM'S SECOND LAW

water and the other with gasoline. When we see the spark of a problem
fire being lit, we can choose to douse it with water and put it out. Or we
can throw gasoline on it and make it worse. If we want to control the
amount of damage Bob can do, we need to use the water.

4. Bob Is a Problem Receiver

Bob is usually a recipient of problems from others, and he encourages
people to bring him more. And of course, sometimes the person is a
Bobbie instead of a Bob. I know of a woman in an organization years ago;
I'll call her "Betty." After putting out a bunch of fires, her supervisor
found that every issue somehow or another was connected to Betty. He
called her into his office to have a talk. He recounted what he had
found, she admitted her part in it, and they talked about it.

"People just bring me their problems all the time," she said. "I don't
ask for them; they just do it."

"Do you want to know why?" he asked.

"Why, yes," Betty answered, "I would."

"People see you as a garbage dump," he answered. "Garbage trucks
take their loads of trash to a place that accepts garbage. And people
with problems take their gripes, gossip, and grumbling to someone
who'll accept it. Because you allow people to dump on you and make no
effort to stop them, they keep dumping. And they won't stop until you
let them know they're not welcome." I'm sorry to say that I heard Betty
didn't change. She continued to let people back up to her desk and
dump their emotional garbage in her lap.

What About Bob?

So what do you do if you have a Bob or Bobbie in your life, someone who finds, creates, and spread problems? Consider these suggestions:

Respond with a Positive Comment

When a negative person tries to drop a problem in your lap, respond with something positive. If the comment is about a situation, try to find the bright side. If it's about a person, point out a positive trait you've observed.

Show Your Concern for Someone Being Criticized

Anytime a person's motives are being critiqued, the best thing is to give him the benefit of the doubt. No one should presume to know the heart of another person. That's something only God can judge. Believe the best in others (and express that belief) unless the individuals prove otherwise to you personally.

Encourage Steps Toward Resolution

Anytime someone brings you a problem he has with another person—and he hasn't personally addressed the problem with the other person—he's really engaging in gossip. And if you listen, you are too.

The best way to deal with gossip is to direct the complainer to talk to the person with whom he has an issue. Encourage him to meet one-on-one and work things out. And if he brings up the issue again, ask him point-blank: "Have you addressed this with him yet?" If the answer is no, refuse to discuss it.

Ask Bob to THINK Before Speaking

Not everyone will respond positively to your suggestions. But if you have a strong connection with Bob or you are in a position of authority with him, then ask him to THINK before he speaks using this acronym:

T   Is it true?

H   Is it helpful?

I   Is it inspiring?

N   Is it necessary?

K   Is it kind?

If he can answer yes to all of these questions, then it's appropriate for him to proceed.

Keep Bob Away from Others

Former major-league baseball manager Casey Stengel had some great advice concerning how to deal with problem people. He said that on most teams, a manager will have fifteen players who will run through a wall for him, five who hate him, and five who are undecided. He believed the trick was to keep the five who hate him away from the five who are undecided.

If you supervise one or more Bobs—and you can't or won't remove them from your team—then do damage control by isolating them. Don't let their negativism spread.

WHAT IF YOU'RE BOB?

I've said a lot about what to do if you have a Bob in your life, but what if *you* are Bob? If you're not sure, ask yourself these questions:

- *Do I experience some kind of conflict almost every day?*

- *Do people often rub me the wrong way?*

- *Do bad things just naturally happen to me?*

- *Do I have few friends and wish I had more?*

- *Do I always seem to say the wrong thing?*

If you answered yes to several of these questions, then you might be Bob (or Bobbie). If that's true, remember the first rule of holes. When you're in one, stop digging.

The first thing you have to do is to admit you're Bob. The second is that you must *want* to change your lifestyle. You can't be like Mrs. Mohler, who was being tried for the murder of her third husband. A lawyer asked, "What happened to your first husband?"

"He died of mushroom poisoning," said Mrs. Mohler.

"How about your second husband?" asked the lawyer.

"He died of mushroom poisoning too," said Mrs. Mohler.

"Well, then," asked the lawyer, "what about your third husband?"

Mrs. Mohler replied, "He died of a brain concussion."

The lawyer asked, "How did that happen?"

Mrs. Mohler replied, "He wouldn't eat the mushrooms."

Changing won't necessarily be easy. And there are no quick fixes. Neil Anderson, author of *Victory Over the Darkness*, says,

> Studies have shown that, in the average home, for every positive statement, a child receives 10 negative statements. The school environment is only slightly better; students hear seven negative statements from their teachers for every one positive statement. No wonder so many children are growing up feeling that they are losers. Parents and teachers are conveying that perception every day in how they talk to their children. These studies go on to point out that it takes four positive statements to negate the effect of one negative statement.[6]

Begin by following the guidelines I've already given. Use the THINK questions before you speak. Try to see the positive in every situation. And ask people to hold you accountable for your attitude and actions. No one has to be a Bob forever.

BOB PRINCIPLE DISCUSSION QUESTIONS

1. Why is gossip so appealing to many people? How can you tell when something you are being told is gossip? What can you do to kindly stop someone from gossiping to you?

2. Think about the last time you were confronted by a people-related problem. How did you respond to it? Did the problem end there, or did it continue to smolder? Would you say that your response put water or gasoline on the "fire"? Why? How could you have responded better?

3. Is every person who brings you a problem without offering solutions automatically a Bob or Bobbie? How often is this problem an attitude? How often is it training related? When you've adequately trained people to seek solutions and an individual insists on pointing out problems without offering solutions, what should you do? What will happen if you ignore the behavior?

4. In the past, how have you handled it when a friend or colleague has come to you saying that someone else has a problem with something you have done? Was the outcome positive or negative? What happened to the relationships? How would you handle it in the future?

5. Do you find it difficult or easy to give people the benefit of the doubt, assuming their motives to be good? Why? Which is worse: accusing a good person of bad motives, or assuming a bad person has good motives? How does your attitude in this area affect your relationships? How will you conduct yourself in the future, and why?

THE APPROACHABILITY PRINCIPLE

BEING AT EASE WITH OURSELVES HELPS OTHERS BE AT EASE WITH US

We can give no greater gift to others than putting them at ease.

> THE QUESTION I MUST ASK MYSELF:
> WOULD MY FRIENDS SAY THAT I AM EASY
> TO APPROACH ABOUT DIFFICULT ISSUES?

Have you ever met anyone famous? What was it like? Was it exciting, or did it turn out to be surprisingly ordinary? Were you disappointed, or was it even better than you expected? Did you connect with the person, or were you treated like a nuisance? Or were you so intimidated that you were unable to even try to talk to the person? The quality of any first-time meeting experience—whether or not people are famous—depends largely on their approachability.

We've all met people who seemed cold and forbidding. And we've all met people who treat us like old friends from day one. This isn't an issue with just high-profile people. How approachable are the most important people in your life? When you need to ask your boss a question, is it easy or difficult? When you need to talk to your spouse about a difficult subject, do you expect a dialogue or a fight? Can you bring up a touchy issue with your closest friend without worrying about being blown out of the water?

For that matter, what about you? Can the people closest to you talk to you about nearly anything? When was the last time someone brought you bad news? Or strongly disagreed with your point of view on an issue? Or confronted you concerning something you did wrong? If it has been a while, you may not be a very approachable person.

Some people treat the idea of becoming approachable as frivolous; it's a nice thing if one can be bothered to cultivate it. But truly it's much more than that. It is a powerful asset to have in one's relational toolbox. Here's the story of someone who's made that quality a $12 million-a-year asset!

WHO COULDN'T TALK TO HER?

Oprah Winfrey calls this person her idol and mentor. For decades she was the highest-paid news personality on television, making more than Peter Jennings, Dan Rather, Tom Brokaw, or anyone else. She has received numerous Emmys, a Peabody Award, the Overseas Press Club's President's Award, the International Radio and Television Society's Broadcaster of the Year Award, the Academy of Television Arts and Sciences Lifetime Achievement Award, numerous honorary degrees, and induction into the Academy of Television Arts and Sciences Hall of Fame. Her specials have run for more than twenty consecutive years. In 1999, she conducted the first interview with Monica Lewinsky, which became the highest-rated newsmagazine show in more than a decade.[1] She is Barbara Walters. And why does she get paid the big bucks? Because *anybody* can talk to her about just about *anything*. She is the most approachable newsperson in America.

OBSCURE BEGINNING

When Walters started out in her career, few people would have guessed her future. Walters herself said, "I was the kind nobody thought could make it. I had a funny Boston accent. I couldn't pronounce my Rs. I wasn't a beauty."[2] After graduating from Sarah Lawrence College with a degree in English, she went to work to help her financially ailing family. She worked first as a secretary and then as a writer on *Jack Parr* and *The Dick Van Dyke Show*. Then in 1961, she got a chance to write and do research for the *Today Show*. Three years later, she started working in front of the cameras as the "Today girl."

During the next thirteen years, Walters built her credibility as a journalist. She was one of a handful of journalists invited to make the historic trip to China with President Nixon in 1972. And in 1976 she became the first female coanchor of a network evening news program. But her greatest recognition came as an interviewer. In fact, Walters has written a book called *How to Talk with Practically Anybody About Practically Anything*.

Walters has interviewed more statesmen and stars than any other television journalist in history. She has interviewed every president since Nixon. She won the first joint interview of Egypt's President Anwar Sadat and Israel's Prime Minister Menachem Begin. She has interviewed foreign leaders such as Jiang Zemin, Boris Yeltsin, and Margaret Thatcher and figures such as Yasser Arafat, Saddam Hussein, Muammar Qaddafi, and Fidel Castro. And she's talked with just about any movie or television star she's wanted to.

Bill Geddie, the producer of her television specials, observes, "She has a way that has matured over the years of getting people to say things on the air that they never thought they were going to say."[3] Walters says that her favorite interviews are with people facing great adversity, such as Steven McDonald, a paralyzed police officer; Dave Dravecky, a baseball pitcher diagnosed with cancer; and Christopher Reeve, an actor who is now quadriplegic. It's said that her skill as an interviewer comes from the empathy and compassion she developed caring for her disabled sister, Jacqueline. Those qualities undoubtedly help, but what it really boils down to is trust. People trust Walters, so they talk to her.

DON'T MISS OUT

People miss many opportunities for connection and the chance to build deeper relationships because they do not make themselves approachable. And notice that I am purposely using the phrase "make themselves." Approachability has little to do with other people's boldness or timidity. It has everything to do with how you conduct yourself and what messages you send to others.

Years ago I saw a piece called "The Art of Getting Along," which stated,

> Sooner or later, a man, if he is wise, discovers that life is a mixture of good days and bad, victory and defeat, give and take. He learns that it doesn't pay to be a too-sensitive soul, that he

should let some things go over his head like water off a duck's back. He learns that he who loses his temper usually loses out, that all men have burnt toast for breakfast now and then, and that he shouldn't take the other fellow's grouch too seriously.

He learns that carrying a chip on his shoulder is the easiest way to get into trouble, that the quickest way to become unpopular is to carry tales of gossip about others, that buck-passing always turns out to be a boomerang, that it doesn't matter so much who gets the credit so long as the job gets done.

He learns that most others are as ambitious as he is, that they have brains as good or better, that hard work, not cleverness, is the secret of success. He learns that no man ever gets to first base alone, and that it is only through cooperative effort that we move on to better things.

He realizes (in short) that the "art of getting along" depends about 98 percent on his own behavior toward others.[4]

If you want to make yourself agreeable and approachable to others, then you need to put them at ease. Here's how.

How to Put People at Ease

Think about all the approachable people you've ever met, and I believe you'll find that they usually exhibit the following seven characteristics:

1. Personal Warmth—They Truly Like People

You can always tell when someone doesn't like people. Conversely, you can feel it when individuals genuinely care for people. They are warm and kind. And as Christian Bovee said, "Kindness is a language the dumb can speak and the deaf can hear and understand."

There's an old *Peanuts* comic strip in which Charlie Brown says, "I love mankind, it's just people I can't stand." To be approachable, it's not enough to love people in theory. You need to generate personal warmth toward the people you meet.

2. Appreciation for the Differences in People

I have to admit, there was a time in my life when I had little patience for people who were very different from me. I tended to look down on people who didn't have my strengths. Then I read *Personality Plus* by Florence Littauer.[5] That book really opened my eyes. My wife, Margaret, and I read it at the same time, and we laughed as we read about each other's weaknesses and celebrated each other's strengths. As we read about each personality type defined in the book—melancholic, choleric, sanguine, and phlegmatic—we recognized friends, family members, and ourselves.

> "Kindness is a language the dumb can speak and the deaf can hear and understand."
> —CHRISTIAN BOVEE

I looked at people differently after that, and I finally understood that different was good. I came to appreciate people for who they were and what they had to offer. I had a better handle on my weaknesses and how people can complement and help each other. Not only has it made me like people more, but it has made me more likable. Appreciating the differences of others can do the same for you.

3. Consistency of Mood

Have you ever worked with or for someone whose moods were up and down all the time, and people tiptoed into the office every morning and whispered to a coworker, "How is he today?" With those kinds of people, you never know what you're going to get. And as a result, those kinds of people are never approachable.

In contrast, approachable people display a consistency of mood. They are even-keeled and predictable. You know what you're going to get because they are basically the same every time you see them.

4. Sensitivity Toward People's Feelings

Although approachable people are emotionally steady, that doesn't mean they expect others to be that way. They recognize that other people's moods are going to be different from their own. Consequently they tune in to the moods and feelings of others, and they quickly adjust how they relate to others. They are like the captain of a sailboat who tests the wind and adjusts the sails according to current conditions in order to get where he desires to go.

Irish novelist George Moore recognized that "our ideas are here today and gone tomorrow, whereas our feelings are always with us, and we recognize those who feel like us, and at once, by a sort of instinct." When people sense that another person is on their wavelength, they are more likely to open up to him because he seems approachable.

5. Understanding of Human Weaknesses and Exposure of Their Own

Nothing is quite as off-putting as someone trying to keep up the pretense of being perfect. I remember one time in a conference I was teaching, I exhorted the leaders in attendance to admit their weaknesses to those working with them. During the break, a man approached me to say that he didn't think my suggestion was a good idea.

"Won't that make my people unsure of me?" he asked.

"No, it won't," I answered. "You see, you're operating under the assumption that they don't already know."

Novelist and editor Ed Howe wisely advised, "Express a mean opinion of yourself occasionally; it will show your friends that you know how to tell the truth." Approachable people are honest about their abilities—and shortcomings. They are willing to be told not what they want to hear but what they need to hear. And they are able to laugh at themselves. They embrace this old Chinese proverb: "Blessed are they who can laugh at themselves. They shall never cease to be amused." And because they can admit their faults, they don't have a problem allowing other people to have faults of their own.

> Approachable people are honest about their abilities and shortcomings. They are willing to be told not what they want to hear but what they need to hear.

6. Ability to Forgive Easily and Quickly
Ask for Forgiveness

An understanding of human weaknesses and a willingness to reveal their own make approachable people humble. And because they're humble, they quickly ask forgiveness and easily grant it to others.

Author and teacher David Augsburger wrote, "Since nothing we intend is ever faultless, and nothing we attempt ever without error, and nothing we achieve without some measure of finitude and fallibility we call humanness, we are saved by forgiveness."[6]

7. Authenticity

One thing that Barbara Walters used to recite to herself anytime she was feeling uncomfortable or insecure is a statement told to her by Mrs. Eugene McCarthy: "I am the way I am; I look the way I look; I am my age."[7]

Approachable people are real. They are who they are. As a result, they engage with others on a genuine level. They don't pretend to be someone they're not. They don't go out of their way to hide what they think and feel. And they have no hidden agenda. They say what they mean and mean what they say. You don't have to worry about where you stand with them.

One of the reasons they can be authentic is that they are secure with themselves. Secure people don't feel that they always have to win, and they don't have anything to prove. Security is the most disarming of all traits. Approachable people are at ease with themselves, and that puts others at ease.

I need to say one more thing about approachability. It is the responsibility of the one in authority! Barbara Walters is the one in authority when she does interviews, so she takes it upon herself to be approachable. Bosses must take responsibility for being approachable to their employees. Parents must make themselves approachable to their children. And spouses must be approachable to each other.

When I began to be successful as a pastor and to receive state and then national recognition for my work, I discovered that some people were intimidated by me. I think the main reason was my confidence.

I certainly didn't want to put people off or make them reluctant to talk to me. So I worked on making myself more approachable. I started to learn how to "walk slowly through the crowd," meaning that whenever I'm out among people, I try to take my time talking to people, connecting with them, being sensitive to their feelings, needs, and wants.

My effort has been richly rewarded. I have experienced the friendliness of people, met many new friends, and developed many rewarding relationships. And I have been able to be myself at the same time. I highly recommend it.

APPROACHABILITY PRINCIPLE DISCUSSION QUESTIONS

1. How at ease are you with yourself? Are you basically secure or insecure? Are you confident in your abilities, or do you deal with a lot of self-doubt? Do you feel good about yourself, or do you wish you were more like someone else? Explain.

2. Do you agree or disagree that the person who is in authority has the responsibility for putting others at ease? Explain. What happens when the weaker person must try to connect with an authoritative person who is uninterested in connection?

3. How can you tell when someone has a hidden agenda? What kinds of things happen when that agenda is revealed? Does the possibility of having to deal with a hidden agenda make you reluctant to be open and approachable?

4. Think about a moody person you've had to deal with in the past. What kind of an impact did that person's moods have on you? How did it affect the relationship? When are you prone to moodiness? What can you do to make your moods fluctuate less?

5. Many people who are not approachable have no idea that others find them intimidating or standoffish. Do a 360-degree survey of your approachability. Find out if your bosses, employees, colleagues, and family members find you easy to talk to. Ask them to tell you the last time they heard you give an honest assessment of yourself. Ask them to share one of your weaknesses with you and see how you react. Your response will reveal a lot.

THE FOXHOLE PRINCIPLE

WHEN PREPARING
FOR BATTLE, DIG A HOLE
BIG ENOUGH FOR A FRIEND

*In poverty and other misfortunes of life,
true friends are a sure refuge. The young they keep out of
mischief; to the old they are a comfort and aid in their weakness, and those in the prime of life they incite to noble deeds.*

—ARISTOTLE

THE QUESTION I MUST ASK MYSELF:
AM I A FRIEND THAT OTHERS
DEPEND ON DURING DIFFICULT TIMES?

A few years ago, I heard pastor and Dallas Theological Seminary Chancellor Chuck Swindoll say that in the U.S. Marines he was taught to dig a foxhole big enough for a friend. That comment stuck with me because I thought it was a great insight.

If you look at an infantry training manual, you'll find that there are several kinds of foxholes (or "fighting holes" as the marines now call them). A soldier may find himself taking up a "hasty fighting position," where he is simply scrambling for cover with no time to prepare. Or if he has time, he can dig in a position for only himself. However, experts advise that a "one-soldier fighting position . . . does not have the security of a two-soldier position." Even better is said to be an arrangement where three people can fight together. The *Army Field Manual* points out its efficiency: "One soldier can provide security; one can do priority work; and one can rest, eat, or perform maintenance. This allows the priority of work to be completed more quickly than in a one-soldier or two-soldier position." It also adds succinctly, "It is more difficult for the enemy to destroy this type position. To do so, the enemy must kill or suppress three soldiers."[1]

The power of people sticking together has been extolled for thousands of years. Solomon of ancient Israel wrote:

> Two are better than one,
> Because they have a good reward for their labor.
> For if they fall, one will lift up his companion.
> But woe to him who is alone when he falls,
> For he has no one to help him up.
> Again, if two lie down together, they will keep warm;
> But how can one be warm alone?

Though one may be overpowered by another, two can
  withstand him.
And a threefold cord is not quickly broken.[2]

Unlike Chuck Swindoll, I never served in the military. But one doesn't
have to be a soldier to appreciate the benefit of having good friends during
tough times. That is of value not only in the army, but also at home or
work. It's indispensable even in the high-tech world of the Internet. A
good example can be seen in the history of the company Yahoo!

At First Just Two Men in the "Foxhole"

Yahoo! started out in February 1994 as the hobby of two Stanford
graduate students: Jerry Yang and David Filo. The two electrical
engineering students created a directory to keep track of their favorite
Internet Web sites. Before long they began sharing it with others. At
first it was called "Jerry's Guide to the World Wide Web." But when
Yang thought that "David was doing all the work and I was getting all
the credit," he changed the name to "David and Jerry's Guide to the
World Wide Web."[3] Later recognizing that they needed something less
cumbersome, they called it simply Yahoo!

At first they offered two basic services: a directory of Web sites
(similar to a book's table of contents) and an Internet search engine
(similar to an index). Using Yahoo!, people were finally better able to
find specific information on the Internet. By the fall of 1994, more than
100,000 people were using their service.

Yang and Filo knew an opportunity when they saw one. They
incorporated Yahoo! in March 1995 and quickly secured $2 million
from Sequoia Capital to bankroll their organization. The friends were
ready to engage in a marketplace battle. They were already practicing
the Foxhole Principle, having decided to work together. But they also
knew they couldn't succeed on their own. So they shopped for a
management team. The person they brought into the organization with
them to become CEO was Tim Koogle (known as T. K.). Koogle brought

in Jeffrey Mallett as COO. The four men worked together closely, but the ones who really made things happen were Koogle, Mallett, and Yang. People called them the three musketeers.

"I'm usually the pragmatic one," said Mallett, "Jerry is the untethered one and T. K. makes the final call. I just know we are always thinking about and anticipating our next moves."[4] And when Yahoo! had to face "Eisner, Welch, and Gates . . . moving directly into our space," as Mallett described it, they stuck together and fought it out. While many other dot-com companies folded, Yahoo! kept going strong.

Koogle and Mallett have since moved on to other ventures, but they have done so with no hard feelings and no regrets. Together with Yang and Filo, they helped to transform Yahoo! from a business with fewer than ten employees to a publicly traded multimillion-dollar enterprise. Today Yahoo! serves the largest worldwide audience—well over 200 million users each month—and serves as a global branded network to its customers.[5]

THE FACTS ABOUT FOXHOLES

We face many kinds of battles in life, and the "foxholes" we sometimes inhabit come in many shapes and sizes. The home is the most important one. (Ideally it should always be a safe haven with people we can depend on.) But others may include a business, a sports team, a small group, a platoon, or something else. And of course, the people who accompany us in these places are as varied as they are.

Before going any further, I need to share with you three assumptions I'm making as I write about the Foxhole Principle:

1. *The foxhole is for you and a friend—not a friend alone.* You can ask a friend to fight with you, but you should never send someone else to fight your battles. When Jerry Yang and David Filo hired Tim Koogle, they didn't walk away from their responsibilities at Yahoo! They partnered with him.

2. *Before the battle, you have developed a friendship.* The Foxhole Principle is not about imposing on distant acquaintances or

using people. You need to be a friend before you ask for the help of a friend.

3. *You have also been in your friends' foxholes with them.* You should be willing to fight for any friend whose help you would request. That's what friends do. Civil rights leader Martin Luther King Jr. said, "In the end, we will remember not the words of our enemies, but the silence of our friends." I don't ever want it to be said that I was a silent friend!

Having established that, here are some truths about "foxholes":

Foxholes Without Friends Are Unhealthy

Separating oneself from others and trying to face the world alone is not healthy or helpful. Several years ago, I read about a campaign initiated by the California Department of Mental Health with the slogan "Friends can be good medicine." Here are just a few findings that prompted the department to embark on the initiative:

- If you isolate yourself from others, you are two to three times more likely to die an early death. This is true independently of whether you take good care of yourself by exercising and refraining from smoking.

- If you isolate yourself from others, you are more likely to contract terminal cancer.

- If you are divorced, separated, or widowed, you have a five to ten times greater chance of being hospitalized for a mental disorder than if you are married.

- If you are a pregnant woman without good personal relationships, your chances of having some kind of complication are three times as great as those with strong relationships, even given the same amount of stress.[6]

Foxhole Experiences Forge Great Friendships

Back in the 1980s when I was looking for someone to help me figure out how to navigate the difficult job of pastoring a large church while leading a national ministry, Jack Hayford entered my life. Jack, who pastors the Church on the Way in Van Nuys, California, was a good friend, a wise counselor, and an unselfish mentor. I could not have succeeded without his help.

More than a decade later, I fought a much more serious battle: I suffered a major heart attack. When Jack heard about it, he called me. He told me that I was working too hard and that I would

> You should be willing to fight for any friend whose help you would request. That's what friends do.

have to learn to say no to people. And then Jack said something I'll never forget: "John, I know you find it difficult to say no to some people. Have them call me; I'll say no for you. And I'll keep you out of those situations." Jack has truly been a foxhole friend to me. And recently when Jack's son-in-law died unexpectedly, I crawled into his foxhole with him. It was the least I could do after all he'd done for me.

Foxholes Prove Friendships

When you face tough times, you find out who your real friends are. When Pepper Rodgers was coaching at UCLA, he had some difficult seasons. Recalling an especially bad year, Rodgers told a reporter, "My dog was about my only friend, and I told my wife that man needs at least two friends. She bought me another dog."

False friends are like our shadows, keeping close to us while we walk in the sunshine but leaving us when we cross into the shade. Real friends stick with us when trouble comes. As the old saying goes: in prosperity our friends know us; in adversity we know our friends.

A FAITHFUL FRIEND

It's said that when Benjamin Franklin signed the Declaration of Independence, he uttered the words, "We must, indeed, all hang together or, most assuredly, we shall hang separately." He understood the power of maintaining strong alliances during times of great conflict. By all accounts, Franklin was a faithful friend and dependable ally to his fellow countrymen throughout his life.

You may have many friends, but not all of them will be foxhole friends. For that matter, you will not be that kind of an ally to everyone in your life either. Foxhole friendships are special. Here are five things you should keep in mind before you agree to do battle with someone:

1. Foxhole Friends Are Few

During the Civil War, President Lincoln received many requests for pardons from soldiers who were sentenced to die for desertion. Each appeal was frequently accompanied by numerous testimonial letters from friends and powerful people.

One day the president received an appeal for a pardon that stood out; it arrived without a single document or letter vouching for the prisoner. Lincoln was surprised by this and asked the officer in charge about it. To Lincoln's amazement, the officer on duty said that the soldier had not one friend and that his entire family had been killed in the war. The president considered that piece of information and told the officer that he would render a decision on the matter in the morning.

Lincoln wrestled with the issue all night. Desertion was no small matter. Overruling a death sentence would send the wrong message to other soldiers. Yet he found it difficult not to have sympathy for someone so alone in the world.

In the morning when the officer asked the president for his decision, he was shocked to hear Lincoln say that the testimony of a friend had sealed his decision on the soldier in question. When the officer reminded the president that the request had come with no letter of reference, Lincoln simply stated, "I will be his friend." He then signed the request and pardoned the man.

If there are people in your life who would go to battle with you, value them, for they are rare indeed.

2. Foxhole Friends Provide Strength Before and During the Battle

Having someone beside you fighting during a battle is a great help. But even before the battle, simply knowing that someone believes in you and will fight for you is uplifting. Greek philosopher Epicurus stated, "It is not so much our friends' help that helps us, as the confident knowledge that they will help us."

Think about a parent, teacher, boss, or coach who went out of the way to express belief in you. Wasn't it great to be trusted? Didn't such a person have a great impact on your life? If so, take the time to thank that individual. And make the same kind of investment of trust in the people for whom you would fight.

3. Foxhole Friends See Things from the Same Perspective

Five-year-old Tracy asked her dad if she could play at the house of a friend who lived next door. Her father told her she could as long as she was home by six o'clock for dinner.

When six o'clock rolled around, Tracy was nowhere to be seen. So her father waited. After about twenty-five minutes, Tracy opened the front door. Her father, working to control his impatience, asked her where she'd been.

> "It is not so much our friends' help that helps us, as the confident knowledge that they will help us."
> —Epicurus

"I'm sorry I'm late, Dad," she responded, "but my friend's doll broke right when I was supposed to leave for home."

"Oh, I see," her dad said. "And I suppose you were helping her fix it?"

"No," replied Tracy. "I was helping her cry."

People who climb down into the foxhole with you see things from your point of view, and they express empathy for your situation. That makes them not only a great help, but also a great comfort.

4. Foxhole Friends Make a Difference in Our Lives

The people who fight the great battles of life with us make a huge impact on our lives. I mentioned that I had a heart attack on December

18, 1998. In the early morning hours while I was battling for my life, a phone call from my assistant, Linda Eggers, prompted a man I barely knew to climb into the foxhole with me and save my life. Months before, I'd had lunch with Dr. John Bright Cage, a Nashville cardiologist who offered to help me "in any way he could" because he was concerned about my health. Linda called him, he called a colleague in Atlanta named Dr. Jeff Marshall, and Dr. Marshall saved my life. It was a case where a relationship literally meant the difference between life and death.

5. Foxhole Friends Love Us Unconditionally

It's said that a friend is someone . . .

- who will keep your secrets and never divulge them—even if tortured or tempted with chocolate (or in my wife's case, Krispy Kreme doughnuts).

- who will quietly destroy the photograph that makes you look like a beached whale.

- who knows you don't know what you're talking about but will let you reach that conclusion independently.

- who goes on the same diet with you—and off it with you too.

Foxhole friends are that—and then some. They'd face any danger with you. They'd do anything for you. They'd give anything of theirs to you.

Author and former pastor of City Temple in London, Leslie D. Weatherhead, wrote about two friends who were literally foxhole friends; they were soldiers together. He said that when one of the soldiers was injured and could not get back to safety, his buddy went out to get him, against his officer's orders. He returned mortally wounded, and his friend, whom he had carried back, was dead.

The officer was angry. "I told you not to go," he said. "Now I've lost both of you. It was not worth it."

The dying man replied, "But it was, sir, because when I got to him, he said, 'Jim, I knew you'd come.'"

Unlike what faced these two men, the conflicts you face may not be on the battlefield. They may not be life and death. But no matter what, wouldn't you prefer to face them with a friend at your side? If so, be a foxhole friend to others, the kind of friend that others can trust, no matter what.

FOXHOLE PRINCIPLE DISCUSSION QUESTIONS

1. What makes a person willing to fight another person's battle with him? Is it always because of unselfish motives? Do motives matter? Do they change the end result?

2. Where does empathy come into play in the Foxhole Principle? Does it develop before the people get together or after they've begun to fight? What other factors, such as values, priorities, vision, etc., might come into play?

3. What kind of a friend have you been to others? Have you been "in the foxhole" with a friend, colleague, or family member? How do you decide whether to become that kind of a friend to somebody?

4. Why do you think some people "climb into the foxhole" alone? Is it something they do because they prefer it or because they have not sufficiently built relationships? What happens to a person who must continually fight alone?

5. In what kinds of situations are you more likely to develop a friendship before doing battle together? In what situations are you likely to find yourself doing battle as a matter of survival and developing a friendship along the way? Do both situations lead to equally deep or long-lasting relationships? Explain.

Before moving on, let's review the People Principles related to the Trust Question . . .

The Bedrock Principle: Trust is the foundation of any relation-ship.

The Situation Principle: Never let the situation mean more than the relationship.

The Bob Principle: When Bob has a problem with everyone, Bob is usually the problem.

The Approachability Principle: Being at ease with ourselves helps others be at ease with us.

The Foxhole Principle: When preparing for battle, dig a hole big enough for a friend.

THE INVESTMENT QUESTION: ARE WE WILLING TO INVEST IN OTHERS?

No man can live happily who regards himself alone;
who turns everything to his own advantage.
You must live for others if you wish to live for yourself.

—SENECA

I ndividuals who learn the People Principles that prepare them to answer the questions in the first three sections of this book—

Readiness: Are we prepared for relationships?
Connection: Are we willing to focus on others?
Trust: Can we build mutual trust?

—can consider themselves to be in pretty good shape relationally. They will have become prepared emotionally for relationships by letting go of their personal baggage. They will be able to connect well with others. And they will be capable of engendering trust when dealing with others. Most people who interact with them will consider them to possess excellent people skills. However, if they stop there, they will miss the best part of relationships.

That brings us to the investment question: Are we willing to invest in others? You may be wondering why I think that is so important. You may even be asking, "Why would anyone take the time and energy to invest in others?" To discover the answer, think about this:

You may build a beautiful house, but eventually it will crumble.
You may develop a fine career, but one day it will be over.
You may save a great sum of money, but you can't take it with you.
You may be in superb health today, but in time it will decline.
You may take pride in your accomplishments, but someone will
  surpass you.

So many people invest in these things, but they are transitory. So what can you possibly invest in that will last? People! When it comes right down to it, is there anything else that really matters in this world compared to people?

Relationships are like anything else. The return you get depends on what you invest. Sometimes when I speak at conferences, young leaders come up to me and say, "I would love to do what you do. How do I get a gig like this?"

Honestly that question makes me chuckle. Sometimes I respond, "You may want to do what I do, but would you like to do what I did in order to do what I do?" They see the bright lights and the big auditorium. But they don't see the decades I spent teaching small groups of people for the mere love of it because it didn't pay anything. They don't see the hundreds of times that Margaret and I hauled grungy boxes filled with books and notebooks on and off airplanes before we could afford to hire any help. They don't consider the thousands of hours we've spent traveling and the uncomfortable hotel rooms and bad meals. The real work has always been behind the scenes. What they see today is really the culmination of thirty years of hard work outside the spotlight.

That's the way the best relationships are. They take work behind the scenes. Once you've gotten to know people, learn to invest in them. The best relationships are always the result of unselfish giving. The following five People Principles offer insight on some of the most important ways we can invest in relationships:

The Gardening Principle: All relationships need cultivation.

The 101 Percent Principle: Find the 1 percent we agree on and give it 100 percent of our effort.

The Patience Principle: The journey with others is slower than the journey alone.

The Celebration Principle: The true test of relationships is not only how loyal we are when friends fail, but how thrilled we are when they succeed.

The High Road Principle: We go to a higher level when we treat others better than they treat us.

If you can answer the Investment Question in a positive way, then your relationships will begin going to a whole new level.

THE GARDENING
PRINCIPLE

─────

ALL RELATIONSHIPS
NEED CULTIVATION

Friendship is like money, easier made than kept.

—SAMUEL BUTLER

THE QUESTION I MUST ASK MYSELF:
DO I OCCASIONALLY OR CONTINUALLY
CULTIVATE MY RELATIONSHIPS?

In 1997, sportswriter Mitch Albom wrote a book called *Tuesdays with Morrie*. It contains wisdom from the recollections of Morrie Schwartz, Albom's former college professor and mentor who was dying of Lou Gehrig's disease. After seeing an interview Schwartz did with Ted Koppel on *Nightline* in 1995, Albom had reconnected with Schwartz after a twenty-year hiatus and cultivated a deeper relationship with him. *Tuesdays with Morrie* came as a result of their meetings. It was a runaway bestseller that stayed on the *New York Times* bestseller list for four years. As of March 2004, it had more than 5 million copies in print, was published in thirty languages in thirty-four countries, and had been made into an Emmy-winning movie.[1]

THE NEXT STORY

Albom's readers were eager to see how he would follow up his bestseller. Most people wanted him to write a sequel. "After *Tuesdays with Morrie*," says Albom, "I was inundated with offers to do *Wednesdays with Morrie*, *Thursdays with Morrie*, *Chicken Soup with Morrie*. I refused because I had said everything that I wanted to say."[2] Accordingly many people were surprised in 2003 when he published *The Five People You Meet in Heaven*, not because it wasn't about Morrie, but because unlike his previous seven books, it was a novel.

The book contains the story of eighty-three-year-old amusement park worker Eddie, who lives what he believes to be an insignificant life, but learns about his impact after he dies and reaches heaven. What's interesting is that the book was inspired by a real person: Albom's Uncle Eddie.

Albom describes Edward Beitchman as a "stumpy, thick-jawed, barrel-chested man born in 1908 to poor immigrant parents in a poor immigrant neighborhood. He was one of nine children, neither the youngest nor the oldest, only the toughest." Albom comments, "He was the champion of my family tree—and stronger than anyone I knew."[3]

Uncle Eddie was Albom's childhood hero. A World War II veteran who worked as a cab driver and factory worker, Eddie had faced down a man in his cab who wanted to kill him. Albom says that when the "nefarious rider tried to slit his throat with a knife, [Eddie] grabbed the blade and squeezed so hard, the would-be killer ran away."[4] And Eddie claimed that during emergency open-heart surgery, he had opened his eyes for a moment to see a group of dead relatives at the edge of the bed waiting for him, to which Eddie responded, "Get the hell out of here, I'm not ready for any of youse yet."[5]

Albom grew up and became a successful journalist. Although he had not kept in contact with his mentor Morrie Schwartz, he always kept in contact with Uncle Eddie. He used to call the older man as he traveled around the country on assignment. And Eddie, whom Albom says had lived a life of unrealized dreams, was always excited and impressed with his escapades.

Uncle Eddie made a profound impact on Albom, but Mitch never really let his uncle know about it before he died. Albom admits, "At his funeral, I delivered the eulogy. I broke down halfway through and started crying uncontrollably. It was sadness, yes, but also regret. I had never said those loving things to his face."[6]

All relationships need cultivation to grow. Mitch Albom did maintain his relationship with Eddie. But he never really took it any deeper than it had been when he was a child. And now he realizes that he missed a great opportunity.

"We all have wonderful people in our lives," notes Albom, "but when they're gone, it seems, all we can do is miss them. I miss Eddie's quiet toughness . . . I realize I have never met anyone as magical as my uncle seemed to me as a boy. He should have known that. And I wish I had told him."[7]

How Does Your Garden Grow?

You cannot neglect a relationship and expect it to grow. That's not to say that all relationships are the same and need the same amount of time and attention. The nature and purpose of the relationship will determine the energy and time needed to cultivate it. Think about some of the many personal and professional relationships you have in your life. How much effort do you give them? Do you treat them the same? Of course not. And you shouldn't. Every relationship is different but can fit into one of three categories:

Some People Come into Our Lives for a *Reason*

Many relationships are very short and occur for very specific reasons. Sometimes they come and then go away forever. Other times they are ongoing but intermittent. These relationships need only brief, periodic cultivation.

> The nature and purpose of the relationship will determine the energy and time needed to cultivate it.

A good example of this kind of relationship is the one with my doctor. I never would have met Dr. Jeff Marshall, my cardiologist, if it hadn't been for the heart attack I suffered in 1998. I consider him my friend as well as my doctor, but I see him only a couple of times a year. And it's always related to my health.

Some People Come into Our Lives for a *Season*

A second type of relationship lasts only for a period of time. These relationships may last only a few weeks or as long as several years. Many times they are related to our current circumstances or situations. But just because they are temporary doesn't mean they're not important. The cultivation of the relationships should just match the season.

Relationships with our children's teachers and coaches are often seasonal. So are many work relationships. Perhaps you work for a boss you enjoy, but the work is the only bond. And when you move on to another job, you have little reason or occasion to keep in touch. Sometimes that's just the way these relationships work out.

Some People Come into Our Lives for a *Lifetime*

The third kind of relationship is ongoing and permanent. These are few and very special. And if we want to keep them healthy and encourage them to grow, we must give them continual cultivation. Otherwise they are likely to shrivel and die.

Our closest friendships are most valuable to us, and like anything of value, they cost us something. We cannot neglect them and expect them to thrive. Playwright George Bernard Shaw once wrote a note to his friend Archibald Henderson, which said, "I have neglected you shockingly of late. This is because I have had to neglect everything that could be neglected without immediate ruin, and partly because you have passed into the circle of intimate friends whose feelings one never dreams of considering." Shaw must have realized that his relationship with his friend was in desperate need of attention, and he desired to save it. What price can you put on a great friendship?

The most important relationship anyone has in this world is the one with a spouse. Men and women are so different that it's not always easy to cultivate a really good relationship. I recently came across a humorous piece that pokes fun at the differences between the genders:

- A man will pay $2 for a $1 item he wants; a woman will pay $1 for a $2 item that she doesn't want.

- A woman worries about the future until she gets a husband; a man never worries about the future until he gets a wife.

- A successful man is one who makes more money than his wife can spend; a successful woman is one who can find such a man.

- To be happy with a man you must understand him a lot and love him a little; to be happy with a woman you must love her a lot and not try to understand her at all.

- Married men live longer than single men, but married men are a lot more willing to die.

- Any married man should forget his mistakes—there's no use in two people remembering the same thing.

- A woman marries a man expecting he will change, but he doesn't; a man marries a woman expecting that she won't change and she does.

- A woman has the last word in any argument; anything a man says after that is the beginning of a new argument.

- There are two times when a man doesn't understand a woman: before marriage and after.[8]

Socrates said, "By all means marry; if you get a good wife, you'll become happy. If you get a bad one, you'll become a philosopher." Selecting the right man or woman to marry is important, but it's only part of the process of developing a good marriage. Before we marry, the focus is on a future mate. After we marry, it's on ourselves. Dating brings out the *best*—marriage brings out the *rest*.

Marriage, like any long-term relationship, requires us to . . .

- wade through a few things that are difficult.

- work for many things that are needed.

- wait on some things that take time.

- watch out for those things that can be harmful.

- wave good-bye to personal things that are selfish.

These are all aspects of cultivation. Marriage partners who don't intentionally cultivate a close relationship will drift apart. It's sad, but after five years of marriage, all some couples have in common is their wedding day. Some marriages may be made in heaven, but their maintenance must be done on earth.

There's a story that illustrates what I mean. A man and a woman who never met before found themselves in the same sleeping carriage of a train. After their initial embarrassment, both managed to get to sleep—the woman on the top bunk, the man on the lower. In the middle of the night, the woman leaned over and said, "I'm sorry to bother you, but I'm awfully cold and I was wondering if you could possibly pass me another blanket."

The man leaned out and, with a glint in his eye, said, "I've got a better idea. Let's pretend we are married."

"Why not?" giggled the woman.

"Okay," he replied, "then get your own blanket!"

WAYS TO KEEP CULTIVATING IMPORTANT RELATIONSHIPS

What does it mean to cultivate a relationship? Whether it's as a spouse, a parent, or a friend, you can start to cultivate a healthy, growing relationship by focusing on the following six things:

1. Commitment

Researcher Dr. Alfred Kinsey observed, "There may be nothing more important in a marriage than a determination that it shall persist. With such a determination, individuals force themselves to adjust and to accept situations which would otherwise seem sufficient grounds for a breakup." Deep commitment to the relationship is one of the greatest assets a married couple can have. But it's also a characteristic of *all* deep relationships.

Political theorist Thomas Paine asserted, "What we obtain too cheaply we esteem too little; it is dearness only that gives everything its value." Every long-lasting relationship suffers strains and setbacks. And no two people agree on everything. Even the best friendships can expect to face conflict. The question is, What are you going to do when trouble comes? How committed are you? Are you more dedicated to maintaining the relationship or to avoiding conflict? Your answer just might determine whether your relationship is lifelong or merely temporary.

2. Communication

How can a relationship form without communication? It often *begins* with easy communication. Sometimes a spark easily ignites a friendship. It *deepens* with more difficult communication. Author Sydney J. Harris believes that "it is impossible to learn anything important about anyone until we get him or her to disagree with us; it is only in contradiction that character is disclosed." And it is *sustained* with intentional communication.

Several years after Margaret and I were married, I realized that when I got home to see her, there was no excitement in our communication. She'd ask about what had happened during the day, and I wasn't very enthusiastic about discussing it. Then I figured out why: during the course of most days, I had shared the most exciting events with a colleague or my assistant. So I was not all that excited about repeating it to Margaret. I knew that needed to change. My solution? Whenever something important or exciting happens during the day, I jot a note about it on a three-by-five card. And then I don't tell other people about it; I save it for the end of the day. That way, Margaret is the first to hear about it, and she is the recipient of my enthusiasm.

3. Friendship

Critic Samuel Johnson remarked, "If a man does not make new acquaintances as he advances through life, he will soon find himself left alone; a man, sir, should keep his friendship in a constant repair." That goes for old friendships as well as new ones. I think we sometimes take for granted the people closest to us, and as a result, we neglect to try being good friends to them first.

For this reason, I remind myself constantly to be Margaret's friend first, before trying to be anything else to her. I try to put her concerns first. And when there is conflict between us or if she is in doubt about making a decision, I tell her, "I'm your best friend," to remind her that I'm looking out for her.

4. Memories

I believe that shared memories are a wonderful source of connection and bonding for people. Have you ever gone to a school reunion or met up with friends you haven't seen for ten, twenty, or thirty years? What helps you to reconnect almost instantly? It's the memories of your shared experiences!

> "What we obtain too cheaply we esteem too little; it is dearness only that gives everything its value."
> —THOMAS PAINE

Today our children are all grown up, married, and living on their own with children of their own. But when they were in their teen years, like many parents, we were worried about their becoming disconnected from us and heading off in a direction that wasn't good for them. At the same time, we knew we needed to give them more and more freedom to be independent. One of the ways we kept the connection strong without trying to force it was by creating a family history. We traveled a lot together and did many activities designed to create positive memories. All of that gave our children something positive to reflect on when their need for independence might have driven them away.

5. Growth

Benjamin Franklin said, "Promise may get friends, but it is performance that keeps them." When you begin any friendship, it is filled with promise. But you have to find ways to keep it fresh and strong so that it continues to have potential and not just good memories. One way to do that is to grow together.

When I was the senior pastor of Skyline Church in San Diego, four staff members worked with me for more than ten years. That is an unusual occurrence in the church world. One reason was that we chose to grow together. Anytime I went to a seminar or conference for personal growth, I always took some of my people with me. They continually shared things they were learning with me. And every month I taught a personal growth lesson to the staff. All of those things created an exciting environment where we enjoyed growing together.

6. Spoiling Each Other

Voltaire wrote, "If the first law of friendship is that it has to be cultivated, the second law is to be indulgent when the first law has been neglected." You can't go wrong spoiling anyone—except perhaps your children. And even that is hard not to do. I try to extend small kindnesses to my friends all the time. Margaret and I continually try to spoil each other. And I won't even talk about how we treat our grandchildren!

Let your friends and family members know how much you care as often as you can. Don't end up living with regrets the way Mitch Albom has concerning Uncle Eddie.

Nancy Reagan, wife of the late former president Ronald Reagan, said, "I am a big believer that you have to nourish any relationship. I am still very much a part of my friends' lives, and they are very much a part of my life. A First Lady who does not have this source of strength and comfort can lose perspective and become isolated." That's true not only of people in the public eye; it's true for all of us. The friendships we develop with others enrich the quality of our lives. But we cannot sustain them if we don't cultivate them. That's why it's important for us to practice the Gardening Principle.

GARDENING PRINCIPLE DISCUSSION QUESTIONS

1. Name some ways in which people in relationships can positively communicate with one another. Does the type of relationship affect which kinds of communication are appropriate? Which methods are most effective for the relationships you value most?

2. How can a person tell the difference between a relationship that is meant to last for a season and one that has the potential to last a lifetime? How did some of your most significant long-term relationships start? With whom do you currently have a short-term relationship that has potential for something deeper? How can you test the waters to see if it can go to the next level?

3. How do you determine with whom you spend your time? Do you think in terms of the importance of the relationship? Do you carve out time for the most significant people and then guard it carefully? Or does your calendar simply fill up on a first-come, first-served basis? Are you satisfied with what you currently do? If not, how can you improve it?

4. The chapter mentioned the importance of wading through difficult issues. Why do people allow difficult issues to remain unresolved in important relationships? Do you think there are ever valid reasons for not dealing with them? Is there an issue between you and someone important that you have not addressed but should? When will you deal with it?

5. When was the last time you spoiled your wife or significant other? Is that something you do often, or is it not something you think much about? Explain why. What could you do to improve in this area?

THE 101 PERCENT PRINCIPLE

FIND THE 1 PERCENT
WE AGREE ON AND
GIVE IT 100 PERCENT
OF OUR EFFORT

If two men on the same job agree all the time, then one is useless.
If they disagree all the time, then both are useless.

—DARRYL F. ZANUCK

> THE QUESTION I MUST ASK MYSELF:
> CAN I FIND COMMON GROUND, AND WILL
> I GIVE IT 100 PERCENT OF MY EFFORT?

Sometimes building relationships is an uphill battle, and connecting with another person can be particularly difficult. How do you connect with people when you seem to have nothing in common with them? Can you build relational bridges in such circumstances? And if so, can the relationships be healthy, long-lasting, and productive? These are legitimate questions. Let's face it. When you see no common ground with another person, it's going to be a challenge to connect. So how do you do it?

The answer can be found in the 101 Percent Principle. When connection is difficult, you must find the one thing the two of you can agree upon. You can do that with just about *anybody*. The problem is that many people naturally take the opposite approach; they look for differences. Why? Sometimes it's due to natural competitiveness; people are often looking for an edge. Sometimes it's to make themselves stand out, to find their own distinctiveness. Other times people focus on differences because they feel threatened by others.

Instead, to make a connection, people need to reach common ground. Most people have many things in common. But even the oddest couple can find something they agree on. Once they do, they need to give it 100 percent of their effort. The greater the differences, the more important it is to focus on what they agree on—and the greater the effort they need to give it. That's not always easy, but the benefits can be remarkably rewarding. This story illustrates that.

GO WEST, YOUNG MAN

Charles Howard was an entrepreneur's entrepreneur. In 1903, after serving in the United States cavalry and then working as a bicycle mechanic in New York, Howard decided to seek his fortune out West. He settled in San Francisco and managed to open a bicycle repair shop downtown.

In those days, automobiles were a new (and often unreliable) addition to the landscape. But there were no auto repair shops. For that reason, car owners began visiting Howard's shop to ask for his help. And Howard was willing to give auto repair a try. It didn't take long for Howard to see a great opportunity. He soon hopped a train to Detroit and wangled a meeting with William C. Durant, head of Buick and future founder of General Motors. Durant liked Howard and hired him. Before long, Howard held the franchise rights to sell Buicks for all of San Francisco, and in 1905 at the age of twenty-eight, Howard opened his first Buick dealership showcasing three vehicles he had purchased while in Detroit.

At first, things didn't go well for Howard, but after the earthquake and fire of 1906, he capitalized on the need for automobiles. Between his natural nose for opportunity and his mastery of promotion, he began to see great success. In 1909, Howard expanded his role in the business. He acquired sole distributorship of Buick, National, and Oldsmobile vehicles for all of the western U.S. The enterprise made the pioneer car man fabulously wealthy. And later when Durant got overextended and faced bankruptcy, Howard bailed him out with a personal loan of $190,000, which Durant later repaid with GM stock and a percentage of gross sales. Howard couldn't have been more successful. Even the crash of the stock market in 1929 didn't destroy him as it did so many others.

In the early 1930s, the old cavalryman-turned-car-magnate rekindled his love of horses, and a friend got him interested in horse racing. He decided that if he was going to own thoroughbreds, he would go first class. He purchased a few horses, then looked for a trainer. The man he found was fifty-six-year-old Tom Smith, a man of the Old West. The two men could not have been more different. Where Howard was a master salesman and promoter, Smith was a quiet man who rarely spoke and could spend literally hours and days watching a horse's every movement. Where Howard was a great businessman used to every luxury, Smith was a former cowboy who was used to sleeping on the ground. Smith had been an experienced mustang hunter and horse breaker from age thirteen. During his career, he had worked as a deer hunter, sheep ranch foreman, mountain lion tracker, farrier, and horse trainer. The Native Americans called him the Lone Plainsman.

Author and racing expert Laura Hillenbrand says of Howard and Smith:

> The two men stood in different halves of the century. Smith was the last of the true frontiersmen; Howard was paving Smith's West under the urgent wheels of his automobiles. Howard was driven by image; Smith remained the Lone Plainsman, forbidding and solitary. But Howard was blessed with an uncanny eye for horsemen. He took one look at Smith and instincts rang in his head. He drove Smith to his barn and introduced his horses to their new trainer.[1]

Added to this unlikely mix was a jockey who had seen better days. John Pollard was a very tough man, even in a profession of tough men. Not only was he a rider, but he had been a prize fighter—although not a very good one. At five feet seven inches, he towered over his rival jockeys. And like many of them, he tortured his body to keep his weight below 115 pounds. In 1928, Pollard had been one of the top-twenty riders in the nation. But his skills had slipped, and by the mid-1930s when Smith hired him, he was winning fewer and fewer races. At that point in his career, his distinction was that he was willing to ride horses other jockeys were afraid to touch.

HOW DID *THEY* GET TOGETHER?

The millionaire, the frontiersman, and the prizefighter—the three men had nothing in common, except one thing: a seemingly worthless racehorse that Smith spotted and Howard purchased. All three had the ability to focus on the one thing they had in common and not their differences.

Hillenbrand describes the horse this way:

> The colt's body, built low to the ground, had all the properties of a cinder block . . . His stubby legs were a study in unsound construction . . . Thanks to his unfortunate assembly, his walk was an odd, straddle-legged motion that was often mistaken for lameness . . . His gallop was so disorganized that he had a maddening tendency to whack himself in the front ankle with his own hind hoof . . . All of this raggedness was not helped by his racing schedule . . . Though only three years old, he had already run forty-three races, far more than most horses contest in their entire careers.[2]

The animal's name was Seabiscuit. What looked to others like an incorrigible nag became one of the world's most famous racehorses— a national hero in the midst of the Depression when people needed to be lifted up. (In 1938, Seabiscuit was the nation's top news maker, generating more press than Franklin D. Roosevelt or Adolf Hitler!) Seabiscuit not only set a record for earnings, but in a head-to-head duel, he went on to defeat War Admiral—a Triple Crown winner and one of the best racehorses of all time. That contest, which most experts at the time believed Seabiscuit could not win, is now considered by many to be the greatest horse race ever run.

When to Practice
the 101 Percent Principle

It is truly remarkable that three such different men were able to find common ground, to find the one thing they could agree upon and invest their energy in it. But that is the value of the 101 Percent Principle. It is an incredible tool in anyone's relational toolbox.

However, it's not something that can be pulled out and used all the time. I say that because this principle takes a big commitment of time, energy, and thinking. Therefore, before practicing this principle, you need to ask yourself some questions:

Is the Person Worth the Commitment?

Every person has worth, but you cannot give every person the time or energy that the 101 Percent Principle requires. So who is "worthy" of this kind of attention? The list begins with your spouse if you're married. In an area where the two of you don't agree, use the 101 Percent Principle. (Margaret and I usually don't see eye to eye on my calendar, but we do agree that we want to spend time together, so we focus on that.) Add your family members to the list. If you own a business and have partners, they must be included on the list. After that, add your friends. Beyond that circle of people, use your judgment. If there is good potential for a mutually rewarding relationship and you can afford to expend the energy, then you might want to give the 101 Percent Principle a try when you find it difficult to agree.

Is the Situation Worth the Commitment?

Most situations where disagreements occur are short-term. In such cases, keep in mind that "this too shall pass." Let it go and save your energy for scenarios where your expenditure of time and attention will have a long-term return.

Is the Issue Worth the Commitment?

When an issue touches on a priority in your life or impacts one of your values, use the 101 Percent Principle. If it doesn't, think twice. And keep in mind the words of clergyman Richard Baxter: "In necessary things, unity; in doubtful things, liberty; in all things, charity."

Is the Return Worth the Commitment?

During the first three years of Seabiscuit's life, many people had the opportunity to find his potential. In fact, before Smith trained him,

Seabiscuit was in the stable of James Fitzsimmons, the most respected trainer of his day. But Fitzsimmons had so many high-caliber horses that Seabiscuit didn't seem worth the effort. Smith saw things differently, and look at the return he received!

A 101 PERCENT RETURN

Practicing the 101 Percent Principle can benefit you in many ways. Here are six:

1. It Allows You to Build a Foundation for Change

If you are in a relationship where you want to influence someone and change the way he sees or does something, then you shouldn't try to initiate the change in an area where you disagree. In relationships, change always begins with common ground. When you practice the 101 Percent Principle, you find that common ground and expand it. It becomes an excellent starting point for change.

2. It Prevents Unnecessary Conflict

I've learned that it's hard to argue with people when they're right. When you focus on the area where you agree with someone else, you are on safe ground because both are right. General Ulysses S. Grant said, "There never was a time, in my opinion, some way could not be found to prevent the drawing of a sword." Why create conflict if you can avoid it?

3. It Reduces the Odds of Making Enemies

Ralph Waldo Emerson observed, "He who has a thousand friends has not a friend to spare, while he who has one enemy will meet him everywhere." Wouldn't you agree that even one enemy in life is more than we would care to have? The best way to get rid of a potential enemy is to make him your friend. When you look for the things you agree on, you increase the odds of doing just that.

4. It Keeps Something of Value That Could Otherwise Be Lost

How many potentially rewarding relationships have you missed because you focused on differences instead of common ground? How many potential friends have slipped through your fingers? How many productive business associations have you forfeited? Former New York Yankees manager Joe McCarthy observed, "Any manager who can't get along with a .400 hitter is crazy." If you want to keep yourself open to potentially rewarding relationships, be pre-pared to try the 101 Percent Principle.

5. It Helps You to Feel Good About Your Part of the Relationship

Novelist Jane Austen quipped in a letter sent to her sister Cassandra, "I don't want people to be very agreeable, as it saves me the trouble of liking them." People who look for the worst in others may try to make themselves *look better* by comparison, but they rarely *feel better* about the way they handle the relationship. In contrast, people who look for the best and focus on what they agree on can take satisfaction in knowing that they did their part.

6. It Enables You to Make the Best of Difficult Situations

The happiest people don't necessarily *have* the best of everything. They just *make* the best of everything. Adopting the 101 Percent Principle makes the best of every relational opportunity. And no one can be expected to do more than that.

> The happiest people don't necessarily *have* the best of everything. They just *make* the best of everything.

In the chapter on the Pain Principle, I told you the story of Tom, the man who sent me a letter criticizing my sermon every week, whom I won over after several years of effort. The way I got him to accept me was by using the 101 Percent Principle. As I mentioned, his kids and ours were adopted. The one thing I could find that we agreed on was that adopted children were special. So whenever we talked, I focused on our kids. I gave his kids special attention, praised them whenever possible, and loved them like they were my nieces and nephews. And *anytime* I was going to be around Tom, if it was appropriate, I brought my children, Elizabeth and Joel Porter, with me.

Tom's children loved me. And his wife warmed up to me quickly. Tom was still a hard nut to crack, but he couldn't hold out forever. It's hard to hold a grudge against someone your whole family likes—especially when that person has never done anything wrong to you in the first place.

Maybe you have a "Tom" in your life, someone you've never gotten along with. You easily see all the person's weaknesses and find it difficult to see anything but differences. I guarantee you that you can agree on *something*. All you have to do is to find it. And once you do, give it 100 percent of your effort. You'll be amazed by the impact it can make.

101 PERCENT PRINCIPLE DISCUSSION QUESTIONS

1. Have you ever met someone who seems to practice the 101 Percent Principle, a person who masterfully finds the common ground in relationships where people don't see eye to eye? If so, describe that person. What do you admire about him or her? What personal qualities do these people possess that make them so good at connecting with others? What percentage of people in your business or career area practice this principle?

2. Why shouldn't you automatically embrace the 101 Percent Principle in every relationship? Which relationships in your life warrant its use? Describe how you will change your interaction with one of these people.

3. Which situations are not worth the effort required to implement the 101 Percent Principle? Which are? Which issues are important to you? How do these issues relate to your values and priorities?

4. Have you allowed an important relationship to slip through your fingers because you didn't find common ground upon which to connect? What are you missing as a result? How could you go about repairing the relationship? Would the return be worth the effort? What is stopping you from taking action?

5. Think of an important relationship in your life that really needs change. Up to now, have you used a common-ground approach to building the relationship before trying to initiate change? What one thing can you and the other person agree on? How can you use that as a springboard for improving the relationship? How can you then take steps toward change that will benefit both of you?

THE PATIENCE PRINCIPLE

THE JOURNEY WITH OTHERS IS SLOWER THAN THE JOURNEY ALONE

*For the friendship of two,
the patience of one is necessary.*

—ANONYMOUS

THE QUESTION I MUST ASK MYSELF:
DO I TAKE OTHERS WITH ME
EVEN WHEN IT'S INCONVENIENT?

Every now and then, you read a story that just seems too wacky to be true. That's the case with this one about Larry Walters, a guy who took the journey alone. It's crazy, but true:

Larry's boyhood dream was to fly. But fate conspired to keep him from his dream. He joined the Air Force, but his poor eyesight disqualified him from the job of pilot. After he was discharged from the military, he sat in his backyard watching jets fly overhead.

He hatched his weather balloon scheme while sitting outside in his "extremely comfortable" Sears lawn chair. He purchased 45 weather balloons from an army-navy surplus store, tied them to his tethered lawn chair dubbed the Inspiration I, and filled the four-foot diameter balloons with helium. Then he strapped himself into his lawn chair with some sandwiches, Miller Light, and a pellet gun. He figured he would pop a few of the many balloons when it was time to descend.

Larry's plan was to sever the anchor and lazily float up to a height of about 30 feet above his backyard where he would enjoy a few hours of flight before coming back down. But things didn't work out as Larry planned.

When his friends cut the cord anchoring the lawn chair to his Jeep, he did not float lazily up to 30 feet. Instead, he streaked into the LA skies as if shot from a cannon, pulled by a lift of 42 helium balloons holding 33 cubic feet of helium each. He didn't level off at a 100 feet, nor did he level off at 1,000 feet. After climbing and climbing, he leveled off at 16,000 feet.

At that height he felt he could not risk shooting any of the balloons, lest he unbalance the load and find himself in real trouble. So he stayed there, drifting cold and frightened with his beer and sandwiches, for more than 14 hours. He crossed the primary approach corridor of LAX, where Trans World Airlines and Delta Airlines pilots radioed in reports of the strange sight.

Eventually he gathered the nerve to shoot a few balloons, and slowly descended. The hanging tethers tangled and caught in a power line, blacking out a Long Beach neighborhood for 20 minutes. Larry climbed to safety, where he was arrested by waiting members of the LAPD. As he was led away in handcuffs, a reporter dispatched to cover the daring rescue asked him why had he done it. Larry replied nonchalantly, "A man can't just sit around."[1]

Fortunately we don't need to go to such lengths to travel—or to get away from people.

TRAVEL TIPS

For twenty-five years I have done a lot of traveling. I've lost track of how many air miles I've logged, but it must be more than 3 million. I've been on just about every kind of aircraft (*except* a floating lawn chair), in all kinds of conditions, on six out of seven continents. And no matter where I was going or what I was doing, I've always found one thing to be true: the journey with others is always slower than the journey alone.

I was reminded of that again recently when I went on a cruise with my family. On a business trip by myself, I blaze on down to the airport, and I'm on a plane *really* quickly. I know the ins and outs of most airports, I know how to avoid lines, and I don't check bags. And if just Margaret and I are traveling together, we still move very quickly. After thirty-five years of marriage and traveling together, we have a great system. But when we go with the whole family—two children, their spouses, and all the grandchildren—believe me, it's a lot slower. And if you add my parents or Margaret's or either of our siblings or their families, it just multiplies. I love the time with family, and I wouldn't trade it, but I go into such trips *knowing* that we're going to be traveling at a slow pace.

I have to admit, patience is not one of my strengths. Every day I find myself wondering, *Why are these people moving so slowly?* It happens in traffic, in stores, at work, on the golf course, and on and on. One long-time friend calls me the Energizer Bunny. The good news is that while I don't have as much energy as I did in my twenties, I still have lots of energy, even though I'm in my late fifties. The bad news is that when I was younger, I constantly cast vision for the people in my organization and then left them behind—not a good thing for a leader. I had to learn to connect with people and develop patience. These are two critical steps in relationship building:

Patience without connection—the relationship lacks energy.
Connection without patience—the relationship lacks potential.
Connection with patience—the relationship has energy and potential.

If you want relationships to last, you need both energy and potential.

MAKING PATIENCE A VIRTUE

Just about everyone would agree that patience is a good quality; we admire it and desire it. Those of us who need it most are least inclined to cultivate it, however. We need patience in order to develop patience. So how do we overcome this catch-22? The answer is to develop a plan. Here are six steps you can take to become a more patient person in relationships:

1. Prioritize Patience As a Virtue Worthy of Developing

Oft-quoted Arnold Glasgow stated, "The key to everything is patience. You get the chicken by hatching the egg, not smashing it." In the long run, you will find that patience with people is beneficial to you. But you may not see a return right away. It may be something you have to wait for. If you are an impatient person and have a hard time prioritizing patience now, then know this: the people around you will benefit from it immediately. As Greek philosopher Aristotle noted, "The greatest virtues are those which are most useful to other persons."

2. Understand That It Takes Time to Build Good Relationships

Anything really worthwhile in this life takes time to build, and that's true of relationships. The more people involved in the relational circle, the longer it takes. For example, think about how long it takes for a work group to develop relationships and chemistry. Two or three people can get to know each other and learn to work together fairly quickly. It takes

> "The greatest virtues are those which are most useful to other persons."
> —ARISTOTLE

five people a lot longer. If you have nine or ten people, it really takes a lot of time for all of them to jell. The bigger the group, the longer it takes.

Relationships of any depth take time as well. Even in the best circumstances, such as when you have instant chemistry with another person, it still takes time to really build that relationship and make it strong. All good relationships take time.

3. Practice the Exchange Principle

To develop patience, you need to appreciate how other people think and be sensitive to how they feel. Every person thinks . . .

- his problems are biggest

- his jokes are the funniest

- his prayers should get special attention

- his situation is different

- his victories are the most exemplary

- his faults should be overlooked

In other words, each of us thinks our circumstances warrant special consideration—people should be extra patient with us. Instead, we should turn the tables: we should put ourselves in the other person's place (as I explained in the Exchange Principle), and be extra patient with them.

The next time you're feeling impatient with someone who is slowing you down, think about this story: a young woman's car stalled at a stoplight. She tried and tried to get it started, but had no luck whatsoever. The light turned green, and there she sat, angry and embarrassed, holding up traffic. The car behind her could have gone around, but instead the driver added to her frustration by laying on his horn.

After another desperate attempt to get the car started, she got out and walked back to the other car. The man rolled down his window in surprise.

"Tell you what," she said. "You go start my car, and I'll sit back here and honk the horn for you."

4. Realize That People *Have* and *Create* Problems

When it comes to people, there is good news, and there is bad news. The good news is that some people in your life are going to be the source of your greatest joy. The bad news is that those same people may be the cause of your greatest problems. That's true not only at home but also at work. And the higher you climb in leadership, the more difficult the problems. The findings of leadership experts Warren Bennis and Burt Nanus bear this out. They state, "What we have found is that the higher the rank, the more interpersonal and human the undertaking. Our top executives spend roughly 90 percent of their time with others and virtually the same amount of time concerned with the messiness of people problems."[2]

When you decide to develop a relationship with another person, keep in mind that it's a package deal. You don't get to take only the good stuff and reject the bad. Everybody has problems, blind spots, and bad habits. Try to give others the same kind of grace you'd like to receive for your shortcomings.

5. Identify Areas Where People Need Patience with You

While we're on the subject of shortcomings, it's a good idea for us to know what *ours* are. For example, I know that the people closest to me need patience to put up with my idiosyncrasies. Ironically, the first one is putting up with my impatience! (I'm working on that one.) But there are plenty of others. Just for fun, I asked my assistant, Linda Eggers, to give me a list of the areas where she has been longsuffering. It didn't take her long. Here are the top things she mentioned:

- I am constantly losing my cell phone and glasses.

- Anytime we're discussing planning, I want lots of options.

- I am constantly changing my travel plans and needs.

- I overschedule myself, and as a result, projects take longer than the time allotted.

- I hate to say no.

- I want to be able to call her twenty-four hours a day, seven days a week.

I'm sure there are lots more, but that's enough. If I can keep in mind that others are being patient with me in multiple areas, it helps me to remember to be patient with others. Doing that may have a similar effect on you.

6. Recognize That All Relationships Have Give-Ups, Give-Ins, and Give-and-Takes

All relationships have difficult times. It doesn't matter how good they are or how long they've lasted. And we can't always have everything our own way. We will experience areas where we have to give:

- *There will be give-ups.* There will be things I like to do but should not do at this time. For example, when my children were small, I gave up golf. The game was just too time-consuming. My relationship with them was more important.

- *There will be give-ins.* There will be things I don't like to do but should do at this time. I don't particularly like to exercise, but I do want to spend more time on earth with my family and friends. So I get on the treadmill almost every day.

- *There will be give-and-takes.* There will be things we do for one another at this time. I remember one time that Margaret had gone to a women's retreat, and she called me because she wished she was at home. After I hung up the phone, I decided to surprise her by picking her up. It was a two-hour drive each way, but the trip was worth it.

I should mention that nobody can make you give up, give in, or give and take. They are voluntary activities. But if you want relationships to last, you've got to be flexible. Take the advice of psychologist Joyce Brothers, who says that relationships should follow one of the rules of watercraft: "The more maneuverable boat should give way to the less flexible craft."

As I worked on this chapter, I got to thinking about my inner circle, the people closest to me who are integral to my satisfaction and success. Some of them are faster than I am; some of them are slower. But with all of them, I try to do these things:

Serve them. Let them lead and do it their way, and assist them when it helps.

Mentor them. Answer their questions, set an example, and direct or correct only when it will make a difference.

Value them. Listen to their ideas, respect their positions, and never undermine their authority.

Reward them. Take good care of those who take good care of you.

Here's the bottom line when it comes to the Patience Principle. If you travel alone, you can probably go faster. But the journey will never be as rewarding, and you probably won't be able to go as far. With some people, we are patient with them because of the relationship. With other people, we are patient with them because of the return. And with still others, we are patient with them because of both. Every relationship requires patience, but in the end, it's worth it.

PATIENCE PRINCIPLE DISCUSSION QUESTIONS

1. Are there particular personality types that are prone to impatience with other people? If so, describe them. Are there certain types who are especially slow? How can these two types learn to interact more positively?

2. Think about the three to five people who are closest to you. How long have you known them? How did your relationships start? When you first met them, did you expect them to become close friends? How intentional was your investment in the relationship? How much time did it take to develop a deeper relationship? Could you have sped up the process, or did it require all of the time spent?

3. What kinds of situations make people impatient with others? What particular situations make you impatient with people? How does that work against you in relationships? How can you change your attitude or actions to make you less impatient and better able to stay connected with others?

4. In what kinds of relationships is it most difficult to give up what you want, give in to what the other person wants, and give and take in order to do what's best for the relationship? Where do goals come into play? How about values? In what situations would it be wrong to give up or give in? What is an appropriate balance of give-and-take? How can you make sure the relationship does not become unbalanced?

5. Which of your quirks, idiosyncrasies, or oddities might cause others to have to be patient with you? (If you think you don't have any, talk to three close friends or family members, and ask them to tell you what they are.) Why should people be patient with you in these areas? Do you *expect* others to be patient and take it for granted, or are you grateful for their patience? Explain.

THE CELEBRATION
PRINCIPLE

THE TRUE TEST OF
RELATIONSHIPS IS NOT ONLY
HOW LOYAL WE ARE WHEN
FRIENDS FAIL, BUT HOW
THRILLED WE ARE WHEN
THEY SUCCEED

*Average people do not want
others to go beyond average.*

> THE QUESTION I MUST ASK MYSELF:
> DO I ENJOY AND ROOT FOR THE
> SUCCESS OF MY FRIENDS?

486

I believe in all the People Principles in this book, and I work at practicing them every day of my life. But the Celebration Principle is especially important to me personally. I was very fortunate early in my career. I've known since I was four years old what I wanted to do in life. And I grew up in a home with a father who was experienced and successful in the profession in which I would follow him. The situation is similar to that of the Manning family in football. Successful NFL quarterback Peyton Manning (and his younger brother, Eli) grew up in the home of Archie Manning, who played for the New Orleans Saints. As a result, they had a jump-start in football that 99 percent of other kids didn't.

In addition to the experiences and exposure I received from just being around my father, I benefited from his strong leadership. He was very strategic in my development, identifying and encouraging my strengths early. He sent me to several Dale Carnegie seminars before I graduated from high school, directed my growth through extensive reading, and took me to see and meet some of the great preachers of the era. The advantages I received are too many to list. I am truly grateful for all of them.

The result of my upbringing was that I saw success early in my career. I achieved a lot of firsts in my denomination. I was the youngest person to be elected to a national office. I was the first pastor to change the name of the church to better reach the community. I was the youngest to write his first book. And I had the first church that averaged more than one thousand in attendance every Sunday.

Unfortunately during those early years, I might have also been the loneliest pastor in my denomination. The good news was that when I failed, plenty of people were glad to commiserate with me. But when I succeeded, few celebrated. I thought my colleagues and I were on the same team, but evidently they didn't see it that way. Many times Margaret and I celebrated alone.

WHAT I LEARNED ABOUT THE CELEBRATION PRINCIPLE

Those early experiences taught us a lot. Many of the lessons we learned are things that you may also find valuable:

The Joy of the Accomplishment Is Diminished When No One Celebrates with You

When I went to my denomination's conference following my first year as a pastor, I was excited about the things that were happening in my church. I was helping people, and I thought I was really making a difference in my community. My enthusiasm was unbounded. Much to my surprise, nobody shared my excitement! People seemed to look at me with skepticism or disdain. It really deflated me emotionally. The words of playwright Oscar Wilde were true: "Anybody can sympathize with the sufferings of a friend, but it requires a very fine nature to sympathize with a friend's success."

After Margaret and I talked about it, we decided that we would never let others' lack of enthusiasm hinder our own. And we also became determined to celebrate with friends when they succeeded—and to be even more enthusiastic when they surpassed us!

That's one reason I love doing conferences for young leaders. It gives me a chance to celebrate with them—and to champion their successes. I want them to feel encouraged and keep pursuing their dreams. There's no telling what they might accomplish with the knowledge that others want them to succeed.

Many People Identify with Failure; Fewer People Identify with Success

Several years ago, I wrote a book called *Failing Forward*. As I was preparing to work on it, I lectured on the subject around the country. And what I found is that *everyone* identifies with failure. In fact, when I told people that they needed to learn how to use their mistakes as stepping-stones for success by *failing forward*, the reaction of the audience was audible. They wanted to learn how to fail forward.

What I've discovered over the years of working with people is the following: you may be able to impress people with your successes, but if you want to influence them, share your failures. Everybody has failed, so it's a great way to connect.

The problem is that because people so readily identify with failure, they sometimes have a hard time connecting with success. And if they don't identify with success, they may resent it.

What Hinders People from Success Often Keeps Them from Celebrating Others' Success

Frequently the very same qualities that prevent people from achieving success—emotional insecurity, a scarcity mind-set, petty jealousy, etc.— prevent them from celebrating others' successes. They constantly compare themselves to others and find themselves wanting. As a result, they have a hard time getting beyond themselves.

Professional speaker Joe Larson once said, "My friends didn't believe that I could become a successful speaker. So I did something about it. I went out and found me some new friends!" It's sad, but sometimes that's what it takes.

The People Who Celebrate with You Become Lifelong Friends

Back during the first years of my career, two people outside my family who celebrated with us when we succeeded were Dave and Mary Vaughn. Dave was a few years ahead of me in his career, and he was always ready to cheer me on when I achieved a goal or passed a milestone. Even when my church grew to be larger than his and I gained more notoriety, he never held back. And thirty-five years later, he and Mary still celebrate with us!

Beware of the Green-Eyed Monster

In October 2003 at *Catalyst,* a conference for young leaders put on by one of my companies, Andy Stanley spoke. Andy is an effective and authentic communicator. He leads Northpoint Community Church, one of the top churches in the country with an attendance of more than fifteen thousand people every weekend. (Just in case you are unfamiliar with the church world, that puts Northpoint in the top 1 percent of all churches in America.)

Andy's second session was about four negative characteristics that can trip up a leader: guilt, anger, greed, and jealousy. Andy confessed that he sometimes experiences moments of professional jealousy when hearing other successful people speak. He said, "I have to make an extra effort to celebrate the success of other people who do what I do."

That potential to jealousy extends even to Andy's closest friends, including Louie Giglio, who directs Choice Resources. Andy explained,

> Louie and I have been friends since the sixth grade . . . We met at youth camp under a bunk bed while seniors battled it out above our heads. Louie is just a phenomenal communicator. When I announce at our church that Louie Giglio is going to be speaking next week, they all start clapping and we have high attendance Sunday. And then for four or five days the rest of the week everyone's going, "Oh, Louie, Louie, Louie."

Andy went on to tell how Louie always teaches to capacity crowds at his events and delivers outstanding material. And every time Andy hears him speak, tiny pangs of jealousy threaten to rear their ugly heads.

Such feelings could destroy Andy and Louie's relationship, and that relationship is deep. Not only do they sometimes work together, but their families are close, and they even go on vacations together. How does Andy handle the envy he feels? By celebrating Louie's accomplishments. When Louie delivers a great message, Andy goes out of his way to praise him and celebrate with him. And Louie does the same with him. Andy said, "It's not enough to think it. I have to say it because that's how I cleanse my heart. Celebration is how you defeat jealousy."

BECOMING A PARTY STARTER

Andy isn't alone. If most people were honest, they would admit to feelings of jealousy or envy when they witness others' success—even when the people succeeding are close friends. I know I've fought feelings of jealousy. Haven't you? So how do you learn to celebrate with others instead of ignoring or undermining them? Start by doing these four things:

1. Realize It's Not a Competition

It's impossible to do anything of real significance on your own. It's very difficult to achieve success without help. And even if you do become successful, you won't enjoy it without friends. Life is better in a community of people you love and who also love you.

When I reflect on the value of community, many thoughts come to mind:

My success can be achieved only with others.

My lessons can be learned only from others.

My weaknesses can be strengthened only by others.

My servanthood can be tested only under others' leadership.

My influence can be compounded only through others.

My leadership can be focused only on others.

My best can be given only to others.

My legacy can be left only for others.

So I should commit myself to and celebrate with others!

Other people have an impact on every aspect of life. Most of the time, I choose with my attitude whether that impact is positive or negative.

Entertainer Bette Midler said, "The worst part of success is trying to find someone who is happy for you." Don't look at your friends, family, and teammates as competition. Be the rare kind of person who is happy when others succeed.

2. Celebrate When Others See Success

Not everyone views success the way you do. When it comes to the Celebration Principle, you must be willing to look at things from other people's point of view. What are their dreams? What goals have they set? What battles are they fighting? When they achieve something that is important to *them*, then celebrate! And be especially careful when a friend accomplishes something that you've already achieved and perhaps find to be old hat. Be sure to celebrate with enthusiasm. Never steal another person's thunder.

3. Celebrate Successes Others Don't Yet See

Sometimes people make great strides and aren't even aware of it. Have you ever started to diet or exercise and after a while felt that you were struggling, only to have a friend tell you how good you look? Or haven't you worked on a project and felt discouraged by your progress, but had a friend marvel at what you had accomplished? It is inspiring and makes you want to work that much harder. If you *haven't* had a friend do that for you, then you may need some new friends—people who practice the Celebration Principle.

4. Celebrate Most with Those Closest to You

The closer people are to you and the more important the relationship, the more you ought to celebrate. Celebrate early and often with those closest to you—especially with your spouse and children if you have a family. It's usually easy to celebrate victories on the job or in a hobby or sport. But the greatest victories in life are the ones that occur at home.

My friend Dan Reiland says, "A genuine friend encourages and challenges us to live out our best thoughts, honor our purest motives, and achieve our most significant dreams." That's what we need to do with the important people in our lives.

I have a confession to make. I haven't always been a practicer of the Celebration Principle at work. I've always done fairly well celebrating at home, but in the early years of my career, I was very competitive. I was driven to achieve, and I was very aware of where I was ranked in comparison to my colleagues. I took secret joy in watching my progress as I rose in those ranks. But as I progressed toward the top, something happened. The achievement of my goals wasn't as rewarding as I expected it to be. I felt that something was missing.

> "A genuine friend encourages and challenges us to live out our best thoughts, honor our purest motives, and achieve our most significant dreams."
> —DAN REILAND

In the late 1980s and early 1990s I finally began to change. When I turned forty, I realized that to accomplish my goals, I would need the help of others. I began to more aggressively develop my employees to lead. At first, my motives were somewhat selfish. But as I helped others to succeed, I found that it brought me great joy, regardless of whether it benefited me personally.

What I discovered is that the journey is a lot more fun if you take somebody with you. It's hard to have that perspective if your own success is the only thing you celebrate. If you want others to succeed alongside you, then you must encourage them and celebrate their successes. Not only does it give them the incentive to keep striving for their dreams, but it also helps them enjoy the journey along the way. As I began reaching out and celebrating others' successes, I found that the success of others brought me more joy than my success.

Now I try to celebrate with as many people as I can—not just my family, friends, and closest colleagues, but also the people farther outside my circle. The more people I can encourage and help to succeed, the better I like it. If you help enough people, the party never stops.

CELEBRATION PRINCIPLE DISCUSSION QUESTIONS

1. Do you agree that most people more readily identify with failure than with success? Explain your answer. What do the people who identify with success possess that others don't? Do they still need the encouragement that comes when friends celebrate their successes? Why?

2. Some people have trouble celebrating even their own accomplishments. Why is that? How are you when it comes to celebrating successes? Do you take time to celebrate the achievement of milestones and goals? If not, why not? If you don't acknowledge your achievements, will you be enthusiastic about celebrating those of others? What must you do to change your attitude toward yourself and others? If you do celebrate your victories and achievements, how much is too much? Why?

3. Who celebrates with you? Do you have friends, colleagues, or family members who cheer you on? If the answer is no, then you need to cultivate new friendships with people who are more encouraging and who focus on your strengths. If the answer is yes, thank them for their support and be sure to celebrate with them.

4. Which is your natural bent: to engage in competition or to foster cooperation? Can people be competitive and still practice the Celebration Principle effectively? Can people be cooperative by nature, yet neglect to celebrate with others? Explain. What things can people do to foster a celebratory spirit in themselves, regardless of their personality types?

5. Think of people you go out of your way to celebrate with. Are there other people in your life who would be especially encouraged and lifted up by celebration on your part? For whom in your life is it your *responsibility* to encourage through celebration? What would you like to start doing differently to help others celebrate?

THE HIGH ROAD
PRINCIPLE

WE GO TO A HIGHER LEVEL
WHEN WE TREAT OTHERS
BETTER THAN THEY TREAT US

Keep a fair-sized cemetery in your back yard,
in which to bury the faults of your friends.

—HENRY WARD BEECHER

THE QUESTION I MUST ASK MYSELF:
DO I TREAT OTHERS
BETTER THAN THEY TREAT ME?

I n 1842, thirteen-year-old William Booth's life changed. His father, Samuel Booth, lost his business. The elder Booth had once been a nail maker, but when his trade became the victim of mass production, he started a business as a small-time builder. Unfortunately, recurring recessions took their toll, and finally Booth went out of business. It put him and his family into difficult circumstances. As a result, William, who had grown up in a household with enough money to have him educated, was sent out to learn a trade. He was apprenticed to a pawnbroker in a seedy part of Nottingham, England.

"Make money," was the advice of Booth's father, who died bankrupt the next year. Booth did learn about making money while learning his trade. But his apprenticeship also gave him another kind of education. Working in a pawnbroker's shop, he was in daily contact with the poor and destitute. One biography noted, "He learned as from a primer what poverty did to people."[1] It's no coincidence that during his years as an apprentice, he became a person of faith—a Christian.

A CHANGE OF HEART

In 1849, Booth moved to London and took a position in a pawnshop in a poor area south of the Thames River. But after only three years, he gave up this trade and became a minister. He saw faith as the solution to the problems of those who were struggling to survive. And he embarked on a lifelong mission that had two objectives: saving lost souls and righting social injustices.[2]

At first he became a Methodist New Connexion minister, then a traveling evangelist. But in 1865 when some people from the area heard him preach in front of the Blind Beggar Pub in East London, he was recruited to become part of a tent ministry that came to be called the Christian Mission.

From there, Booth ministered to the poorest people in London. The East End contained half of the paupers, homeless, and starving in London.[3] His early converts were some of the most desperate types of people: thieves, prostitutes, gamblers, and drunkards. He was trying to make a difference, but his efforts were not met with appreciation, even from the very people he was trying to help.

He and his fellow workers were harassed and brutalized. Local tavern keepers worked especially hard to undermine his efforts. Even street children threw stones and fireworks through the windows of their meeting hall. Booth's wife, Catherine, said that he would "stumble home night after night, haggard with fatigue. Often his clothes were torn and bloody, bandages swathed his head where a stone had struck."[4] But Booth would not retaliate in kind. And he refused to give up.

Booth worked to feed the poor, house the homeless, and share his faith. His organization continued to grow. By 1867, he had ten full-time workers. By 1874, more than one thousand volunteers and forty-two evangelists worked with him. In 1878 when they reorganized, Booth gave the group a new name. From then on, the organization would be called the Salvation Army.

Unfortunately that didn't stop the group's opponents. Booth was labeled "anti-Christ" by the reformer Lord Shaftesbury.[5] An opposition group formed to try to stop Booth and his associates. They came to call themselves the Skeleton Army. An article in the *Bethnal Green Eastern Post* in November 1882 described them:

> A genuine rabble of "roughs" pure and unadulterated has been infesting the district for several weeks past. These vagabonds style themselves the "Skeleton Army" . . . The object of the skeleton army was to put down the Salvationists by following them about everywhere, by beating a drum and burlesquing their songs, to render the conduct of their processions and

services impossible . . . Amongst the skeleton rabble there is a large percentage of . . . loafers and unmitigated blackguards . . . [and] the disreputable class of publicans who hate the London school board, education and temperance, and who, seeing the beginning of the end of their immoral trafic [sic], and prepared for the most desparate [sic] enterprise.[6]

Despite the horrible treatment they received, the officers and volunteers in the Salvation Army persevered, and they helped hundreds of thousands of people.[7] Often, they converted the very individuals who had persecuted them.

In 1912, William Booth, then age eighty-three, delivered his last public address. In it he stated his commitment to investing in people:

While women weep as they do now, I'll fight; while little children go hungry as they do now, I'll fight; while men go to prison, in and out, in and out, as they do now, I'll fight; while there is a drunkard left, while there is a poor lost girl on the streets, while there remains one dark soul without the light of God, I'll fight—I'll fight to the very end.[8]

Three months later, he died. As one observer put it, the "general" who had led the Salvation Army for more than thirty years was "promoted to glory."

William Booth spent a lifetime practicing the High Road Principle. He continually treated others better than they treated him. And as a result, he lived on the highest level, personally and professionally. I greatly admire William Booth, but I must say I didn't always believe in the High Road Principle. When I was a teenager, my father, Melvin Maxwell, was the president of a Bible college. I often watched in frustration as the college's board of directors was difficult to work with and treated him poorly. Yet no matter how the directors

> ". . . while there remains one dark soul without the light of God, I'll fight."
> —WILLIAM BOOTH

treated him, my father never retaliated; he always took the high road. At the time, his response made me furious.

As I got older and worked with more difficult people, I better understood my father's actions. I realized that if you're slinging mud, you're losing ground. There are really only three roads we can travel when it comes to dealing with others. We can take . . .

> the low road—where we treat others worse than they treat us
> the middle road—where we treat others the same as they treat us
> the high road—where we treat others better than they threat us

The low road damages relationships and alienates others from us. The middle road may not drive people away from us, but it won't attract them to us either; it is reactive rather than proactive and allows others to set the agenda for our lives. The high road helps to create positive relationships and attracts others to us; it sets a positive agenda with others that even negative people find difficult to undermine. Taking the cue from my father, I decided to work at taking the high road with others every day.

HIGH ROAD TRAVELERS

The high road truly is the path less traveled. I say that because taking the high road requires thinking and acting in ways that are not natural or common. However, those who practice the High Road Principle become instruments of grace to others and recipients of grace. And I've observed that "high roaders" have several things in common:

High Roaders Understand That It's Not What Happens to You but What Happens in You That Really Matters

During the Civil War, Confederate General W. H. C. Whiting was jealous of rival general Robert E. Lee. Consequently Whiting spread many rumors about him. But there came a time when General Lee could have gotten even. When President Jefferson Davis was considering

Whiting for a key promotion, he asked General Lee what he thought of Whiting. Without hesitation, Lee endorsed and commended Whiting. The other officers who witnessed the exchange were astonished. Afterward, one of them asked Lee if he had forgotten all the unkind words that Whiting had spread about him.

"I understand that the president wanted to know my opinion of Whiting," responded Lee, "not Whiting's opinion of me."

Newscaster David Brinkley observed, "A successful man is one who can lay a firm foundation with the bricks others have thrown at him." That's what high road travelers do. They stay true to their core values and treat people according to them, not according to external circumstances.

High Roaders Commit Themselves to Traveling the High Road Continually

Nearly anyone can be kind in the face of unkindness every once in a while. It's more difficult to sustain a high road attitude all the time. Hector LaMarque remarked, "Most people make some good choices every day, but they don't make enough good choices to create momentum and obtain success." That's a good insight on what happens for people who take the high road all the time: they create momentum. They also cultivate relational success. Why? Because responding best today puts them in the best place tomorrow.

High Roaders See Their Own Need for Grace, and Therefore, They Extend It to Others

I once saw a sign that read, "To err is human, to forgive—is not company policy." It's funny, but it also hints at people's natural inclination not to give individuals a break when they act in a way that shows their human frailty. Let's face it. We're all human and make mistakes. People who take the high road recognize their humanness, know that they need to be extended grace, and are accordingly more likely to extend it to others.

One of the most dramatic stories I've ever read illustrating this idea came from the life of Corrie Ten Boom, author of *The Hiding Place*. She and her family worked with the underground and hid Jews from the Nazis in their home during World War II. When their actions were discovered, they were arrested by the Gestapo and sent to the Ravensbruck death camp. Every one of her family members died, and only because of a paperwork error did she survive and obtain her release.

A strong woman of faith, Ten Boom lectured often after the war. In 1947, she returned to Ravensbruck to speak about God's grace and forgiveness to the German people. After she spoke, she found herself face-to-face with the cruelest guard she had encountered at Ravensbruck.

"It could not have been many seconds that he stood there—hand held out," she wrote, "but to me it seemed hours as I wrestled with the most difficult thing I ever had to do." Finally she extended her hand and forgave him. She took the most difficult of all high roads.

High Roaders Are Not Victims; They Choose to *Serve* Others

People who take the high road don't do so because no other roads are open to them. They do it as an act of will according to a desire to serve others. They are like the grandmother at her golden wedding anniversary celebration who told the guests the secret of her happy marriage. "On my wedding day," she said, "I decided to make a list of ten of my husband's faults that, for the sake of our marriage, I would overlook." As the guests were leaving, a young wife asked the older woman to name some of the faults that she had overlooked.

"To tell you the truth," the grand-mother said, "I never did get around to making the list. But whenever my husband did something that made me hopping mad, I would say to myself, 'Lucky for him that's one of the ten!'" Because the high road is uphill, no one travels it by accident.

High Roaders Set Higher Standards for Themselves Than Others Would

James Michener, the author of *Tales of the South Pacific*, *Texas*, *Centennial*, *Space*, and many other novels, was a prolific writer who gained respect for his literary prowess and sales success. However, he always had one detractor who remained a thorn in his side for years.

Abandoned as an infant, the author never knew his biological parents. Fortunately he was taken in and raised as a foster son by a widow. He became a Michener, adopting the name of his new family. But each time he published a new book, he received nasty notes from one of the Michener clan. The relative chastised him for besmirching the good Michener name, which he said the novelist had no right to use, despite the fact the writer won a Pulitzer Prize.

Despite the berating, Michener did agree with one thing the relative said. The novelist particularly remembered the comment: "Who do you think you are, trying to be better than you are?" Michener said. "I've spent my life trying to be better than I was, and I am a brother to all who share the same aspiration."

People who embrace the high road make excellence their goal. That's something that can be accomplished if we . . .

> care more than others think is wise
> risk more than others think is safe
> dream more than others think is practical
> expect more than others think is possible
> work more than others think is necessary

When we conduct ourselves according to our highest standards, we are less likely to be defensive and take the low road when attacked by others. I say that because when you know you've done all you can do, you can let criticism roll off your back like rain.

High Roaders Bring Out the Best in Others

Have you ever heard the fable of the lion and the skunk? A proud, loud, and especially obnoxious skunk challenged a lion to a fight. The lion promptly and emphatically declined the challenge.

"Hah!" sneered the skunk. "You're afraid to fight me!"

"No," answered the lion, "but why should I fight you? You would gain fame from fighting me, even though I gave you the worst beating of your life—which I would do. But how about me? I couldn't possibly gain anything by defeating you. On the other hand, everyone I met for a month would know that I had been in the company of a skunk."

The high road is the only path that brings out the best in others. Philosopher-poet Johann Wolfgang von Goethe advised, "Treat people as though they were what they ought to be and you will help them become what they are capable of becoming."

High Roaders Bring Out the Best in Themselves

Making it your practice to always treat others the best that you can affects the way you see the world—and yourself. President Abraham Lincoln said, "Die when I may, I want it said of me by those who knew me best that I always plucked a thistle and planted a flower where I thought a flower would grow." That is what the High Road Principle does to a person's heart over the course of time: it plants flowers where thorny weeds once thrived. The way that you treat others is your statement to the world of who you are. Are you making the kind of statement you desire?

If you don't already practice the High Road Principle, I hope you will embrace it from this day forward. It is probably the best investment you can make in a relationship. If you need a little help moving to the high road, then follow these "directions":

1. Stay on Kindness Street as long as possible.

2. Turn right on Forgiveness Avenue.

3. Avoid Get Even Alley because it is a dead end.

4. Climb to the top of the hill, for there you will see the high road.

5. Take it and stay on it; and if you lose your way, ask God for help.

The high road is often not the easiest road, but it is the only one that leads to the highest level of living.

HIGH ROAD PRINCIPLE DISCUSSION QUESTIONS

1. How would you define the *high road*? Why is it difficult to take the high road with someone who is taking the low road with you? What particular low road actions by others do you find difficult to overcome or ignore?

2. Why do most people take the middle road? How does that affect their relationships? Can a person stay on the middle road and still be an investor in people? Explain.

3. What happens to relationships when people have a get-even mind-set? Can a person desire revenge in one area of life without its affecting other relationships? What does harboring the desire for revenge do to a person emotionally, physically, and spiritually?

4. Describe a difficult situation where you chose to take the high road in a relationship. Why was it difficult? How were you able to overcome your desire to respond in kind? Is that a strategy you use effectively very often? Where did you learn it, or how did you develop it?

5. Do you agree that taking the high road brings out your best? Explain your answer.

Before moving on, let's review the People Principles related to the Investment Question . . .

The Gardening Principle: All relationships need cultivation.

The 101 Percent Principle: Find the 1 percent we agree on and give it 100 percent of our effort.

The Patience Principle: The journey with others is slower than the journey alone.

The Celebration Principle: The true test of relationships is not only how loyal we are when friends fail, but how thrilled we are when they succeed.

The High Road Principle: We go to a higher level when we treat others better than they treat us.

THE SYNERGY QUESTION: CAN WE CREATE A WIN-WIN RELATIONSHIP?

*Win/Win is a frame of mind and heart that
constantly seeks mutual benefit in all human interactions . . .
Win/Win is based on the paradigm that there is plenty
for everybody, that one person's success is not achieved
at the expense or exclusion of the success of others.*

—STEPHEN R. COVEY

If we're honest about relationships, we'll admit that there are some people with whom we want to spend time, and others with whom we don't. What separates the good relationships we desire from the ones that don't do anything for us? The answer is synergy. Some relationships are a win-win. They add value to both parties, and that is rewarding.

I believe that every relationship has the *potential* to be win-win, though not all relationships achieve that quality. But when both parties enter into a relationship with an investment mind-set—after having connected and built trust with each other—a win-win relationship is often the result.

The wonderful thing about win-win relationships is that they can be forged in every area of life and in all kinds of relationships: between husbands and wives, parents and children, friends and neighbors, bosses and employees. If both parties sustain a giving attitude and both are having their needs met, then the relationship can become something truly special. The "currency" that they give each other doesn't have to be the same. They may provide each other unconditional love. Or one person may provide loyal admiration, and the other security. One may provide mentoring, and the other gratitude. One may build the business, and the other may provide a paycheck. One may provide humor, and the other may be a great audience. As long as both people experience consistent wins in areas they value, they develop synergy.

The following People Principles answer the question, "Can we create a win-win relationship?" and will help anyone who practices them create relationships with synergy.

The Boomerang Principle: When we help others, we help ourselves.

The Friendship Principle: All things being equal, people will work with people they like; all things not being equal, they still will.

The Partnership Principle: Working together increases the odds of winning together.

The Satisfaction Principle: In great relationships, the joy of being together is enough.

In the long run, lopsided relationships don't last. If one person is doing all the giving and the other is doing all the receiving, the giver will eventually become worn out. And ironically the taker will become dissatisfied because he will feel he is not receiving enough. The only way to build a positive, long-lasting, synergistic relationship is to make sure everybody wins!

THE BOOMERANG
PRINCIPLE

WHEN WE HELP OTHERS,
WE HELP OURSELVES

No man becomes rich unless he enriches others.

—ANDREW CARNEGIE

> THE QUESTION I MUST ASK MYSELF:
> DO I EXPERIENCE A RETURN
> WHEN I HELP OTHERS?

I n the early years of my career, I did not have a correct view of life. I approached life as if it were a slot machine. I wanted to put as little as possible into it, and I always hoped to hit the jackpot. I'm embarrassed to say that I often had a similar approach in my interaction with people. I was more focused on what people could do for me than what I could do for *them*. As a result, I would try to make relational "withdrawals" without ever having made any "deposits." Needless to say, I was not very successful.

As I spent more time working with others, my thinking slowly began to change. I began to learn the Big Picture Principle, to see people in a different light, and to place a higher value on them. Once my attitude started changing, so did my actions. I started to invest in people simply because they had value. They were important. And I found that when I focused on what I could give rather than what I could get, people blossomed, relationships matured, and life was more rewarding. After I started to make giving my goal, I often felt that I received more from people than I was able to give.

Over the course of many years, I began learning to invest in people first and often. Somebody has to make the first move in relationships. So I figured, *Why not me?* I started to take a giver's approach to life, focusing on what I could give in relationships. And I often tried to do it without an expectation of receiving something in return. I discovered that when I added value to people, many desired to add value back to me. When that happened, the relationships developed an incredible synergy and went to a new level.

What Goes Around . . .

Where do you stand on the subject of giving to others? I believe there are only three kinds of people when it comes to this subject:

1. TAKERS RECEIVE AND NEVER GIVE. Many people focus on themselves and rarely go out of their way to do anything for others. Such people are takers. They worry only about what they can get, and they are never satisfied.

2. TRADERS RECEIVE AND THEN GIVE. Some people focus on keeping score. They are willing to give, but their primary motivation isn't to help others. They see relationships as an exchange. Often they give because they think they owe something to someone who has helped them, and they desire to make things "even." I was like that early in my career. I was grateful to people who helped me, but I didn't understand the value of adding value to others. And I didn't initiate giving.

3. INVESTORS GIVE AND THEN RECEIVE. In this third group, people focus on others. They give first and then receive if something is offered in return. They believe that success comes from being helpful, caring, and constructive. They desire to make everything and everyone they touch better, and they understand that the best way to accomplish that is to give of themselves. Ironically, by possessing an agenda to give first, they are the ones who most often experience the synergy of win-win relationships.

People who invest in other people have some things in common:

Investors Understand That People Are of Great Value

Once when I was speaking to employees at BellSouth, an executive for the company stated, "People are our company's most appreciable asset."

I heard good news and bad news in that statement. The good news is that he truly valued his people and cared about their well-being. The bad news is that what he said is only partly true. People are an *appreciating* asset only if we are willing to *invest* in them. Most people, if left alone, remain much the same.

Investors Embrace the Boomerang Principle

People who invest in others know that the best way to help themselves is to help others. They start that investment process by investing in relationships. They see everyone as a potential friend. Counselor and author Alan Loy McGinnis noted:

> In research at our clinic, my colleagues and I have discovered that friendship is the springboard to every other love. Friendships spill over onto the other important relationships of life. People with no friends usually have a diminished capacity for sustaining any kind of love. They tend to go through a succession of marriages, be estranged from various family members, and have trouble getting along at work. On the other hand, those who learn how to love their friends tend to make long and fulfilling marriages, get along well with the people at work, and enjoy their children.[1]

> People are an appreciating asset only if we are willing to invest in them.

When you invest in a friendship, you open the door to investment—and ultimately the possibility of a return.

Investors Practice the Principle of Sowing and Reaping

There has never been a person who gave that did not receive in return! You may not believe that, but it is a fact. The Boomerang Principle is true: when we help others, we help ourselves. Here's why I say that. Whenever you give to another person, you will receive something in return that affects your valuables, your values, or your virtues.

- VALUABLES: *the things that provide financial worth*. When people think about receiving something in return for giving, their thoughts often turn to material benefits. Sometimes when you help others, you do receive something of financial worth. But that is only one kind of benefit and perhaps not the most common kind.

- VALUES: *the things that bring fulfillment*. Have you ever given anonymously? If so, then you understand that while you received nothing tangible in return, you benefited emotionally or spiritually. Anytime you do something to fulfill your values, you benefit.

- VIRTUES: *the things that develop character*. Many benefits we receive from giving come in the area of character. Every time you overcome the inclination to be greedy by giving, you become less selfish. Every time you help someone and don't see an immediate return, you become more patient. Such things build character.

In nature, if you sow, you reap. What you reap depends on what you plant. And you always reap later than you sow. The same is true when it comes to relationships. As in nature, they take time.

Investors Believe That Helping Others Is the Divine Work of People

American literary giant Ralph Waldo Emerson advised:

> Don't be a cynic . . . [and] bewail and bemoan. Omit the negative propositions . . . Don't waste yourself in rejection, nor bark against the bad, but chant the beauty of the good . . . Set down nothing that will not help somebody. It is one of the beautiful compensations of life that no man can sincerely try to help another without helping himself. To help the young soul, to add

energy, inspire hope, and blow the coals into a useful flame; to redeem defeat by new thought and firm action: This, though not easy, is the work of divine man.[2]

TAKE INVESTING IN OTHERS TO A NEW LEVEL

Investing in others is one of the most noble and productive things we can do. Whatever we can do to help others makes the world a better place. As President Woodrow Wilson said, "You are not here merely to make a living. You are here in order to enable the world to live more amply, with greater vision, with a finer spirit of hope and achievement. You are here to enrich the world, and you impoverish yourself if you forget the errand."

So how do you enrich the world and become someone who invests in others? Begin by taking these five steps:

1. Think "Others First"

Good, healthy, growing relationships begin with the ability to put other people first. Remember the Big Picture Priniciple, and work to develop an attitude of kindness toward everyone. Begin every relationship by giving the other person respect—even before he has had a chance to earn it. Initiate acts of kindness with everyone.

2. Focus on the Investment, Not the Return

Novelist Herman Melville believed that "we cannot live only for our-selves. A thousand fibers connect us with our fellow men; and along those fibers, as sympathetic threads, our actions run as causes, and they come back to us as effects." We are intimately linked with other people, and our destinies are interwoven. As a result, when we help others, we will benefit. But that is not where we should place our focus.

> Good, healthy, growing relationships begin with the ability to put other people first.

Investors in people are like investors in the stock market. In the long haul, they will benefit, but they have little control over what that return will look like or how it will occur. But they *can* control what and how they invest. And that's where they should focus their time and energy.

3. Pick Out a Few People with Great Potential

In 1995 when I began investing in people full-time, I felt called to invest strategically in ten people. My desire was to pick people with great potential and invest in them to help them become better leaders. The list of people has changed over the years, but my commitment to serving others has not. If anything, it has intensified. In 1995, I simply wanted to add value to others. Now ten years later, I want to multiply value to others by adding value to leaders.

When people prepare to make financial investments, the wise ones don't put all their money into a single stock or fund. They diversify by investing in several areas. (If you invest in only one and it doesn't perform well, you're in trouble.) But good investors don't spread themselves too thin, either. They know they can give only so much time and attention to each particular investment. Wise investors in people follow a similar pattern. Pick only as many people as you can handle with intensity, choose only people with great potential for growth, and choose only people whose need for growth matches your gifts and talents.

4. With Their Permission, Begin the Process

You cannot help someone who does not want your help. That seems so obvious that I hesitate to say it, but I feel that I must because I see people with good intentions trying to initiate the process without getting the buy-in of the person they're trying to help.

In *The 21 Irrefutable Laws of Leadership*, the Law of Buy-In says that people buy in to the leader, then the vision. Mentoring relationships possess a leader-follower dynamic. The people being mentored must trust and believe in their teachers. The stronger the relationships and the greater the trust, the higher the likelihood that the investment process will work. But it must begin with agreement.

5. Enjoy a Return in Due Season

Poet Edwin Markham wrote,

> There is a destiny that marks us as brothers;
> No one goes his way alone:
> All that we send into the lives of others
> Comes back into our own.

I am convinced that when people's motives are pure and they genuinely desire to add value to others, they cannot help others without receiving some benefit. The return may be immediate, or it may take a long time, but it will occur. And when it does, the relationship begins to resonate with synergy.

You are probably familiar with the story of Helen Keller, the deaf and blind girl whose life was transformed thanks to the efforts of Anne Sullivan. Keller, who was only seven when Sullivan came into her life, lived almost like an animal. But Sullivan taught her to communicate and opened the world to her. By the time Keller was an adult, she was able to take care of herself. She went on to receive a degree from Radcliffe College and to become a famous author and lecturer.

What you may not know is that when Anne Sullivan became ill years later, the person who took care of her was none other than Helen Keller. The helper became the one who needed help, and the one to whom she had added value turned around and added value to her. Invest in others, and like a boomerang, it will come back to you, sometimes in a most unexpected way.

BOOMERANG PRINCIPLE DISCUSSION QUESTIONS

1. In the past, how have you approached relationships: as a taker, a trader, or an investor? If you have been a taker, why do you think you have been reluctant to give of yourself to others? If you have been a trader, in what ways have you "kept score" with other people? If you have been an investor, in what specific ways have you invested in others? Do you desire to change the way you see relationships? If so, why?

2. Is it possible to add value to people if you don't value people? Explain your response. Describe the characteristics of someone who values people and puts others first. Think of someone you know who fits this profile. How do you measure up?

3. How should one go about the process of selecting people to invest in? What traits should all people to be invested in possess? What specific needs or characteristics should a person you would mentor possess? Why?

4. What are your greatest talents and gifts? Are these traits that can be shared? In what way can you use them to add value to others?

5. What is your plan for intentionally investing in others? Do you have a process already in place? If so, how has it worked? What do you need to change? What have others done that might work for you? If you have not yet created a plan, what do you think it should include? Have you observed a model that works? If so, what parts of it will you embrace? When will you start?

THE FRIENDSHIP
PRINCIPLE

ALL THINGS BEING EQUAL, PEOPLE WILL WORK WITH PEOPLE THEY LIKE; ALL THINGS NOT BEING EQUAL, THEY STILL WILL

The most I can do for my friend is simply be his friend.

—HENRY DAVID THOREAU

> THE QUESTION I MUST ASK MYSELF:
> AM I A FRIEND TO
> THE PEOPLE I WORK WITH?

I f you were suddenly faced with a huge project that had a tough deadline and you needed to pull together a group of people to help you accomplish it, who would you ask for help? Would you enlist the aid of the people in your office who give you the most trouble? Would you go out of your way to partner with people who rub you the wrong way? Of course not!

What if you became aware of a business opportunity that you knew was the chance of a lifetime? How would you pursue it? Would you use the Yellow Pages to find people to help you? Would you put an ad in the newspaper looking for a business partner? Certainly not! You would mentally review the friends and associates qualified to help, and you would choose the people with whom you have the best relationships. And if two people had the same level of skill, you'd pick the person you most like to work with.

All that may seem painfully obvious to you as you read it. However, I believe that most people underestimate the power and importance of relationships in regard to business and career. They try to learn the most recent management fad. They focus on product quality. They create programs and systems to improve productivity or increase repeat business. They collect e-mail addresses. These things may be helpful, but the real key is relationships. Never underestimate the power of friendship and likability when it comes to doing business.

To see an excellent example of the Friendship Principle, look at the life of Bill Porter. If ever there was a person with obstacles to succeeding in business, he was it. Porter was born with cerebral palsy. As a child, he was always physically behind his peers. From birth his right hand has been nearly useless, and verbal communication has always been difficult. The so-called experts thought he was retarded and advised his parents to institutionalize him. They refused. Instead they made major adjustments to their lifestyle, worked with him, and helped him to cultivate independence. Porter worked hard and completed high school, receiving his diploma.

DETERMINED TO MAKE IT

After high school, he looked for work with the aid of the Oregon Department of Employment. He took a job as a stock clerk and was fired after only one day. He worked as a cashier for Goodwill and lasted only three days. He took jobs at the Salvation Army working on the loading dock and at the Veterans Administration answering phones. After more firings, the Department of Employment deemed him "unemployable."

But Porter wouldn't give up. He didn't want to live his life accepting a government disability check. When he got an opportunity to sell household items to raise money for United Cerebral Palsy, he loved it. He decided to make sales his career. He had a hard time finding a company that would give him a try, though. Finally he persuaded the director of Watkins Incorporated to give him a chance. He was reluctantly offered a territory that no other salesman would accept—working for straight commission. Porter would be selling household products door to door.

That was in the 1950s. Today, Porter is in his seventies, and he still works for Watkins. For decades he got up in the morning at 5:45, took two hours to laboriously get ready and dressed, caught buses across town to his territory, and haltingly walked seven to ten miles every day, going door to door selling products such as vanilla, spices, and detergents. He won his first sales award more than forty years ago and long ago became Watkins' number one salesman in the Northwest. In an era when door-to-door salesmen faded away, he continued to thrive.

How did he do it? His first asset has always been persistence. His second has been friendship. How else could you explain the continued success of a salesman whom people find difficult to understand, selling products that can be bought cheaper at discount stores, being sold in a method that went out of style decades ago, from a man who asks his customers to complete their own order forms because he has trouble writing? As Shelly Brady, who has assisted Porter since she was seventeen, says, "He snuck into people's hearts."[1]

THE FOUR LEVELS OF BUSINESS RELATIONSHIPS

As soon as you understand the way that relationships affect business, you begin to realize that all business relationships are not created equal. As I have studied the subject, I've found that there are four levels:

1. People Knowledge—Your Understanding of People Helps Build Your Business

In the introduction of this book, I discussed the importance of people skills in business relationships. They are absolutely essential to success. All the product knowledge in the world won't help someone without people skills. Nor will technical expertise. Nor will the ability to build a brilliantly efficient organization. If individuals don't possess people skills, they very quickly hit a ceiling in their effectiveness.

An interesting way that some people overcome a lack of expertise in people knowledge is to partner with someone who possesses it in abundance. For example, people like Steve Wozniak and Steve Jobs brought together technical skill and people knowledge in a way that has made Apple computers a household name.

I believe there are thousands and thousands of technically talented people whose businesses would turn around overnight if only they mastered—or partnered with someone who possessed—people knowledge.

2. Service Skills—Your Treatment of People Helps Build Your Business

Barry J. Gibbons, author of *This Indecision Is Final*, maintains, "Between 70 percent and 90 percent of decisions not to repeat a purchase of anything are not about product or price. They are about some dimension of the service relationship." Many businesses today recognize this fact, and as a result, they place greater emphasis on service to their customers. How you treat the people you do business with really matters, especially in a competitive marketplace. The more competitive the industry, the more important the service.

3. Business Reputation—Your Reputation for Relationships Helps Build Your Business

Writer Howard Hodgson said, "Whatever business you are in, you are in a business of relationships. That's why your reputation is your greatest asset." Because of Bill Porter's physical disabilities, many people under-estimated his people skills—until they got to know him. Porter knew how to connect with people and understand their needs. For that reason, he was a good salesman. He also conducted his business in such a way that his customers *always* got what they were promised, when it was promised. Over time, his reputation grew. And as a result, he has sold products to three and sometimes four generations of some families!

4. Personal Friendship—Your Friendship with Others Builds Your Business

The highest level of business relationships is reached when people like your business, but more important, they like you! When there is a heartfelt personal connection to another person, it becomes stronger than any other kind of business bond. That's why I say all things being equal, people will work with people they like; all things not being equal, they still will. Friendship is the difference maker! Even when the odds are stacked against you, friendship many times will still give you the edge with the customer. Why? People like being and working with their friends.

> Even when the odds are stacked against you, friendship many times will still give you the edge with the customer.

I read a story about when General William Westmoreland was in Vietnam, and he was reviewing a platoon of paratroopers. As he walked down the line, he asked each of them a question: "How do you like jumping, son?"

"Love it, sir!" was the first answer.

"The greatest experience in my life, sir!" exclaimed the next paratrooper.

But when he came to the third one, the soldier's response surprised him.

"I hate it, sir," the young man replied.

"Then why do you do it?" asked Westmoreland.

"Because I want to be around the guys who love to jump."

THE VALUE OF FRIENDSHIP

Although I've been examining the Friendship Principle solely in the context of business, it applies much more broadly. People want to engage in activities with people they like. Once again, this probably seems obvious, but I mention it because I want to emphasize the value—and power—of true friendship in every context and situation.

One person who had incredible insight about relationships was King Solomon of ancient Israel. It's said that he was the wisest person who ever lived. During the course of his lifetime, he wrote many wise things about friendships, and we can learn from them today. Here are a few of those truths about real friends:

Real Friends Are Scarce

Solomon wrote, "Friends come and friends go, but a true friend sticks by you like family."[2] When you develop a deep friendship with someone, value it, because real friends are rare. A true friend . . .

is someone who sees you at your worst but never forgets your best.

is someone who thinks you're a little bit more wonderful than you really are.

is someone you can talk with for hours or be with in complete silence.

is as happy for your success as you are.

trusts you enough to say what he really means when talking to you.
doesn't try to know more, act smarter, or be your constant teacher.

In short, a real friend is a friend all the time. Value the real friends you have. They are precious. More important, try to become a real friend to others. There are few gifts greater than being a friend.

Real Friends Are Refreshing

Solomon observed, "Just as lotions and fragrance give sensual delight, a sweet friendship refreshes the soul."[3] Every situation in life improves when a friend is involved. When you want to share a fun experience, there's nothing like having a friend with you. When you're facing a crisis, a friend shares its weight. C. S. Lewis said, "Friendship is born at the moment one person says to another, 'What, you too? I thought I was the only one.'" That kind of connection is refreshing, no matter what's happening in your life.

How do others respond to you? When people see you coming, do they expect to be refreshed and energized? Or do they have to expend energy to sustain their interaction with you? Everyone should be a breath of fresh air to someone in his life.

Real Friends Make Us Better

In the best kinds of friendships, the people improve one another simply by being together. As Solomon said, "You use steel to sharpen steel, and one friend sharpens another."[4]

Automaker Henry Ford was having lunch with a person and asked him, "Who is your best friend?" As Ford waited for his response, the man hesitated. He wasn't sure.

> "Friendship is born at the moment one person says to another, 'What, you too? I thought I was the only one.'"
> —C. S. Lewis

"I will tell you who your best friend is," Ford jumped in. "Your best friend is the one who brings out the best that is within you."

That's what real friends do. They bring out each other's best.

Real Friends Remain Faithful

Have you heard this one? What do you get if you cross Lassie with a pit bull? You get a dog that bites your face off and then goes for help. Real friends aren't like that. In this world there are plenty of people who don't care about others. Solomon remarked, "Calloused climbers betray their very own friends; they'd stab their own grandmothers in the back."[5] But real friends remain faithful no matter what.

Author and pastor Richard Exley said, "A true friend is one who hears and understands when you share your deepest feelings. He supports you when you are struggling; he corrects you, gently and with love, when you err; and he forgives you when you fail. A true friend prods you to personal growth, stretches you to your full potential. And most amazing of all, he celebrates your successes as if they were his own."

You cannot sustain a deep friendship with everyone, nor should you try. But you should cultivate genuine, deep friendships with a few people. And you can be a friendly, kind, supportive person to everyone you meet. You can treat every person as an individual, not simply a business "contact." If you put others first as people and then worry about business second, you're on your way to practicing the Friendship Principle.

No matter what kind of business or industry you're in, the Friendship Principle can help you. It doesn't matter if you're the salesman or the customer, a boss or an employee, an executive or a stay-at-home mom. Whatever work you do, people will be more inclined to do it with you when you treat them like a friend.

FRIENDSHIP PRINCIPLE DISCUSSION QUESTIONS

1. How can you tell when people place business ahead of friendship? How can you tell when they approach relationships the other way around? What motivates people to place business first? What motivates others to place friendship first? Which is your natural inclination?

2. Do you agree that if you look at people in terms of friendship first and business second, then you have a chance of making a friend *and* succeeding in business? Explain your answer.

3. Consider the four levels of business relationships:

   - People knowledge
   - Service skills
   - Business reputation
   - Personal friendship

   On what level are most of the people you do business with? Does it matter whether the person is a colleague or client? Where would you like them to be? What is preventing you from taking your business relationships to the next level?

4. Have you ever worked in a company or industry with a bad business reputation? What was it like? Is it possible to practice the Friendship Principle in such an environment? What kinds of things work against you in such a situation? What must you do to succeed and practice the Friendship Principle?

5. Do you agree that true friends are people who bring out the best in you? If so, how does that work? Do people who bring out your best *become* your friends? Or because people *are* your friends, they bring out your best? How do the encouragement from and sharpening by friends apply in the work environment?

THE PARTNERSHIP
PRINCIPLE

WORKING TOGETHER
INCREASES THE ODDS OF
WINNING TOGETHER

You can do what I cannot do. I can do what you cannot do.
Together we can do great things.

—MOTHER TERESA

> THE QUESTION YOU MUST ASK YOURSELF:
> ARE OTHERS BETTER OFF BECAUSE OF
> THEIR PARTNERSHIP WITH ME?

Some people just naturally approach life with a partnership mind-set. And as a result, they reap unusual success. Benjamin Franklin was one such person.

Franklin is remembered as a printer, statesman, inventor, writer, and Founding Father of the United States. He was born in Boston, the fifteenth of seventeen children, the son of a candle maker. His formal schooling lasted less than two years. At age twelve, he apprenticed to his brother to learn the trade of printing. At seventeen, with no resources other than his talent and hard work, he moved to Philadelphia to seek his fortune, starting out as a printer and journalist. By 1730, at age twenty-four, he owned his own business. In 1748, he was wealthy enough to retire.

The reason Franklin wanted to retire was to devote himself to scientific research. His experiments with electricity made him world famous. Beginning in the 1750s, he became heavily involved in community affairs and politics. Once again, his accomplishments were incredible. He was one of a handful of influencers who shaped the American Revolution and the creation of the new country. A cowriter of the Declaration of Independence and the Constitution, he was the only person to have signed the four documents that helped to create the United States: the Declaration of Independence (1776), the Treaty of Alliance, Amity, and Commerce with France (1778), the Treaty of Peace between England, France, and the United States (1782), and the Constitution (1787).[1]

PARTNERSHIP MAKER

A quick review of Franklin's accomplishments might tempt one to believe that Franklin was the kind of person inclined to work alone.

Nothing could be further from the truth. Franklin embraced the Partnership Principle from early in his career. Despite his meager education, Franklin was a lifelong learner. But he knew his greatest progress would not come working alone. So in 1727, at the age of twenty-one, he founded a group called the Junto. Franklin described it as "a club of mutual improvement" composed of "most of my ingenious acquaintance." The original group included printers, surveyors, craftsmen, a clerk, and a merchant. "We met on Fridays," Franklin said. "The rules that I drew up required that every member, in his turn, should produce one or more queries on any point of Morals, Politics, or Natural Philosophy, to be discuss'd by the company; and once in three months produce and read an essay of his own writing, on any subject he pleased."[2] Franklin's Junto eventually evolved into the American Philosophical Society, which still exists today.

An important part of Franklin's continuing self-education was reading books. Often short of funds when he was young, Franklin came up with a partnership approach to acquiring books. He convinced a group of people to pool their money and buy a library of books to be shared. By 1731, the idea evolved into the nation's first lending library.

Franklin used a similar partnership approach again and again. Because of the threat of fire in Philadelphia, he convinced a group of colonists to come together to form the city's first volunteer firefighting club in 1736. In the event of a fire threatening the property of any club member, all of the other members would come to his aid. In 1751, he helped to found the first public hospital in the country. In 1752, he encouraged a group of colonists to share financial risks by partnering in the Philadelphia Contributorship, America's first fire insurance company. He got people to work together to hire street sweepers and to employ local policemen. Time after time, Franklin teamed up with others so that all could achieve success.

No matter how successful Franklin became, he never abandoned his partnership approach to achievement. He employed it on national and international scales. When the United States was seeking its independence, its founders knew that the country would not survive without the help and partnership of other nations. Franklin was dispatched to Europe as the nation's first minister to France. He was successful in persuading the French to partner with America against the British. Scholar Leo Lemay called Franklin "the most essential and successful American diplomat of all time"[3]

And after the young nation had secured its independence and was attempting to write its constitution in 1787, when delegates could not agree on the structure of the legislature, Franklin proposed the "great compromise" that created our current two-house congressional structure. Few men have had a greater impact on the United States. And few people have understood the power of partnership the way Franklin did.

LEARNING TO LOOK TO OTHERS

From his youth, Ben Franklin understood that working together increases the odds of winning together. I wish I had been as wise. It took me a long time to learn the Partnership Principle. In this area of life, I have gone through four stages:

1. I Want to Make a Difference . . .

Like many people, I started out in what I call the self stage. My focus was on me and what I could do. That's not to say I was doing anything wrong. My motives were positive. It's just that my perspective—along with my effectiveness—was so limited. I worked hard, and I got a lot done. But I couldn't do anything of real significance by myself. What I later discovered and wrote in *The 17 Indisputable Laws of Teamwork* is really true: one is too small a number to achieve greatness.

If you think that you can make a difference on your own, then you need to read the words of the poet who wrote "The Indispensable Man":

> One is too small a number to achieve greatness.

Sometime when you're feeling important;
Sometime when your ego's in bloom;
Sometime when you take for granted,
You're the best qualified in the room.

Sometime when you feel that your going
Would leave an unfillable hole;
Just follow this simple instruction,
And see how it humbles your soul.

Take a bucket and fill it with water,
Put your hand in it up to the wrist;
Pull it out and the hole that's remaining,
Is a measure of how you'll be missed.

You may splash all you please when you enter,
You can stir up the water galore;
But stop and you'll find in a minute,
That it looks quite the same as before.

The moral in this quaint example
Is to do just the best that you can;
Be proud of yourself, but remember
There's no indispensable man![4]

My personal definition of *high morale* is "I make a difference." Conversely, my definition of *low morale* is "I make no difference at all." If your personal sense of well-being is affected by your ability to make a positive impact on others, then you need to think beyond what only you can do.

2. I Want to Make a Difference with People . . .

When I began to look beyond myself, I discovered that I could go farther and achieve more when others joined me on the journey. As a result, I wanted to take *everybody* with me. It didn't take me long to realize that was a mistake. Here's why:

- *Not everyone* should *take the trip—passion*. Have you ever worked with people who said they were on board with you and believed in what you were trying to accomplish, yet you kept having to talk them into doing their part? Those people have no passion for the work. They may want to take the ride, but they have no interest in pedaling. Take them on, and they will wear you out.

- *Not everyone* wants *to take the trip—attitude.* Some people simply don't believe in you or what you're doing. That doesn't mean you're wrong, nor does it make them wrong. It just means you shouldn't try to take them with you.

- *Not everyone* can *take the trip—ability.* The difference between a partnership and a rescue mission is capacity. Some people may want to make a difference, but they have no ability to affect what you're doing. You cannot afford to partner with someone with whom there is no fit.

The main lesson I learned during this phase is that I should try to build relationships with everyone, but I should forge partnerships with only a few.

3. I Want to Make a Difference with People Who Want to Make a Difference . . .

English statesman Henry Van Dyke observed, "In the progress of personality, first comes a declaration of independence, then a recognition of interdependence." When I turned forty, I entered a season of life where I finally started to realize this truth: those closest to you determine your level of success. It was then that I moved from simply working with good, capable people to partnering with difference makers. And let me tell you the secret of going to the next level in this area: find capable people with the same passion and mission as yours who also need others to make a difference. When you create partnerships with these people, there's no telling what you can do together.

4. I Want to Make a Difference with People Who Want to Make a Difference Doing Something That Makes a Difference

Only at this time of my life have I entered what I call the significance stage. I have many rewarding relational partnerships, and together we are doing many things that are making a positive impact by helping others. I can't imagine anything more rewarding.

Rabbi Harold Kushner remarked, "The purpose of life is not to win. The purpose of life is to grow and to share. When you come to look back on all that you have done in life, you will get more satisfaction from the pleasure you have brought into other people's lives than you will from the times that you outdid and defeated them."

The Power of Partnership

As you read the previous pages, you may have noticed something about the progression I experienced:

I want to make a difference (self stage) . . .
with people who want to make a difference (sharing stage) . . .
doing something that makes a difference (significance stage)!

Between the self stage and the significance stage lies the sharing stage with people. Incredible power comes from discovering partnership with others. It can be one of the most rewarding experiences of life. It has so many benefits:

When You Partner with Others, You Lose Nothing

Thomas Jefferson observed, "A candle loses nothing when it lights another candle." That is the real nature of partnership. I find that many people don't think that way. They believe that sharing means losing something. But I don't think that's true.

> "A candle loses nothing when it lights another candle."
> —THOMAS JEFFERSON

Every person possesses one of two mind-sets: scarcity or abundance. People with a scarcity mind-set believe that there's only so much to go around, so you have to scrap for everything you can and protect whatever you have at all costs. People with an abundance mind-set believe there's always enough to go around. If you have an idea, share it; you can always come up with another one. If you have money, give some of it away; you can always make more. If you have only one piece of pie, let someone else eat it; you can bake another one.

I believe that in this area, you get from life what you expect. You can hoard what little you have and receive no more. Or you can give what you have, and you will be rewarded with abundance. Your attitude makes the difference. So if you partner with another person and give generously, one way or another you're going to get back more than you gave.

When You Partner with Others, You Help Yourself

Novelist Mark Twain said, "The best way to cheer yourself up is to cheer everybody else up." What he knew instinctively is that when you help others, you help yourself. At the very least, you will receive the satisfaction of helping another human being. But more likely than not, when you help other people, they desire to turn around and help you.

Richard Shipley, president and CEO of Shipley Associates, offers this advice: "Work well with others to help them achieve their own victories; yours will follow. Share ownership with the right people. You'll spend many hours with these colleagues, so select associates you really enjoy working with. Allow successful colleagues to share the equity in your mutual efforts."

When You Partner with Others, You Are Rewarded with Hope

In 2003, Dave Sutherland, who had been the president of one of my companies, INJOY Stewardship Services (ISS), was ready to make a transition and move to the West Coast where his children and grandchildren live. Dave had done a wonderful job of building the company for almost a decade, and I wondered how I was going to replace him. It didn't take me long to realize who needed to succeed him in leading the company: Kirk Nowery.

Kirk, a former pastor, had come aboard years before at ISS and had worked with hundreds of pastors and churches. He has a passion for adding value to pastors, his skills are tremendous, and no one has worked harder. And he is an excellent leader. I couldn't think of anyone I'd rather partner with in helping churches fulfill their vision. So Margaret and I talked with Kirk, and after several lengthy discussions, I offered him the job.

A few days later, Margaret and I got a card in the mail. The printed message read, "For all that has been, Thanks. For all that will be, Yes.— Dag Hammarskjold." Below it Kirk had handwritten,

> *Dear John and Margaret, with the deepest respect and honor,*
> *I accept.*

That moment brought me great joy, and I was so grateful. Why? Because I knew that the future of ISS was bright.

If you desire to cultivate win-win relationships, embrace the Partnership Principle. You probably know in your heart that what you can do alone pales in comparison to what you can do with others. The most rewarding relationships are always partnerships. I've found that it's true in business, it's true in marriage, and I believe it will be true for you.

Partnership Principle Discussion Questions

1. What does "making a difference" mean to you? Have you considered whether or how you desire to make a difference in your lifetime? What is your dream? What steps must you take to accomplish it?

2. In what stage are most of the people you know: the self stage, the people stage, or the significance stage? How can you tell? Must everyone go through the first two before entering the third? What stage are you in currently? Explain your answer.

3. How much control do you have over the people you work with most closely? Does that make an impact on your ability to achieve your goals and fulfill your dreams? If you have little control, what could you do to change that situation? In what areas could you currently surround yourself with make-a-difference people? How can you go about finding people with the same passion, a similar mission, talent, and a need for partnership?

4. Describe a marriage that functions as a true partnership. What are the advantages of such a relationship? What happens when marriage partners don't work together? If you are married, describe your attitude toward matrimonial partnership. Describe your spouse's. What can the two of you do to increase your ability to work together?

5. Should leaders try to cultivate relational partnerships with people who work with them? Explain. If so, when would that be appropriate? If you are a leader, what kinds of people have you surrounded yourself with? Do you think of those closest to you as working *with* you or working *for* you? What, if anything, would you like to change in how you interact with them?

THE SATISFACTION PRINCIPLE

IN GREAT RELATIONSHIPS, THE JOY OF BEING TOGETHER IS ENOUGH

A joy shared is a joy doubled.

—JOHANN WOLFGANG VON GOETHE

THE QUESTION I MUST ASK MYSELF:
DO MY CLOSEST FRIENDS
ENJOY JUST BEING WITH ME?

D uring the fourteen years that I led my church in San Diego, every December we put on a big charity show to reach the community and raise money for a local child abuse foundation. I always participated, acting as master of ceremonies and sometimes doing a comic cameo in one of the scenes. Most years we did at least twenty-four performances. It was an exhilarating, yet exhausting, experience.

Before every performance, I used to go out and warm up the crowd by talking to everyone and interacting with the audience. One of the things I liked to do was to find the couple in the audience who had been married the longest. I still remember the one couple who held the record from all the years I did it. They had been married seventy-seven years!

As the couple stood and the audience applauded them, their eyes sparkled.

"Do you want me to give you two marriage counseling?" I asked, getting a quick laugh from the audience.

The old gentleman looked at me, smiled, and said almost confidentially, "It just gets better and better."

THE GREATEST SATISFACTION

Most of us admire and respect people who sustain solid, long-term relationships. A marriage of more than seventy-five years is remarkable. And friendships of any kind that last for decades are the envy of many.

One of the great friendships in Hollywood, a city that is often criticized for its superficiality, was developed between George Burns and Jack Benny. Burns's thirty-eight-year marriage to Gracie Allen (until her death in 1964) was admirable. But his friendship with Jack Benny lasted even longer. After Benny's death in 1976, Burns characterized their relationship this way:

> Jack and I had a wonderful friendship for nearly fifty-five years. Jack never walked out on me while I sang a song, and I never walked out on him while he played the violin. We laughed together, we played together, we worked together, we ate together. I suppose that for many of those years we talked every single day.[1]

I think all of us would love to have a relationship like that of Benny and Burns or like that of an older married couple we've met. But how do we get there? The foundation is built upon all the previous People Principles in this book. A lasting relationship begins as a healthy relationship. Beyond that, I believe that four factors help to create the right climate for relationships where simply being together is enough:

1. Shared Memories Create a Bonded Environment

In March 2004, Margaret and I took a seventeen-day trip to Africa with EQUIP, the nonprofit organization I founded to teach leadership to people overseas. It was a grueling trip. We traveled long distances to four different countries on the continent. Many mornings we were up teaching by seven o'clock, and we went nonstop until midnight or 1:00 A.M. During those two and a half weeks of teaching, we had only one break. We took a two-day safari to see the magnificent wildlife of the bush country.

One person who accompanied us on this trip was Tom Mullins. Tom is a good leader and a highly successful pastor of a large church in Florida, and he was helping the team with the teaching responsibilities. Tom and I have been friends for about eight years, and the longer I know him, the deeper my respect and affection for him have become.

The afternoon that we got home to Atlanta from Africa, Margaret and I dragged ourselves home from the airport and went to bed. All we wanted to do was sleep. Even the next day, we were still jet-lagged and worn out. As I sat at my desk sorting though mail and catching up on work, I got a phone call. It was Tom. It had been only a day since we'd seen each other, but already he wanted to reminisce. We laughed about our safari. (The other tourists came loaded with expensive cameras with zoom lenses, while Tom and I were armed with nothing but a disposable camera!) We recalled the difficult travel. And we marveled at the response of the thousands of people we taught.

"John," Tom finally said, "let's do it again!" Tom and I will never forget that trip together. And the memories we share will forever provide a common bond between us.

Those kinds of experiences are invaluable in our deepest relationships. Margaret and I tried to create many memories with our children as they were growing up. And from the time we got married, we vowed that we would do whatever it took so that when we created our greatest memories, we would be together.

2. Growing Together Creates a Committed Environment

Back in the 1970s when we lived in Lancaster, Ohio, Margaret and I became involved in our first business. She and two friends decided that they wanted to become partners and open a floral shop. We didn't have any money in those days, so we created a business plan and talked to a local banker about a loan. I still vividly remember sitting across from him in his office.

"There's good news and bad news," he said. "The good news is that I'm going to give you the loan." We were elated. "The bad news is that if you're like most new business owners, your partnership will break up in a couple of years. Many start together; few stay together."

That can be said of all kinds of relationships. Beginnings and endings are often much easier than the hard work of sustaining a relationship. Why?

Beginning relationships possess the *excitement* of *starting* together.
Continuing relationships possess the *commitment* of *sticking* together.
Lasting relationships possess the *joy* of *staying* together.

So what is the bridge that spans the gap between relationships that start together and those that stay together? The answer is growth. People who grow together become more committed to one another. And they are usually happier too.

In truth, all relationships grow—they grow apart or they grow together. If we are intentional about growing together, then we are much likelier to stay together. Unfortunately what the banker told us back in Lancaster turned out to be true. By the end of the second year, one of the partners was no longer committed to the business and bowed out.

3. Mutual Respect Creates a Healthy Environment

Respect within a relationship creates a healthy environment because it produces two things. First, it creates trust, and as you know, trust is the foundation of all relationships. Second, it engenders servanthood. People almost can't stop themselves from helping and serving someone they deeply respect. And as Albert Einstein said, "Only a life lived for others is worthwhile."

4. Unconditional Love Creates a Safe Environment

Children's author Dinah Maria Mulock Craik wrote, "Oh, the inexpressible comfort of feeling safe with a person; having neither to weigh thoughts nor measure words, but to pour them all out, just as they are, chaff and grain together, knowing that a faithful hand will take and sift them, keep what is worth keeping, and then, with the breath of kindness, blow the rest away." When somebody loves you with no strings attached and no personal agenda, it's the most freeing thing in the world. It creates a safe environment wherever you are.

Recently Margaret and I were traveling together on a plane, and we struck up a conversation with another couple seated across the aisle from us. When the woman asked, "Where's home?" without even thinking, I said, "Wherever she is," pointing to my wife. And that's true. Margaret loves me unconditionally. I can be myself with her like I am with no other person in the world. She is my safe harbor. There is nothing sweeter in this life than the unconditional love of your closest friend.

I feel very fortunate to have Margaret. I tell people all the time that the greatest decision I ever made was to ask her to marry me. I think about that daily. And I try to tell her as often as I can. On Valentine's Day 2004, I wrote her a note reflecting on our relationship. She has given me permission to share it with you:

> Margaret,
>
> It was about this time forty years ago that we started dating. Although each year seems to be going by quicker than the previous one, our lives have been filled with memories. At fifty-six, I have forgotten many, but the special ones are still today very real to me. I ask myself, "Were the memories special because of what we did or because we experienced them together?" The answer is . . . both. The specialness was greater because we were together.
>
> When we are apart I look forward to our telephone time each evening. It's the highlight of my day. Why? Is it because we both share our list of things that have happened to us that day? No. It is because we are once again together.
>
> I can well remember the anticipation I felt when we were courting as I drove from Circleville to Chillicothe for a date night with you. I could hardly wait! The years have not diminished the anticipation to once again see you after I have been gone. That's why I call you as I leave the airport on my way home. Margaret, the joy you display when you see me again has stayed strong over all these years. Each time I call, you answer the phone with an excitement that expresses to me that I am loved.
>
> I'll never forget the time you sold some of your Ohio State textbooks and bought a bus ticket so you could surprise me and we could have an evening together. Or the time you traveled from Nepal to Delhi to spend an extra night with me. Those extra efforts to be together are what have made our marriage so successful.

A relationship never stays the same. It either grows closer or apart. Forty years after ours began, we still like to be together. Let's take a walk to the mailbox.

Love,

John

Taking a walk to the mailbox for us means spending time together just for the joy of it. And that's what all great relationships provide: joy.

I hope you have people in your life with whom you can share the Satisfaction Principle. If you do, be grateful. If you don't, then begin by practicing the People Principles in this book. Then cultivate rewarding relationships where you create shared memories, grow together, and give each other mutual respect and unconditional love. Do that, and it's only a matter of time before you experience the joy that comes from deep, long-lasting relationships.

> When somebody loves you with no strings attached and no personal agenda, it's the most freeing thing in the world.

SATISFACTION PRINCIPLE DISCUSSION QUESTIONS

1. Can a person be standoffish and still develop a rewarding win-win relationship? Explain your answer. What is the price a person has to pay to develop deep relationships? What would make the price worth paying for you?

2. Think about people you know personally who have sustained a good relationship for more than twenty years. (It can be any kind of relationship, such as a married couple, business partners, or friends.) Describe their relationship. What do they do to keep the relationship going? What can you learn from them?

3. In relationships with a high degree of safety, how do mutual respect and unconditional love come into play? Think about the closest relationship in your life. Do you feel safe with that person? Can you say anything you want? Can you express your feelings? Are you comfortable with long silences? If not, how can you change the environment and make it more positive?

4. Describe some ways that married couples can grow together to make sure that they do not grow apart. How difficult is it to make growth part of a marriage? What challenges or obstacles do most couples face? How can they overcome them? What is the reward of perseverance? Have you succeeded in this area in your marriage?

5. How have shared experiences and their memories affected your closest relationships? Describe a memory that you hold dear. Do your friends or family members value the same memories? How often do you talk about them and relive them? Do you think doing that would be beneficial? How intentional are you about creating new memories together? How can you improve in this area?

Final Review of the People Principles for Winning with People

The Readiness Question:
Are We Prepared for Relationships?

The Lens Principle: Who we are determines how we see others.

The Mirror Principle: The first person we must examine is ourselves.

The Pain Principle: Hurting people hurt people and are easily hurt by them.

The Hammer Principle: Never use a hammer to swat a fly off someone's head.

The Elevator Principle: We can lift people up or take people down in our relationships.

The Connection Question:
Are We Willing to Focus on Others?

The Big Picture Principle: The entire population of the world—with one minor exception—is composed of others.

The Exchange Principle: Instead of putting others in their place, we must put ourselves in their place.

The Learning Principle: Each person we meet has the potential to teach us something.

The Charisma Principle: People are interested in the person who is interested in them.

FINAL REVIEW OF THE PEOPLE PRINCIPLES

The Number 10 Principle: Believing the best in people usually brings the best out of people.

The Confrontation Principle: Caring for people should precede confronting people.

THE TRUST QUESTION: CAN WE BUILD MUTUAL TRUST?

The Bedrock Principle: Trust is the foundation of any relationship.

The Situation Principle: Never let the situation mean more than the relationship.

The Bob Principle: When Bob has a problem with everyone, Bob is usually the problem.

The Approachability Principle: Being at ease with ourselves helps others be at ease with us.

The Foxhole Principle: When preparing for battle, dig a hole big enough for a friend.

THE INVESTMENT QUESTION: ARE WE WILLING TO INVEST IN OTHERS?

The Gardening Principle: All relationships need cultivation.

The 101 Percent Principle: Find the 1 percent we agree on and give it 100 percent of our effort.

The Patience Principle: The journey with others is slower than the journey alone.

The Celebration Principle: The true test of relationships is not only how loyal we are when friends fail, but how thrilled we are when they succeed.

The High Road Principle: We go to a higher level when we treat others better than they treat us.

THE SYNERGY QUESTION:
CAN WE CREATE A WIN-WIN RELATIONSHIP?

The Boomerang Principle: When we help others, we help ourselves.

The Friendship Principle: All things being equal, people will work with people they like; all things not being equal, they still will.

The Partnership Principle: Working together increases the odds of winning together.

The Satisfaction Principle: In great relationships, the joy of being together is enough.

Notes

Introduction

1. Zig Ziglar, *Top Performance: How to Develop Excellence in Yourself and Others* (New York: Berkley Publishing Group, 1991), italics added.

The Mirror Principle

1. "Pete's Records," www.peterose.com (accessed 20 January 2004).
2. Pete Rose, www.baseball-reference.com (accessed 20 January 2004).
3. Lieber and Neff, "The Case Against Pete Rose."
4. Rose, www.baseball-reference.com (accessed 20 January 2004).
5. "Pete Rose: 'I bet on baseball,'" excerpt from *My Prison Without Bars*, in *Sports Illustrated*, 5 January 2004, www.si.com.
6. Craig Neff and Jill Lieber, "Rose's Grim Vigil," *Sports Illustrated*, 3 April 1989, www.si.cnn.com (accessed 5 January 2004).
7. Lieber and Neff, "The Case Against Pete Rose."
8. "Pete Rose: 'I bet on baseball.'"
9. Ibid.
10. Ibid.
11. Ibid.
12. John C. Maxwell, *The 21 Irrefutable Laws of Leadership* (Nashville: Thomas Nelson, 1996).
13. Phil McGraw, *The Ultimate Weight Solution* (New York: Free Press, 2003), 25.

The Hammer Principle

1. Proverbs 15:1.
2. Marshall Goldsmith, "How to Learn the Truth About Yourself," *Fast Company*, October 2003, 127.

The Elevator Principle

1. George W. Crane, *Dr. Crane's Radio Talks*, vol. 1 (Mellot, IN: Hopkis Syndicate, Inc., 1948), 7.
2. Ibid., 8–9.
3. Ibid., 16.

4. Ella Wheeler Wilcox, "Which Are You?" *Custer, and Other Poems* (Chicago: W. B. Conkey Company, 1896), 134.

5. Anonymous.

The Big Picture Principle

1. "Meet the New Angelina Jolie," www.cnn.com/2003/showbiz/movies/10/25/jolie.ap (accessed 13 January 2004).

2. "Child Changes Everything," ABCNews.com, 17 October 2003.

3. Ibid.

4. Ibid.

5. Ibid.

6. "Meet the New Angelina Jolie."

7. Author unknown.

8. Bob Buford, *Halftime* (Grand Rapids: Zondervan, 1997), 138.

The Exchange Principle

1. Art Mortell, "How to Master the Inner Game of Selling," vol. 10, no. 7.

The Learning Principle

1. Tom Seligson, "How a Wiseguy Set Me Straight," *Parade*, 18 January 2004, 18.

2. Ibid.

3. Joe Pantoliano with David Evanier, *Who's Sorry Now* (New York: Plume, 2002), 243.

4. Ibid., 14.

5. Ibid., 289.

6. Philip B. Crosby, *Quality Is Free: The Art of Making Quality Certain* (New York: Mentor Books, 1992), 68.

The Charisma Principle

1. Reprinted with permission from "Dr. Zimmerman's Tuesday Tip," a weekly Internet newsletter, www.drzimmerman.com, Tip #171, 23 September 2003.

2. Marcus Buckingham and Donald O. Clifton, *Now, Discover Your Strengths* (New York: Free Press, 2001), 116.

The Number 10 Principle

1. Marilyn Haddrill, "Lessons in Learning: Ex-Marine-turned-teacher Shapes up Her Tough High School Class," *Chicago Tribune*, 3 March 1996, http://internet.cybermesa.com (accessed 22 January 2004).

2. Ibid.

3. Ibid.

4. LouAnne Johnson, *The Girls in the Back of the Class* (New York: St. Martin's Press, 1995), 61.

5. LouAnne Johnson, *Dangerous Minds* (New York: St. Martin's Press, 1993), 7.

6. Johnson, *The Girls in the Back of the Class,* ix–x.

7. Haddrill, "Lessons in Learning."

8. LouAnne Johnson, "My Posse Don't Do Homework," http://members.authorsguild.net/louanne/work4.htm (accessed 22 January 2004).

The Bedrock Principle

1. Dan Barry and others, "Correcting the Record: Times Reporter Who Resigned Leaves Long Trail of Deception," *New York Times*, 11 May 2003, http://query.nytimes.com (accessed 9 March 2004).

2. Elizabeth Kolbert, "Tumult in the Newsroom," *New Yorker*, 30 June 2003, www.newyorker.com (accessed 9 March 2004).

3. Barry et al., "Correcting the Record."

4. Paul D. Colford, "More Blair Faults at Times," *New York Daily News*, 13 June 2003, www.nydailynews.com (accessed 9 March 2004).

5. Barry et al., "Correcting the Record."

6. Peter Johnson, "'Times' Execs Address Blair Scandal," *USA Today*, 14 May 2003, http://usatoday.printthis.clickability.com (accessed 9 March 2004).

7. Barry et al., "Correcting the Record."

8. Ibid.

9. Macarena Hernandez, "What Jayson Blair Stole from Me, and Why I Couldn't Ignore It," *Washington Post*, 1 June 2003, www.washingtonpost.com (accessed 9 March 2004).

10. "Burning Down My Master's House: My Life at The New York Times," *Publishers Weekly,* 8 March 2004, 58.

11. "Numbers," *Time,* 29 March 2004, 19.

12. Barry et al., "Correcting the Record."

13. Maxwell, *The 21 Irrefutable Laws.*

14. William M. Boast with Benjamin Martin, *Masters of Change* (Provo, UT: Executive Excellence Publishing, 1997).

15. D. Michael Abrashoff, *It's Your Ship* (New York: Warner Business, 2002), 65.

The Situation Principle

1. "Willams Sisters Display Loving Sibling Rivalry at Australian Open," *Jet*, 9 February 1998, www.findarticles.com (accessed 5 February 2004).
2. L. Jon Wertheim, "We Told You So," *Sports Illustrated*, 5 April 1999, http://sportsillustrated.cnn.com (accessed 4 February 2004).
3. Timeline: Venus and Serena Williams, http://sportsillustrated.cnn.com/tennis/features/williams/timeline (accessed 4 February 2004).
4. Wertheim, "We Told You So."

The Bob Principle

1. Tobias Seamon, "The All-Bastard Athletic Club," *The Morning News*, 10 June 2002, www.themorningnews.org/archives/personalities (accessed 28 January 2004).
2. *Sports Illustrated*, 30 March 1981, quoted on http://espn.go.com/classic/s/quotesbmartin000806.html (accessed 23 January 2004).
3. Ibid.
4. Interview, *New York Times*, 15 July 1982.
5. Neil T. Anderson, *Victory Over the Darkness* (Ventura, CA: Regal Books, 1990).

The Approachability Principle

1. "Biography of Barbara Walters," us.imdb.com/name/nm0910181/bio (accessed 19 February 2004).
2. Tina Gianoulis, "Barbara Walters," *St. James Encyclopedia of Popular Culture*, 2002, www.findarticles.com (accessed 17 February 2004).
3. Ibid.
4. Alberta Civil Service Association *News*.
5. Florence Littauer, *Personality Plus: How to Understand Others by Understanding Yourself* (Grand Rapids, MI: Fleming H. Revell, 2003).
6. *Simpson's Contemporary Quotations*.
7. Barbara Walters, *How to Talk with Practically Anybody About Practically Anything* (Garden City, NY: Doubleday, 1970), xv.

The Foxhole Principle

1. *Army Field Manual* number 7–8, Headquarters, Department of the Army, Washington, DC, 22 April 1992, www.adtdl.army.mil/cgibin/atdl.dll/fm/7-8/ch2.htm#s2p6 (accessed 17 March 2004).

2. Ecclesiastes 4:9–12.

3. Tom and David Gardner, "Motley Fool Radio Interview with Yahoo! Co-Founder Jerry Yang," www.fool.com/Specials/1999/ sp990303YangInterview.htm (accessed 11 March 2004).

4. Jon Swartz, "Yahoo's Other Dynamic Duo: Jeff Mallett and Tim Koogle Have Transformed the Service into the Web's Most Popular Site," *San Francisco Chronicle*, 6 August 1998, www.sfgate.com (accessed 12 March 2004).

5. http://docs.yahoo.com/info/pr/faq.html (accessed 12 March 2004).

6. Robert Lauer and Jeanette Lauer, *Watersheds* (Boston: Little, Brown, 1988), 69.

The Gardening Principle

1. "Mitch Albom Bio," www.albom.com (accessed 11 March 2004).

2. Tracy Cochran, "Everyone Matters," *Publishers Weekly*, 18 August 2003, www.publishersweekly.com (accessed 12 March 2004).

3. Mitch Albom, "He Was a Champion," *Parade*, 14 September 2003, 4–5.

4. Ibid., 4.

5. Cochran, "Everyone Matters."

6. Albom, "He Was a Champion," 5.

7. Ibid.

8. Author unknown.

The 101 Percent Principle

1. Laura Hillenbrand, *Seabiscuit: An American Legend* (New York: Random House, 2001), 29.

2. Ibid., 33–34.

The Patience Principle

1. "Lawn Chair Larry: 1982 Honorable Mention," www.darwinawards.com/ stupid/stupid1997-11c.html (accessed 10 February 2004).

2. Warren G. Bennis and Burt Nanus, *Leaders: The Strategies for Taking Charge* (New York: HarperBusiness, 1985), 52.

The High Road Principle

1. Richard Collier, *The General Next to God: The Story of William Booth and the Salvation Army* (London: Collins Clear-Type Press, 1965), 27.

2. Steve Artus, "General William Booth—Salvation Army," *Claves Regni*, October 1994, www.stpetersnottingham.org (accessed 25 February 2004).

3. "William Booth," www.spartacus.schoolnet.co.uk/rebooth.htm (accessed 25 February 2004).

4. "The Founder—William Booth," http://archive.salvationarmy.org.uk (accessed 25 February 2004).

5. Collier, *The General Next to God*, 110.

6. "The Skeleton Army," www1.salvationarmy.org/heritage.nsf (accessed 15 March 2004).

7. "History," www.salvationarmyusa.org (accessed 25 February 2004).

8. Artus, "General William Booth—Salvation Army."

The Boomerang Principle

1. Alan Loy McGinnis, *The Friendship Factor* (Minneapolis: Augsburg Fortress, 1979), 9.

2. Quoted in Patrick Flaherty, *Scout Law: Quotes for Life* (Iowa City: Penfield Books, 2002), 29.

The Friendship Principle

1. Bethany Broadwell, "Bill Porter: Selling His Uplifting Attitude," 9 August 2002, www.ican.com/news/fullpage.dfm (accessed 4 March 1004).

2. Proverbs 18:24 *The Message*.

3. Proverbs 27:9 *The Message*.

4. Proverbs 27:17 *The Message*.

5. Proverbs 16:29 *The Message*.

The Partnership Principle

1. "Ben Franklin As a Founding Father," http://sln.fi.edu/franklin/statesman/statsman (accessed 1 March 2004).

2. "Ben Franklin: Networker," www.pbs.org/benfranklin/13_citizen _networker.html (accessed 1 March 2004).

3. "Ben Franklin: France," www.pbs.org/benfranklin/13_citizen_france.html (accessed 1 March 2004).

4. Anonymous.

The Satisfaction Principle

1. O. S. Hawkins, *Tearing Down the Walls and Building Bridges* (Nashville: Thomas Nelson, 1995), 27.

About the Author

JOHN C. MAXWELL is an internationally recognized leadership expert, speaker, and author who has sold over 13 million books. His organizations have trained more than 2 million leaders worldwide. Dr. Maxwell is the founder of EQUIP and INJOY Stewardship Services. Every year he speaks to Fortune 500 companies, international government leaders, and audiences as diverse as the United States Military Academy at West Point, the National Football League, and ambassadors at the United Nations. A *New York Times*, *Wall Street Journal*, and *Business Week* bestselling author, Maxwell was named the World's Top Leadership Guru by Leadershipgurus.net. He was also one of only 25 authors and artists named to Amazon.com's 10th Anniversary Hall of Fame. Three of his books, *The 21 Irrefutable Laws of Leadership, Developing the Leader Within You*, and *The 21 Indispensable Qualities of a Leader* have each sold over a million copies.

BOOKS BY DR. JOHN C. MAXWELL
CAN TEACH YOU HOW TO BE A REAL SUCCESS

RELATIONSHIPS

Be a People Person

Becoming a Person of Influence

Relationships 101

The Power of Influence

The Power of Partnership in the Church

The Treasure of a Friend

Ethics 101

Winning with People

25 Ways to Win with People

ATTITUDE

Be All You Can Be

Failing Forward

The Power of Thinking Big

Living at the Next Level

Think on These Things

The Winning Attitude

Your Bridge to a Better Future

The Power of Attitude

Attitude 101

Thinking for a Change

The Difference Maker

The Journey from Success to Significance

EQUIPPING

Developing the Leaders Around You

Equipping 101

The 17 Indisputable Laws of Teamwork

The 17 Essential Qualities of a Team Player

Partners in Prayer

Your Road Map for Success

Success One Day at a Time

Today Matters

Talent Is Never Enough

LEADERSHIP

The 21 Indispensable Qualities of a Leader

Revised & Updated 10th Anniversary Edition of *The 21 Irrefutable Laws of Leadership*

The 21 Most Powerful Minutes in a Leader's Day

Developing the Leader Within You

Leadership 101

Leadership Promises for Every Day

The 360 Degree Leader

The Right to Lead

The Power of Leadership

Leadership Gold

Go for Gold

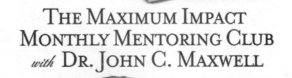

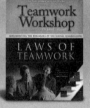

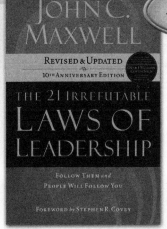

JOHN C. MAXWELL has combined his insights from leadership successes, mistakes and observations from the worlds of business, religion, politics, sports, and the military in *The 21 Irrefutable Laws of Leadership*.

Now, this 10th anniversary edition's additional practical applications and revised content make this book stand out above the best-selling original.

21 Irrefutable Laws of Leadership (978-0-7852-8837-4)

Leadership expert John C. Maxwell brings an in-depth look at God's laws for leaders and leadership.

Includes:
+ New articles and notes
+ Revised indexes
+ New interior page design

Available in hardcover and black bonded leather.

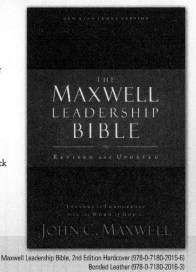

Maxwell Leadership Bible, 2nd Edition Hardcover (978-0-7180-2015-6)
Bonded Leather (978-0-7180-2016-3)

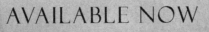
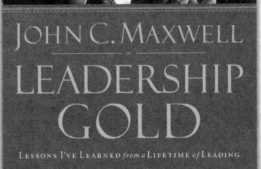